The Poor Law of Lunacy

The Poor Law of Lunacy

THE ADMINISTRATION OF PAUPER LUNATICS IN MID-NINETEENTH-CENTURY ENGLAND

PETER BARTLETT

Leicester University Press
London and Washington

First Published 1999 by Leicester University Press, a Cassell imprint
Wellington House, 125 Strand, London WC2R 0BB
370 Lexington Avenue, New York, NY 10017-6550

British Library Cataloguing-in-Publication Data

A catalogue record for this book is available from the British Library.

ISBN 0 7185 0104 7

Library of Congress Cataloging-in-Publication Data

Bartlett, Peter.
    The poor law of lunacy : the administration of pauper lunatics in
mid-nineteenth-century England / Peter Bartlett.
    p. cm.
    Includes bibliographical references and index.
    ISBN 0-7185-0104-7 (hardback)
    1. Mentally ill—Institutional care—Government policy—England—
History—19th century. 2. Insane—Commitment and detention—
England—History—19th century. 3. Psychiatric hospitals—England—
History—19th century. 4. Poor laws—England—History—19th
century. I. Title.
HV3009.B37 1999
362.2'1'094209034—dc21   98–51388
                                   CIP

Typeset by Bookens Ltd, Royston, Herts

Printed and bound in Great Britain by
Bookcraft Ltd, Midsomer Norton, Somerset

FOR MY PARENTS

Contents

Figures

Tables

Acknowledgements

I owe tremendous debts to a wide variety of people who have assisted, encouraged, cajoled and otherwise put up with me throughout the creation of this book. It started life as a dissertation in the Faculty of Law at University College London. Acknowledgement must first go to my supervisors, David Nelken and William Twining, who provided solid encouragement and sound advice from the beginning. It was a delight to work with them, and I offer both my deepest thanks. Both my examiners, Lucia Zedner and Peter Fitzpatrick, provided encouragement and advice regarding publication. Dr Zedner, acting well beyond the call of duty, provided further detailed comments on revision of the dissertation for publication.

It became clear early in the project that advice from historians of lunacy would be of great assistance, and to that end I was tremendously fortunate to have been put in touch with the Wellcome Institute for the History of Medicine. It would be difficult to understate their assistance. Roy Porter and Bill Bynum have read numerous papers and drafts, and provided invaluable assistance. I have been fortunate to read various papers both to Institute 'Work in Progress' seminars, and to less formal meetings of graduate students and postdoctoral fellows. In addition, Professor Bynum was kind enough to arrange a desk for me at the Institute, which provided me with a stimulating community of colleagues. That community made the creation of the thesis much more intellectually fulfilling and personally enjoyable than would otherwise have been the case. More recently, the Department of Law at the University of Nottingham has arranged my teaching to allow for trips to the Public Record Office, in the process of turning the dissertation into a book.

Throughout the development of this work, I have been fortunate to develop a number of close collegial relations. Early in the project, Alexander Zahar, Timothy Morrison and Javier Moscoso were particularly helpful. More recently, I have benefited considerably from the advice and collegial support of David Wright. Throughout, it has been a particular delight to work with Akihito Suzuki, from whose wisdom, insights and friendship I have benefited greatly. In this, as in all my work, my colleague and friend Alan Yoshioka has been both advocate and critic. Rick Savage has provided a cheerful check on potential obsession, in an endearing mix of bemusement and befuddlement.

After the completion of the dissertation, a number of projects were funded by the Wellcome Trust which examined topics relevant to my work. Of particular relevance to me were the projects of David Wright in Buckinghamshire, Pamela Michael and David Hirst in Wales, Len Smith on pre-1845 county asylums and Jo Melling, Bill Forsythe, Richard Adair and Robert Turner in Exeter. Two-day annual symposia for those involved in those projects and related work have now been sponsored by the Trust for several years. Thanks are extended to the participants in those events, and particularly to Elizabeth Malcolm, who provided perceptive comments regarding the transfer of the dissertation to book form, and to Len Smith, who provided advice and a few gentle warning shots on substantive points.

I must also thank the staffs of various archives and libraries: the British Library, the Public Record Office, and the Wellcome Institute. Particular thanks are extended to the staff of the Leicestershire Record Office, whose consistent competence and good cheer made the local study a particularly pleasant aspect of the project.

The realities of doctoral research require cash, and I have been fortunate to have received generous funding. During my doctoral studies, much of my tuition for three years was funded through the Overseas Research Students Award Scheme, administered by the Committee of Vice-Chancellors and Principals. The Wellcome Trust was also very generous in funding the remainder of my tuition fees and providing a generous stipend for two years. The Department of Law at the University of Nottingham kindly funded research assistance for four weeks and covered incidental travel expenses. Throughout the project, the staff at Cassell have been both enthusiastic and professional. I am grateful particularly to Veronica Higgs, Alan Worth and Dominic Shryane, who had charge of the general production of the book, and to Sarah Bragginton, who handled the minutiae of copy editing.

Finally, particular thanks are extended to my parents. Not only have they provided steadfast emotional encouragement; their integrity, standards of human decency and intellectual curiosity have also proved an inspiration to me. They also taught me much about history. Many thanks to them both; and to them this volume is respectfully dedicated.

Note on citations and terminology

The names of the authorities responsible both for lunacy-related matters and the Poor Law generally changed at various times, so the following guide may be of assistance.

From 1834 to the end of 1847, the central authorities with responsibility for Poor Law matters were the Poor Law Commissioners. They were replaced from the beginning of 1848 by the Poor Law Board. They, in turn, were replaced in 1871 by the Local Government Board, a body with a broader jurisdiction. In the following chapters, I have used the generic term 'Poor Law central authority' for these authorities.

As for the lunacy central authority, the Metropolitan Commissioners in Lunacy were created in 1828 with jurisdiction to license and inspect private madhouses in the greater London area. They were authorized in 1842 to conduct a nationwide inspection of madhouses and county asylums, preliminary to the enactment of new lunacy legislation in 1845. The 1845 acts continued this national inspection role, and renamed them the Commissioners in Lunacy. Prior to 1845, the name 'Commissioners in Lunacy' had referred to officials at the Court of Chancery; the 1845 statutes renamed this latter group 'Masters in Lunacy'. As there is no call to refer to the Chancery jurisdiction in this dissertation, the phrase 'Commissioners in Lunacy' has been used to refer both to the post-1845 commissioners and, when a generic term is required, to the Metropolitan Commissioners as well.

There is one brief comment about the citation of parliamentary papers. These papers were published separately, and incorporated into bound volumes, paginated by hand. In some archives and libraries, the unbound papers continue to exist. I have adopted the practice that the first page reference in a citation refers to the handwritten pagination within the volume, while page references within the parliamentary paper itself refer to the printed pagination in the report. For example, in the citation 'PP 1850 (735) xxiii 393 at 26', the '393' refers to the handwritten pagination of Volume 23 and the '26' refers to the printed pagination within the paper itself.

Finally, Crown copyright material in the Public Record Office is reproduced by permission of the Controller of Her Majesty's Stationery Office, and copyright material contained in the Leicestershire Record Office is reproduced by kind permission of that archive.

Table of cases and statutes

CASES

STATUTES

Titles have been abbreviated. For full titles. see bibliography.

Introduction

Twentieth-century scholars have generally viewed the care of the insane in modern England in the context of the history of psychiatry. In these accounts, the bestial images of lunacy which accompanied the whips and chains of seventeenth-century establishments gave way by the nineteenth century to new forms of treatment which acknowledged the humanity of the lunatic. This transition was concurrent with the rise of the medical profession. Metaphors of demonic possession gave way to diagnoses of illness as doctors consolidated their sole authority in the field of lunacy.[1] Concurrent in turn with this professionalization had been the rise of a trade in madness in eighteenth-century England, as medical men turned their authority to business advantage by opening profit-motivated private madhouses for the care of the insane. The care provided in these private facilities was increasingly challenged by humanitarian reformers as cruel in nature and inadequate in scale. Asylums established as philanthropic endeavours on the model of voluntary hospitals were unable to provide care on a sufficient scale. As governments were convinced of the need for more and better regulated care, new county asylums were built, staffed by medical specialists. It was, at least initially, a triumph of reform.

This factual structure is remarkably consistent between traditional 'Whiggish' and revisionist accounts. Those versions differ not on the basic factual structure but rather on the interpretation to be put on those facts, or the subsequent implementation of the system. Apologists for the changes emphasize the horrors of earlier periods and the humanitarian objectives of the reformers.[2] Critics may stress the unfortunate results of these benevolent motivations,[3] the professional interests of the psychiatrists[4] or the social control implications of the process.[5] Either way, the medical professionals and the asylums and madhouses which they ran are central to the analysis. The fact of the attainment of power by these medical specialists is never questioned. At issue has been how, not whether, this occurred.

When that basic fact is challenged, it is shown to be remarkably tenuous. The chapters which follow review the statutes and administrative structures involved in the construction of county asylums and the confinement of the insane in them. This analysis shows that the asylum doctors had little role in deciding how asylum construction would occur, and who would be placed in or removed from county asylums. The Lunacy Commissioners, the central authority credited with providing focus to the reform movement, similarly had almost no formal power. Throughout the nineteenth century, decisions regarding the construction of county asylums and confinement in them rested with local Justices of the Peace and Poor Law officials. In addition, the vast bulk of those confined in county asylums were paupers. The county asylum was essentially a Poor Law institution. As such, it is juxtaposed, not with the private madhouse and the charitable hospital, but with the union workhouse and the system of doles which constituted outdoor poor relief. At issue is not simply a question of segregating the mad, for the insane poor were cared for under each of these branches of the Poor Law. It is rather a matter of understanding the relationships between these institutions as they related to the pauper insane.

That is the focus of this research. What is being considered is how pauper lunacy was administered, and how lunacy fits into the broader scheme of the nineteenth-century Poor Law. Inconsistent administrative models contained in the statutes conferred authority on a variety of local officials. Two central authorities inspected and reported on the local situation, but had little legal authority to require change. The result was not hierarchical power structures based on legal fiat but rather webs of influence between the various administrators. Where other histories of nineteenth-century county asylums have tended to focus on the asylum medical professionals essentially in isolation from the officials who administered the relevant legislation, they are placed here in their context as a part of an administrative network, and a relatively unimportant part at that.

The work focuses on England, not on Britain or the United Kingdom. Scotland and Ireland had entirely different administrative structures and criteria for admission. Wales had the same legislation as England, but had a different set of social traditions. Institutional

2

provision was quite different, with boarding out remaining significant well after it ceased to be a major force in England. Pam Michael and David Hughes are currently engaged in research on asylum provision in Wales, and discussions with them furthered my resolve that Wales is sufficiently different that it should be excluded from my work.

The work which follows focuses on the period from 1834 to 1870. The association between Poor Law and lunacy extends back into the eighteenth century and before, and continues into the twentieth. The temporal focus was chosen for various reasons. A logical starting point seemed to be 1834, with the enactment of the new Poor Law. The legislative basis of the county asylum movement predates this by a quarter of a century, but asylums constructed prior to 1834 tended to be small and few in number. The twenty years after the enactment of the new Poor Law, and particularly the period after county asylums became mandatory in 1845, represents the beginnings of large-scale identification and specialized treatment of the insane poor. The 1845 Act also established a Lunacy Commission which published annual reports and whose archives survive, and changed record-keeping procedures at the local level. The result is that most remaining lunacy documents date from after this period.

The study ceases in 1870. By that time, the county asylum system was well established, allowing for consideration of its relatively large-scale operation, not merely its formative years. The central Poor Law administrative structure changed in 1871 with the introduction of the Local Government Board, so that extending this study further would require addressing a somewhat different administrative structure. On the other hand, extending the research through the 1860s allowed access to a wider variety of documents in Leicester, my area of local study. A complete set of admission documents and casebooks survive for the period 1861 through 1865, and a close study of these forms the basis of Chapter 5 below.

In addition, 1870 seems to provide a dividing point in Poor Law history. The founding of the Charity Organization Society began to suggest the acknowledgment within the Poor Law of a more structured and formal role for private benevolence. Garland cites social work, criminology and eugenics as having their genesis at about that time.[6] With the advent of charity work, mixed with social work and criminology, a new intellectual structure centring on the individual as a 'case' appears. While the study of admission documents and casebooks in Chapter 5 suggests some similarity to these later phenomena, a full-scale history of the transitions in case reporting and recording is outside the scope of this work. The rise of eugenics in the last thirty years of the century has obvious bearings on lunacy policy, such that continuation after 1870 would considerably expand this project. Further, commencing in the 1880s with the Idiots Act,[7] there begins an institutional diversification of the Poor Law and asylum movement. To continue beyond 1870 would require these developments to be addressed, and thus the expansion of the time-frame well into the twentieth century.

That said, the characters and processes described in the chapters that follow will not be entirely foreign to the modern reader. The current English Mental Health Act[8] has never escaped its nineteenth-century origin. Prior to the arrival of the National Health Service, separate processes applied to public/pauper and private admissions to psychiatric facilities. The latter involved an application by the next of kin, supported by medical certificates and, after 1890, approved by a Justice of the Peace.[9] The former, the process discussed in the work which follows, was in the hands of the Poor Law relieving officers and medical officers and, from the foundation of the system at the beginning of the nineteenth century, the Justices of the Peace. It would stretch the truth only marginally to suggest that, with the arrival of the National Health Service, the public and private systems were simply forced into one, with minimal concern as to the coherence of the detail. While the admission would no longer require the sanction of a Justice of the Peace, it would require, for all patients, the involvement of the family and a public official. The names of the official have changed over time. The relieving officer became a 'duly authorized officer', then a 'mental welfare officer', before becoming an 'approved social worker', the current title. As will become clear from the material which follows, the job itself has remained remarkably unchanged.

Much of the modern legislative provision similarly flows directly from nineteenth-century legislation. With the unification of admission processes and the move to the NHS, the original rationale for much of the detail has been rendered nonsensical. Thus the right of a nearest relative to discharge a patient currently contained in section 23(2) of the Mental Health Act flowed both from the right of the nineteenth-century nearest relative to discharge the private patient for whom he or she was paying[10] and also from the right of the family of a pauper patient to discharge the patient, on the undertaking that he or she would no longer be a charge on the Poor Law.[11] This latter measure

4

used the broad antipathy to pauper status in the nineteenth century to further fiscal restraint in public finance. Both the original clauses allowing discharge by next of kin flow from fiscal reasons which no longer exist: the family no longer pays for confinement in the psychiatric facility and pauper status has been abolished. Yet they remain in the 1983 statute. The corresponding limitation of the right of the family member to discharge a patient centres on the dangerousness of the individual. It is contained in section 25(1) of the 1983 Act, but similarly flows directly from nineteenth-century legislation.[12]

The point here is not that nothing has changed; if anything, quite the reverse. The economic and political context, the nature of the family and the institutional frameworks have all varied markedly. The history of mental health legislation demonstrates the force of legislative inertia, and a history of cut-and-paste law-making over periods of considerable change. The point is instead that the study of the nineteenth-century administrative networks has much to say about the roots of the twentieth-century statute.

The nineteenth century none the less presented a remarkably similar set of options to the twentieth, when confronted with an insane person: provide a cash handout to live in the community (called 'outdoor relief' in the nineteenth century); admit to an asylum (now a 'psychiatric hospital'); or admit to a different form of social service housing — boarding out or workhouse care in the nineteenth century, nursing home provision and group homes in the twentieth. The most significant legal difference is that nineteenth-century admissions to asylums were always legal confinements; there was no equivalent to 'voluntary' or 'informal' admission. The debates between therapeutic need and dangerousness as standards of confinement in an asylum and the controversy surrounding costs are equally as much a part of the nineteenth-century debate as of the twentieth. Without wishing to press the point too far, the similarities between the centuries are striking.

And so, on with the show. Chapter 1 looks at the premisses of other asylum history, and discusses why this book focuses on legal structures and administrative mechanisms. Chapter 2 makes the fundamental claim of the book, that the nineteenth-century county asylum is to be understood in terms of the Poor Law. Chapter 3 examines the legislative history of pauper lunacy, in the context of nineteenth-century Poor Law. Chapters 4 and 5 are based on a local study of the Leicestershire and Rutland County Lunatic Asylum. The first of these is an examination of the interrelations between the key officials involved in the confinement process: Justices of the Peace, Poor Law relieving officers and Poor Law medical officers. The casebooks and admission documents are examined in Chapter 5, as they provide particular insights into how the choice between asylum, workhouse and outdoor relief was understood by the actors of the period. Chapter 6 considers the role of the Commissioners in Lunacy. While highly visible, these individuals had remarkably little real power, and it will be argued that they hesitated to use what power they in fact did have. The chapter will examine how they used gentler techniques of persuasion to influence decision-making. The final chapter draws some of the previous themes together, in an assessment of the significance of the research in understanding the work of French theorist Michel Foucault.

NOTES

1   The timing of these events remains somewhat controversial. Until relatively recently, the view was that most intellectual and humanitarian reform occurred in the nineteenth century: see Andrew Scull, *Museums of Madness* (Harmondsworth: Penguin, 1982); Kathleen Jones, *Law, Lunacy, and Conscience 1744–1845: The Social History of the Care of the Insane* (London: Routledge, 1955). More recently, eighteenth-century historians of medicine have objected to this view, based on the uncritical use of what they see as a nineteenth-century caricature of the eighteenth-century treatment of the insane: see, for example, Roy Porter, *Mind-Forg'd Manacles* (1987; reprinted Harmondsworth: Penguin, 1990) at pp. 276 ff. and *passim*. The precise timing of these events is not significant for current purposes, since all would agree that large-scale asylum provision, the subject of the present research, was a nineteenth-century phenomenon.

2   See, for example, Kathleen Jones, *Law, Lunacy and Conscience, 1744–1845*, and *Asylums and After: A Revised History of the Mental Health Services* (London: Athlone, 1993).

3   For example, David Rothman, *The Discovery of the Asylum* (Boston: Little, Brown and Co., 1971); and *Conscience and Convenience* (Boston and Toronto: Little, Brown and Co., 1980).

4   Andrew Scull has argued this position most forcefully in the context of nineteenth-century England; see for example *Museums of Madness* (1979; reprinted Harmondsworth: Penguin, 1982); 'Humanitarianism or control? Some observations on the historiography of Anglo-American psychiatry', in *Social Control and the State*, ed. Cohen and Scull (1983; reprinted Oxford: Blackwell, 1985); 'Mad-doctors and magistrates: English psychiatry's struggle for professional autonomy in the

nineteenth century', *Arch. Europ. Sociol.*, **17** (1976): 279; *Social Order/ Mental Disorder* (London: Routledge, 1989); *The Most Solitary of Afflictions* (New Haven and London: Yale University Press, 1993). For a continuation of these themes into the twentieth century see Scull, *Decarceration* (2nd edn., Englewood Cliffs, NJ: Prentice Hall, 1984; and Oxford: Basil Blackwell Ltd., 1984).

5 See the works by Scull in note 4 above. Michel Foucault can also be viewed in this vein: *Madness and Civilization*, trans Richard Howard (New York: Random House, 1965), especially in Chapter 9.

6 David Garland, *Punishment and Welfare* (London: Gower, 1985) in Part II.

7 Idiots Act 1886, 49 Vict. c. 25.

8 1983, c. 20.

9 Lunacy Act 1890, 53 Vict. c. 5.

10 This is contained expressly in legislation, commencing in 1845: 8&9 Vict. c. 100 s. 72. It was, no doubt, assumed by both proprietors of madhouses and those responsible for payment, well before that time. The significance of its express inclusion lies in the provisions of section 75, which limit its application in cases of dangerousness: see below.

11 This provision is expressly contained in legislation beginning with 9 Geo. IV c. 40 s. 39 (1828), which empowers the Justices in charge of the county asylum to release an individual upon application of a relative or friend 'if they think fit, upon the Undertaking of such Relative or Friend as aforesaid, to the Satisfaction of the Overseers of the Parish to which such Pauper Lunatic belongs, that he shall no longer be chargeable to such Parish'.

12 The release of privately confined persons upon application of next of kin was introduced in 1845, where the medical officer of the institution could force a hearing before Justices of the Peace or Commissioners in Lunacy if the patient were 'dangerous and unfit to be at large': 8&9 Vict. c. 100 s. 75. Cf. the wording of the modern statute, 'where the medical officer certifies that 'the patient, if discharged, would be likely to act in a manner dangerous to other persons or to himself': Mental Health Act 1983, s. 25(1). As paupers were released by Justices anyway, the analogous provision was not applied to them in the nineteenth century, except when they were confined in private facilities.

CHAPTER 1

Socio-legal history and asylums

'[M]ental health law is more than simply a matter of the legal framework of admission and discharge and patients' rights, but also provides the designation and management structure of the institutions where patients are treated.'[1]

The history of insanity, of asylums and of psychiatric confinement is appropriately placed not merely within the history of medicine, but also within the history of law. Fennell's comment regarding modern mental health law is equally applicable to the historical context: the history of the administration of the insane and the history of management structures of the resulting institutions are matters for legal analysis. Law also provides the constitutional framework. It articulates understandings of rights, power, political process, social control and policing through legislation, case law and convention. Law is of course not the only factor in these structures. If we have learned anything from Foucault, it must be the inadequacy of a mono-dimensional analysis of power; but law is certainly relevant to understanding these issues.

It thus seems strange that socio-legal analysis has been relatively absent in the history of the nineteenth-century asylum movement. There have, of course, been the chronicles of the struggle towards reform, most notably Kathleen Jones's *Lunacy, Law, and Conscience, 1744–1845*[2] and *Mental Health and Social Policy 1845–1955;*[3] but the reform motif which provides the structure for such works tends to influence the view of the legislation. The law becomes the passive result of reform, rather than dynamic in the construction of institutional frameworks. Even in revisionist accounts such as Rothman's *Discovery of the Asylum*[4] and *Conscience and Convenience,*[5] which take a relatively broad view of the influences on asylum development, the emphasis is on broad political and ideological

8

structures rather than on legal, administrative or constitutional contexts. In any event, the emphasis is on the macro level. The processes of admission and discharge are not analysed; yet it is here that the law interacted with the individual in the most direct fashion.[6]

Wherever there is law, there is lunacy. Legal discourses of civil and criminal liability revolve around responsibility. Analyses of incapacity, a close cousin of insanity, are thus never far away. This omnipresence is not of marginal importance in this book. The Poor Law was not designed with the insane in mind; yet their presence in Poor Law structures was by no means marginal to the care of the insane in the nineteenth century. None the less, for present purposes, particular mention might be made of four distinct legal structures directed towards confinement of control of the insane specifically.

The first grew out of the *parens patriae* jurisdiction of the Crown, codified first at the beginning of the fourteenth century.[7] Much refined by statute over the course of the nineteenth century, this was a power conferred directly by the Crown. By the nineteenth century, tradition had been established that it would be granted to the Lord Chancellor.[8] The power allowed the holder to empanel a jury to try whether an individual was lunatic or idiot. If such a finding was made, the goods, person or both of the insane person were placed in the care of the Crown. By the nineteenth century, the tradition had developed that care of both the person and the estate would be delegated to a member of the insane person's family.

Criminal lunatics presented a different set of problems. Here, the difficulty was that an individual might be acquitted of a criminal offence on the basis of insanity, or found insane at the time of trial. Without some form of intervention, the right to hold the individual following the acquittal was dubious. In response to *Hadfield's Case*,[9] legislation to address this difficulty was passed.[10] Again refined over the course of the nineteenth century, it allowed these individuals to be held for an undetermined period.

Private madhouses were subject to separate regulation commencing in 1774.[11] This Act required licensing of madhouses, by the College of Physicians if in London or by the Justices of the Peace if outside the metropolis. More significant was legislation of 1828 which set the administrative pattern for the remainder of the century.[12] Houses were licensed and inspected by Justices of the Peace outside London, but by a new board of commissioners, the Metropolitan Commissioners in

Lunacy, within London. Admission to these facilities was on application of a family member, upon certification of two doctors.

Finally, there were the county asylums. Their legislative form was set in 1808.[13] They were constructed on the county rates, and administered by the county Justices of the Peace in Quarter Session. The Justices further controlled both admission and discharge to the facilities. Although a medical certificate was required from 1811 onwards,[14] the application was itself in the hands of the Overseers of the Poor. In any event, confinement was within the discretion of the Justice, unless the individual were actually dangerous.[15]

These four legal strands continued throughout the century.[16] In law, they operated quite separately. The administrators and processes surrounding each were quite different. The inquisition process was, generally, in the control of Chancery. The criminal process was in the court handling the case – usually Queen's Bench, if in the superior court, and certainly not Chancery. Admission to private madhouses was in the control of families, with medical involvement. Admission to county asylums was controlled by the Justices of the Peace, supported by Poor Law authorities. Given the divergence of administration and of institution, it is questionable in what sense one can speak of lunacy law as a coherent package in the nineteenth century. The failure to take account of the specifics of process has led to a variety of misconceptions and half-truths about nineteenth-century confinement.

There is a sense, for example, that lunacy was an overarching status. Clive Unsworth, after noting the variety of laws relating to the Lord Chancellor's jurisdiction, capacity to enter legal transactions, criminal responsibility and confinement in the nineteenth century, notes:

With the arrival of the carceral era, ... a massive tapestry of laws was spread over provision for the mentally disordered. The new system combined an extensive network of lunatic asylums, public and private, in which patients were legally detained, the construction of a tutelage whereby the mentally disordered were subjected to a modified status of citizenship, the secure dominance of the medical profession in the therapeutic management of the asylum population and the establishment of administrative machinery, in particular a central Lunacy Commission, to oversee the conduct of lunacy practice.[17]

Unsworth acknowledges here his debt to Castel's work on France,[18] but the legal and historical contexts are markedly different. The demise of *lettres de cachet* and the rise of a radical liberal social ideology following the revolution is pivotal in Castel's account of medical authority in

France. French society was touchy about arbitrary confinement, but the insane remained a problem. Medical expertise provided the authority to allow the confinement of the insane on a non-political basis. There is no equivalent crisis in England, which remained much more socially hierarchical and paternalist throughout the nineteenth century. The judicial personhood of French law has no obvious English equivalent. Where it is not surprising that the French law of 30 June 1838[19] makes appointment of administrators of affairs of the inmate automatic upon admission, and includes curatorship (personal guardianship) as part of the same process as admission,[20] this was not the English way.

English law was instead specific. Admission to an asylum did not per se preclude signing a will or contract.[21] Nor did a finding that a specific contract was invalid per se invalidate subsequent contracts. The finding of insanity by the Lord Chancellor did not warrant confinement in a madhouse or asylum, nor did it preclude execution of a will.[22] A finding of incapacity by the Lord Chancellor was to be noted on admission documents to facilities; it was by no means an automatic corollary, nor a prerequisite. English law may have been a 'massive tapestry', as Unsworth suggests; but its application was a matter of precision, specificity and subtlety.

Failure to recognize the specificity and the differences between the various strands of legal lunacy has led to misconceptions about the period. This is clearest in the failure to distinguish between confinement in public and private facilities. A variety of scholars have seen the Victorian period as one of concern over wrongful confinement, culminating in scrutiny over confinements by Justices of the Peace commencing in 1889.[23] Thus Kathleen Jones refers to the reforms at that period as 'the triumph of legalism'.[24] Clive Unsworth entitles his chapter on the 1890 Act 'Lunacy, Liberty and the Rule of Law',[25] referring to the 'intricate legalism' of the Act.[26] Peter McCandless explains the Victorian dilemma between civil liberty and care and removal of the insane through the following quotation from Wilkie Collins's Victorian novel, The Woman in White, as spoken by the hero after unwittingly helping the title character to escape from her private madhouse:

What had I done? Assisted the victim of the most horrible of all false imprisonments to escape; or cast loose on the wide world of London an unfortunate creature whose actions it was my duty, and every man's duty, mercifully to control?[27]

There was no doubt much concern about wrongful confinement in the Victorian period. By mid-century, civil rights protections were being laid down for those in the private sector.[28] But that is the private sector. The application of the civil rights attitude to those in the public county asylum system is problematic. The 1890 Act made virtually no difference to public confinements. From 1808, the poor had been received into asylums on the application of Poor Law officers, approved by Justices of the Peace. So it remained after 1890. Certainly, there were some paupers who were not pleased at being sent to the county asylum;[29] but they did not seem to perceive their situation in terms of civil rights. Whether because their pauper status left them understanding that they had no rights, or because the cost of enforcement of those rights through the legal system would be prohibitive or because, however much they did not like the asylum, they were without reasonable alternative, the discourse does not appear. This is in a way not a surprise. As will be discussed further below, the asylum might be portrayed in a flattering light, a good provided to the poor by a benevolent and paternalist society. The state of the poor living outside the asylum makes its appeal credible. Relative to their accommodation outside, the furnishings might be a better standard, the food sufficient, the work moderate and the rooms warm in the winter and cool in the summer. In so far as this vision was shared by the inmates of the asylum, it is not obvious that they would object to 'wrongful' confinement.[30] Even Louisa Lowe, the author of *The Bastilles of England, or the Lunacy Laws at Work* and critic of lunacy law in many forms, perceived the problems of public confinement in terms of exploitation of labour, maltreatment and indignity, rather than wrongful confinement.[31] Protection from wrongful confinement was a middle-class matter, relating to private madhouses. The 1890 Act may have been a triumph of legalism in the political realm, but for the public, county asylums it made minimal change to the status quo.

This study deals with the fourth strand of law, the county asylum system. It is thus not a study about 'lunacy and law' as a universal construct, for such a construct is at least as much a hindrance as a help. At issue is how the county asylum is to be contextualized, and how it was administered. What are the legal and administrative structures which created the nineteenth-century asylum, and how were these structures used by the people involved in administering the system?

PREVIOUS HISTORIES

This approach indicates both a reliance upon and a departure from previous histories of institutions. These can be seen to be influenced to a considerable degree by Erving Goffman, and in particular his 1961 work, *Asylums*.[32] Notwithstanding the modern resonances of the title, that was not merely a work about psychiatric facilities. It was instead about 'total institutions', institutions such as hospitals, psychiatric asylums, boarding schools, prisons and monasteries, which separated the inmates from broader society and imposed upon them a régime of daily living. It was Goffman's thesis that these institutions had a variety of characteristics in common. They were often as total for staff as for the inmates. Inmates became reliant upon them, and far from fitting the inmate for the world outside, they had quite the reverse effect. Recidivism was a corollary of the system. Power relations were likely to be similar between the institutions as well, with staff adopting parental roles and inmates infantalized.

Goffman's work has of course been tremendously influential in social policy, in many of the areas where total institutions had held sway for so long. In mental health, his arguments are significant to the movement towards 'care in the community' and the hesitation to confine individuals for long periods. His ideas have also been influential on historians. David Rothman's *Discovery of the Asylum*,[33] published in 1971, is a history of the creation of these total institutions in the United States in the first half of the nineteenth century. Rothman perceives the rise of the penitentiary, lunatic asylum, child reformatory and almshouse as flowing from parallel theories as to social reform. Social causes of deviance, whether based in inadequate parenting, cultural angst or stresses inherent in the frontier mentality, would be corrected by an intensive period in a curative institution. Poverty, crime and insanity would be cured. In a relatively short space of time, however, the need for large-scale management of the deviant poor swamped the ethos of cure. The institutions became focused on control, not reform, of individuals.

Rothman appropriately places his work squarely in the context of the United States. Even when examining the colonial roots of social policy, he is at pains to stress the independence of the American situation.[34] There are certainly points of divergence between England and the United States in the social, political and intellectual factors he mentions. Thus he perceives immigration and lack of classification of inmates to be significant to the move from curative to custodial institution.[35] These were not obvious factors in England. There are none the less distinct similarities between Rothman's tale and accounts of the English experience. The broad movement from curative to custodial institution, based to a considerable degree on economic factors, is reflected in Andrew Scull's work on the asylum.[36] Overcrowding and the prevalence of chronic cases in asylums, occupying so many beds that curable cases could not be admitted, were certainly much complained of in English facilities, as they were in America, and while the specific social causes of deviant behaviour such as insanity might have differed from America, the causes were perceived as social in both. In America, overwork leading to insanity was associated with colonial life and the frontier, where in England it was more likely to be associated with factories and commerce; but these seem to be distinctions of detail.

If Rothman may overstate the uniqueness of the American experience regarding social factors generally, he certainly does not do so regarding the legal and administrative differences. Most of North America never adopted the English Poor Law, and a perusal of American statutes indicates that, whatever the key clientele may have been, the admission processes were not expressly in the hands of Poor Law officers, but instead with the family of the individual.[37] American admission criteria frequently referred specifically to dangerousness of the individual, where the English instead referred to the 'appropriateness' of confinement. Facilities were generally centrally managed in America, by the state governor. American society had a very different structure. There is no role analogous to the landed gentry, so much in evidence on the benches of English magistrates which controlled the county asylums here. Law is defined by its jurisdiction. Even more fundamentally than in Rothman, the approach in the chapters that follow is similarly defined by national boundaries. By focusing on the specifics of legal intervention, the application of statutes and local practice, my approach suggests a specifically English study.

The focus on legal relationships further problematizes the study of institutions in several ways. Rothman's approach, like Goffman's, treats total institutions as broadly comparable. The focus on the legal relations between institutions forces a closer examination of their similarities and differences. Given that an insane pauper might be cared for either in the county asylum or the union workhouse, how was a relieving officer, Poor Law medical officer, workhouse master or Justice of the Peace to decide between the two institutions?[38] Certainly there are parallels; but equally there are differences. In addition, there was a third option: outdoor relief. This option was chosen for roughly a quarter of the insane poor in 1850, falling slowly to about 8 per cent in 1890. If outdoor relief were chosen, the institution would be avoided completely. The implied view in Rothman's work is that institutions monopolized care. Whatever may have been the case in the United States, this was not true in England.

In Rothman's work, the prevalence of the poor is a central cause of the downfall of the curative asylum. He cites George Chandler, the superintendent of the Worcester state hospital, regarding the prevailing views of the poor insane in the mid-1850s:

When ... the patients, instead of being partly drawn according to the original purpose from an intelligent and educated yeomanry, are drawn mainly from a class which has no refinement, no culture, and not much civilization even — that hospital must certainly degenerate.[39]

Rothman continues, 'The predominance of the poor and the immigrant in the institutions made observers question the reform program's basic assumptions about the character of American society.'[40] A custodial institution was the result.

Again, the distinction with the English situation is significant. As will be shown in Chapter 2, the English county asylums were always primarily for the poor. The presence of the poor in these English asylums cannot therefore be understood as indicative of failure. Rothman can further coherently criticize American asylum super-intendents for colluding, albeit with the best of intentions,[41] with the change from the curative to the carceral, for they generally had the authority to select or reject patients. Their English counterparts had no such power: they took whomsoever the Poor Law officers and Justices of the Peace sent them.

At the same time, Rothman's references to poverty indicate a basic difference between his project and this one. He views the dispatch of the poor to the asylums unproblematically, in that he does not examine the reason why the asylum was chosen for these individuals in preference to other instituional or non-institutional responses. For Rothman, the issue was a simple one of isolation of the poor and immigrants:

From the perspective of the community's officials, the pauper and the immigrant insane, especially the troublesome and dangerous ones, were a convenient and practicable group to incarcerate.... The reform ideology not only sanctioned but encouraged isolation, so that later administrators could enforce it with good conscience. And to the degree that overseers and judges used the asylum instead of a poorhouse or jail for the insane, they could better adopt a humanitarian pose.[42]

Such a technique equally meshed with social expectations:

These groups, many observers believed, produced many of the dangerous lunatics and the lower the social standing of the inmates, the easier for other ranks to incarcerate their most troublesome cases there. Granted, this arrangement was not without drawbacks. By giving the asylum over to the least desirable elements, the middle and upper classes restricted their own ability to utilize it. They might well hesitate to incarcerate the peaceable but still bothersome relative in such a setting. But in the end they made their choice. The returns of a custodial operation seemed worth the price.[43]

This all fits very neatly: the interests of social administrators and the respectable public intersect, and doctors are carried along, lacking any obvious alternative. The reform ideology even provides a sugar coating, through its earlier claims of the benefits of incarceration.

This model is enticing in its elegance. It does not fit precisely onto the English situation, since the English county asylums were designed for the poor. At the same time, it has some points of similarity. The English insane poor were certainly confined in large numbers, and pressures filtered through much of the nineteenth century to keep pauper and private lunatics separated, even when for reasons of convenience or history they were in the same institutions. Yet Rothman's relatively brief account begs the questions of primary interest in the remainder of this book. The Victorians did not confine most of the poor: those on outdoor relief always vastly outnumbered those in institutions. While a majority of the insane poor were confined, the rationales of confinement deserve close scrutiny.

Many similar themes appear in Andrew Scull's work on English asylums and madhouses.[44] Unlike Rothman, Scull's work focuses specifically on the insane. For Scull, as for Rothman, the nineteenth century saw the creation of the mad as a distinct deviant population. Where Rothman sees the rise of the asylum in tandem with the rise of other institutions, however, Scull focuses on the history of confinement in the context of the rise of the medical profession:

At the outset of the period [i.e., in the mid-eighteenth century], mad people for the most part were not treated even as a separate category or type of deviants. Rather, impoverished madmen were assimilated into the much larger, more amorphous class of the morally disreputable, the poor, and the impotent, a group which also included vagrants, minor criminals, and the physically handicapped; and their richer (though not necessarily more fortunate) counterparts were for the most part coped with by their families.... By the mid-nineteenth century, however, virtually no aspect of this traditional response remained intact. The insane were clearly and sharply distinguished from other 'problem populations'. They found themselves incarcerated in a specialized, bureaucratically organized, state-supported asylum system which isolated them both physically and symbolically from the larger society. And within this segregated environment, now recognized as one of the major varieties of deviance in English society, their condition had been diagnosed as a uniquely and essentially medical problem. Accordingly, they had been delivered into the hands of a new group of professionals, the so-called 'mad-doctors'.[45]

The Act which made county asylums mandatory in 1845 is perceived as a triumph of humanitarian reform, a movement which allied medical professionals and lay reformers. The asylum, under the control of the medical superintendent, was the result.

The consideration of the administrative approach noted above indicates its problems, however. People continued to be cared for at home, both rich and poor. Private patients were not generally contained in the 'bureaucratically organized, state-supported asylum system'; they were in private madhouses. And confinement in the public county asylum movement were not controlled by the so-called 'mad-doctors', but by Poor Law officials and the Justices of the Peace.

So far, Scull's analysis may be less sympathetic to medical professionals, but is otherwise factually similar to that of traditional nineteenth-century medical historians. Scull departs from previous histories in his emphasis on the effect of economic changes on the creation of the asylum, and his assessment of the implementation of reform. He is also much less flattering in his view of the rise of the medical profession. After having manoeuvred their way to power in the care of the insane, the medical professionals were unable to fulfil their promises of high cure rates. In Scull's view, as in Rothman's, the curative asylum was increasingly shown to be a chimera, and asylums became mere 'museums for the collection of insanity', 'warehousing' patients.[46] This failure of the ideals of reform did not stop the growth of the asylums, nor did it challenge the authority of the medical superintendents of the asylums, who had already secured their position as the sole persons qualified to treat the insane. Changed economic circumstances had left the poor little option but to send their insane and enfeebled relatives to the asylum, turning the asylum into 'a handy place to which to consign the disturbing, the vaguely menacing, the unwanted, and the useless – those potentially and actually troublesome people who posed threats to the social order and to the business of daily living which were not readily subject to control by the legal system.'[47] Scull's work is thus an account of the rise of professional power of doctors, and the failed promise of humanitarian reform.

There is much in Scull's account which is convincing. Asylum doctors were certainly attempting to consolidate their position in the care of the insane, and Scull's work has many useful insights into that process. Scull largely assumes rather than demonstrates the centrality of the medical profession to the care of the nineteenth-century insane, however, and yet his own work provides a challenge to that assumption. When asylum doctors crossed the county Justices, they were dismissed or forced to resign.[48] He claims that a specialized alienist literature in the first half of the nineteenth century 'made it difficult for outsiders to avoid concluding that considerable expertise had already been developed in the handling and treating of the insane, and that existing knowledge was in the process of being further refined and extended'.[49] Certainly there was a burgeoning medical literature on insanity through the eighteenth and nineteenth centuries, but it was largely written by doctors for other doctors. The degree to which outsiders were influenced by this literature is at best uncertain. Even the Lunacy Commissioners, argued by Scull to be supporters of the medical cause,[50] defended the presence of lawyers and lay persons in their number,[51] suggesting that the Commissioners were loath to acknowledge a medical monopoly in the field of insanity. Scull himself quotes their chairman, Ashley (after 1851, the seventh Earl of Shaftesbury), as stating that 'it having been once established that the insanity of a patient did not arise from the state of his bodily health, a man of common sense could give as good an opinion as any medical man he knew [respecting the treatment and the question of his sanity]'.[52] Scull eventually comments:

At the close of the nineteenth century, however, the professional status of asylum doctors remained distinctly questionable. Conspicuously mired in the status of salaried employees, and forced to confront and cope with a clientele consisting almost entirely of the least attractive members of the lower orders of society, they shared with similarly situated groups like workhouse doctors and public health officers at best a tenuous hold on social respectability and but a paltry measure of the autonomy usually granted to those engaged in professional work.[53]

For Scull, the medico-humanitarian vision went somehow horribly wrong. Instead of humanitarian care, reform resulted in 'the creation of vast receptacles for the confinement of those without hope'.[54] The medical and humanitarian aspects became almost a sham, as Scull claims that 'the medical control of asylums, and the propaganda about treatment rather than punishment, served to provide a thin veneer of legitimation for the custodial warehousing of these, the most difficult and problematic elements of the disreputable poor'.[55] If the development of the law relating to lunatics in the nineteenth century was not merely the function of humanitarian and medical pressures, however, so the 'success' or 'failure' of the reforms could not reasonably be expected simply to conform to those models. If, as will be argued below, doctors and reformers were not central to the growth of the asylum, if cures were not necessarily the concern and perhaps not even particularly expected and if asylums were actually about something else, the gap between the aspirations of reformers and medical men and the implementation of the system would not be illuminating.

Scull points out that the medical profession was unable to produce cures,[56] a fact chronicled in the annual and special reports of the Lunacy Commission. He argues, however, that neither the public nor the Poor Law officials were interested in cures:

If the attractions of a convenient institution in which to dump the troublesome and undesirable sufficed to ensure at least the passive acquiescence of the asylum doctors' true clients, the families and parish officials, in their continued existence, their nominal clients, the asylum's inmates, had little choice but to cooperate in sustaining their definition of the situation.... Once they [the medical professionals] had secured control over asylums, they no longer had to attract clients – the institution did that for them. And once patients were obtained, they formed literally a captive audience held in a context which gave immense power to their captors.[57]

If the interests of the 'true clients' lay elsewhere, however, why should the medical profession and reformers occupy a central place in the history of the asylum? Scull is right to place the rise of the asylum in the broader context of economic disruption of the eighteenth and early nineteenth-centuries; but such a placement argues for consideration of the asylum in the context of other nineteenth-century social policy, which grew out of precisely the same circumstances; and given that the lunatics confined in the nineteenth century were overwhelmingly poor, the Poor Law should be central to that analysis.

ASYLUMS AND ADMINISTRATION

Adoption of an approach based on administrative and legal structures creates a marked change in focus in the history of asylums. The key administrative players cease to be the specialist medical profession involved in insanity. They were generally uninvolved in the committal processes, and even if they held posts in a county asylum, were subject to the administrative authority of a local committee of Justices of the Peace. Instead, it was Justices and the Poor Law officers who were in control of admission, and Justices who were in charge of the asylum. For reasons which will become clearer in the next chapter, the county asylums were Poor Law institutions.

In both Scull's and Rothman's accounts, the asylum is portrayed, eventually, as a failure – a 'convenient place to dump the troublesome' for Scull,[58] a 'dumping ground for social undesirables' and a 'snake pit' for Rothman.[59] One must here question the criteria of success and failure. It is fair to say that whatever criteria these scholars are using, it is not related to the asylum's administrative context as a Poor Law institution. It is easy to question the logics of the Poor Law system as a whole, and the place of the asylum within it, but it is less obvious that passing judgement post hoc is helpful. Without wishing to minimize the lessons history brings for the present, it is open to question the benefit of retrospective moralizing. Such a view's relevance would be based in its ahistoricism. For that reason, the objective of this work is to understand, not to judge the past.

Clearly there were radical changes in the social policy relating to lunacy in the nineteenth century, but the explanation of those changes is not to be found in the rise in status and humanitarian interventions of the medical profession; it is rather to be understood in the context of the great nineteenth-century Poor Law reform, and the introduction of the new Poor Law in 1834. The 1834 Act in theory did not affect lunacy. The county asylums legislation was essentially unamended between 1828 and 1845, and even the 1845 Act did not alter the basic managerial structure of asylums. The 1834 Act was pivotal in other ways.

First, it replaced the old system of relief based on parishes with a new administrative unit, the union. Management of the Poor Law was therefore changed from local Justices of the Peace to boards of guardians, elected by the ratepayers. While magistrates continued to have a place ex officio on rural boards of guardians, their powers were significantly curtailed. At least in theory, the new Poor Law also signalled an ideological movement away from the paternalist notions of the old Poor Law, toward a system of faceless administration, imposing moral choices and moral judgements on the poor. The exclusion of the county asylum from these provisions meant that it remained one of the few remaining points of magisterial control in the Poor Law. In this context, the asylum became a reaction to the new Poor Law, even from within the Poor Law itself, a fiefdom for the magistrates. A discourse appeared, portraying the county asylum as humanitarian, juxtaposing it with the rigours of the punitive workhouse, and reflecting the paternalism of the old Poor Law.

Secondly, the new Poor Law ideology imposed a moral judgement onto the pauper. Paupers were deemed to be individuals capable of deciding in their own best interests, and the Poor Law system was structured to induce the pauper to choose a life of morality and wage labour. This was reflected in the appeal of moral management in the asylum: work had therapeutic value and the pauper insane were to be taught a trade. The people sent to the asylum were often portrayed in the asylum casebooks in morally judgemental ways reminiscent of the new Poor Law discourse. The causes of insanity might be viewed in moral terms. Notwithstanding the paternalist attitudes noted above, this constituted an intersection in the attitudes of the asylum aims and the Poor Law.

Thirdly, and consequent on the new administrative divisions, the 1834 Act created a professional Poor Law staff at the local level. Gone were the voluntary parish overseers of the old Poor Law. Most significant for present purposes was the creation of paid relieving officers and medical officers, as these officials were in charge of preparing the documentation to go to the Justice for the admission of a pauper to the asylum. Furthermore, it was Poor Law medical officers in 1845 who were charged with the duty to visit every pauper lunatic not in an asylum on a quarterly basis. Administration of pauper lunacy became a matter of routine within the new Poor Law bureaucratic structures.

The association of the county asylum with Poor Law is not an entirely novel approach: Busfield,[60] Rothman, Scull and Jones[61] all refer to the importance of the Poor Law in the roots of the care of the insane. Yet even Scull, who places himself in opposition to the 'naive Whiggish view of history [of the asylum movement] as progress'[62] and who turns to the language of Marxism and the theory of the Poor Law for part of his argument regarding the growth of asylums, does not examine the practical interrelations between the administration of Poor Law and lunacy law. For Scull and others, the specifics of the Poor Law were something from which the administration of the insane was to be distinguished and with which it was to be juxtaposed. There is the occasional remark about 'lunatics who had formerly starved and rotted in workhouse cellars',[63] but serious analysis of the care of the insane under the Poor Law is entirely lacking. This is particularly surprising since, as the nineteenth century progressed, the insane in workhouses increasingly outnumbered those in the private madhouses which are an important part of Scull's analytical structure.[64]

The closer focus on the administrative actors in this process has ramifications for the context of discussion. At issue is not merely, as for example in Foucault, an abstract formulation of power, but rather the creation and uses of power by the specific individuals involved, in their specific political context. Part of this involves interclass relations: the asylum, like the rest of the Poor Law, was directed to the appropriate treatment of the poor, and the strategies of power used in this context are certainly relevant. At the same time, there are intra-class issues, the strategies of the various actors to protect or increase their power or authority vis-à-vis other actors. As a concrete example, it will be argued that one reason for the success of the county asylums was their control by the Justices, whose authority was under threat from the Poor Law. In some sense, the rise of the asylum was a symbol of the power of the Justices of the Peace.

Studies of English administration are more relevant, and particularly those concerning the administrative wrangles associated with the Poor Law. The so-called nineteenth-century revolution in government has provided sporadic discussion for much of the twentieth century. The debate flows from A. V. Dicey at the beginning of the twentieth century, and has trundled along with varying degrees of enthusiasm since that time. As befits a tradition of that longevity, various themes have developed. Dicey divided nineteenth-century administration into three periods. From 1800 to 1830 was a period of 'quiescence' and minimal legislative intervention of any sort; 1830 to 1870 represented a period of individualism, where legislation focused on the removal of constraints to individual liberty; and 1870 to 1900, a time of collectivist legislation.[65] Subsequent scholars pointed out that 1830 to 1870 was in fact a period of considerable government intervention.[66] Anthony Brundage claims that between 1830 and 1837, 'the Whigs presided over one of the most extraordinary periods of government growth in British history',[67] an enthusiasm which continued for much of the remainder of the century. In the middle years of the century, Westminster was active in legislating over a wide range of issues: nuisances, factories, child welfare, labour law, education, local government, criminal law, matrimonial law, public health, vaccination, censuses, birth and death registration and, of course, Poor Law and lunacy law.

Scholars have not necessarily challenged the view of individualism as the prevailing ideology. One strand of debate developed as to how laissez-faire as the prevailing ideology could be understood alongside the growth in government intervention that the legislation and resulting bureaucracy implied.[68] In some cases, this has involved marginalizing the ideological debates, and positing the rise in government intervention as related primarily to a response to practical situations.[69] Other scholars seem to have moved away from the fixation on laissez-faire as the controlling ideology for the mid-nineteenth century. Thus for Martin Wiener the state was to provide guidance, not merely to punish offences, and law became 'the most powerful national schoolmaster'.[70] Mitchell Dean claims, 'Police becomes no longer simply the condition of order in a community but the prosperity, health, welfare, and security of the totality of human life within that community, the population.'[71]

Some formulations have implicitly or explicitly associated the revolution with centralization of power at Westminster. Such accounts focus not merely on the legislative activity at the central level, but also on the growth of a centralized bureaucracy. Oliver MacDonagh's five-step model of legislative reform,[72] for example, sees the creation of these bureaucracies in terms of increasing centralized responses to situations perceived as intolerable, after a realization that simple legislation without an enforcement mechanism was insufficient to correct the impropriety. Henry Parris claims that in the new alignment of power in the nineteenth century, 'the monarchy rose above party, so the civil service settled below party. Constitutional bureaucracy was the counterpart of constitutional monarchy.'[73] A second strand of the debate surrounding the revolution in government challenges this centripetal movement of power. William Lubenow's work in the early

1970s[74] instead placed the issue of division of power between local and central authorities as central in the understanding of nineteenth-century administration.

Lubenow's formulation is not without its persuasive merit. The central bureaucracy remained numerically small by continental standards in the early and mid-Victorian period, and, at least in the cases of the Poor Law and lunacy central authorities, had minimal concrete power. Centralization was a long-standing battle, waged on a variety of fronts and far from a foregone conclusion in the period of this study. Thus, for example, it was not until 1877 that the central government assumed control over local prisons,[75] and not until 1867 that the Poor Law Board was made permanent.[76] The central control over both Poor Law and lunacy did not come from the creation of the central bureaucratic structures, as these never had the legal or financial resources to require compliance with their orders. Rather, the control resulted from the contribution of funds to pay for Poor Law and lunacy, providing a motivation for local authorities to co-operate with the central government. Thus contributions were made to the salaries of Poor Law medical officers and teachers commencing in 1845 and 1848 respectively.[77] A per diem contribution from the central government for the upkeep of lunatics in asylums commenced in 1874. These payments no doubt increased the influence of central government at the local level. They were perceived to do so and were controversial in some quarters as a result,[78] but these payments did not result in a complete loss of local control. Local authorities maintained control over admission to facilities well into the twentieth century.

Power thus remained largely within the local élites, with the local boards of guardians and Justices of the Peace in Quarter Sessions. The Justices were drawn early in the nineteenth century from the ranks of the local gentry and clergy, with local merchants and factory owners increasingly replacing clerical appointments as the century progressed.[79] The boards of guardians seem to have been drawn from similar ranks.[80]

A more recent twist to the debate squarely addresses the question of administrative efficacy. In his analysis of the nineteenth-century factories and mines inspectorates, P. W. J. Bartrip[81] argues that the number of inspectors hired to enforce legislation was sufficiently small that it is doubtful whether the legislation had a significant effect at all, and that perhaps Dicey was correct all along in portraying the period as one of essentially laissez-faire. The difficulty with taking the argument to this extreme is that efficacy is judged in terms of the size of the budget for enforcement:

It is difficult to judge the extent of industrial regulation in a totally convincing way. Perhaps the best quantitative guide to intervention is through assessment of the level of state resources devoted to implementation.[82]

Bartrip is right that efficacy cannot be assumed from the passage of legislation; but it does seem equally capricious to dismiss the possibility of statutory compliance absent enforcement mechanisms in a note, because it is 'unmeasurable'.[83] It will be argued in Chapter 6 that the Lunacy Commission used their annual and special reports as vehicles to press publicly for improved institutional standards. The efficacy of such an approach is difficult to measure with any specificity, but it cannot be assumed to be negligible. In addition, it will be argued that the inspections and reporting by the Lunacy Commission acted along with other factors to create the sense of county asylums as constituting a national system of institutions, rather than a collection of local facilities. Such changes in perception are not measurable, but they are not thus rendered insignificant.

The nineteenth-century revolution debate tends to adopt an essentially benign view of the state. As in the examples cited above, the state at least attempts to remedy social ills. There may be debate as to whether it was successful, but not about its basic motivation. This may in part result from the fact that much of this literature stems from a trend of work written in the 1960s examining the roots of the welfare state, a time when that concept enjoyed broad public and academic appeal. After the social control arguments of the 1970s and 1980s, this simply benign vision of the state appears curiously naive. The social control literature envisaged social organization as the control of the poor and deviant. Where the nineteenth-century revolution literature spoke of administration, the social control literature spoke of power.

The argument hereinafter has been influenced by the social control literature in this regard. Both the asylum law and the broader Poor Law placed the poor person in an administrative structure where the decision-makers were the magistrates and the Poor Law authorities. That is not merely an administrative relationship; it is also a power relationship, but several caveats are appropriate. It would be naive to think that the relationship was a simple one. While the attitudes of paupers and their families are difficult to judge as there is virtually no documentation left from them as to how they approached the system, it will be argued from anecdotal evidence in asylum casebooks that poor people may well have been at least occasionally manipulating the system to their own advantage. Poor people cannot simply be portrayed as inanimate. Further, no claims are made as to how successful the mechanisms were, and in particular whether the lower classes became more docile as a result of their implementation.[84] This question is particularly problematic, since in so far as the workhouse may be understood as representing the punitive side of the Poor Law and the asylum the benevolent side, they represented different strategies for social control.

The phrase 'social control' is itself problematic, as it seems to mean different things to different people.[85] Its own historical roots in twentieth-century sociology have even been used to argue that its use in understanding earlier states is anachronistic.[86] For these reasons, the phrase appears likely to create more problems than it solves, and its use has been avoided hereafter.

NOTES

1 Phil Fennell, 'Law and psychiatry: the legal constitution of the psychiatric system', *Journal of Law and Society*, **13** (1986): 35, at p. 36.

2 London: Routledge, 1955.

3 London: Routledge, 1960. This, along with her 1955 work above, has recently been revised and reissued as *Asylums and After* (London: Athlone, 1993).

4 Boston: Little, Brown, 1971.

5 Boston: Little, Brown, 1980.

6 More recent scholars have begun to consider admission and discharge documentation and the processes by which asylums were administered. In an English context, see for example Walton, 'Casting out and bringing back in Victorian England: pauper lunatics 1840–70' in Bynum *et al.* (eds), *The Anatomy of Madness*, Vol. II (London: Tavistock, 1985), pp. 132 ff.; Charlotte Mackenzie, 'Social factors in the admission, discharge, and continuing stay of patients at Ticehurst Asylum, 1845–1917', in Bynum *et al.*, *ibid*; David Wright, 'Getting out of the asylum: understanding the confinement of the insane in the nineteenth century', *Social History of Medicine*, **10** (1997): 137; Forsythe, Melling and Adair, 'The new Poor Law and the County Pauper Lunatic Asylum – the Devon experience 1834–1884', *Social History of Medicine*, **9** (1996): 335; and, regarding a somewhat earlier period, J. Andrews, 'The politics of committal to early modern Bethlem', in R. Porter (ed.), *Medicine in the Enlightenment* (Amsterdam: Clio Medica, 1995), p. 6.

7 *De Prerogativa Regis*, 17 Edw. II stat I. (1324).

8 The power was also granted to Vice-Chancellors when they began being appointed. The first such appointment was in 1813; in 1843, the number of Vice-Chancellors was raised to three.

9 (1800) 27 Howell's St. Tr. 1281.

10 39 & 40 Geo. III c. 94 (1800).

11 14 Geo. III c. 49 (1774).

12 9 Geo. IV c. 41. Again, this statute was much modified over the course of the century: see list of statutes contained in bibliography.

13 By 48 Geo. III c. 96.

14 By 51 Geo. III c. 79.

15 This was made explicit by 51 Geo. III c. 79 (1811), and apart from a brief period in 1845–6, remained the case throughout the century. See further Chapter 3.

16 They were consolidated into one statute in 1890: 53 Vict. c. 5. The consolidation was merely a compilation, however, and the strands remain clearly visible in the modern Mental Health Act 1983. The remnants of the old inquisitorial process, now placed entirely on a statutory footing and applying to the estate only, are contained in part VII of the Act. Criminal patients are dealt with in part III. Civil admission to facilities (with the distinction between public and private abolished since the Mental Health Act 1959) are contained in part II.

17 Unsworth, 'Law and lunacy in psychiatry's "Golden Age"',' *Oxford Journal of Legal Studies*, **13** (1993): 479 at p. 481.

18 Unsworth, 'Law and lunacy', p. 479, citing Castel, *The Regulation of Madness: The Origins of Incarceration in France*, trans. Halls (Cambridge: Polity, 1988).

19 Contained as Appendix A to Castel.

20 Arts 31 to 38.

21 See *Martin* v. *Johnston* (1858), 1 F. & F. 122; and *Lovatt* v. *Tribe* (1862), 3 F. & F. 9.

22 See, for example, *Bannatyne and Bannatyne* v. *Bannatyne* (1852), 2 Rob. Ecc. 472. The finding of incapacity did reverse the onus in the case, however, so that the party propounding the will would have to demonstrate capacity.

23 52 & 53 Vict. c. 41; consolidated in 53 Vict. c. 5.

24 K. Jones, *Mental Health and Social Policy 1845–1955* (London: Routledge, 1960) at Ch. 7; *Asylums and After* (London: Athlone, 1993) at Ch. 6 (see note 3 above).

25 *The Politics of Mental Health Legislation* (Oxford: Clarendon, 1987), Ch. 4.

26 Ibid., p. 80.

27 P. McCandless, 'Dangerous to themselves and others: the Victorian debate over the prevention of wrongful confinement', *Journal of British Studies* **23**(1) (1983): 84.

28 See, for example, *Nottidge* v. *Ripley* (QB, 1849), a case of wrongful

confinement in a madhouse. Chief Baron Sir Frederick Pollock instructed the jury that 'It is my opinion that you ought to liberate every person who is not dangerous to himself or others ... and I desire to impress that opinion with as much force as I can': quoted by Scull, 'The theory and practice of civil commitment', in *Social Order/Mental Disorder* (London: Routledge, 1989), pp. 283 f. It would be incorrect to say that this was a universally adopted view. The Lunacy Commissioners, for example, issued a strong objection: see PP 1849 (620) xlvi 381, discussed in Chapter 6 below.

29 See further, Chapter 4 below.

30 Regarding those feigning lunacy to gain admission to the asylum, see further Chapter 4.

31 See her introduction to *The Bastilles of England; or the Lunacy Laws at Work* (London: Crookenden, 1883). The body of this work is devoted to private asylums, including problems of wrongful confinement in that type of institution.

32 1961; reprinted Harmondsworth: Penguin, 1968.

33 Boston and Toronto: Little, Brown, 1971.

34 This is as true for his view of legislation as it is for social factors:

> Although American statutes were firmly based on English precedent, they did not mechanically repeat every stipulation and faithfully duplicate the system. Rather, assemblies selected from the English corpus those sections that they found most consistent with their own attitudes and most relevant to their own needs, and in so doing they gave a discernibly American quality to the result. (Rothman, *Discovery of the Asylum* (1971), p. 20)

35 Ibid., pp. 250, 254, 273.

36 Regarding Scull, see further below.

37 Connecticut is a notable exception to this model. The system there appears much more similar to the English model than typical for America.

38 This will be discussed in Chapters 4 and 5.

39 Rothman, *Discovery of the Asylum*, p. 285.

40 Ibid., p. 285.

41 Rothman argues that collusion was based on a choice between sending the incurable patient back to 'primitive conditions' in the community, or retain them, 'sacrificing the goals of moral treatment' (p. 274).

42 Ibid., p. 285.

43 Ibid., pp. 246f.

44 The following discussion is based primarily on Scull's book, *The Most Solitary of Afflictions* (New Haven: Yale University Press, 1993). This is a much revised and extended second edition of his pioneering *Museums of Madness* (1979; reprinted Harmondsworth: Penguin, 1982).

45 Scull, *Most Solitary of Afflictions*, pp. 1f.

46 *Most Solitary of Afflictions*, particularly Chapter 6.

47 *Most Solitary of Afflictions*, p. 352.

48 *Most Solitary of Afflictions*, pp. 247 f., 251n.

49 *Most Solitary of Afflictions*, p. 234. For a similar claim about the late eighteenth century, see p. 184.

50 *Most Solitary of Afflictions*, for example, pp. 230, 246.

51 See, for example, testimony of Robert Lutwidge before the Select Committee on Lunatics, PP 1859 2nd sess. (156) vii 501, at questions 2090–2095.

52 *Most Solitary of Afflictions*, p. 211, quoting *Hansard*, Vol. 61, 3rd ser., 1842, col. 806. Square brackets in Scull's text. Scull further acknowledges, 'Actually, this was far from being the last occasion on which he [Shaftesbury] cast doubt on the medical profession's capacities in the diagnosis and treatment of insanity', citing further examples from 1859 and 1862: *Most Solitary of Afflictions, supra*, at 211n.

53 *Most Solitary of Afflictions*, p. 382.

54 *Most Solitary of Afflictions*, p. 333.

55 *Most Solitary of Afflictions*, p. 332.

56 *Most Solitary of Afflictions*, pp. 245 f.

57 *Most Solitary of Afflictions*, p. 245.

58 *Most Solitary of Afflictions*, p. 245.

59 Rothman, *Discovery of the Asylum*, pp. 286 and xv.

60 Busfield, *Managing Madness: Changing Ideas and Practice* (London: Hutchinson, 1986).

61 Jones, *Lunacy, Law, and Conscience, 1744–1845: The Social History of the Care of the Insane*, (London: Routledge & Kegan Paul, 1955); Jones, *Asylums and After* (London: Athlone, 1993).

62 Scull, *Museums of Madness*, p. 14.

63 *Most Solitary of Afflictions*, p. 133.

64 On 1 January 1859 there were 5,016 insane persons in private madhouses, and 7,963 in workhouses; by 1 January 1891 the numbers in private madhouses had slightly decreased to 4,547 and the insane persons in workhouses had more than doubled to 17,825. Source of statistics: *Thirty-Sixth* and *Forty-Fifth Annual Reports of the Commissioners in Lunacy*, respectively PP 1882 (357) xxxiii 1 and PP 1890–1 (286) xxxvi 1.

65 Dicey, *Lectures on the Relation between Law and Public Opinion* (London: Macmillan, 1905).

66 See, for example, Henry Parris, *Constitutional Bureaucracy* (London: George Allen & Unwin, 1969), pp. 258 ff.; Derek Fraser, *The Evolution of the British Welfare State*, 2nd edn. (Basingstoke: Macmillan, 1984) pp. 110 f.; William C. Lubenow, *The Politics of Government Growth* (Newton Abbot: David & Charles, 1971); Oliver MacDonagh, *Early Victorian Government*, (London: Weidenfeld and Nicolson, 1977); Oliver MacDonagh, 'The nineteenth-century revolution in government: a re-appraisal', *The Historical Journal*, 1 (1958): 52.

67 Brundage *England's 'Prussian Minister'* (London and University Park: Pennsylvania State University Press, 1988), p. 13.

68 e.g., Burn, *The Age of Equipoise: A Study of the Mid-Victorian Generation* (1964; reprinted New York: Norton, 1965), Chapter 4, especially pp. 132 ff.; Henry Parris, *Constitutional Bureaucracy*, pp. 268 ff.

69 e.g., Fraser, *Evolution of the British Welfare State*, pp. 117, 120 f.

70 Wiener, *Reconstructing the Criminal* (Cambridge: Cambridge University Press, 1990), at Chapter 2. The quotation is on p. 46.

71 Dean, *The Constitution of Poverty* (London: Routledge, 1991), p. 62. Note that for Dean, 'police' is a term of art which does not refer primarily to crime control or police forces in the twentieth-century sense, but rather to the science for the maintenance of social order generally.

72 In MacDonagh, 'The nineteenth-century revolution in government: a re-appraisal'.

73 Parris, *Constitutional Bureaucracy*, p. 49.

74 Lubenow, *The Politics of Government Growth*.

75 Garland, *Punishment and Welfare* (London: Gower, 1985), p. 10. Corporal punishments remained in local control until even later.

76 30 & 31 Vict. c. 106. Prior to this, the Board was subject to renewal every three to five years.

77 For medical officers, see Ruth Hodgkinson, *The Origins of the National Health Service: Medical Services of the New Poor Law, 1834–1871* (London: Wellcome Historical Medical Library, 1967), p. 476. For teachers, see M. A. Crowther, *The Workhouse System 1834–1929*, (1981; reprinted London: Methuen, 1983), p. 131.

78 At the 1876 Poor Law District Conference, for example, a motion passed to ask government to make the per diem payments for the insane also payable for insane persons in workhouses. One of the key issues at that time was the loss of local control this would entail for the local boards of guardians: *Report of Poor Law District Conferences, 1875* (London: Knight, 1876), pp. 177 ff.

79 Philips, 'Black Country magistracy 1835–60', *Midland History*, 3 (1976): 161; and H. E. Zangerl, 'The social composition of the county magistracy in England and Wales, 1831–1887', *Journal of British Studies*, 9(1) (1971): 113. With regard to the general point about the slowness of centralization, the former article is also pertinent.

80 See Brundage, *Prussian Minister*, p. 32; Brundage, Eastwood and Mandler, 'The making of the new Poor Law *Redivivus*', *Past and Present* **127** (1989): 185.

81 Bartrip, 'State intervention in mid-nineteenth century Britain', *Journal of British Studies*, **23** (1983): 63.

82 Bartrip, 'State intervention in mid-nineteenth century Britain', p. 81.

83 Bartrip, 'State intervention', p. 81n.

84 See F. M. L. Thompson, 'Social control in Victorian Britain', *Economic History Review*, **34** (2nd ser.) (1981): 180. Thompson criticizes the trend in the 1970s to extend the use of social control methodology into any situation where bourgeoisie and lower orders met. His prime example is

education of the poor, but he also refers to control of lower-class leisure and the regulation of public fairs. Apart from the efficacy question, he argues that in this sort of context, social control becomes indistinguishable from socialization, a criticism not particularly applicable to Poor Law and lunacy, where co-operation by the pauper was not necessarily optional in any meaningful sense. Regarding more blatantly coercive measures, a category in which Poor Law and lunacy seem to fit more closely, he comments, 'If social control is used simply as another name for law and order it is scarcely a great leap forward' (p. 199). That may well be true, so long as the coercive nature of the facility is acknowledged. It is less telling regarding institutions such as the workhouse, which were designed to create social effects, but were not overtly coercive: no one was legally forced to go into a workhouse, and anyone in a workhouse was entitled to leave. A level of sophistication is at work in such institutions beyond the mere perpetuation of 'law and order'.

85 See John Mayer, 'Notes towards a working definition of social control in historical analysis', in *Social Control and the State*, ed. Stanley Cohen and Andrew Scull (1983; reprinted Oxford: Blackwell, 1985), p. 17; Gareth Stedman Jones, 'Class expression versus social control?', in the same volume, p. 39; A. P. Donajgrodzki, 'Introduction', *Social Control in Nineteenth Century Britain*, ed. A. P. Donajgrodzki (London: Croom Helm, 1977).

86 Dario Melossi, *The State of Social Control* (Cambridge: Polity, 1990) p. 1 ff. and *passim*.

CHAPTER 2

Poor Law and asylum law as a single strand

Previous studies of nineteenth-century asylums have considered them in a package with private madhouses, in the context of the history of medicine. This book instead takes as a starting point that the nineteenth-century asylum is to be understood in the context of the nineteenth-century Poor Law. Others have referred to the Poor Law as part of the general intellectual background of the asylum movement, marking the social ideas and attitudinal tide which made the rise of large-scale confinement in the asylum attractive to the nineteenth century.[1] The nineteenth century is perceived in such studies as a period where social problems were seen in abstract and theoretical terms, and where broad administrative solutions to these problems were developed. Thus in these studies poverty (and also criminality, although this is less directly relevant here) is perceived as a parallel to lunacy: they were social problems to be solved. These studies do not attempt to extend the relationship beyond this point.

The relationship between administration of lunacy and Poor Law was much closer than these studies suggest. The asylum's legislative roots were in the old (i.e, pre-1834) Poor Law, and throughout the nineteenth century it remained an institution directed towards the poor. Far from being administratively separate from the nineteenth-century Poor Law, both shared an administration at the local level. And far from the nineteenth-century asylum ousting Poor Law jurisdiction in insanity, large numbers of the insane remained on other forms of poor relief, usually residing in the workhouse or living on outdoor relief. The picture which emerges is of various organs of the Poor Law, including the asylum, acting in tandem.

This closer relationship is at the core of the argument in this book;

but as it is a new departure, it warrants further discussion and justification.

THE LEGISLATION OF LUNACY AND POVERTY

The first statute allowing county asylums to be built on the rates was passed in 1808.[2] The birth of the county asylum system can reasonably be said to have occurred at that time, thus well before the enactment of the new Poor Law in 1834. To understand the legislative roots of the asylum, it is therefore necessary to make a few remarks about the old Poor Law.

The legislative foundation of the old Poor Law had been laid originally by a 1601 statute,[3] extensively modified by the end of the eighteenth century. The original policy had been threefold: those who would work, but could not get work, were to be provided with work; those who could not work were to be offered charity; and tramps, vagrants and those who refused to work were to be punished. Administration was through the more than 15,000 parishes of England and Wales. Unpaid parish overseers were directly responsible for the administration of relief, under the supervision of local Justices of the Peace.

The thrust of the policy was to keep the poor in their own communities. Relief could only be given in the parish where the pauper was 'settled', and parishes were authorized to remove paupers to their parish of settlement for relief.[4] By the eighteenth century, settlement was attained in various ways. Legitimate children received the settlement of their father; illegitimate children received the settlement of their place of birth. Women became settled in their husband's parish upon marriage, and men became settled in the parish where they were apprenticed, or then in a parish where they paid an annual rent of more than ten pounds per year. Such a tenancy was well beyond the means of the common labouring man, who thus retained for life the settlement of his father.

The 230 years following the enactment of the Elizabethan Act were full of legislative innovation. Amendments to the law of settlement were one such set of innovations. Local exemptions and requirements were another, and by the beginning of the nineteenth century, there were hundreds of these local acts. Administration, originally local, had become more centralized in the period before the Commonwealth, and more localized again afterwards. Perhaps more important for present purposes, changes in legislation and practice led to a diversification of relief. Almshouses for the aged and disabled poor had been part of the original Elizabethan Poor Law.[5] A 1722 statute allowed parishes to construct a workhouse to provide work for their able-bodied paupers,[6] and almost 2,000 such houses had been constructed by 1776.[7] These were small institutions, usually containing between 20 and 50 persons, and unlike their nineteenth-century namesakes, not normally designed to be punitive. Each county was required to build a house of correction in 1744, for the correction of various sorts of ruffians, beggars and vagabonds, including those who 'refuse to work for the usual and common Wages given to other Labourers in the like Work, in the Parishes or Places where they then are'.[8]

Gilbert's Act of 1782[9] allowed parishes to unite for purposes of poor relief, and roughly 1,000 parishes united in this way. The intention of the legislation was for workhouses to be constructed in these unions for the relief of the aged and infirm. The able-bodied were to be relieved outside the workhouse, where employment was to be provided, and wages supplemented from the poor rates if necessary. Such relief in aid of wages had become common practice in some parishes prior to this time, but this was its first legislative authorization. It was not until 1796[10] that such a practice received general legislative approval; by 1832, 10 per cent of the population was in receipt of such benefits.

Poor relief prior to 1834 was thus a patchwork of local solutions, administered by local justices and parish officers, under a jumbled accumulation of special and general statutes.

The 1808 statute was not the first English legislation to deal with lunatics. The power of the king as *parens patriae* to control and protect the persons and property of lunatics and idiots was so enshrined as far back as the fourteenth century.[11] This was appealed to only where significant property was at stake, however, and it was not until the beginning of the eighteenth century that statutes began to address the insane more generally.

A 1714 Act[12] was apparently the first instance in which committal of lunatics was mentioned specifically in a modern English statute. Its title makes clear its Poor Law character:

An Act for Reducing the Laws relating to Rogues, Vagabonds, Sturdy Beggars, and Vagrants, into one Act of Parliament; and for the more effectual Punishing such Rogues, Vagabonds, Sturdy Beggars, and Vagrants, and sending them whither they ought to be sent.

This reflects the old Poor Law policy of punishment of those who could work but refused to do so, the undeserving poor.

The Act dealt with the insane only tangentially. It allowed commitment of persons 'of little or no Estates, who, by Lunacy, or otherwise, are furiously Mad, and dangerous to be permitted to go Abroad' by two Justices, for such time as the madness continued. The reference here was explicitly to the poor. Hunter and Macalpine argue that the effect of the Act was to treat the mad differently from other categories of sturdy beggar: the mad would no longer be liable to be whipped as a punishment for their vagrancy.[13] A relatively high standard of lunacy was required by the statute. This can be seen as an extension of the common-law standard. There had long been a common-law defence to an action for trespass against people committing or restraining mad people, but the defence applied only when the lunatic was detained 'in his fury'.[14] The statute can thus be seen as carrying the common-law standard over into the statutory realm.

The 1714 provisions regarding the confinement of the mad were re-enacted in 1744.[15] This latter Act was also clearly a Poor Law statute. Its most important clause required the construction of houses of correction in all counties. Its focus was once again on controlling the unruly poor, creating offences for sheltering vagabonds and defining the powers of Justices of the Peace to deal with 'incorrigible Rogues'.

Thus the first statutes authorizing committals of the insane by the state were contained within the Poor Law. This eighteenth-century legislation had not indicated where the lunatics were to be confined, but the Poor Law seems to have been heavily involved. Some workhouses constructed under the old Poor Law had accommodation designed for lunatics.[16] The returns to the Select Committee on the State of Criminal and Pauper Lunatics in 1807 indicated that of the 2,398 pauper lunatics reported, 1,765 were in workhouses and a further 113 in houses of correction.[17]

This is broadly consistent with studies of the care of the insane under the old Poor Law. Unless the individuals were dangerous, they would be kept with their families.[18] Outdoor relief might be provided either to assist in purchasing of necessaries for the insane person, or sometimes to hire a nurse to provide supervision to allow the breadwinner(s) to continue work.[19] These cases appear to have been dealt with primarily at the parish level. The dangerously insane poor in the seventeenth and eighteenth centuries, on the other hand, would generally be sent by Quarter Sessions to some sort of secure place.

Sometimes, this would be a private madhouse, or Bethlem, which was until the mid-eighteenth century the only charitable facility in England for the care of the insane. Bethlem catered primarily to the metropolis. The dangerously insane poor in the provinces would more likely end up in a house of correction, workhouse or, occasionally, the local gaol.[20] Interestingly, Suzuki notes no change in practice with the introduction of the Vagrants Act in 1714.[21] Instead, he shows a practice of confining the dangerously insane poor by Quarter Sessions throughout the seventeenth and eighteenth centuries, suggesting that, at least in his local study of Middlesex, the 1714 Act was merely codifying a pre-existing practice.

The result of the 1807 Select Committee was enabling legislation, allowing counties to construct lunatic asylums, for their pauper lunatics.[22] Prior to this legislation, asylums had been built by private subscription and were few in number. Under the 1808 legislation, they could be built on the rates. In the history of the asylum movement, this was a significant development. Some of the arguments used by the Select Committee are reminiscent of arguments later to be employed for the removal of the insane from workhouses to asylums: conditions in the workhouses were said to be 'revolting to humanity'; lunatics needed an environment conducive to cure; asylums could cure, with the York Asylum boasting a 50-per-cent cure rate; and the inmates of the workhouse were without the legal safeguards afforded to lunatics in private madhouses.[23]

The Act was also a natural development in the Poor Law. By its terms, it was directed to the confinement of paupers. It made no provision at all for the admission of privately paying patients to the facilities. Statutory provision for the admission of such patients was made in 1815,[24] but this clause applied only if there were excess capacity in the asylum. The 1808 Act did not repeal the 1744 Act, but specifically incorporated it: persons detained under the 1744 legislation were to be kept in the county asylum, if one were constructed, otherwise in a licensed madhouse.[25] The funding and administrative mechanisms, by which Justices of the Peace superintended the asylum, were essentially the same as those used for the construction of the Poor Law houses of correction, required by the 1744 Act.[26] The old Poor Law had established a number of institutional foci for relief, including houses of correction, workhouses and almshouses. To the observer in the early nineteenth century, the county asylum must have been perceived as just another in this series.

In 1774, a second stream of statutes was commenced, designed to regulate private madhouses.[27] The original act set the tone for those which followed: all persons boarding at least two lunatics had to get a licence; houses were to be inspected, initially by representatives of the College of Physicians in London, or local Justices accompanied by a physician or surgeon in the provinces; all persons detained in such houses had to be certified by a physician, apothecary or surgeon; and the names of persons confined were to be forwarded to the College of Physicians to be included on a register. This line of statutes, like the asylum acts, was much developed over the course of the nineteenth century. In 1828, the Metropolitan Commissioners in Lunacy were established. The Commissioners took over the inspection and licensing functions from the College of Physicians; outside London, these functions remained under the control of local Justices of the Peace.[28] Following a national inspection of facilities for the insane by the Metropolitan Commissioners in 1842–4, the jurisdiction of the Lunacy Commissioners was extended in 1845 to include inspection of all private madhouses in England and Wales.[29]

Private madhouses were permitted to admit pauper patients, paid for by Poor Law authorities, and prior to the explosion in asylum building after the 1845 Asylum Act, madhouses actually contained more pauper than paying patients.[30] The actual numbers were small: in 1844, for example, roughly 18 per cent of the pauper insane were in madhouses, and by 1890, this proportion had decreased to 2 per cent. This reflects the statutory priorities: paupers could be admitted to private madhouses only when no space was available in the county asylum.[31] The removal of the poor from private asylums and the separation of paupers from other classes of insane was also reflected in the objectives of the Lunacy Commission.

The two streams of acts were not consolidated into one statute until the 1889/1890 legislative revisions, and even then the statute treated paupers and private patients quite differently.[32] The continuation of the two legislative streams reinforces the sense of the asylums as juxtaposed to the private madhouses. There was not one lunacy law system, but two.[33] The county asylum acts referred specifically to pauper lunatics throughout the century. The vestiges of the Poor Law roots of the asylum system can thus be seen as remaining in the character of the legislative framework.

THE NEW POOR LAW AND THE ASYLUM

By the first third of the nineteenth century, the Poor Law had reached a point of political crisis. Costs were soaring: poor rates increased an average of 62 per cent between 1802–3 and 1832–3.[34] At the same time, there was civil unrest among the poor. This reached a political crisis point with the Swing Riots in the south of England in the early 1830s. The Poor Law was a target of this unrest: 13 workhouses were attacked and two destroyed.[35] There were calls in Parliament for the complete abolition of the Poor Law, as an interference in the labour market and as instilling moral vice in the poor. The Whig government appointed a Royal Commission in 1832 to investigate the operation of the Poor Laws, and to recommend reform. The Commission reported in 1834, and the resulting legislation was enacted that same year.

This is not the place to examine the advent and implementation of the new Poor Law in detail, although some of the relevant issues will be discussed in subsequent chapters. Some basic information and argument here is however necessary to understand the continuing close relationship between lunacy and the Poor Law in the remainder of the century.

The new scheme involved the formation of the 15,000 parishes into roughly 600 unions. The focus of reform was the relief to be given to the able-bodied pauper, and the basis of the new structure was the so-called 'principle of less eligibility', stated by the commissioners in the following terms:

The first and most essential of all conditions, a principle which we find universally admitted, even by those whose practice is at variance with it, is, that his [i.e., the able-bodied pauper] situation on the whole shall not be made really or apparently so eligible as the situation of the independent labourer of the lowest class.[36]

Poor law was to relieve indigence, not mere poverty. To attain this end, outdoor relief to the able-bodied was to be abolished. The wage supplements of out-relief were seen as a subsidy to employers, undercutting the labour market, leading to depressed wages and the need for further supplementation of wages by the Poor Law. Such supplements were also thought to be open to abuse by dishonest poor, who might through fraud receive relief in more than one parish. Outdoor relief to the able-bodied was thus to be prohibited. Relief to the able-bodied was to be afforded only in a well-regulated union workhouse.

Notwithstanding the similar nomenclature, the workhouse of the new Poor Law was intended to bear little resemblance to its old Poor Law predecessor. The Commissioners trod a very fine line in the explanation of what a workhouse was to be. On the one hand, life in the workhouse had to be 'less eligible' than the situation of the independent labourer. On the other hand, starvation could not be countenanced, and the so-called 'independent labourers' were already living close to starvation. The result as the system developed in the early years was an attempt to make the workhouse unappealing through the use of discipline. Workhouse uniforms were required to be worn, making the inmates readily identifiable by the public and removing individuality. Husbands and wives were housed separately from their families and from each other, and could communicate only with permission of the master. Food was adequate, but plain and lacking variety. Work was tedious, for example stone-breaking for the men, laundry work and mending for the women, and the treadmill and picking oakum[37] for both. None the less, notwithstanding *Oliver Twist* and aberrations such as the Andover scandal of 1845, a case where inmates were in fact kept close to starvation, it would appear that few people starved in the workhouses.

A two-pronged attack was thus put in place. The individual pauper would be discouraged from applying for relief by the principle of less eligibility and, at the same time, the termination of outdoor relief in aid of wages would cause wages to float back up to their pre-intervention levels. This combination involved an aim more ambitious than mere relief: the aim was to terminate pauperism, at least for those morally responsible enough to live within their means. For those lacking such moral fibre, the system would at least confront them and hold them accountable for their indiscretions.

The new system was an administrative departure from the old. The new unions were to be administered by boards of guardians, mainly elected by local ratepayers, but with the local Justices of the Peace serving ex officio in rural areas. Where the old Poor Law had been administered by local volunteer parish officials, the new required each union to hire relieving officers. Some workhouse staff were also hired full-time. Originally, these included a master and a matron, but as the century progressed they grew to include nurses, schoolteachers and medical staff. Medical assistance, both inside and outside the workhouse, might be provided on a fee-for-service basis, or by salary, usually with the expectation that the physician or surgeon would carry on a private practice as well. Originally, staff costs were met entirely through the local rates, but, as time passed, the central government intervened to contribute both to the salaries of schoolteachers and medical officers of workhouses. These payments were significant, as they allowed greater central control of the employment of these people.

The movement towards greater centralization was also reflected in the formation of a central board of Poor Law Commissioners who were in charge of the implementation of the new law. A group of Assistant Commissioners was formed to inspect implementation in local unions, and report back to this central board. Centralized audit control further ensured the compliance of local jurisdictions, and annual reports from the Poor Law Commissioners provided a running commentary on the operation of the new law.

The 1834 report repeatedly indicated that the workhouse test was to apply only to the able-bodied poor. In fact, the Commissioners went so far as to praise outdoor relief of the so-called 'impotent' poor, stating that 'even in places distinguished in general by the most wanton parochial profusion, the allowances to the aged and infirm are moderate'.[38] Some of the Assistant Commissioners favoured a system of discretion, whereby the aged or infirm could be subject to the workhouse test in some circumstances 'so as not to take away altogether the apprehension of this punishment or disgrace, such as it is, from the minds of persons who might be induced by this motive to exert themselves, so as to escape the workhouse'.[39] The eventual legislation granted such discretion to the local board of guardians.

A reading of the 1834 report suggests that the workhouse was to be primarily a deterrent for the able-bodied poor, although the administrative discretion afforded to the guardians regarding the infirm complicates this image. In fact, presumably from the beginning and certainly when the first statistics were published by the Poor Law Commissioners, able-bodied adults were a minority of those in workhouses. Between 1848 and 1870, they usually represented somewhere between 13 and 17 per cent of workhouse inmates.[40] Non-able-bodied adults, other than the insane, accounted for an additional 30 to 40 per cent, and children for roughly 40 per cent. The bulk of able-bodied adult paupers continued to receive outdoor relief throughout this period.[41]

The county asylums were not directly referred to in the 1834 legislation.[42] None the less, the Poor Law connotations did not disappear. Pauper lunacy had been within the scope of the 1832 Royal Commission's examinations of the workings of the old Poor Law. While the focus of the eventual report was the able-bodied poor, various Assistant Commissioners also discussed peripherally the care of the mad and the desirability of county asylums.[43] Somewhat sporadically at first, the annual reports of the Poor Law Commissioners contained statistics relating to pauper lunacy and, from 1860, the percentage of pauperism ascribable to lunacy was calculated. In the accounts appended to these reports, asylum expenditures were categorized as 'Expenditures for Relief to the Poor, and Purposes connected therewith', and not, for example, as related to the public health functions of the Poor Law Commission.

The statistics regarding those who were confined in asylums bears out this Poor Law connection. County asylums became mandatory in 1845, and the number of paupers confined therein rose from 4,224 in 1844 to 9,966 in 1852. The number of paupers then increased more than fivefold between 1852 and 1890, that is, to 51,910. The proportion of private patients in county asylums fell from about 3.6 per cent in 1849, to less than 2 per cent by 1855, and remained under 2 per cent until at least 1890.[44]

This raises the question of what a pauper was. Technically, a 'pauper' was a person whose maintenance was paid for by his or her local parish or union. It was alleged that, for many of the people in asylums, this was a misleading designation, as the families of the inmates reimbursed the Poor Law authorities for the costs of their care. The Lunacy Commissioners in 1855 claimed that 'not infrequently tradesmen, or thriving artisans' had relatives admitted to the asylum on this basis.[45] This has led to some discussion as to whether 'paupers' in asylums can rightly be considered comparable to other paupers under the Poor Law.[46]

In Poor Law jargon, the individual had to be 'chargeable' to the parish or union. In 1875 an opinion of the Law Officers of the Crown stated that persons were 'chargeable' in this context if unable to provide themselves with the treatment necessary for their position, provided that no persons legally compellable to support them were competent to provide such treatment.[47] This provided some support for the legality of the reimbursement, so long as the family was unable to afford the costs of care of a private patient. The opinion also made it clear that the issue was eligibility for relief; individuals did not actually have to have been on the Poor Law rolls prior to the admission to the asylum, although they were afterwards.

The consideration of the Leicestershire and Rutland documents below will show that some patients were admitted on this basis, although it is open to question how significant the numbers were. It should not be taken as displacing the image of the asylum as a place for the poor, however. There was correspondence on the issue in 1863, when at the request of the Lunacy Commission, Home Secretary Sir George Gray asked the Poor Law Board for an opinion as to 'what course should be taken with reference to Lunatics being sent to the Asylum as Paupers when they are not really so'.[48] This issue arose out of a concern that families of persons in the Sussex Asylum were reimbursing the Poor Law officials for the costs of their care. The opinion of the Board did not address what constituted chargeability, and whether partial payment still left an individual chargeable, and therefore a pauper in the eyes of the statute, but it was unambiguous on the need for pauper status:

No person should be sent to an Asylum by the Justices on the application of the Relieving Officer, unless such person be a pauper Lunatic, that is, one who is chargeable on the Poor Rate. This fact should be established to the satisfaction of the Justices before they make the Order, but if a Lunatic, not chargeable to the Poor Rates, be sent to the Asylum as a pauper lunatic, it would be competent to the Visitors of the asylum to discharge such Lunatic, and such a proceeding, if threatened, or adopted, would probably prevent the recurrence of what appears to be an abuse.[49]

The Committee of Visitors of the asylum were in entire agreement, particularly since the asylum was full at the time:

The Committee cannot imagine that the legislature when providing an Asylum for paupers ever intended that persons not paupers should be permitted by collusive arrangements between Unions and their friends to participate in the benefits the asylum affords whilst those for whom it was erected are excluded.[50]

Even the Lunacy Commissioners, who supported the admission to the asylum by this system of discreet reimbursement so long as the pauper or their family could not afford the whole cost, acknowledged this argument:

This course of proceeding is stated to prevail to a considerable extent in the

Asylums of Metropolitan Counties, and its effect in occupying with patients, not strictly or originally of the pauper class, the space and accommodations which were designed for others who more properly belong to it, has more than once been the subject of complaint.[51]

The restriction to actual paupers might further be reflected in asylum admission forms. Thus both Yorkshire asylums in the 1860s included the following clause in their admission documents, in italics:

The asylum is for paupers only, and the justices are earnestly requested not to permit overseers or relieving officers to send any lunatics who are not actually chargeable as paupers.[52]

To avoid this restriction, charities were established in some counties, catering to those who were poor but not actually paupers. In Leicestershire, the justification for the charity was explained as follows:

The public can scarcely be aware of the extent of the benefit to the indigent Insane this charity confers; THE LAW PROVIDES ONLY FOR *ACTUAL PAUPERS*: but the numerous class of the population who are poor, and many of them the poorest, whose families have struggled not to be upon the parish, would in cases of insanity be totally without assistance, if the Institution did not open its doors to afford it to them.[53]

This would suggest that both by the central authorities and the local administrators the asylum was seen as a Poor Law institution, with its target clientele the poor of the county.

The characterization of the county asylum as a Poor Law institution was not without its critics in the nineteenth century. John Arlidge, a physician in the charitable hospital sector, was such a critic:

If, on the contrary, our public asylums were not branded by the appellation 'Pauper;' if access to them were facilitated and the pauperizing clause repealed, many unfortunate insane of the middle class in question, would be transmitted to them for treatment; the public asylum would not be regarded with the same misgivings as an evil to be avoided, but it would progressively acquire the character of an hospital, and ought ultimately to be regarded as a place of cure, equivalent in character to a general hospital, and as entailing no disgrace or discredit on its occupant.[54]

These critics do not appear to have swayed the administrative mentality, however. Thus even in 1908, the Royal Commission on the Care and Control of the Feeble-Minded dealt with county asylums in a section entitled 'Poor Law Institutional Relief Outside the "Workhouse"',[55] and both majority and minority reports of the Royal Commission on the Poor Laws and Relief of Distress in 1909 consider county asylums in the context of poor relief.[56] The Poor Law character of the asylum remained firm throughout the nineteenth century.

THE CONTINUATION OF WORKHOUSE CARE

At the same time, insane paupers continued to be cared for in the workhouses of the new Poor Law. From 1842[57] to 1890, a fairly steady 25 per cent of poor persons identified as insane were institutionalized in the workhouse, an increase from 3,829 in 1844 to 17,825 in 1890.[58] Many of these people were housed with the general workhouse population. However, by mid-century they were increasingly classified within the workhouse environment itself, and special wards were built to house them. In 1859, the Lunacy Commissioners reported that about one-tenth of the workhouses in England and Wales had such wards.[59] By 1865, 104 of the 688 workhouses in England and Wales had these dedicated wards.[60]

This workhouse care was given explicit statutory recognition over the course of the century. The Poor Law Amendment Act of 1834 had prohibited the detention of dangerous lunatics in the workhouse for longer than 14 days.[61] This was taken by implication as allowing the continued accommodation of non-dangerous insane persons in workhouses,[62] a reasonable interpretation given the history of workhouse accommodation of the insane. Commencing in 1862, statutory authority was provided for the removal of chronic cases to the workhouse from the asylum.[63] In 1867, the Metropolitan Poor Act mandated the construction of large Poor Law facilities in London for the insane,[64] resulting shortly thereafter in accommodation in two new facilities for a total of 3,000 insane paupers.

Prior to 1867, there was no statutory power to confine the insane in workhouses. The common law had traditionally provided a defence for those confining insane persons dangerous to be at large.[65] This had theoretically been overridden by sections of the madhouse acts, although the courts could be slow to apply these sections.[66] The 14-day proviso in the Poor Law Amendment Act presumably provided some legal authority for detention for the 14 days. Those who were not actually dangerous were in theory free to leave the workhouse at will, like any other pauper, although according to the Lunacy Commission, local Poor Law authorities might discourage this. This rather awkward situation was clarified by the Poor Law Amendment Act 1867, which provided workhouses with formal committal powers for the first time.[67]

There has been a tendency to consider workhouse care of the insane as substandard and particularly unpleasant. Certainly, there is anecdotal evidence to support such a vision. The annual reports of the Lunacy Commission recited instances of restraint, inadequate accommodation, insufficient exercise, substandard food, occasional cruelty, insufficient or non-existent record-keeping, poor locations and lack of curative treatment directed towards the insane.[68] These images will be discussed in greater detail below.[69] Suffice it here to say that the Poor Law authorities contested the claim that such conditions were in any way typical, and occasionally the Lunacy Commissioners themselves might acknowledge reasonable standards of workhouse care in their annual reports, as for example in their *Fifteenth Annual Report*:

In many Workhouses the Lunatic Wards are evidently intended to supersede the County Asylum. The Patients are under the care of experienced attendants. The buildings are specially constructed for the Insane, and include baths, padded rooms, &c. The dietary is on a more liberal scale than that of the ordinary inmates; and the general treatment of the Patients is in some measure assimilated to that adopted in County Asylums, although some of the most important provisions are wanting. The class of Patients found in these wards differs little, if at all, from those met with in County Asylums; and the changes of Patients which take place (and which is shown in some of the Workhouses by a record of the admissions, discharges, and deaths), are as frequent as those met with in ordinary Asylums.[70]

Indeed, there might be reasons why workhouse care might be preferable for the lunatic, depending on the individual asylum or workhouse ward where the lunatic would be kept. The asylum in the lunatic's county might be located miles from his or her family, rendering visits a practical impossibility. Visiting hours might also be more liberal in the workhouse. In some cases, notwithstanding the pride of the asylum in providing a liberal diet, the lunatic might actually receive more food in the workhouse.[71] Some workhouses put lunatics under the care of other workhouse paupers, some of whom were old and feeble-minded themselves, but an increasing number in the 1850s and 1860s provided qualified and professional attendant care similar to the asylums, and regular medical visitation. For lunatics contained in general wards, the workhouse offered the possibility of mixing with the general inmate population, providing arguably less stigma than confinement in the asylum, and perhaps a more interesting existence.

The Lunacy Commission's general expectation was that the workhouse would contain chronic cases only. There were indications of the success of workhouses as curative institutions as well, however. Samuel Gaskell, a physician and Lunacy Commissioner, was questioned in this regard with reference to an unnamed workhouse ward in his testimony before the 1859 House of Commons Select Committee on Lunatics, in which 35 of 90 insane inmates had recovered completely, and an additional 35 had 'derived great benefit'. Gaskell accounted for these numbers by speculating a high number of the cases being of delirium tremens, or caused by a temporary and minor domestic irritation or 'slight cases of temporary insanity'. The apparently curative effect of the workhouse was explained as follows:

[I]n all probability they were cases arising from temporary causes, which were readily removed by admitting the patient into any place away from his home, where he would have the benefit of change of scene; he would rapidly recover.[72]

The difficulty with this admission was that the distinction from the asylum became blurred: if the issue was removal from home, why removal to the asylum rather than to the workhouse?

The comments regarding the St Pancras workhouse in the annual report of the Lunacy Commissions for 1860 provides a further indication of a curative image for the workhouse. In 1860, 423 insane people were admitted, including 50 persons with delirium tremens or other alcohol-related problems, 73 with acute mania and 40 melancholics. That same year, there were 449 discharges, being 127 persons who had recovered or were much improved, 147 sent to asylums, 46 deceased and 129 other discharges.[73]

There was even by 1859 some ambiguity as to whether the workhouse might offer a better chance of cure than the county asylum. Dr George Webster, a medical practitioner and member of the board of guardians for Camberwell Union, in his testimony to the 1859 Select Committee stated on the one hand that curable cases ought to be sent to the asylum, but not entirely consistently that the workhouse offered a better chance of cure for some people:

2318. Is there any other advantage in that [i.e., in the accommodation of incurable and chronic cases in the workhouse] besides the economy? – Yes, there is this advantage, that they would be with their friends; they can see them more, and they can occasionally mix with the inmates of the house; and indeed, they are more likely to be curable than otherwise by being in a small number than in a large house.

2319. Did you not say that you did not propose to retain any curable patients? — Yes; but now and then even these imbeciles, even the chronic cases are cured and become more probably curable. There are not 20 patients in the lunatic asylum at Wandsworth that are probably curable out of 950.[74]

Dedicated lunatic wards of workhouses were thus not necessarily mere warehouses where the insane were allowed to fester out of the public eye.

Outdoor relief also continued for the pauper insane. Such relief for the insane is consistent with the policy of the new Poor Law, which was in theory concerned most immediately with confinement of the able-bodied poor in workhouses. The statistical significance of such relief waned under the new Poor Law, however, from roughly a quarter of the insane poor at mid-century to only about 6 per cent in 1890. Thus while it is doubtful whether the institutional solution to pauper insanity may be equated with care in county asylums, the decreasing importance of outdoor relief does suggest that the institutional solution was adopted for the pauper insane in the nineteenth century.

The care of the insane in workhouses and on outdoor relief survived the nineteenth century. Thus the Minority Report of the Poor Law Commission estimated in 1909 that nearly 70,000 mentally defective persons were under the jurisdiction of these branches of the Poor Law, compared to no more than 120,000 in asylums.[75] Indeed, their argument that such a large group of persons ought to be withdrawn from the Poor Law was taken by them as entailing the break-up of the entire Poor Law system.[76]

ADMINISTERING THE SYSTEM

The asylums and the remainder of the Poor Law were not two systems operating in parallel. They were instead parts of the same system. They were, after all, administered by the same people. Notwithstanding the creation of the Poor Law and lunacy central authorities, most administrative duties rested with the local boards of guardians and their staff, and apart from the signing of the actual order authorizing admission to the asylum, the administration of pauper lunacy relied almost entirely on the Poor Law staff.

Thus it was Poor Law medical officers who after 1845 were to keep lists of insane paupers not in asylums, and visit them quarterly.[77] This provision was a supplement to a requirement dating back to 1828 that overseers of the poor under the old Poor Law to make annual lists of pauper lunatics.[78] Medical officers were also under a duty to report any pauper lunatic they encountered to the Poor Law relieving officer within three days.[79]

The statutes seem to envisage that this would be the standard entry route into the committal system. Indeed, the statute tended to suggest an image of Poor Law officers combing the shires for insane paupers. The reality was somewhat different, as will be seen in subsequent chapters. In fact, it appears generally to have been the lunatic's family or occasionally neighbours who approached the Poor Law officials.[80] Thus the initial contact was normally with the Poor Law relieving officer.

It was the Poor Law relieving officer who completed the particulars of the order for reception. These particulars were not merely basic personal facts such as name and address, but also included some describing features of the insanity: length of time insane, whether first attack, age on first attack, whether suicidal or dangerous to others and, after 1853, the supposed cause. It was the relieving officer who had carriage of the application from this stage. The statute imposed a duty to bring the alleged lunatic before a Justice within three days.

Next, medical certificates were necessary. Until 1853, Poor Law medical officers were precluded from signing these certificates, but after 1853 their involvement quickly became the norm. In theory, it was the responsibility of the Justice to arrange for the medical examination; in practice, it would appear that this was done prior to approaching the Justice.

It was at this stage that the Justice was called upon to sign the order for admission. If two medical certificates were presented to the Justice, one signed by the Poor Law medical officer and another by an independent doctor, the Justice in theory had no discretion not to confine the pauper.[81] This was the extremely rare case.[82] Normally, confinement was discretionary on the part of the Justice. Discharge from the asylum was within the powers of the Committee of Visitors, Justices nominated annually by Quarter Sessions to superintend the running of the asylum.

It was theoretically compulsory for relieving officers to bring all pauper lunatics before a Justice, except for a brief period from 1853 to 1862 when discretion was given not to report a lunatic if not 'a proper person to be sent to an asylum'.[83] After 1853, the duty of the medical officer to commence committal proceedings through notifying the relieving officer was also discretionary. The 1862 statute gave the workhouse medical officer an additional authority to certify a lunatic as 'a proper Person to be kept in a Workhouse',[84] suggesting no diminution of the responsibility of Poor Law staff to determine the place where lunatics were to be kept. In any event, it appears clear that Poor Law staff were not bringing all lunatics before Justices, but were diverting paupers off into other systems of relief.

Even at the level of the Justices, the division between the asylum and the remainder of the Poor Law was not as great as might first appear. While the new Poor Law limited the direct role of the individual Justice in the administration of poor relief, it did not oust the jurisdiction of Justices in Quarter Sessions, particularly in the important matter of disputes between unions over settlement and thus liability for payment. Furthermore, local Justices in rural unions sat ex officio on boards of guardians. The indications are that, in some unions, these ex officio members were less active than the elected members,[85] but their continued membership suggests a closer administrative relationship between asylum admission and the remainder of the Poor Law than might be first apparent from the statutes. The Justices must be taken to have been aware of the relief to the insane being offered in other branches of the Poor Law. They must at least tacitly have approved of such relief, as the statutes gave them a clear power to intervene and remove insane paupers to the asylum howsoever knowledge of that pauper came to them.[86]

The integration of the asylum admission procedures with the remainder of the Poor Law continued if the lunatic pauper was placed on poor relief outside the asylum. For paupers on outdoor relief, the system of quarterly visitation by Poor Law medical officers continued, with the resulting duties to report to relieving officers. Those admitted to the workhouse would be placed immediately in a probationary ward, pending examination by the medical officer of the facility. The rules then stated:

If the medical officer, upon such examination, pronounces the pauper to be labouring under any disease of body or mind, the pauper shall be placed either in the sick ward, or the ward for lunatics and idiots not dangerous, as the medical officer shall direct.[87]

The medical officer was required periodically to visit insane paupers in the workhouse, to provide all necessary instructions for their diet and treatment and to report them to boards of guardians.[88] These provisions allowed for the continued identification of paupers for removal to an asylum. In Leicestershire, as will be shown below, a little over a quarter of asylum admissions in the first half of the 1860s were admitted from the workhouse.

Given the administrative focus of the care of lunatic paupers, it is not a surprise that Poor Law administrative manuals tend to include the duties of the Poor Law officials regarding lunacy.[89] William Golden Lumley, a barrister and assistant secretary to the Poor Law Commissioners, devoted an entire book to the 1845 Lunacy Acts.[90]

The administrative processes focus on the Poor Law officials to the exclusion of both the central authorities and the asylum staff. The involvement of these bodies was not completely ousted. Thus while the asylum staff had no role in the admission of patients, they did have an advisory role in patient discharge from the asylum.

The central authorities' involvement was more formalized. They received copies of the lists compiled by the medical officers along with the medical officers' comments about the individuals on those lists, and they did follow up with queries about dubious cases. The Poor Law central authority might be quite tenacious in advocating asylum admission where there was some reason to believe an individual on outdoor relief might actually be dangerous, but their effectiveness lay more in persuasion than in the threat of legal intervention. The Lunacy Commissioners and Poor Law inspectorate both visited workhouses regularly, and might recommend the removal of individuals to the asylum. Lunacy Commissioners also made annual visitations to the county asylums, and recommended alterations in accommodation. The legal powers of the central authorities were limited, however, and they tended to rely on persuasion.

The asylum system was built on the Poor Law administrative infrastructure. The new Poor Law made the growth of the county asylum a real possibility. Prior to the introduction of the new Poor Law, county asylums were few and small.[91] The introduction by the new Poor Law of a professional administrative staff created the bureaucratic machinery to make a national system of asylums feasible.

This may not have been a sufficient condition for the creation of large county asylums, but it was certainly a necessary one, as it is difficult to see the voluntary officers of the old Poor Law, with its haphazard and patchwork variety of relief, as yielding the relatively consistent approach of the post-1834 bureaucracy.[92]

INITIAL OBJECTIONS AND RESPONSES

The existing history of madness provides a number of orthodoxies as to the motivating factors of the local Poor Law decision-makers. Some of these are themes, such as the behaviour of the individual and the possibility of cure, which will be elaborated in the chapters which follow. Others have been influential, but are in the end unsatisfactory: the relative expense of asylum care, the lack of space in county asylums, and the distinction between idiocy and lunacy. These are discussed now.

Expense

Expense is the most common factor cited. Anne Digby's comment that care of the mentally ill was 'stifled by financial pressures within a destitution authority' is typical of the approach.[93] This approach reflects the attitude of the Lunacy Commissioners. Their chairman, Lord Shaftesbury, in his testimony to the 1859 Select Committee on Lunatics referred to 'the dogged and passive resistance which is offered by the [local Poor Law] authorities, who are determined that they will not incur what they consider will be an increased expense'.[94] Needless to say, these allegations were firmly denied by the Poor Law authorities. As one put it, 'they [the guardians] would not trifle with the brains of any fellow-creature to save themselves a few shillings'.[95]

There was no question that the asylum was more costly than the workhouse, although different accounting practices made (and make) it difficult to assess the precise degree of the difference. According to Lord Shaftesbury in 1859, a typical asylum would pay three shillings eight-and-a-half pence per pauper per week for food, and an additional eight-and-a-quarter pence for clothing, for a total of just under four shillings and five pence a week maintenance.[96] Shaftesbury argued that this compared not too unfavourably with workhouse maintenance charges of four shillings per week, which referred to the same items of expenditure.[97]

The view that economy was a pervasive motivation of the Poor Law administrators must none the less be viewed critically. The Lunacy Commission claimed at its most critical that lunatics were not placed in the care of their friends because the guardians believed that 'the cheapest way is to get them within the walls of the workhouse, and there stint them, and starve them.... They say, "We will keep them very quietly here, and almost for nothing."'[98] Outdoor relief would generally have been cheaper than workhouse confinement, however. In Billesdon Union in Leicestershire in 1863, for example, maintenance charges in the workhouse were roughly three shillings and sixpence per week. Outdoor relief ranged from one shilling and ten pence per week to four shillings and ten pence, but only one of the ten insane persons receiving outdoor relief received more than three shillings.[99] Any reluctance of the Poor Law authorities to place people on outdoor relief thus cannot simply be ascribed to parsimonious motives.

Instead, the evidence seems to point to a rather startling willingness of the Poor Law authorities to spend money on the care of the insane. This is easiest to see with reference to county asylums, where accounts were kept separately from the remainder of the Poor Law. The nineteenth century after the new Poor Law represented a veritable explosion in asylum care and construction. In 1832, there had been 13 county asylums. By 1858, that number had tripled, and by 1890, the total had reached 66. The average size of asylums grew from 116 inmates in 1826, to 298 in 1850, to 387 in 1860, and would surpass 800 in 1890.[100] In 1856, 17 of the 32 asylums open at that time had some form of building programme in operation.[101] Hanwell Asylum in Middlesex had been constructed in 1831 for 500 patients. Within two years, it was full. Within a further two years, it contained an excess of 100 people, and within a further two years, it was enlarged to accommodate 800. By 1851, it contained over 1,000 patients, and a second Middlesex asylum, Colney Hatch, was built to accommodate 1,200 patients. By 1856, the Lunacy Commissioners had been asked to expand Hanwell by a further 600 to a total size of 1,620, and Colney Hatch by more than 700, to almost 2,000.[102] Asylums were being built and people were being sent to them. It is difficult, given this explosion, to see where the reluctance of the Poor Law decision-makers to spend money on pauper lunatics was manifest.

The expenditure on asylums in real terms reflects this. By 1863, the Poor Law authorities were spending over half a million pounds per year on county asylum charges, a figure which grew to £1.2 million in

1890. From 1857 to 1890, total expenditures on asylum charges were almost £27.5 million. This figure grew from 8 per cent of the total expenditures in relief of the poor in 1857, to 14 per cent in 1890.[103] By the early 1860s, expenditures on pauper lunatics in county asylums were more than double the amounts spent on all medical relief to the poor; by 1877, they were more than treble.[104] These sums do not include monies expended in the erection and staffing of workhouses and the maintenance of insane persons in them, expenses which were not accounted separate from other workhouse expenses, but which must have been considerable and increasing in proportion to other workhouse expenses with the construction of more and more sophisticated lunatic wards in workhouses in this period. Payments for lunatics on outdoor relief would have added additional expenses.

The asylum expenses cited do not include collateral costs of asylum admission, such as transportation to the asylum, costs which were not insignificant. Burbage Parish in Leicestershire, for example, paid from one pound to two pounds ten shillings for conveyance of a lunatic the 11 miles to the Leicester asylum in the second half of the 1840s. The medical examination prior to 1853, when Poor Law medical officers were authorized to complete the required certificates, would cost the parish an additional ten shillings. As a point of comparison, the asylum charged seven shillings per week for maintenance at this stage. In the event that the asylum was full, the parish sent paupers to a private asylum, Haydock Lodge. Transportation of a pauper from Haydock Lodge cost the parish about four pounds ten shillings in 1846.[105]

Thus the financial commitment made by the Poor Law authorities was considerable. The question can always be asked whether enough money is being spent. Particularly given the considerable expenditures being made, it would be surprising if Poor Law authorities were not concerned about the costs of pauper lunacy. This is particularly true given that one of the justifications for the introduction of the new Poor Law was the previous escalation in the cost of poor relief. None the less, the patterns of confinement and payment do not support the claim that the decision-making regarding lunacy was simply driven by concerns about economy.

Overcrowding

The lack of space in asylums is also touted as a reason for workhouse accommodation of the insane,[106] and once again such claims are not without their support in the nineteenth-century documents.[107] Again, it is not suggested that this was never a factor, but rather that it is not entirely satisfying as a comprehensive explanation. According to figures provided in the *Eleventh Annual Report* of the Lunacy Commissioners, only ten of the 37 asylums turned anyone away in 1856. In London, 618 people were turned away that year, but, outside London, the number was much smaller: only 304 for the entire country. In total, on 1 January 1857, the system was operating at approximately 91 per cent of capacity.[108]

The opening of two new county asylums in Lancashire in 1851 further suggests that a low vacancy rate in asylums was not the only factor in sending people to workhouses. There was already an asylum in Lancashire, Lancaster Moor. In 1850, it can be estimated that there were roughly 1,807 insane paupers in Lancashire: 758 in the existing county asylum, 380 in private madhouses or hospitals and roughly 673 in workhouses.[109] With the opening of the two new asylums, available asylum accommodation rose to approximately 1,658 places, enough to accommodate almost all lunatics then in asylums, workhouses and private madhouses in the county. The Lunacy Commissioners reported gleefully in their *Sixth Annual Report* (1851):

The happy effect of these judicious arrangements is already very sensibly felt. The Workhouses in the County of Lancaster, many of which, until the last year, contained numerous cases of insanity in its various forms, and more especially of dangerous epilepsy and idiocy, have now been in a great measure relieved from a charge which ought never to have been imposed on them.[110]

The statistics tell a somewhat different story. In 1852, there were approximately 1,976 insane paupers in the various facilities. The three asylums contained a total of 1,277, private madhouses and hospitals four and workhouses 695.[111] The *Sixth Annual Report* provides some anecdotal evidence that paupers were transferred from the Manchester workhouse to the new asylum at Prestwich.[112] The new asylums had removed pauper lunatics from private madhouses in Lancashire, at least temporarily, consistent with the priority accorded by the Commissioners to removing pauper lunatics from establishments motivated by profit. Haydock Lodge, a private asylum which had housed 355 pauper patients prior to the opening of the new county asylums, was entirely closed down and renovated to receive private patients, although, by the end of 1854, it was once again housing 53 paupers.[113] What is relevant for the present discussion is that, notwithstanding that the asylums were operating at only 77 per cent capacity, the total number of insane in workhouses was continuing to grow.

It is much too simplistic to ascribe the continued accommodation of the insane in workhouses to a lack of available accommodation in asylums. The Commissioners in Lunacy themselves recognized this in their *Eleventh Annual Report* (1857), and ascribed a desire of the local officials to keep the rates down as an additional reason for the continuation of the insane in workhouses.[114]

WORKHOUSE IDIOTS

The Commissioners commented upon the opening of the new asylums in Lancashire that the people remaining in the workhouses might 'correctly be described as, nearly all, persons whose unsoundness of mind has the character of harmless idiocy or imbecility'.[115] The implication that it was idiots that were left in the workhouses, while cases of lunacy were the proper province of the asylum, appeared fairly frequently in the mid-nineteenth-century documents,[116] and it is therefore appropriate to ask whether the distinction between idiocy and lunacy is a useful one.

In law, the distinction between idiocy and lunacy had been important for hundreds of years.[117] There were three points of distinction useful for the present discussion. Idiocy commenced at birth or very shortly after, while lunacy could commence at any time in a person's life. Idiocy was a permanent state, whereas lunacy in law always allowed the possibility of cure. Finally, lunacy always allowed the possibility of a 'lucid interval', a period of time when notwithstanding the continuation of the disease, the subject functioned normally; such a possibility was not consistent with idiocy.

By the nineteenth century, medical theory was creating different categorizations. First, a range of conditions had been developed, from idiocy, which affected all mental faculties, to imbecility, a less extreme condition.[118] By 1824, leading alienist physician Alexander Morison was articulating these concepts in terms of both congenital and acquired conditions.[119] By mid-century, the traditional categories were being criticized as unhelpful by leading members of the medical establishment. The physician Samuel Hitch, first head of the Association of Medical Officers of Asylums and Hospitals for the Insane, remarked in his report on Leicester Workhouse:

I have used, as expressive of the forms of disease under which I found the patients suffering, the terms which are now recognized by Medical men conversant with Insanity, those of 'Lunatic', 'Idiots' and 'Insane person', though still retained in Lawbooks not being descriptive of any distinct form of mental disease, nor capable of conveying any definite idea of the state or the prospect of his or her restoration.[120]

Along with dementia, melancholia, moral insanity and epilepsy, Hitch did refer to idiocy and imbecility, but in the revised categorization only two persons fell into each of these classes of the 31 people identified as insane on the annual returns and remaining in the workhouse at the time of his report. This compares with 17 of the 36 people identified as idiotic, imbecilic, 'half-witted' or (in one case) 'childish' on the return itself, completed a year before Hitch's report.[121]

The Lunacy Commissioners also claimed that the term 'idiot' was not being used in its medical sense:

The Poor Law Commissioners have, in their return of Pauper Lunatics in England and Wales for the year 1842, returned the numbers of Lunatics belonging to Parishes formed into Unions, at that time, 6451, and of idiots 6261. In these Returns, the word 'Idiot' is used in a more extensive sense than that in which it is usually employed by medical men, and we think that the term ought to be confined to cases of congenital idiocy. This will account for the very large numbers which have been returned under this description, and which, in point of fact, includes a large number of lunatics of every class. The return would represent that the lunatics of all descriptions belonging to Parishes in Unions, throughout England and Wales, exceeds that of the idiots only by 190.[122]

If the Poor Law authorities were not adopting the medical definitions, it was still not the case that they were using the old legal criteria with any consistency. Thus it is clear that idiocy did not necessarily originate at or near birth. The returns provided to the Poor Law Commissioners in 1837 required 'born idiots' to be distinguished. Those returns indicate that of 5,060 idiots in Poor Law unions created at that time, only 3,710 (73 per cent) were born idiots. This is consistent with the testimony of H. B. Farnall, a Poor Law inspector, to the Select Committee on Lunatics in 1859:

1599. What do you think is the malady, in the greater number of those cases, if there be one, which would not justify you in saying that they ought to be sent to an asylum? – I think that they are harmless, idiotic, and incurable people.

1600. Would many of them come under the description of infirm people from age? – Generally they would not. Generally they would be persons who are attacked by fits, and who suffer from fits severely, and therefore are very much weakened in their minds.[123]

A view of the statistics casts further doubt on whether a consistent theoretical structure was adopted at all by local Poor Law officials. In an introduction to the statistics relating to insanity in the *Twelfth Annual Report* of the Poor Law Board, the Principal of the Statistical Department, Frederick Purdy, remarked on the difficulties of classification. The returns that year had generally classified directly according to idiocy or lunacy, but a wide variety of other classifications had been included on some returns. These had ranged from relatively technical terms, such as *maniae potu*, to lay terms such as 'silly'. The distinction drawn by the statistical department was that everyone who was congenitally insane would be classified as an idiot, while other insane people would be classified as lunatics. This classification was to be irrespective of the age at which the insanity commenced.[124]

It is not clear, given the variety of designations listed in the report, how the statistical department was in a position to ascertain who was congenitally insane and who not. It is also not clear that this was the distinction uniformly adopted by the individuals completing the returns. The variation in the frequency of idiocy relative to lunacy does not give cause for optimism. Mr Purdy summarized:

12. The proportion of Idiots to the total number of Insane Paupers is between ONE THIRD and ONE FOURTH, i.e., 29.3 per cent. for the whole Country. But there is considerable variation from this proportion in different Union Counties, and in different Divisions. In the Metropolis, where it is the lowest, the ratio is 9.5 per cent.; and in North Wales, where it is the highest, it is 52.3 per cent.[125]

London and Wales were the extremes. The remaining regions gave an appearance of greater consistency, ranging from 28.2 per cent to 35.7 per cent. The consistency disappears, however, when individual counties are considered. Five English counties reported that over 40 per cent of their insane were idiots, and, in an additional 15, the ratio was greater than one in three. Two counties outside London, Rutland and the East Riding of Yorkshire, reported that less than 20 per cent of their insane persons were idiots, and Cornwall and Durham reported less than 25 per cent. These figures are not decisive. Local variations may occur. None the less, the proportional range of idiots to lunatics does little to inspire confidence that uniform criteria were applied in the distinction between idiots and lunatics.

The Lunacy Commissioners themselves recognized the difficulty in distinguishing between the terms 'idiocy' and 'lunacy':

These terms, which are themselves vague and comprehensive, are often applied with little discrimination, and in practice are made to include every intermediate degree of mental unsoundness, from imbecility on the one hand, to absolute lunacy or idiocy on the other.[126]

The usefulness of the categorization is correspondingly limited.[127]

CONCLUSION

This chapter has been a justification of a starting point. In my view, the administration of the mad by the state in nineteenth-century England was a part of the Poor Law. It relied upon Poor Law administration and it confined paupers. Roy Porter argues against an 'epistemological rupture' in medical treatment of the mad between the eighteenth and nineteenth centuries.[128] Rupture in medical theory there may not have been, but rupture in administration there was, in the creation and flourishing of county asylums. As a result, the poor represented roughly 90 per cent of those mad people in institutions by the end of the nineteenth century. In nineteenth-century county asylums, private patients, including those relatively poor people placed through charitable schemes such as the one in Leicester, were always a minuscule percentage of the patients. After 1855, they never accounted for more than 2 per cent of the inmates.

The nineteenth century manifested a change in administrative attitudes. In the eighteenth century committals were few, and only of the dangerous. As Porter has said, 'In Georgian times public authorities had no brief systematically to police the mad.'[129] The nineteenth century changed that. The Lunacy Acts provided the legal authority for the close policing of the mad poor, and the new Poor Law provided the administrative machinery. While the policing may never have been as close as the statutes intended, it was of a fundamentally different sort from that of the eighteenth century.

And yet if there was rupture, there was also continuity. The old Poor Law had generated a variety of institutional responses to poverty: workhouses, almshouses, houses of correction, dispensaries and medical services being obvious examples. The county asylum, with its legislative roots pre-dating the introduction of the new Poor Law by a quarter of a century, was a part of that diversification, and its authority structures continued to reflect those old Poor Law roots. The rupture cannot therefore be considered in isolation, but instead as relative to the alteration in Poor Law theory and practice which occurred in the nineteenth century. The interplay between this reform and continuity is a theme which will recur in the chapters which follow.

NOTES

1 See, e.g., Andrew Scull, *Museums of Madness* (1979; reprinted Harmondsworth: Penguin, 1982), Ch. 1; and Joan Busfield, *Managing Madness* (London: Hutchinson, 1986), Ch. 7; Berrios and Freeman, 'Introduction', *150 Years of British Psychiatry*, (London: Gaskell, 1991), p. x.

2 48 Geo. III c. 96 s. 19.

3 43 Eliz. I c. 2.

4 The eighteenth-century law of settlement was based in a 1662 statute, 13&14 Car. II c. 12.

5 Their legislative authorization was 39 Eliz. I c. 5, thus pre-dating the 1601 Act by four years.

6 Knatchbull's Act, 9 Geo. I c. 7.

7 Anne Digby, *The Poor Law in Nineteenth-Century England and Wales* (London: Historical Association, 1982), p. 6.

8 17 Geo. II c. 5 s. 1.

9 22 Geo. III c. 83.

10 36 Geo. III c. 23.

11 *De Prerogativa Regis*, 17 Edw. II, stat. I, cap. ix (1324). It would appear that even this was merely codifying existing legal doctrine: see Ontario, *Final Report of the Enquiry on Mental Competency* (D. Weisstub, chair) (Toronto: Queen's Printer, 1990), Appendix III at note 551; and Heywood and Massey, *Court of Protection Practice*, 9th edn., (London: Stevens and Sons, 1961). The power was much amended by statute in the nineteenth century.

12 12 Anne c. 23 (1714).

13 Richard Hunter and Ida MacAlpine, *Three Hundred Years of Psychiatry, 1535–1860* (1963; reprinted Hartsdale, NY: Carlisle Publishing, 1982). p. 299.

14 See Sir John Comyn, *Digest of the Laws of England*, 5th edn., 8 vols, ed. Anthony Hammond (London: Strachan, 1822), at Vol. 6, p. 544, pl. 3.M.22; Sir Matthew Brook, *A New Abridgement of the Law*, 7th edn., 8 vols, ed. H. Gwillim (Vols 2–4) and C. Dodd (Vols 1, 5–8) (London:

Strachan, 1828), at Vol. 7, p. 664; Robert Brook, *La Grande Abridgement*, 2 vols (n.p., 1573), 'Faux Imprisonment', pl. 28, Vol. 1, p. 330; *Brookshaw v. Hopkins* (1773), Lofft. 240 at 243 (KB).

15 17 Geo. II c. 5 s. 20.

16 See, for example, the House of Industry of the Flegg incorporation in Norfolk, constructed between 1775 and 1777, which had separate accommodation for lunatics: cf. Anne Digby, *Pauper Palaces* (London: Routledge, 1978), p. 37. St Peter's Workhouse in Bristol also housed lunatics, and went so far as to provide for their weekly visitation by a medical practitioner: cf. Roy Porter, *Mind-Forg'd Manacles* (London: Athlone, 1987), p. 118.

17 *Report of the Select Committee on the State of Criminal and Pauper Lunatics and the Laws Relating thereto, 1807*, PP 1807 (39) ii 69, at 12. These figures do not include criminal lunatics, who were committed under 39&40 Geo. III (1800) c. 94. The figures are not clear as to how many of the individuals shown as lunatics were detained pursuant to the 1744 legislation, and how many were merely housed in the establishments without formal legal authority. The overwhelming presence of lunatics in the Poor Law facilities, compared with 37 people in gaols, 115 people in madhouses, 23 in hospitals or asylums, 108 privately lodged and 78 on out-relief suggest that the workhouse had established itself as the pre-eminent place for the state to house mad people at this time. The Committee believed that the numbers reported were far below the actual numbers of pauper lunatics in the country. They did not explicitly challenge the distribution of those lunatics, however, between the various methods of care.

18 See Akihito Suzuki, 'Lunacy in seventeenth- and eighteenth-century England: analysis of Quarter Sessions records Part I', *History of Psychiatry*, 2 (1991): 437; Peter Rushton, 'Lunatics and idiots: mental disability, the community and the Poor Law in north-east England 1600–1800', *Medical History*, 32 (1988): 34; A. Fessler, 'The management of lunacy in seventeenth-century England: an investigation of Quarter-Sessions records', *Proceedings of the Royal Society of Medicine*, 49 (1956): 901. Rushton associates the dangerous–not dangerous distinction with the lines between idiocy and lunacy. Whatever the merits of that association for the seventeenth and eighteenth centuries, it will be argued below that it is generally unhelpful in a nineteenth-century context.

19 Suzuki, 'Lunacy in seventeenth- and eighteenth-century England, Part I', pp. 453 ff. This practice of providing nursing care through outdoor relief structures continued in Leicestershire at least into the mid-nineteenth century: see Chapter 4, below.

20 Akihito Suzuki, 'Lunacy in seventeenth- and eighteenth-century England, Part II', *History of Psychiatry*, 3 (1992): 29.

21 Suzuki, 'Lunacy in seventeenth- and eighteenth-century England, Part II', p. 35.

22 *An Act for the better Care and Maintenance of Lunatics being Paupers or Criminals in England*, 48 Geo. III (1808) c. 96.

23 *Report of the Select Committee on the State of Criminal and Pauper Lunatics and the Laws Relating thereto, 1807*, PP 1807 (39) ii 69.

24 55 Geo. III (1815) c. 46 s. 12.

25 48 Geo. III (1808) c. 96 s. 19.

26 17 Geo. II (1744) c. 5 ss. 30, 33.

27 The first statute in the series is 14 Geo. III (1774) c. 49.

28 See 9 Geo. IV c. 41.

29 See 8 & 9 Vict. c. 100. Their licensing powers remained restricted to the metropolitan madhouses. The Lunacy Commissioners also received authority to inspect, but not license or approve, workhouses and county asylums at this time as well: 8 & 9 Vict. c. 126.

30 In the late 1840s, paupers represented up to 60 per cent of those in private madhouses. By 1860, this proportion had decreased to 31 per cent, following the explosion in asylum growth of the 1850s. It varied between a quarter and roughly a third of those in private madhouses until the end of the century. Note, however, the declining significance of this form of care: numbers in madhouses were 6,931 (4,178 paupers) in 1849; by 1890, these numbers had fallen to 4,547 (1,509 paupers). For all these statistics, see William Parry-Jones, *The Trade in Lunacy* (London: Routledge and Toronto: University of Toronto Press, 1972), p. 55.

31 Indeed, according to an 1844 Queen's Bench decision, Justices had no jurisdiction to send insane persons to private madhouses at all if a county asylum had been constructed, even if the asylum was full: *R. v. Ellis* (1844), 14 LJ (NS) MC 1. This jurisdiction was provided explicitly in 1845: see 8 & 9 Vict. c. 126 s. 48.

32 52 & 53 Vict. c. 41 and 53 Vict. c. 5. The latter statute was a consolidation, not merely of the county asylum and madhouse acts, but also of the provisions relating to the care of lunatics in workhouses and on outdoor relief, and the procedures for determination of lunacy in the Chancery Court.

33 Or actually four, since an administrative and legislative structure directed towards criminal lunatics developed contemporaneously with the county asylum and madhouse systems, and the Chancery jurisdiction continued, increasingly subject to legislation, throughout this period. These four streams were consolidated in 1890 by 53 Vict. c. 5, the predecessor of the current Mental Health Act. Although combined into the same statute at that time, much of the distinctness of the four strands remained. These were separate and distinct from litigation relating to testamentary capacity and contractual competence. Such litigation was also active in the nineteenth century, but not subject to statutory regulation.

34 Anne Digby, *The Poor Law in Nineteenth-Century England and Wales*, p. 6.

35 See M. A. Crowther, *The Workhouse System 1834–1929* (London: Methuen, 1981), p. 21.

36 *Report from His Majesty's Commissioners for Inquiring into the Administration and Practical Consequences of the Poor Laws*, PP 1834 (44) xxvii 1, at 127.

37 i.e., picking apart old rope, so the hemp could be reused as caulking for ships.

38 *Report from His Majesty's Commissioners for Inquiring into the Administration and Practical Consequences of the Poor Laws*, PP 1834 (44) xxvii 1, at 24.

39 Report of Alfred Powers, contained in Appendix I to the *Report from His Majesty's Commissioners for Inquiring into the Administration and Practical Consequences of the Poor Laws*, PP 1834 (44) xxvii 1, at 258.

40 For the proportions of able-bodied compared to non-able-bodied adults in the workhouse, see Appendix 1. Note that the figures contained therein refer to adults only, and roughly 40 per cent of workhouse inmates were children.

41 See Appendix 1. In January 1849 for example, 28,058 adults classed as able-bodied were in the workhouse; 171,472 were relieved outside the workhouse: *Eleventh Annual Report of the Poor Law Board*, PP 1859 1st sess. [2500] ix 741, at app. 33. In January 1870, the numbers were respectively 30,389 and 163,700, and in January 1890, 25,917 and 71,828: *Ninth Annual Report of the Local Government Board*, PP 1880 [2681] xxvi 1, at app. D(71); and *Twentieth Annual Report of Local Government Board*, PP 1890–1 [6460] xxxiii 1.

42 The reasons for their exclusion will be discussed in Chapter 3, below.

43 Assistant Commissioners' reports, in *Report from His Majesty's Commissioners for Inquiring into the Administration and Practical Consequences of the Poor Laws*, PP 1834 (44) xxvii 1, at 429 f. The Assistant Commissioners' reports are not contained in the Checkland edition of the 1834 report.

44 Statistics are drawn from the annual reports of the Commissioners in Lunacy for the relevant years. Regarding total institutionalization of private and pauper insane persons, see Appendix 1.

45 *Ninth Annual Report of the Lunacy Commissioners*, PP 1854–5 (240) xvii 533, at 34.

46 Hodgkinson, for example, argues that outside the class of able-bodied, the new Poor Law increasingly relieved a broader segment of the poor over the course of the mid-century: *Origins of the National Health Service* (London: Wellcome, 1967), especially at Chapter 10. There is a factual query about this. Certainly in Leicestershire and Rutland, the application of the provisions of the lunacy legislation requiring visitation of insane paupers by Poor Law medical staff was restricted to those actually on outdoor relief. It will be acknowledged in Chapter five that some non-paupers were admitted to the asylum under a provision allowing the confinement of those 'not under proper care and control' or as 'cruelly treated', but the numbers of these were relatively small.

Technically, to be a pauper meant to be in receipt of relief, as the poor who received medical relief were. That therefore cannot be the meaning of 'pauper' which Hodgkinson adopts. It is not clear what other definition she uses, however. Does she mean 'respectable', not part of the 'residuum' of the poor, and thus not appropriately characterized by the moralizing language of pauperism adopted by the new Poor Law? If so, she may well be correct, but it is then an open question whether she has distinguished the poor receiving medical or asylum relief from the bulk of paupers, or instead shown the gap between the new Poor Law mythology and actual paupers relieved. Thus numbers of able-bodied people on relief were significantly greater in January, when there was no agricultural labour to be had, than in June, suggesting an inference that their relief was necessitated by a lack of work available, not a lack of will to work. Are these 'real' paupers in Hodgkinson's scheme?

The more important point is instead that the distinction is dubious. Large numbers of the poor were on minimal wages, unable to provide more than a hand-to-mouth existence for themselves and their families. Acquisition of significant savings was not a real possibility, and thus any financial interruption, whether based on lunacy, industrial injury, seasonal variation or economic recession would equally result in a turn to relief and resulting pauperization.

Where a distinction can be noted is that medical relief was provided to people who were working, without requiring admission of the family to the workhouse. This was also true of admission to an asylum, which did not result in the confinement of the remainder of the individual's family. It would thus frequently be relief where the household head remained employed, and was thus essentially relief in aid of wages. In that context, the question becomes less one of whether the individuals were 'paupers', than on whether the hard lines of pauperism implied by the 1834 report and its mythology were pervasive, or whether broader views of poor relief more similar to those of the old Poor Law continued into mid-century.

47 Opinion of Richard Baggallay and John Holker, dated 24 July 1875, PRO MH/51/772.
48 PRO MH/51/755.
49 PRO MH/51/755.
50 PRO MH/51/755.
51 *Ninth Annual Report of the Lunacy Commissioners*, PP 1854–5 (240) xvii 533, at 33.
52 Copies of these admission forms are contained for persons transferred from these asylums to the Leicestershire and Rutland County Lunatic Asylum, in the collection of admission documents at LRO DE/3533.
53 *Twenty-Eighth Annual Report of the United Committee of Visitors, Leicester and Rutland Lunatic Asylum* (1864), LRO DE 3533/13. Emphases in original.

54 *On the State of Lunacy and the Legal Provision for the Insane* (London: John Churchill, 1859), p. 35.

55 PP 1908 [4202] xxxix 159, at 16.

56 In majority report, see initial statistics at UK, *Report of the Royal Commission on the Poor Laws and Relief of Distress* (London: Queen's Printer, 1909), p. 30. The majority did not discuss asylums in any detail, instead referring to the 1908 report of the Royal Commission on the Feeble-Minded. The minority report discussed lunacy in somewhat greater detail, advocating for the removal of the insane from the purview of the Poor Law. While it was clear that the minority report did not favour the pauperization of the insane, which it perceived as the status quo, they equally limited their criticisms of county asylums, perhaps because they favoured such specialized institutions for the care of the insane. See generally UK, *Minority Report of the Poor Law Commission, 1909* (London: National Committee to Promote the Break-Up of the Poor Law, 1909), p. 296. Both these published sources are reprintings of PP 1909 [4499] xxxvii 1.

57 The figures for the 1840s are not reproduced annually in the Commissioners' reports, and the statistics in Appendix 1 start at 1849. Such earlier figures as there are do not suggest a significantly different proportion in workhouses in the 1840's however: Poor Law returns showed that, of the 13,870 pauper lunatics identified on relief in August 1842, 3,829 (28 per cent) were living in workhouses: PP 1844 (172) xl 189. For 1844, it was 4,224 of 16,896 (25 per cent): PP 1845 (333) xxxviii 133.

58 Source of statistic: annual reports of Poor Law Commissioners and Poor Law Board, reprinted annually in Parliamentary Papers. Consistent with the local administrative control of the new Poor Law, different unions adopted different practices regarding choice of care, resulting in a variation of institutional responses: see Bill Forsythe, Joseph Melling, and Richard Adair, 'The new Poor Law and the County Pauper Lunatic Asylum – the Devon Experience 1834–1884', *Social History of Medicine*, **9** (1996): 335.

59 *Supplement to the Twelfth Annual Report of the Commissioners in Lunacy*, PP 1859 1st sess. (228) ix 1, at 9.

60 David Mellett, *The Prerogative of Asylumdom* (New York, London: Garland, 1982), p. 156.

61 4 & 5 Will. IV c. 76 s. 45.

62 See, for example, the position of the Poor Law Commissioners and the opinion of the Law Officers of the Crown regarding the scope of s. 45, contained in the *Eighth Annual Report of the Poor Law Commissioners*, PP 1842 [359] xix 1, at 111.

63 25 & 26 Vict. c. 111 s. 8.

64 30 Vict. c. 6.

65 See Sir John Comyn, *Digest of the Laws of England*, 5th edn., 8 vols, ed.

Anthony Hammond (London: Strachan, 1822), at Vol. 6, p. 544, pl. 3.M.22; Sir Matthew Brook, *A New Abridgement of the Law*, 7th edn., 8 vols, ed. H. Gwillim (Vols. 2–4) and C. Dodd (Vols. 1, 5–8), (London: Strachan, 1828), at Vol. 7, p. 664; Robert Brook, *La Grande Abridgement*, 2 vols. (n.p., 1573), 'Faux Imprisonment', pl. 28, Vol. 1, p. 330; *Brookshaw v. Hopkins* (1773), Lofft. 240 at 243 (KB).

66 Essentially, the madhouse acts restricted confinement of the insane outside county asylums to licensed premises, and required procedures prescribed in the Act to be followed. Even when such procedures were followed imperfectly, however, the courts tended to hesitate to intervene: see for example, *R. v. Inhabitants of Minster* (1850), 14 QB 349 at 362, where Lord Chief Justice Campbell held that once a lunatic had been received on improper documentation, there was a continuing obligation to continue the confinement until the discharge of the lunatic by proper authority. In a similar vein, see *In Re Shuttleworth* (1846), 16 LJ (NS) MC18; 9 QB 651, which holds at LJ (NS) MC 21 that the court has a residual discretion not to release dangerous lunatics, notwithstanding flaws in committal documents.

67 30 & 31 Vict. c. 106 s. 22. Under this section, an insane person could be detained in the workhouse if the medical officer of the house certified that 'such Person is not in a proper State to leave the Workhouse without Danger to himself or others'. The wording of the amendment is to be understood in its context. A question had been raised as to whether a union might detain a weak-minded pauper who applied for discharge but would not be safe without supervision. The legal opinion which resulted stated that the common law power to detain would be satisfied if the guardians 'could establish the insanity of the Pauper, and his unfitness to be at large': *Twentieth Annual Report of the Commissioners in Lunacy*, PP 1866 (317) xxxii 1, at 23. This was a broader meaning than would have been understood by the word 'dangerous' in the context of the 14-day limitation on detention of dangerous insane persons in the workhouse under the 1834 Act, a limitation which remained in effect. The committal standard for the workhouse appears to have been directed instead at those insane persons who could not survive outside the workhouse.

68 Many of the annual reports contain such allegations about particular workhouses, and some about workhouses in general. Particularly vehement denunciations are contained in the *Supplement to the Twelfth Annual Report of the Commissioners in Lunacy*, PP 1859 1st sess. (228) ix 1. See also the testimony of Lord Shaftesbury, chairman of the Lunacy Commission, to the Select Committee on Lunatics, 11 April 1859, reported at PP 1859 1st sess. (204) iii 75, at questions 629 sq.

69 See especially Chapter 6.

70 *Fifteenth Annual Report of the Lunacy Commissioners*, PP 1861 (314) xxvii 1, at 47 f. The contradictions in Lunacy Commission policy regarding

workhouse care of the insane will be discussed in detail in Chapter 6.

71 See, for example, the case of Leicester, discussed below. The dietaries for the Leicester workhouse and the Leicestershire and Rutland Lunatic Asylum are reproduced in Appendix 3.

72 PP 1859 1st sess. (204) iii 75, at question 1687.

73 *Fifteenth Annual Report of the Commissioners in Lunacy*, PP 1861 (314) xxvii 1, at 48.

74 PP 1859 2nd sess. (156). vii 501.

75 UK, *Minority Report of the Poor Law Commission, 1909* (London: National Committee to Promote the Break-Up of the Poor Law, 1909), p. 297. These figures include 'over 11,000 certified lunatics, imbeciles, and idiots' in general mixed workhouses, and over 5,000 on out-relief. In addition, there were said to be 'at least 40,000' in workhouses and 12,000 on out-relief described as 'feeble-minded, epileptic, or requiring special treatment'. They do not include 47,000 children in schools for mental defectives, and a variety of persons in inebriate asylums and institutions for epileptics who might well have been classed as insane in the previous century.

76 Ibid., p. 306.

77 See 8 & 9 Vict. c. 126 s. 55. At least, according to the Lunacy Commissioners, these lists were notoriously inadequate until a fee of two shillings and sixpence was required to be paid for each visit in 1853 pursuant to 16 & 17 Vict. c. 97 s. 66.

78 9 Geo. IV c. 40 s. 31, re-enacted in the various statutory consolidations for the remainder of the century.

79 8 & 9 Vict. c. 126 s. 48, re-enacted in the various consolidations throughout the century. The scope of this duty is discussed further in Chapter 3.

80 See Chapter 5, below. Regarding the role of families in certification processes, see also David Wright, '"Childlike in his Innocence": lay attitudes to "idiots" and "imbeciles" in Victorian England', in Wright and Digby, *From Idiocy to Mental Deficiency* (London: Routledge, 1996), p. 118; and David Wright, 'A beam for mental darkness: a history of the National Asylum for Idiots, Earlswood, 1847–1886', University of Oxford dissertation, 1993, especially Chapters 2 and 3. While Dr Wright's work does not focus on the Poor Law issues, insanity specifically, many of his insights apply equally in that context.

81 This provision in effect commenced in 1846: see 9 & 10 Vict. c. 84 s. 1. This provision was re-enacted in subsequent consolidations.

82 My research in Leicestershire did not turn up a single case where this rule applied.

83 16 & 17 Vict. c. 97 s. 67; rep. 25 & 26 Vict. c. 111 s. 19.

84 25 & 26 Vict. c. 111 s. 20.

85 See Anne Digby, *Pauper Palaces*, pp. 5 and 78. Digby states that in Norfolk and Durham, Justices were less active as ex officio guardians

than their elected counterparts, but acknowledges that in North-amptonshire, at least in the early stages of the new Poor Law, the Justices and the elected guardians were equally active.

86 This power dates from at least 1819: 59 Geo. III c. 127 s. 1. When the application procedures became more explicit in 1845, the power of the Justice to act on his own knowledge continued: see *R. v. Inhabitants of Rhyddlan* (1850), 14 QB 327. This power was made more explicit in the 1853 statute: 16 & 17 Vict. c. 97, s. 67.

87 *First Annual Report of the Poor Law Commission*, PP 1835 (500) xxxv 107, at 59.

88 See articles 12 and 37 of the original rules, reprinted as Appendix A(9) to the *First Annual Report of the Poor Law Commissioners*, PP 1835 (500) xxxv 107, and articles 78 (2) and (3) of General Workhouse Rules of 1842, printed as Appendix A(3) to the *Eighth Report of the Poor Law Commissioners*, PP 1842 [359] xix 1.

89 See, for example, Michael Nolan, *A Treatise of the Laws for the Relief and Settlement of the Poor*, 4th edn., 3 vols (London: Butterworth, 1825), pp. 352 ff., 375 ff. and 408 ff.; William Golden Lumley, *Manuals of the Duties of Poor Law Officers: Master and Matron of the Workhouse* (London: Knight, 1869) and *Manuals of the Duties of Poor Law Officers: Medical Officer* (London: Knight, 1849); *Shaw's Union Officers' and Local Boards of Health Manual for 1858*, ed. W. C. Glen (London: Shaw and Sons, 1858); and *Archbold's Poor Law*, 12th edn., ed. W. C. Glen (London: Shaw and Sons, 1843).

90 *The New Lunacy Acts* (London: Shaw, 1845).

91 Only 13 county asylums were built prior to the enactment of the new Poor Law: Bedford (1812), Nottingham (1812), Norfolk (1814), Lancashire (1816), Staffordshire (1818), Wakefield (1819), Cornwall (1820), Gloucester (1823), Cheshire (1825), Middlesex (1831), Suffolk (1829), Dorset (1932) and Kent (1833).

92 The fact that rate-financed county asylums become dominant as compared to public subscription asylums, which had little effect in England but rose to prominence in Scotland, is referred to as 'one of the oddities of the institutionalization of insanity in England' by Roy Porter: *Mind-Forg'd Manacles*, p. 135. Viewed in the context of poor relief, it is not an oddity at all. Scotland, with its poor relief administrative system much more similar to the old Poor Law, did not develop the professional poor relief bureaucracy which made the county asylum system possible. Nor did it have a system of mandatory taxation to fund poor relief, a mechanism which had been part of the English tradition for centuries. Instead, poor relief was funded by voluntary contribution: R. A. Cage, *The Scottish Poor Law 1745–1845* (Edinburgh: Scottish Academic Press, 1981). It is thus hardly surprising that Scots' asylums were funded in this fashion.

93 Anne Digby, *The Poor Law in Nineteenth-Century England and Wales*, pp.

34 f. See also for example Marlene Arieno, *Victorian Lunatics: A Social Epidemiology of Mental Illness in Mid-Nineteenth-Century England,* (Selinsgrove: Susquehanna University Press; and London and Toronto:
94 Associated University Presses, 1989), p. 27; Kathleen Jones, *Lunacy, Law, and Conscience, 1744–1845: The Social History of the Care of the Insane* (London: Routledge & Kegan Paul, 1955) pp. 17, 160–7; David Mellett, *The Prerogative of Asylumdom: Social, Cultural and Administrative Aspects of the Institutional Treatment of the Insane in Nineteenth-Century Britain,* (New York, London: Garland, 1982), pp. 52, 134.
95 Testimony of Shaftesbury before the Select Committee on Lunatics, 17 March 1859, PP 1859 1st sess. (204) iii 75, at question 615.
96 H. B. Farnall (a Poor Law Inspector for the Metropolitan District, and previously for Lancashire and Yorkshire) to the Select Committee on Lunatics, 24 March 1859, PP 1859 1st sess. (204) iii 75, at question 1616. See also the evidence of Andrew Doyle (Poor Law Inspector for North Wales, Cheshire, Shropshire, Staffordshire, etc.) to the Select Committee on Lunatics, 28 July 1859, PP 1859 2nd sess. (156) vii 501, at questions 1836–7.
97 See his testimony before the Select Committee on Lunatics, PP 1859 1st sess. (204) iii 75, at questions 592 to 599.
98 Other workhouse maintenance charges might be somewhat less expensive, however: Billesdon Union in Leicester charged three shillings and sixpence per week in 1863, and Barrow Union three shillings in 1859: see PRO MH 12/6415, 'List of Chargeable Lunatics', dated 27 February 1863; and PRO MH 12/6401, 'Annual Return of Lunatics for 1859' respectively, somewhat increasing the differential identified by Lord Shaftesbury.
99 Testimony of Shaftesbury before the Select Committee on Lunatics, 17 March 1859, PP 1859 1st sess. (204) iii 75, at questions 678 and 679.
100 PRO MH 12/6415, 'List of Chargeable Lunatics', dated 27 Feb. 1863 (no further accession number). The workhouse statistic does not include any contribution to capital or staff costs, which were paid from a separate account, so the real costs of workhouse care would have been higher.
101 Andrew Scull, *Museums of Madness,* p. 198.
102 *Eleventh Annual Report of the Lunacy Commissioners,* PP 1857 2nd sess. (157) xvi 351. An additional five asylums were near to completion at that time.
103 *Eleventh Annual Report of the Lunacy Commissioners,* PP 1857 2nd sess. (157) xvi 351.
104 Figures drawn from the *Twentieth Annual Report of the Local Government Board,* PP 1890–1 [6460] xxxiii 1, at Appendix F(118). See also Appendix 1. In 1860, paupers in county asylums had represented 2 per cent of the total paupers relieved; by 1890, they represented 7 per cent of total paupers relieved.
105 Figures for medical relief drawn from *Twentieth Annual Report of the Local Government Board,* PP 1890–91 [6460] xxxiii 1, Appendix F(116).

106 Burbage Parish Receipt and Disbursement Book, 1838–47, LRO DE 3120/1. The expenses and inconvenience of removal could be such in 1841 that the Metropolitan Commissioners in Lunacy complained that they 'not infrequently occasion his [i.e., the pauper lunatic's] being improperly continued in confinement': *Annual Reports of the Metropolitan Commissioners in Lunacy 1835–41*, PP 1841 2nd sess. (56) vi 235, at 7f.

107 See, for example, Marlene Arieno, *Victorian Lunatics*, pp. 32 f.; Ruth Hodgkinson, 'Provision for pauper lunatics, 1834–71', *Medical History*, **10** (1966): 138 at 150.

108 See, for example, the report of the Lunacy Commissioners to the Poor Law Commissioners reproduced as Appendix (A) to the *Supplementary Report of the Lunacy Commissioners*, PP 1847 [858]; *in octavo* 1847–8 xxxii 371, at 262; *Fifth Annual Report of the Commissioners in Lunacy*, PP 1850 (735) xxiii 393, at 12 f.; *Eleventh Annual Report of the Lunacy Commissioners*, PP 1857 2nd sess. (157) xvi 351, at 22; *Ninth Annual Report of the Poor Law Commissioners*, PP 1843 [468] xxi 1, at 21; *Tenth Annual Report of the Poor Law Commissioners*, PP 1844 [560] xix 9, at 19 f.; *Report of the Commissioners for Administering the Laws for Relief of the Poor in England, 1848* [i.e., first annual report of the Poor Law Board], PP 1849 [1024] xxv 1, at 8.

109 *Eleventh Annual Report of the Commissioners in Lunacy*, PP 1857 2nd sess. (157) xvi 351, at Appendix D.

110 The numbers for the asylum, the licensed madhouses and the hospital are taken directly from the appendices to the *Fifth Annual Report of the Commissioners in Lunacy*, PP 1850 (735) xxiii 393. The figure for workhouses is more problematic, since all workhouses were not visited by the Commissioners in any given year. The Commissioners did tend to visit more regularly the workhouses containing specialized lunatic wards, of which there were seven in Lancashire, or large numbers of lunatics. The figure included in the body of the text is the sum of insane in workhouses visited in 1849–50, from the *Fifth Annual Report* (570 in number); those in workhouses visited in 1848–99 and not in 1850, from the *Fourth Annual Report*, PP 1850 (291) xxiii 363 (99 in number); and those in 1847–8 for those not visited in the two later years from their *Third Annual Report*, PP 1849 [1028] xxii 381 (4 in number), for a total of 673.

111 *Sixth Annual Report of the Commissioners in Lunacy*, PP 1851 (668) xxiii 353, at 5 f.

112 1851 statistics are not used for comparison because the two new asylums open on the cusp of the statistical year, on 1 January 1851. The statistics contained in the *Sixth Annual Report* (1851) showed no persons accommodated in the two new asylums; as regards the asylums, the situation represents the status quo on 31 December 1850. It would appear that this is also true of the madhouse statistics. The workhouse

statistics until 1853 reflect visits made between 1 July and 30 June of the following year, so it is not possible to tell which workhouses were visited before and which after the asylums opened. The figures from the following annual report are used here, to avoid these accounting ambiguities.

The 1852 statistics have a comparable weakness to the 1850 statistics, discussed above. The figures for the three asylums, for licensed houses and for hospitals are drawn directly from the *Seventh Annual Report of the Lunacy Commissioners*, PP 1852–3 xlix 1, and reflect the situation on 1 January 1852. The workhouse figures reflect the number of insane persons in workhouses visited by the Commissioners in 1851–2, as presented in the *Seventh Annual Report* (totalling 287) plus those in workhouses visited by the Commissioners from July 1852 to December 1853, as reflected in the *Eighth Annual Report*, PP 1854 (339) xxix 1 (totalling 393); and those visited in 1854 and not in the previous two years from the *Ninth Annual Report*, PP 1854–5 (240) xvii 533 (totalling 15), for a combined total of 695.

113 *Sixth Annual Report of the Commissioners in Lunacy*, PP 1851 (668) xxiii 353, at 6. A comparison of the figures in the fifth and seventh annual reports does indicate a fall of 30 paupers, from 131 to 101.

114 See *Ninth Annual Report of the Lunacy Commissioners*, PP 1854–5 (240) xvii 533, at 24, and Appendix A. The county asylum at Lancaster Moor at this time had 664 patients, 94 less than in 1850.

115 *Eleventh Annual Report of the Lunacy Commissioners*, PP 1857 2nd sess. (157) xvi 351.

116 *Sixth Annual Report of the Commissioners in Lunacy*, PP 1851 (668) xxiii 353, at 6.

117 See, for example, the report of the Lunacy Commissioners to the Poor Law Commissioners, reproduced as Appendix (A) to the *Supplementary Report of the Lunacy Commissioners, 1847*, PP 1847 [858]; *in octavo 1847–8 xxxii 371, at 257 ff.; Fourth Annual Report of the Commissioners in Lunacy*, PP 1850 (291) xxiii 363, at 16; *Supplement to the Twelfth Annual Report of the Commissioners in Lunacy*, PP 1859 1st sess. (228) ix 1, at 13; and the testimony of Andrew Doyle (Poor Law Inspector) before the Select Committee on Lunatics, 28 July 1859, PP 1859 2nd sess. (156) vii 501, at 1716.

118 The distinction was included, for example, in the 1324 Royal Prerogative statute, 17 Edw. II stat. 1, Chapters 9 and 10.

119 See Edgar Millar, 'Idiocy in the nineteenth century', *History of Psychiatry*, 7 (1996): 361.

120 See Janet Saunders, 'Quarantining the weak-minded', in Bynum, Porter and Shepherd (eds), *The Anatomy of Madness*, Vol. III (London: Routledge, 1988), p. 274.

121 Correspondence between Leicester Union and the Poor Law Commissioners, PRO MH 12/6470 18259/44, at p. 10.

122 The return is at PRO MH 12/6470 14532/43.

123 UK, *Report of the Metropolitan Commissioners in Lunacy to the Lord Chancellor*, (London: Bradbury and Evans, 1844), pp. 96 f. Reprinting PP [HL] 1844 xxvi 1.

124 Testimony of H. B. Farnall to the Select Committee on Lunatics, 24 March 1859, PP 1859 1st sess. (204) iii 75.

125 Frederick Purdy, 'Remarks on the Return of Insane Paupers, chargeable on the 1st January 1859 (No. (E.) Sess. 1859)', being Appendix 32 to the *Twelfth Annual Report of the Poor Law Board*, PP 1860 [2675] xxxvii 1, at 267.

126 Frederick Purdy, 'Remarks on the Return of Insane Paupers, chargeable on the 1st January 1859 (No. (E.) Sess. 1859)', being Appendix 32 to the *Twelfth Annual Report of the Poor Law Board*, PP 1860 [2675] xxxvii 1, at 270 f.

127 Annual report of the Lunacy Commissioners for the year ending 1855, quoted by Andrew Doyle (Poor Law Inspector) in evidence before the Select Committee on Lunatics, 28 July 1859, PP 1859 2nd sess. (156) vii 501, at question 1716.

128 This view is consistent with Janet Saunders's claim for later in the century, that 'in the workhouse as in the asylum, the variability of classification makes it difficult to discover how many inmates were insane, idiot, or weak-minded at any one time': 'Quarantining the weak-minded', p. 282.

129 Roy Porter, *Mind-Forg'd Manacles*, pp. 277 and 142.

130 Porter, *Mind-Forg'd Manacles*, p. 121. Porter apparently agrees that the new Poor Law and the 1845 County Asylum Act changed this for the poor: See p. 278.

CHAPTER 3

The Legislation of Pauper Lunacy

The previous chapter argued that the law relating to the insane in the nineteenth century was in essence a branch of nineteenth-century Poor Law. The Poor Law, in turn, underwent a revolution of its own with the introduction of the new Poor Law in 1834, and understanding the development of the care of the insane therefore requires an understanding of that transition.

The 1834 amendments focused on the able-bodied poor. The principle of less eligibility, their linchpin, lay at the intersection of the versions of utilitarianism, paternalism, and evangelicalism espoused by the members of the 1832 Royal Commission. The resulting ideological framework was tremendously influential. It was not that it was generally agreed upon. Objectors ranged from workers who rioted, to *The Times*, which ran a campaign against the 1834 provisions for at least a decade. It was more that the principles of 1834 articulated a new orthodoxy. Arguments may have been for or against, but the 'principles of 1834' were what the dispute was about, and those in opposition defined themselves less according to some unifying and coherent alternative theory than simply in juxtaposition to the 1834 programme.

The Poor Law of lunacy, like the provisions for the non-able-bodied poor, was not expressly included in the 1834 statute. It had its own largely distinct statutory history. While the Poor Law of lunacy retained much of its legal form inherited from the old Poor Law, it relied on new Poor Law bureaucratic personnel, and was required to fit into the structure of the new Poor Law workhouses and outdoor relief. The result was a peculiar hybrid, and the tensions implied will form a recurrent theme in the remainder of this book.

This chapter examines these developments with a relatively broad brush, tracing developments in the legislation and administrative structures relating to pauper lunacy in the context of those of the nineteenth-century Poor Law. This is not the place to write a history of the nineteenth-century Poor Law; yet some background is necessary to make sense of the developments in the lunacy sphere.

THE COMING OF THE NEW POOR LAW

In the first quarter of the nineteenth century, it appeared clear that a reform of the Poor Law was essential. The English population had grown roughly from 5.5 million to 8.9 million in the eighteenth century; by 1831, it had reached 13.9 million. The economic forces of the industrial revolution in agriculture resulted in increased mechanization and more economically efficient management of estates, and the country remained more or less self-sufficient in food, but at the cost of considerably increased pauperism. The passing of roughly 4,000 Enclosure Acts forced the poor off their traditional lands and terminated their traditional rights. The resulting surplus of labour was made worse with the return of soldiers at the end of the Napoleonic wars in 1815. Annual hiring in agriculture gave way to monthly or weekly terms. The result was an increase in pauperism generally, and particularly seasonally.[1] By the beginning of the 1830s, 10 per cent of the population was on relief.

The result was civil unrest. Luddites attacked industrial machinery from 1811 to roughly 1816. In 1816–17 and 1819, bad harvests led to strikes. A meeting advocating parliamentary reform was suppressed by the military in 1819, resulting in the Peterloo massacre in which eleven died and 400 were injured. In the early 1830s, there was further rioting in the south by the followers of Captain Swing, and in particular rioting in response to the initial rejection of the first Reform Bill in 1831.

The civil strife was mirrored by intellectual discord. On the one hand, the tradition of poor relief was firmly established in England. Whether one views it as an outgrowth of Christian charity, a ruse of the rich to purchase the loyalty of the poor, a paternalist's duty or an investment to encourage the growth of the labour force, the old Poor Law, with its the handouts, almshouses, bridewells and houses of industry had engrained itself into the English psyche.

The origins of this system were in a vision of society based in hierarchical duties and obligations. That vision continued to have its adherents through the nineteenth century: paternalism may have changed to reflect the times, but it certainly did not die out. In David Roberts's analysis, nineteenth-century paternalism centred around four assumptions.[2] First, government was to be authoritarian, but limited by the civil rights of Englishmen. Secondly, and related, society was hierarchical, and usually seen as reflecting a divine creation. In Roberts's words, 'At the heart of a paternalist's outlook is a strong sense of the value of dependency, a sense that society could not exist without those who are dependent having an unquestioned respect for their betters.'[3] The duty of the rulers of society was to rule, to guide and to help. The rulers were identified generally in terms of property, and the new factory-owning class was gradually and grudgingly accepted into the vision. 'Property has its duties as well as its rights' was a hallmark phrase of paternalism. Thirdly, society was organic, in the Durkheimian sense: to quote the old maxim, the paternalist vision was of 'everyone in his place, and a place for everyone'. Finally, there was an assumption of pluralism, in the sense that since society was composed of a variety of social spheres, there would be a corresponding variety of hierarchies.

While this social vision remained in evidence throughout the nineteenth century, it had become controversial. For Adam Smith and the Scots Enlightenment thinkers of the eighteenth century, society was instead a harmony of individuals acting in their own interests. This conceptualization applied as much to the poor as to the rich. As Mitchell Dean points out, 'the poor' in Smith's vision became 'labourers who ought be treated, like all other groups, as rational subjects of exchange', acting in their own self-interest and seeking to better their condition.[4]

Smith himself never attacked the Poor Laws directly, but his unseen hand was at work in critiques first by Townsend and then Malthus. Townsend argued[5] that, in a state of nature, without state intervention, there was an equilibrium between population and food supply. The Poor Laws upset this equilibrium, providing value in excess of the labours of the poor, resulting in excess population growth among the poor. This in turn necessitated the provision of more relief and a spiral of poverty was created. The argument was therefore abolitionist: the provision of poor relief in fact aggravated the problem it was designed to solve, and the solution to the problem of poverty was to put a stop to this spiral by the removal of poor relief.

Malthus, by comparison, argued for a natural disequilibrium between food supply and population. His formula has become famous:

It may be safely pronounced therefore, that population when unchecked goes on doubling itself every twenty-five years, or increases in a geometrical ratio.

* * *

It may be fairly pronounced therefore, that, considering the present average state of the earth, the means of subsistence, under circumstances the most favourable to human industry, could not possibly be made to increase faster than in an arithmetical ratio.[6]

The crisis of poverty was thus contained within nature itself. It was certainly aggravated, but not created, by the intervention of the Poor Law, and the abolition of the Poor Law was not in itself an entire solution to the problem. In addition, moral restraint was necessary among the poor, and failure to abide by that restraint was to yield both harsh consequences and moral judgement:

When nature will govern and punish for us, it is a very miserable ambition to wish to snatch the rod from her hands, and draw upon ourselves the odium of executioner. To the punishment, therefore, of nature he [i.e., those poor marrying improvidently] should be left, the punishment of severe want.... He should be taught to know that the laws of nature, which are the laws of God, had doomed him and his family to starve for disobeying their repeated admonitions....[7]

The abolition of poor relief would better the lot of the average labourer, but it would equally force the poor, at their peril, to a life of moral restraint. Where the eighteenth-century poor had been a fact of life, an unavoidable reality or even in some formulations the basis of social wealth, in Malthus's view they were a threat to social prosperity, needing to be made responsible for their own fate.

Malthus's *Essay on the Principles of Population* was published in 1798 and, in the same year, Jeremy Bentham published his culminating work on Poor Law, *Pauper Management Improved*. For Bentham, the need for organized provision for the poor was not merely concerned with the wealth of the nation. He, like the early nineteenth-century politicians, saw the problem of the poor as one of the stability of the state: provision had to be made for the poor because of the practical threat they posed to political stability in the event of a rebellion. The issue was one of security.[8] Here, Bentham's work displays an unaccustomed conservatism with hints of paternalism. Bentham favoured the preservation of the social order and the continued distinctions between rich and poor, but as the rich expected their enjoyment of their property as a matter of right, so the English poor had corresponding expectations to be free from starvation and provided with a minimal subsistence.

Bentham's theory was thus not Malthusian in its direction; and while certainly containing implied moral precepts, it was not moralistic in the Malthusian way. Population was not a 'problem' for Bentham, in the way it was for Malthus. While it may be jarring to the modern reader to see the poor referred to as 'that part of the national live stock which has no feathers to it and walks with two legs',[9] it does suggest a continuation of the view that the poor were the basis of the nation's wealth, rather than a threat to it.

If Bentham was not impressed with Malthus, he found Smith more convincing, so that he could not ignore the low wage arguments of the economists of the period. The problem therefore became a practical one of providing subsistence for the poor, ensuring security for the social order and not upsetting the market. The solution here was to be found in the system of 'less eligibility': while life under poor relief was to be sufficient to keep the pauper alive and healthy, it was also to be sufficiently undesirable that no pauper would choose to apply for relief, without real need. As a life in employment outside the relief system would thus be preferable to the new, rational pauper, the relief system would not undercut the labour market.

Poor Law reform thus placed the Whigs, newly elected in 1830, in a predicament. Political opinion ranged from cries for a strengthening of the old Poor Law, to its outright abolition. The civil unrest had shown that failure to reform was not a practical option; yet if reform was essential, it was also perceived as impossible, running the risk of a full-scale revolt. The appointment of a Royal Commission on the Poor Laws in 1832 can thus be seen in part as an act of desperation, and in part a political manoeuvre to avoid the appearance of inaction.

The circumstances surrounding the creation of the Royal Commission put a particular direction onto its work. As S. G. and E. O. A. Checkland have said, 'The Commissioners were aware that the Government expected them to produce the basis for reform. A kind of teleology would thus operate: the very need for a programme could hardly have failed to affect the writing of the report, giving it greater simplification and directness.'[10] The report was not merely to describe, it was also to convince.[11] Civil unrest gave the impression that matters had reached an impasse in the Poor Law, a matter not downplayed by the Commissioners themselves.[12] Nassau Senior, the Commissioners' liaison with the government, emphasized the connection between poor relief and social stability in his discussions with the Cabinet.[13]

The Commission itself has traditionally been seen as a triumph of Benthamism.[14] Certainly, there are elements of similarity. Outdoor relief in aid of wages was to be forbidden. The Committee recommended the nationwide construction of workhouses, where the principle of less eligibility would apply. Outdoor relief of the able-bodied was to be prohibited. Instead, the able-bodied pauper and his family would be 'offered the house'. The system was to limit fraud and administrative discretion: 'If the claimant does not comply with the terms on which relief is given to the destitute, he gets nothing; and if he does comply, the compliance proves the truth of the claim – namely, his destitution.'[15] No appeal mechanisms would be necessary, and no complicated administrative machinery. The fabled 'clever pauper', who received outdoor relief from several parishes through administrative oversight, would be stymied, and jobbing by the parish officials would be made significantly more difficult. Administrative discretion, which had purportedly allowed parish officials and Justices to corrupt the beneficial purposes of the old Elizabethan statute, would be at an end.[16]

The Commissioners claimed to be reverting to the principles of the Elizabethan legislation, which they suggested had been corrupted through the years. It is certainly true that the old Poor Law had little sympathy for those able but unwilling to work: they were to be whipped. It is similarly inappropriate to romanticize the generosity of the old Poor Law to the aged and infirm. As Akihito Suzuki notes, few were exempted from work in that system:

Once [eighteenth-century] workhouses started, the aged, orphans, the lame, the blind, idiots, lunatics, etc., were put together and were set to various kinds of work. Such labour did not require skill nor physical strength, so everyone could do something for the workhouse. In the workhouse of St. Andrew's, Holborn, 'nine old men and women pick ockam [sic], four women and boys spin noyl, nine knit noyl yarn into caps, two make the woolen cloathes, to make linel cloaths, two cooks constantly attend the kitchen, two make beds, three nurse those that are sick'. The governor of the workhouse wrote that they employed even an idiot for the task of picking oakum, and they found that even the lame and the blind could pick oakum.[17]

The new system was none the less to be different in fundamental respects. Notwithstanding the Commissioners' claim that their work-houses were similar to the pre-1834 houses of industry, 'places where they [the poor] may be set to work according to the spirit and intention of the 43 Elizabeth',[18] the two institutions were to be fundamentally different. The pre-1834 institution had not operated expressly on a principle of less eligibility; they were instead to be places where work could be provided for the poor. The post-1834 workhouse was by its nature to be governed by the principle of less eligibility. Their aim was not to provide employment as a form of relief, but rather as a moral rule. The intention was not to provide assistance in plying one's trade, but to turn the tedium of the work into an aspect of the régime of less eligibility, and to reinforce a work ethic onto the poor. This moral side was more Malthus than Bentham, and reflected the Malthusian concern that without moral inculcation, a proliferation of poor would sap the nation's wealth. The new Poor Law would further abolish the old threefold categorization of the poor. The non-able-bodied would still be considered a separate class, but the distinction relating to the willingness of the pauper to work disappeared: all able-bodied were to be 'offered the house'. The refusal to work ceased to be criminal, and the eighteenth-century distinction between deserving and undeserving poor was abolished, in theory if not in practice; but the removal of this distinction did not imply a move away from the consideration of the poor in moral terms. Where the eighteenth century had allowed that some would be unemployed through no fault of their own, the theory of the nineteenth-century Poor Law equated unemployment and the need to seek relief with immorality.

Along with the substantive amendments to the Poor Law, the Commissioners recommended a new system of administration. The reformulation of Poor Law in the sixteenth and seventeenth centuries had placed responsibility at the parish level, with local Justices supervising volunteer overseers in the provision of relief paid for generally from a parish rate. In order to reach the scale necessary to justify a workhouse, the 1834 Commissioners recommended that roughly 18,000 parishes would be formed into 600 unions. The new system would not be run by Justices of the Peace, but by a separate and elected board of guardians, although as a sop to local élites, Justices of the Peace were placed ex officio on these boards in rural areas when implementing legislation was actually enacted. These boards would supervise a professional staff of relieving officers, Poor Law medical officers and workhouse staff. Supervising the whole system would be the new, national, Poor Law Commissioners, with their staff of inspectors.

The new Poor Law was enacted by the Whig government in 1834, within months of the presentation of the report of the Royal Commission. The logjam had been broken. A compromise position had been found which acknowledged the economic arguments of the anti-Poor Law forces; yet Poor Law was maintained, in deference to traditionalist views. The Whigs had been faced with practical problems of social unrest. The gross coercion of law could no longer be relied upon to maintain social order, and capitulation to the mob was unthinkable. Reliance on market forces seemed the ideal option, and it was introduced in legislation with due dispatch.

THE IMPLEMENTATION OF THE NEW POOR LAW

The early years of the New Poor Law arouse that peculiar fascination which comes with watching an elaborately devised machine fail to start.[19]

So M. A. Crowther commences her discussion of the implementation of the 1834 Act. On one understanding of the Act, the image is apt, for the intention was to introduce a uniform system, a system which would remove administrative discretion at the local level, a system which would lower poor rates and eventually terminate pauperism. Good harvests for the first few years of the new scheme provided cause for optimism, but the depression of the 1840s once again sent poor rates and numbers relieved soaring. Not only that, but however popular the Act was with Whigs in Parliament, it was highly controversial in the country. *The Times* vehemently opposed the new system for over a decade. Especially in the north of England, riots against the Poor Law, particularly during a trade depression following 1837, made implementation particularly difficult. By that date, 350 workhouses had been constructed under the new Act, mainly in the south of England,[20] but in 1854, twenty years after the enactment, 13 unions still had no functioning workhouse, and, as late as 1870, somewhere between 15 and 24 per cent of unions still had no workhouse constructed since 1834, and thus intended for the purposes of the 1834 Act.[21] Parishes which had united in so-called 'Gilbert Unions' under 1782 legislation were not required to enter the new Poor Law and, in 1847, 1.5 million people remained outside the 1834 Act. This number dwindled to 180,000 in 1868.[22] And while most reorganization of parishes into unions had been completed by 1837, union boundaries were not finalized in the West Riding of Yorkshire until the 1860s.[23]

Crowther's mechanical image is somewhat misleading, however, in that, notwithstanding the imagery of the uniform system and the removal of discretion, much decision-making was left at the local level. The central Poor Law Commission could not require the construction of a workhouse, nor even require alterations costing more than fifty pounds to existing facilities.[24] There was no consistency as to relations between local unions and the commission, nor between local unions as to their application of the law. Whatever the intent of the legislation, discretion had not been removed from local boards of guardians in the granting of relief.

Whether for reason of lack of space in the workhouse, or for reasons associated with the power of local élites and paternalism, outdoor relief to the able-bodied simply did not disappear: able-bodied adults on outdoor relief always vastly outnumbered those in workhouses.[25] The result was a continuation of discretion, along lines not dissimilar to the old Poor Law, as David Roberts points out:

The vestry, the parish overseer, and the local magistrate had managed the old law while the assistant poor-law commissioners, union guardians, magistrates, and union relieving officers administered the new law. Both administrations, Richard Oastler and John Walter II notwithstanding, were but two forms of paternalism. The much abused workhouse, like the dismal and easily forgotten poorhouse of the old law, formed a perfect instrument of paternalism. It combined that mixture of severe discipline and kindly benevolence that was desired in those local spheres where squire and parson thought they could distinguish between the unworthy and worthy poor.[26]

Given the continuation of local discretion, it is not surprising to find variation in practice. Thus Apfel and Dunkley in their study of Bedfordshire find that the workhouse test was applied for two-thirds of the able-bodied poor, with the remaining third mainly widows and deserted wives with dependants.[27] Anne Digby, by comparison, in her study of Norfolk finds the continuation of outdoor relief, and a scepticism of the workhouse test.[28] The principle of less eligibility was also inconsistently applied. During a fever epidemic in 1842, the guardians of Ashby de la Zouch Union in Leicestershire offered outdoor relief to 44 workhouse inmates. The epidemic was serious, and five people eventually died. None the less, seven people refused the outdoor relief, preferring to risk death in the workhouse rather than face life outside it.[29]

More significant for current purposes, and whatever the intention of the Commissioners may have been, no class of able-bodied was ever the majority of those on poor relief, either inside or outside the workhouse. From the beginning, most workhouse inmates and most people on outdoor relief were classed as 'not able-bodied'. Between 1849 and 1890, the non-able-bodied ranged from 60 to 80 per cent of those on outdoor relief, and generally constituted more than 60 per cent of those in the workhouse.[30]

The aim of the 1834 legislation had been to create a deterrent workhouse. While the uniformity of administration envisaged by the report did not occur, and despite conditions in the workhouse being such that few starved, a mythology did develop around the workhouse which itself provided a deterrent. This was no doubt due in part to the language of the 1834 report and its resulting protests, but the implementation of the Act and the development of the nineteenth-century vision of the poor also encouraged the creation of this imagery.

THE NEW POOR LAW AND THE NON-ABLE-BODIED

The members of the Royal Commission were able to reach a consensus on their view of the able-bodied pauper. Outside this area of agreement, the Commissioners were highly circumspect. The report said virtually nothing about the non-able-bodied poor. This may be at least in part because the able-bodied were considered of paramount importance. The Assistant Commissioners had enquired about the care of the non-able-bodied, however, so the exclusion should not be quite so quickly dismissed. It is reasonable to suggest that the Commissioners were unable to formulate a coherent and mutually acceptable policy.

On the one hand, the non-able-bodied were the appropriate objects of charity. At the same time, the reports of the Assistant Commissioners show some of the moral ambiguity associated with the non-able-bodied poor. Illness, old age and infirmity were matters for which the poor were to plan, and accordingly judgement could not be entirely removed from this class.[31] Charity should be dispensed only with great care and reserve in such situations. Further wrath was reserved for the families of such persons. The duty of supporting parents and children was performed 'even among savages, and almost always so in a nation deserving the name of civilized. We believe that England is the only European country in which it is neglected.' They advocated that, where such duties were not observed, 'it might be proper to replace them, however imperfectly, by artificial stimulants, and to make fines, distress warrants, or imprisonment act as substitutes for gratitude and love'.[32] The result is ambiguous: feelings were mixed between the realization that the non-able-bodied were unable to support themselves, and a moralizing tendency to view them or their families as responsible for their economic situation.

In the end, the Commissioners recommended no change in care. The non-able-bodied were placed outside the labour market structure. They were said to have no economic value, for 'no use can be made of the labour of the aged and sick', so there was no issue of forcing them to choose a life of virtue and wage labour, and the Commissioners found that 'even in places distinguished by the most wanton parochial profusion the allowances to the aged and infirm are moderate'.[33] Even this was not a view universally shared in the intellectual milieu. Bentham, for example, would have been content to see virtually all the poor at work:

Those with no eyes can knit: those who have no feet can work at any sedentary employment. Those who have but one hand can write. Those who have none can carry a message.... In the pin and other manufactories employment is found for children of four years old.[34]

The silence of the Commissioners did not of course mean that the introduction of the new Poor Law did not effect the care of the non-able-bodied. The failure to prescribe a theoretical approach to the relief of this class instead allowed their care to evolve solely within the administrative system, developed largely at the local level. That system was staffed by people working otherwise in the new Poor Law structure, and influences from Poor Law doctrine and from the various ideological frameworks of paternalism, utilitarianism and Malthusianism might reasonably be expected to be found.

Since no guidance was provided on how the distinction between able-bodied and non-able-bodied was to be made, this was an area where discretion was particularly rife among the local guardians. As Peter Wood explains, the punitive imagery of the punitive workhouse was pivotal to the exercise of this discretion:

In dealing with the able-bodied the workhouse was invariably offered to those regarded as of bad character, such as aged or diseased prostitutes, ex-criminals, mothers with more than one illegitimate child, known alcoholics and vagrants. In addition the workhouse test was often applied in case of doubt; where it was believed that savings or casual earnings were being concealed, in dubious sickness claims and in the case of deserted wives and their children. It could also be used as a means of putting pressure on relatives to contribute towards the maintenance of an applicant for relief. Where space remained for other able-bodied it was the single of both sexes and widows with one child who were most likely to be offered the house. In practice one of the most feared characteristics of the workhouse was the supposed nature of its inmates. Regarded as a refuge for undesirables, the workhouse gave its inmates a greater stigma than applied to those in receipt of outdoor relief.[35]

The system of moralization was thus not self-acting, as the Commissioners had proposed, and the categories of deserving and undeserving poor did not disappear. At the base of that distinction was the question of responsibility; and for those not responsible for their poverty, proactive responses might be introduced. A few examples will illustrate.

Children under 16 represented roughly 40 per cent of those in the workhouse. They were housed apart from their parents, both to add to the ineligibility of the situation for their parents, and to protect them from the evil moral influences of the other, hardened paupers. Here, the Poor Law Commissioners made a real attempt at a proactive solution. Schooling was to be provided for pauper children, and attempts were made to get them apprenticeships. Costs of school teachers were defrayed by the central government from 1848 onwards,[36] suggesting that the commitment here was a serious one.

It might similarly be understood that responsibility fell chiefly upon male paupers. Women were to rely on their husbands.[37] As Dean points out, if the husband was to be exposed to the naked power of natural economic law, the wife was to ensure her own protection by reliance on her husband:

If for Blackstone the wife places herself under the 'wing, protection, and cover' of her husband, for Malthus the poor wife must be left exposed if that cover is lifted or is threadbare. The Malthusian prescription for the poor is about allowing those laws of nature to operate which bind the poor man to the yoke of wage-labour and the poor woman to the yoke of conjugal dependence.[38]

The treatment of women by the new Poor Law apparently flowed from the moral assessment of the woman in that context. Thus the putative father of an illegitimate child had no obligation to aid in the support of that child until a Poor Law amending statute of 1844,[39] and an application for poor relief by a woman with more than one illegitimate child would normally result in admission to the workhouse.[40] In these situations, the woman would be held responsible. The woman who lost her husband through death or desertion was treated more leniently, through a grant of outdoor relief.[41]

The general lack of responsibility accorded to women might none the less result in a more lenient attitude of Poor Law officials. Indeed, the Poor Law Commissioners and their successors, the Poor Law Board, were not averse to reformative action. The following comment from the 1859 edition of the consolidated rules of the Poor Law Commissioners and Poor Law Board suggests more than a mere judgement of poor women:

Any measures which appear likely to rescue abandoned women from a profligate life, and to hold out to them a prospect of earning an honourable livelihood when they leave the Workhouse, are not only desirable, but are highly to be commended. It has been suggested that with this view the mothers of illegitimate children when in the Workhouse, who are of sufficient capacity and ability, should be trained under the direction of the Medical Officer as sick nurses, and attend upon women in their confinement.[42]

The Poor Law authorities were also sympathetic to intervention when inability to work was based in poor health. The Commissioners actively encouraged the formation of friendly societies to protect the poor against unemployment and illness.[43] Attempts were made to improve medical relief, for example through the imposition of standards for Poor Law medical officers and the construction of Poor Law infirmaries. On a systemic level, Poor Law authorities were responsible for vaccination, for control of public nuisances and for various public health measures.

It is not clear how widely such redemptive activity was undertaken. The attitudes regarding health and illness, education and apprenticeship of pauper children, and redemption of fallen women would suggest, however, that the Poor Law was not merely about forcing paupers to be responsible for themselves. That may have been the primary policing technique, particularly for the able-bodied adult men, but it was not the only one.

LUNACY, ASYLUMS AND THE PRINCIPLES OF 1834

County lunatic asylums were not included in the 1834 Act. Indeed, apart from the condition that dangerously insane people could not remain in the workhouse for more than 14 days, management of the insane was conspicuously absent from that statute. On one level, this is not surprising. The 1834 report and legislation, as distinct from their implementation, were largely silent on the question of the non-able-bodied poor, and the tradition of the old Poor Law seems to have acknowledged that lunatics were incapable of work. As noted in Chapter 2, the first legislative mention of pauper lunatics was in the 1714 vagrancy statute, which provided that their failure to work should result in confinement rather than whipping.[44] Bentham had considered lunatics capable of work;[45] but it is not unreasonable to speculate that the Commissioners departed from the Benthamite model here, as they had for the other non-able-bodied poor.

While this goes a considerable distance in explaining the silence of the Commissioners' report and the resulting legislation, it is not entirely sufficient. The care of poor lunatics had been surveyed on the questionnaires returned by individual parishes, and had further been considered by the Assistant Commissioners during their fieldwork. The incorporation of asylums for the pauper insane into the Poor Law structure remained Poor Law Commission policy into the 1840s.[46] And while the 1834 legislation had been largely silent on doctrine relating to the non-able-bodied, it had none the less included their relief in the new system. The county asylum is notable as perhaps the only major institution of the old Poor Law not incorporated directly under the 1834 scheme.

Pauper lunatics would not have been easy to integrate into the system proposed by the Commissioners. The objective of the new Poor Law had been a categorical realignment of poor relief, to harmonize moral and economic systems. Following Smith, Malthus and Bentham, Poor Law theory presupposed rational, choosing paupers, able to select courses of action for their benefit, and thus liable to moral censure when they required relief. This assumption of rationality could not obviously be applied to the insane, at least when they were insane, and thus the argument for moral censure was undercut. Yet many were believed to have become insane because of excessive alcohol consumption, or because of immoderate and sinful lives prior to becoming insane. For these, moral judgement seemed more appropriate. The insane were morally ambiguous in the Poor Law taxonomy.

If considered moral, the appropriate choice under the principles of the new Poor Law would presumably be a grant of outdoor relief. This option might well prove impractical for the lunatic pauper,

85

however, who might be unable to survive outside an institution. If considered immoral, the workhouse should logically have been offered. This too led to a theoretical problem. The workhouse was to be a deterrent, and to operate by structuring the choice of the immoral pauper, forcing by economic mechanisms a return to the moral life of wage labour. Yet the return to normal life of the lunatic pauper, if such return were possible at all, was not by structuring the individual's choice, for the individual was *ex hypothesi* insane and thus incapable of making the rational choice. Instead, the return of the insane to society would be effected by the redemptive power of the care and treatment. It was what the institution had to offer, in the form of 'cure', which would restore the insane pauper to a productive life, not the institution as merely serving as a less desirable alternative to a different life.

The insane did not fit the taxonomy which was the basis of the 1834 report. Bryan Green has argued that the taxonomy of that report could not accommodate the concept of a rehabilitative institution,[47] and his argument is not without merit. The case of the insane is more complex. It was not merely that they were problematic because some (but by no means all) might be cured, but also that they did not clearly divide into the moral and the immoral, or the able-bodied and non-able-bodied. They were, in a sense, a counter-example to the new Poor Law taxonomy. The strength of the new Poor Law was its articulation of a strong theory; pauper lunacy ran counter to that theory. Following Green, it is arguable that the administrative issues remained unaddressed, because they could not easily be articulated in the Poor Law taxonomy.[48]

There was also a subtle shift between the 1834 report and the policy regarding its implementation. The 1834 report had expected each union to have a variety of workhouses, organized according to the type of pauper contained:

Each class might thus receive an appropriate treatment; the old might enjoy their indulgences without torment from the boisterous; the children be educated, and the able-bodied subjected to such courses of labour and discipline as will repel the indolent and vicious.[49]

The general mixed workhouse which was usually constructed following the 1834 Act was not intended by the Royal Commissioners. The Act itself was ambiguous as to which model was to be followed.[50] The Royal Commissioners saw county asylums as an existing instance of this categorization of paupers between buildings. The above quotation from the 1834 report continues as follows:

The principle of separate and appropriate management has been carried into imperfect execution, in the cases of lunatics, by means of lunatic asylums; and we have no doubt, with relation to these objects, the blind and similar cases, it might be carried into more complete execution under extended incorporations acting with the aid of the Central Board.[51]

The asylum was not incorporated into the 1834 legislation, because it was already an example of what the reforms were attempting to achieve.

In the period after the 1834 legislation, policy changed to encourage mixed workhouses. Pragmatic considerations would have militated against incorporating asylums into the Poor Law structure in this period, however. Unlike the alteration from specialized to mixed workhouses, the inclusion of county asylums after 1834 would have involved legislative amendment. The introduction of the 1834 Act was already sufficiently controversial that politicians would not have been attracted to the controversy which incorporating asylums might bring. The mechanics of this would not necessarily have been easy. The administrative basis of the pauper asylum was the county; and the new Poor Law unions did not follow county boundaries. Incorporation of the asylums into the new system would therefore involve complex financial negotiations as to how transfer of ownership would be effected. The incorporation of the insane into mixed workhouses would be similarly problematic. Some form of coalitions of Poor Law unions would be necessary in many cases, to attain the scale required to justify proper insane wards within workhouses. The capital outlay on the construction of workhouses was already such that local ratepayers would not obviously welcome such further construction.

The Poor Law authorities were frantically busy getting the administration of the existing legislation operational, without embarking on new conquests. To begin with, unions had to be formed and the new administrative structures put into place. Construction of workhouses had to be overseen, as well as the sale or other disposition of existing almshouses and other Poor Law property in the parishes. Here, too, civil disobedience during implementation would have been a further discouragement to pressing for the expansion of the system. On the substantive side, consistent with the 1834 report, the first priority of the Poor Law Commissioners was the reorganization of relief for the able-bodied poor. That occupied their time in the initial years of the Poor Law; it is unsurprising, given the complexity of incorporating asylums, that they did not press this other priority.

In any event, despite the general change in focus of the Poor Law to mixed workhouses, the Poor Law central authorities do not seem to have given up the notion that separate facilities for the pauper insane were desirable. In their instructional letter to the boards of guardians in 1842, they went on to praise the county asylums:

It must, however, be remembered, that with lunatics, the first object is their cure, by means of proper medical treatment. This can only be obtained in a well-regulated asylum; and therefore the detention of any curable lunatic in a workhouse is highly objectionable on the score both of humanity and economy. The Commissioners indeed believe that most of the persons of unsound mind, detained in workhouses, are incurable harmless idiots. But although the detention of persons of this description in a workhouse does not appear to be liable to objection on the ground of illegality or of defective medical treatment, they nevertheless think that the practice is often attended with serious inconveniences, and they are desirous of impressing upon the guardians the necessity of the utmost caution and vigilance in the management of any persons of this class who may be in the workhouse.[52]

Further integration of the institutions was thus not desirable for managerial reasons. This view is consistent with a bill in 1839, which would have allowed unions to unite for the purposes of building an asylum.[53] The bill would have brought these asylums under the jurisdiction of the Poor Law; by its terms, however, the concept of separate facilities for the insane was affirmed. By 1839, as will be discussed below, the energy had gone out of Whig reforms in any event, and it is not surprising that the bill was not pursued.

LUNACY LEGISLATION IN POOR LAW CHRONOLOGY

For the Poor Law generally, the report and legislation of 1834 were a watershed. The abolitionist forces were dissipated. The foundations were laid for a new image of poverty and of paupers, an image centred on individual responsibility and market forces. Whatever the implementation may have been, the policy of less eligibility was manifest both in the language of government policy and in the popular perception of the punitive workhouse. The logjam of Poor Law reform was broken, and, in a remarkably short space of time, a new and powerful orthodoxy of poor relief was born.

The exclusion of lunacy from the report meant that the the Poor Law of lunacy lacked such a moment of catharsis. Instead there was a series of acts and official reports, none particularly pivotal or revolutionary in its theoretical outlook. While these reports might sometimes be triggered by scandals in the care of the insane, there was never the immanent threat of broad social upheaval: the care of the insane was never a rioting issue, in the way that Poor Law triggered the Swing Riots in the early 1830s. There were changing political winds with the resurgence of the Tories in 1841, but there was no immediate social or political crisis which required circumvention. There was no fundamental theoretical re-evaluation corresponding to the 1832 Poor Law Commission, and broad theoretical issues were unarticulated.

A brief sketch of the development of county asylum legislation may assist here. The early legislative development was discussed in the previous chapter. By an 1808 statute, the Justices in Quarter Sessions were empowered to construct asylums for their pauper lunatics, and to charge the costs to the local rates. Consistent with the old Poor Law, the management of these facilities, including admission and discharge provisions, remained with these local Justices. A series of statutes throughout 1828 made only minor modifications to this scheme, and despite the introduction of the new Poor Law in 1834, the focus on magisterial authority remained until 1888, when, along with many of the magistrates' other Poor Law functions, it was transferred to the new local authorities. Magisterial control over asylum admissions continued even later, until 1959.[54]

There was a legislative silence in the realm of pauper lunacy through the 1830s. By the 1840s, the new Poor Law was in place, and the asylum legislation passed between 1845 and 1870 reflected its presence. While the hierarchy left Justices in charge, an increased administrative role was created for the new professional Poor Law officers. It was the Poor Law relieving officer who had carriage of the committal application before the Justice. Commencing in 1828, the Overseers of the Poor under the old Poor Law had been required to present lists of pauper lunatics annually to the local Justice in Petty Sessions. Compliance with this provision was apparently inadequate, and in 1845, Poor Law medical officers were instead required to visit quarterly all insane paupers not in county asylums, and send a list of these persons to the Commissioners in Lunacy. A fee of two shillings and sixpence per visit was provided for this task in 1853. The 1853 statute also gave these medical officers the authority to sign the medical certificate which accompanied the committal application, and their involvement in this way quickly became the norm. Legislation in 1862 gave the medical officer of the workhouse the duty to determine whether a lunatic therein was 'a proper Person to be kept in a workhouse', and an 1867 Poor Law statute gave him the power actually to confine the insane pauper in the workhouse. Thus, while the mid-century legislation maintained the position of the Justices as established under the old Poor Law, it also gave the new Poor Law officials an increasingly influential role in administration.

These foci were essentially local, and the practical decision-making in the Poor Law of lunacy remained at the local level. The legislative structures did involve central authorities in the system, however, and they were quite active on issues of pauper lunacy.[55] The Poor Law Commissioners were introduced by implication, as they had responsibilities over Poor Law staff, and particularly medical staff.[56] The statutes, however, gave authority to the Poor Law officers directly, not as agents of the Poor Law central authority, nor of the boards of guardians. As a result, issues arising from the lunacy statutes formed a site of dispute between the Poor Law officers, particularly the medical officers, who asserted their independence, and the other Poor Law authorities, who were endeavouring to enforce the Poor Law administrative hierarchy.

The Commissioners in Lunacy were given a permanent mandate to inspect county asylums and workhouses in 1845, but their legal authority was very limited. While they did have powers relating to transfer of patients between institutions, these did not include transfers from workhouses until 1862.[57] From the 1840s, the Commissioners in Lunacy took it upon themselves as part of their inspections of county asylums to examine committal documents and exert pressure for the discharge of persons confined on deficient documentation. In 1853, they acquired the power to allow the amendment of such admission documents within 14 days of the admission,[58] and in 1862, a statute clarified this to allow them to order the release of those confined according to incomplete or inadequate documents.[59] They never had the power to release paupers from county asylums on the basis that the individual had recovered, or had never been insane.[60] They had the power, commencing in 1853, to request the Home Secretary either to enforce the mandatory construction of asylums for jurisdictions that had not complied at that time, or to require enlargement of existing county asylums, although these provisions were used only rarely.[61] Beginning in 1862, they had general authority to stipulate the forms of records which would be kept in the county asylums.[62] From 1853, they had specific authority to prosecute violations of the asylum acts,[63] although fiscal and personnel limitations made this an exceptional course of action. Beyond this, their authority was generally limited to receiving notification of admissions and discharges, inspection and reporting.[64] Other than persuasion, they had only limited powers to enforce their views on local authorities.

The flurry of legislation in mid-century came to a halt in the mid-1860s. Thereafter, apart from the introduction of the Idiots Act in 1886, there was a legislative silence until the 1889–90 revisions.[65]

The legislation of pauper lunacy in the nineteenth century thus fell into three fairly distinct periods. The first, from roughly 1808 to 1828, occurred before the period under study here. It saw the creation of county asylums and began the articulation of processes for committal to those asylums. The second, from the 1840s to the 1860s, corresponds in large measure to the temporal focus of this book. It saw the county asylum become mandatory in 1845, and the introduction of administrative roles for the Lunacy Commission and the local Poor Law officers. The legislative directions of the 1845 statute were continued in major legislative initiatives in 1853 and 1862,[66] and in a flurry of minor legislation as well. There was then a period of relative legislative calm, until the consolidation of lunacy legislation in 1889–90.[67]

The preceding section of this chapter has accounted for the legislative silence of the 1830s. It remains to explain the flurry of legislative activity from the 1840s to the 1860s; and how to account for the return to legislative silence in the mid-1860s. Essentially, it will be argued that the periods of legislative action and inaction correspond to the practical and political fortunes of the new Poor Law. In the 1830s, under the Whig reformers, the new Poor Law was relatively successful at asserting itself politically. It was challenged politically in the 1840s, however, resulting in the replacement of the Poor Law Commission by the less doctrinaire Poor Law Board at the end of 1847. The hard edges of the Poor Law were down played from this time to the late 1860s, when there was something of a Poor Law revival.

As the 1830s drew to a close, so did the administration of the Whigs. As David Roberts says,

The English electorate in the summer of 1841 was in a Tory mood. A decade of innovations had exhausted the popularity of the Whigs. Chartism had been suppressed. Europe lay quiet. The Reform Act had not ruined England. Church reform allayed the louder cries of dissent. And Sir Robert Peel's Tory government had a majority of seventy-six in the House of Commons.[68]

This change in political mood was coincident with challenges to the new Poor Law. As noted above, the new Poor Law had been highly controversial in its implementation. There had been riots, particularly in the north of England, during its early implementation in the 1830s. During the trade depression of the early 1840s, the discontent spread, and the riots widened to include the Midlands and Wales. At least one Assistant Poor Law Commissioner was dismissed as a result.[69] The Andover scandal, where hungry workhouse inmates were found to be sucking the rotting marrow from chicken bones they had been set to break for fertilizer, eventually forced the replacement of the Poor Law Commissioners at the end of 1847.

The result, unsurprisingly, was a move away from the Whiggish grand schemes of the previous decade, and a resurgence of Tory paternalism. In 1844, the country squires launched a particularly aggressive campaign against the new Poor Law, as not truly protecting the poor.[70] Roberts argues that the objective here was not necessarily a simple return to the old ways:

The New Poor Law presented an ambiguous issue to all paternalists. The law did weaken the prerogatives of locality, but it also defended property from exorbitant rates and systematized the landed classes' control of the poor.... The paternalist mentality of the country squire was a curious mixture of prejudice, self-interest, local loyalties, and benevolence. They hated the new and the alien, they liked secure rents and low rates, they were jealous of their local prerogatives, and they wanted their own elderly married couples, when in the workhouse, to live together.[71]

The result was thus not an abolition of the new Poor Law, but a softening of its hardest edges. Thus under the Tory government, the Poor Law Board, which replaced the Poor Law Commissioners, was viewed as conciliatory in their administrative style, and elderly married couples were permitted to live together when in the workhouse.

In this political climate, it is not surprising that the government turned to consideration of the law of lunacy in 1842, nor that the Poor Law Commissioners were not to be the investigating body. Instead, the Metropolitan Commissioners in Lunacy were given this investigative function. The Metropolitan Commissioners were a mixed bunch, but a group which would have been attractive to the political climate of the day. They included not merely barristers and medical men, but also Members of Parliament and Justices of the Peace.[72] Their previous jurisdiction had related solely to licensing and inspection of private madhouses in London.[73] They had no previous national authority, nor previous authority to inspect county asylums or workhouses.

The inspection of county asylums was not to be the sole focus of the 1842 investigation. Much of the Commissioners' 1842 mandate still concerned private madhouses throughout the nation, which they were also to inspect. Consistent with the prevailing political winds regarding care of the poor, however, county asylums were central to the eventual report. And notwithstanding that the Commissioners had no mandate to visit and report on workhouse care of the insane, they took it upon themselves to visit workhouses when it was convenient for them to do so.[74] The result, submitted in 1844, was a report much more focused on the care of the insane under the Poor Law than may have been the intent of the government.

Unlike the report of the Poor Law Commissioners a decade earlier, the report of the Metropolitan Commissioners was not an expressly visionary document. It was concerned instead with practical issues such as fireproofing of asylums and desirable locations. There was some discussion of classification of lunatics and condition of paupers on admission, but only in the context of concern that they be admitted quickly to the asylum, when the chances of cure were believed to be greatest. The treatment offered, and particularly the desirability of minimizing physical restraint of inmates, was also debated, not from the perspective of the theory of 'moral management' (although humanitarianism was raised), but rather from the perspective of the pragmatics of kind patient care and administrative peace. The foundations of moral management may have been in the belief that the insane might be influenced through their understanding, and 'by this means the spark of reason will be cherished',[75] but this style of argument was generally absent from the 1844 report. The social organization of the institution, essential to the early conceptions of moral management, was largely not discussed. Where the 1834 Poor Law report had drawn a bold theoretical picture, the Metropolitan Commissioners' report a decade later was dry, atheoretical and mechanical.

New legislation followed in 1845. Its content was consistent with the Tory paternalism of the 1840s. County asylums were not placed under the jurisdiction of the increasingly criticized Poor Law Commission. The introduction of the national Lunacy Commission as a central inspectorate was accepted because of the view that pauper lunatics as a group required particularly strong protection.[76] More significant here, the authority of local Justices was maintained. As will be shown in subsequent chapters, the practicalities of the system were becoming increasingly reliant on the staff of the new Poor Law; yet if the system could not do without the involvement of the Poor Law staff at the local level, the 1845–6 legislation continued the Justices' traditional role, overseeing the admission and discharge of inmates and serving as the management board of the asylum.

The enactment of the 1845 Act can be seen as an implied challenge to the new Poor Law. The move to a system of unions had been a direct challenge to the power of the magistrates.[77] Their administration of the old Poor Law was roundly attacked by the 1834 commissioners.[78] Rural Justices continued to sit as ex officio guardians under the new system, but even here their voice was but one in a board of otherwise elected officials. Regarding the administration created by the 1834 Act, Mandler is essentially correct when he speaks of 'the elimination of magisterial authority'.[79]

The tenor of the 1845 Act was quite different. Despite the interest of the Poor Law central authorities in developing an asylum system, they were essentially excluded, in favour of a plan administered by local Justices of the Peace. Where the new Poor Law had restricted the authority of the Justice in favour of elected boards of guardians, the 1845 Act perpetuated county asylums as a magisterial fiefdom. Where the 1845 Act had initially limited magisterial discretion in the committal decision, such discretion was expressly restored by 1846 legislation,[80] a statute which gave the magistrates the same sort of paternalist authority regarding asylums they had possessed under the old Poor Law. This was Tory legislation passed by a Tory government.

What is surprising, therefore, is not that the 1845 legislation was passed; it is rather that the basic legislative system did not change during the near uninterrupted years of Whig administration, from 1852 to 1874.[81] This can partly be explained by historical accident. The major legislative initiatives were promoted chiefly by Lord Ashley (from 1851 the seventh Earl of Shaftesbury), the chairman of the Lunacy Commission. He was a Tory of some note himself, but a Tory with impeccable Whig connections: he was son-in-law of Viscount

Palmerston.[82] Thus Ashley had contacts whichever administration was in power. More fundamentally, issues of public policing did not create a neat split between Whigs and Tories. They were allied, for example, in the legislation allowing creation of local police forces in the provinces, in the late 1830s,[83] and in at least some parts of the country, local Tories supported the 1834 Poor Law policy of the Whigs.[84] The Poor Law Board adopted a lower profile than its predecessor, and was not particularly pressing for expansion of its role in lunacy legislation. Finally, the county asylum system was already entrenched by the 1850s, based on the county or borough as the administrative unit. Any attempt to move to a system based on combinations of unions would have been fraught with administrative difficulties.

As the advent of the period of legislative activity regarding the Poor Law of lunacy in the 1840s corresponded with the retreat from the hard edges of the new Poor Law, so the termination of this legislative activity roughly corresponded to the return of political focus to the Poor Law. This was reflected administratively in the replacement of the Poor Law Board by the Local Government Board in 1871. Where the Poor Law Board had been conciliatory, the Local Government Board has been seen, at least initially, as reaffirming the paramountcy of deterrence. The result was a prolonged ideological attack on outdoor relief. For the first time, the workhouse test was applied to single women in a systematic way, and the number of able-bodied women on outdoor relief dropped from 166,407 in 1871 to 55,036 in 1891.[85] Where outdoor relief had constituted more than half of Poor Law expenditures in the 1860s, it fell to 35 per cent in the second half of the 1870s.[86]

It is misleading in the present context to consider this alteration as simply a return to the 'principles of 1834'. Certainly there was a reduction in the numbers on outdoor relief, but the numbers of able-bodied poor relieved in the workhouse similarly declined. The result of the policies of the 1870s was a reduction in the total number of able-bodied relieved, from 410,811 on 1 January 1869 to 280,348 on 1 January 1879, and a reduction in the number relieved in the workhouse in the same period from 29,826 to 22,650.[87] The proportion of able-bodied relieved in the workhouse, however, remained almost constant in this period, being 7.3 per cent in 1869 and 8.1 per cent a decade later. The tightening of relief in this period is the more startling, as the so-called 'Great Depression' of 1873 to 1896 presumably significantly increased need. In so far as implementation is a guide to policy, therefore, the issue was not so much a return to the workhouse test for the able-bodied, as restricting availability of relief to the able-bodied across the board. At the same time, there appears to have been a movement to place the able-bodied under the care of private charities.[88] While it is not possible to tell whether or how much charity increased after 1870 to care for those removed from poor relief, it does appear that the Poor Law central authorities supported and encouraged this increased role for private charity,[89] and consideration of the reduction in poor relief in this period must take that into account.[90]

The new régime had a very different effect on the non-able-bodied poor. In the same period, the number in this class dropped from 434,476 to 349,629, a drop of only 20 per cent, compared to 32 per cent in the able-bodied class. While non-able-bodied on outdoor relief dropped from 370,130 to 266,317, a drop of 28 per cent, non-able-bodied in the workhouse actually increased considerably, from 64,346 to 83,312, a rise of 29 per cent.

As Hodgkinson notes, the workhouse system had itself begun to recognize accommodation of the non-able-bodied poor as an explicit part of its role:

Also, the gradual realization of the importance of institutional treatment for the sick led to a decline in the provision of domiciliary attendance. Therefore the workhouses assumed more and more the role of hospitals. *The chief concern of the Poor Law administration in 1834 was the able-bodied labourer; by 1871 this administration had developed into the State medical authority for the poor.*[91]

Consistent with this shift had been the construction of new and specialized facilities for the non-able-bodied poor, and the introduction of professional attendant care, commencing in the 1860s on a fairly major scale. In 1849, there had been 171 professional nurses in workhouses; by 1872, there were 1,406, and by 1906, 6,094.[92] Where the 'principles of 1834' had directed workhouses particularly at the able-bodied poor, the Poor Law of the late 1860s and the 1870s saw workhouse care increasingly in terms of the pauper who could not survive alone.

Outside London, the diversification and professionalization of the Poor Law institutions in the 1860s occurred at the encouragement of the Poor Law Board, but apparently within the structures of the existing Poor Law. In London, the process was assisted by the passage of the Metropolitan Poor Act, 1867.[93] This Act is reminiscent of the unsuccessful 1839 bill, in that it allowed unions in the London area to combine for purposes of building asylums for the insane paupers and hospitals for ill paupers, under the authority of the Poor Law Board.[94] Two such Poor Law asylums were constructed immediately. Within two years of their opening in 1870, they together contained over 3,000 paupers.[95]

The statistics relating to pauper lunatics are more complex, as county asylums must be taken into consideration, but they do generally mirror the situation with other non-able-bodied poor. Thus outdoor relief to the insane dropped from 6,987 on 1 January 1869 to 6,230 a decade later, a comparatively modest drop of 11 per cent, but a reduction none the less. Insane paupers in workhouses rose from 11,181 to 16,005 in this period (43 per cent), a somewhat faster rise than for the class of non-able-bodied poor. The total pauper insane in all types of institution rose from 40,015 to 55,877, a rise of 40 per cent.[96]

The legislative initiatives of the late 1860s can be seen as consistent with this new emphasis on the workhouse as a place of care. The 1867 legislation allowing the construction of Poor Law asylums mentioned above is an obvious example of a legislative emphasis shifting from the asylum administration back to the workhouse. Consistent with this trend was the grant of detention powers to workhouses, also in 1867.[97] Equally telling is the absence of significant legislative reform to county asylum legislation until the end of the 1880s. The county asylum system was not attacked by legislation, but, in a time of emphasis on workhouse care, nor was it given legislative extension.

The legislation of the Poor Law of lunacy thus followed the trends in other Poor Law legislation. Legislation supporting the county asylum structure was passed when the Poor Law was in disfavour; when the trend was to a stronger workhouse system, however, legislation over county lunatic asylums was conspicuously absent from the statute books.

MODELS OF ADMINISTRATION IN ASYLUM ADMISSIONS

The asylum statutes can be understood as both protecting the jurisdiction of magistrates and consolidating the new Poor Law administration. Where the magistrates were left in a position of supervision, at the top of the administrative hierarchy, the statutes also provided increasingly defined roles for the various Poor Law officers. In practice, it became a situation where the magistrates would understand themselves as being in control of the asylum and its administration, but equally were increasingly reliant on the Poor Law staff for the daily mechanics of investigation and carriage of applications for admission of paupers.

Within this division of power, the asylum legislation established two essentially inconsistent models regarding the admission of paupers to the asylum. The first of these envisaged a local bureaucracy of professional Poor Law officers and Justices of the Peace sending all pauper lunatics to the new county asylums. While this was not a 'self-acting' system, as the new Poor Law was intended by the 1832 Commission to be, it was as close as the lunacy system could come: removal of the insane pauper was to be automatic. The second model again relied on these local authorities, but acknowledged a considerable administrative discretion throughout the process. This suggests a parallel to the way in which the 1834 Poor Law was actually implemented, where local paternalism remained a pivotal factor. The articulation of these models will facilitate discussion of the relationships between the various groups involved in lunacy administration.

County asylums became mandatory in 1845, and administrative mechanisms for locating, monitoring and confining pauper lunatics became increasingly refined. When a union medical officer became aware of a pauper lunatic as defined by the statute, he was to notify the relieving officer within three days, who was in turn within three days to bring the individual before a Justice. Medical certificates were obtained, and the Justice then had the power to confine the individual in an asylum. Constables similarly had a duty to bring lunatics found wandering to the notice of the relieving officer, thus triggering a committal application. The 1845 Act made these provisions mandatory, in law if not in practice: failure to notify the relieving officer, or failure of the relieving officer to bring the individual before a Justice, made the constable, medical officer or relieving officer liable to a fine of up to ten pounds per case.[98] Under the 1845 Act, the Commissioners in Lunacy and the Poor Law Commissioners were united in their view that the Justices had no discretion in their decision as to whether a committal was to occur: given the appropriate completion of forms by the relieving officer and the medical man, committal was to occur in a county asylum, if there were space, otherwise in a licensed madhouse.[99]

98

These provisions were buttressed with a set of procedures to ensure that all pauper lunatics were drawn to the attention of Justices. The quarterly visits of pauper lunatics outside asylums by Poor Law medical officers has already been noted. In addition, workhouse rules required the medical officer to examine all paupers upon admission for signs of physical or mental disease.[100]

These procedures represented a remarkable change from the processes and attitudes of the old Poor Law. Under the 1828 Act, while the parish overseer of the poor had been responsible for the legwork of the application, the Justices were involved throughout the process and the overseer acted under the Justice's direction.[101] The system in 1828 had been the result of a slow progression, which made concessions to increasing formality, but only in so far as it remained consistent with the discretion of the Justices. The 1808 Act provided that admission to county asylums was to be by warrant of the Justices.[102] An 1811 statute made it clear that the Justices could refuse to commit a pauper lunatic if the lunatic were not dangerous, reinforcing that discretion.[103] In 1815, the Justices were given authority to order lists of insane people to be compiled by the parish overseer, accompanied by a certificate from a medical practitioner as to the 'state and condition' of the 'lunatic or dangerous idiot', but, once again, this was a discretionary power of the Justice.[104] These procedures were consolidated in the 1828 Act.[105]

The 1845 and subsequent legislation focused the administration instead on the Poor Law staff directly. Justices continued to administer the asylums, and they did have the power to begin the committal processes when knowledge reached them through channels other than the Poor Law staff. In the usual case, however, they became involved in the admission processes only at the point where the order for admission was to be signed; the Poor Law staff themselves administered the acts up to that point. These changes reflected the new administrative structures and functioning of the new Poor Law. The old Poor Law had relied upon volunteer parish appointees for administration of relief. The result was administration with varying degrees of competence and enthusiasm, creating the need for supervision by the Justices. The provision of a professional staff employed to administer the new Poor Law regularized administration, reducing the need for this supervision. Whether the statute recognized the status quo of relations between Poor Law staff and the Justices in 1845, or whether it represented a departure from the status quo and awarded new powers to the Poor Law staff which they then went on to use, probably depended on the particular unions and the individuals involved. What is relevant for the discussion here is the increasing reliance of the system on professional administration of the new Poor Law, away from the involvement of the Justices.

The 1845 processes also reflected a new view of the state's role as regards to pauper lunacy. This can be seen by juxtaposing the mid-nineteenth-century law with the situation a century earlier. Roy Porter comments on the narrow scope of the 1744 Act which allowed committal of the insane poor:

It made clear that madness was to fall under the magistrates' gaze as part of the control of the vagrant poor. Yet the lunatic was to be a problem only if 'dangerous', and dangerous lunacy was expected to be sufficiently visible to be decided by JPs not physicians. Such nuisances could be confined in whatever secure place was available, be it workhouse, lock-up, private madhouse, bridewell or gaol.[106]

The mid-nineteenth-century legislative vision entailed the systematic surveillance of the mad, a system designed to ensure that all those that came within the purview of the statute would be watched, documented and, where appropriate, confined. The image is of the Poor Law officers combing the shires in search of lunatics. The vision is less reminiscent of the haphazard administration of the old Poor Law, and more similar to Bentham's plans for admission to the panopticon.[107]

The administration of the Poor Law of lunacy can also be juxtaposed with the administration of relief to the able-bodied in the workhouse. Both were intended as comprehensive in their respective spheres. The broader Poor Law was to be self-administering, however: the workhouse test was to ensure that only those in need of relief would apply, and the relief to be offered would automatically be the workhouse. By comparison, the Poor Law of lunacy placed increasing reliance on the Poor Law staff to identify lunatics, and to bring them into the system. While the comprehensiveness of the lunacy procedure was reminiscent of the broader Poor Law, the Poor Law of lunacy was unlike the general Poor Law in that it was certainly not to be self-administering. They were, however, to be automatic and universal, without discretion on the part of those administering the statute.

These mandatory processes for asylum admission were overlaid in the statutes by a completely different administrative model, a model of discretionary action by both Justices and Poor Law staff. This was the result of both the implied and explicit statements that decision-making under the Act was discretionary, and of the limited application of the Act.

The 1845 Act had presented a system where the committal of the pauper insane would be mandatory. Even the Justice would have no discretion. This was directly undercut by an 1846 statute, which made it clear that the Justice was to admit an individual to the asylum only if satisfied of the propriety of confining the lunatic.[108] The actions of the Justice were therefore clearly discretionary, and remained so into the twentieth century.[109] While the administration had changed from Tory to Whig between the 1845 and 1846 Acts, Parliament remained essentially Tory, and local paternalists had a strong voice. The continuation of discretion of the Justices was part of the reaction against the new Poor Law, in favour of the old system of administration. The local élites had not been prepared to give up their discretion in the administration of the new Poor Law; they were equally not prepared to give it up in the administration of pauper lunatics. Local paternalism remained secure.

Equally significant was the restriction of the application of the Acts. The sections concerning admission procedures in the 1853 statute referred to a pauper 'deemed to be a lunatic, and a proper person to be sent to an asylum'.[110] That these words should exist for the Justices is not a surprise: the decision of the Justices was discretionary in any event. From 1853 to 1862, however, this same formulation affected the duty of the Poor Law officials to commence an application for admission to the asylum.[111] The phrase 'and a proper person to be sent to an asylum' was repealed in 1862 in so far as it affected relieving officers,[112] but it continued to modify the duty of the medical officer to notify the relieving officer. Similarly, the medical certificate prescribed by the 1853 statute and not altered in 1862 required the medical man to attest that the insane person was 'a proper person to be taken charge of and detained under care and treatment'.[113] This wording introduced an element of judgement into the decisions, not only of Justices, but also of these other officers.

Discretion was also implied from legislative ambiguities. Section 45 of the Poor Law Amendment Act (1834) provided that 'nothing in this Act contained shall authorize the Detention in any Workhouse of any dangerous Lunatic, insane Person, or Idiot, for any longer Period than Fourteen Days'.[114] The issue of the scope of this section was raised with the Law Officers of the Crown. The Poor Law Commissioners explained the resulting opinion to the local boards of guardians in the following terms:

The words 'dangerous lunatic, insane person or idiot' in this clause, are to be read 'dangerous lunatic, dangerous insane person or dangerous idiot,' according to the opinion of the Law Officers of the Crown given to the Poor Law Commissioners.

* * *

From the express prohibition of the detention of dangerous persons of unsound mind in a workhouse, contained in the clause just cited, coupled with the prevalent practice of keeping insane persons in workhouses before the passing of the Poor Law Amendment Act, it may be inferred that persons of unsound mind, not being dangerous, may legally be kept in a workhouse.[115]

The letter went on to praise county asylums, but the point was clear: removal of non-dangerous lunatics to the asylum was discretionary. The section upon which this statement relied remained in force, notwithstanding the enactment of the 1845 admission procedures. By 1862, the accommodation of lunatics in workhouses was given specific sanction in the asylum legislation[116] and, in 1867, the Poor Law expanded to allow detention of the insane in workhouses against their will.[117]

Each of these models had its effect. Shaftesbury claimed that mandatory asylum admissions were the law well after this position could be reasonably sustained.[118] The discretionary model was extraordinarily influential at the local level, as Chapters 4 and 5 will demonstrate.

The remainder of this book considers these administrative relations in detail. Chapter 4 examines the roles of the individual administrators. Chapter 5 examines the documents relating to persons admitted to the Leicester and Rutland Lunatic Asylum. The administrative role of the Lunacy Commission is considered in Chapter 6.

NOTES

1 The able-bodied adult paupers relieved on 1 January of a year might be half as much again as those relieved on 1 July of the same year: see Appendix 1.

2 See Roberts, *Paternalism in Early Victorian England* (London: Croom Helm, 1979), pp. 2 ff.

3 *Paternalism in Early Victorian England*, p. 3.

4 Dean, *Constitution of Poverty* (London: Routledge, 1991), p. 135; see also Himmelfarb, *Idea of Poverty* (London: Faber, 1984), p. 57.

5 Townsend, *A Dissertation on the Poor Laws by a Well-wisher of Mankind* 2nd edn (London: Dilly, 1787).

6 Malthus, *An Essay on the Principle of Population*, 1803 edition, ed. D. Winch and P. James, (Cambridge: Cambridge University Press, 1992), pp. 17, 19.

7 Malthus, *Essay on the Principle of Population*, pp. 262 f. With regard to the process of abolishing poor relief, Malthus advocated a system where relief would be denied for those poor born after a specific, publicized date. The passage quoted is drawn from his defence of this transition provision.

8 See Dean, *Constitution of Poverty*, p. 187; Lea Campos Boralevi, *Bentham and the Oppressed* (Berlin and New York: de Gruyter, 1984), Ch. 5 and especially at p. 99.

9 Quoted in Charles Bahmueller, *The National Charity Company* (Berkeley: University of California Press, 1981), p. 129.

10 'Introduction', *The Poor Law Report of 1834*, ed. Checkland and Checkland, (Harmondsworth: Penguin, 1974), p. 31 f.

11 A provocative account of the rhetorical structures used by the 1834 report which made it so convincing is contained in Bryan Green, *Knowing the Poor* (London: Routledge & Kegan Paul, 1983).

12 See Bryan Green, *Knowing the Poor*, p. 84; Checkland and Checkland, 'Introduction', *The Poor Law Report of 1834*, p. 25.

13 Peter Dunkley, 'Whigs and paupers', *Journal of British Studies*, **20** (1980–1): 124 at 128.

14 More recently the influence of the evangelical members has been taken more seriously. Peter Mandler has associated the evangelical Commissioners with the 'Noetic' movement, composed of followers of Edward Copleston, Provost of Oriel College, Oxford, from 1814 to 1826: 'Tories and paupers', *The Historical Journal*, **33** (1990): 81. These were 'liberal Tories' who united natural theology and political economy, evangelicals keen on Malthusian theories of nature and responsibility. Certainly, there was a strong evangelical component to the Commission, including Bishops Blomfeld and Sumner, and Revd Henry Bishop. Whether Mandler is also correct in including Sturges Bourne and Nassau Senior as part of this cadre is less clear. The Noetics are of interest here, because they serve as a reminder of the cross-fertilization between the different ideological schools. Thus while they were strong on restoration of the natural order established by the Creator, suggesting a point of connection with nineteenth-century paternalism, this was viewed in a Malthusian framework, including the need to enforce responsibility on the poor. Mandler argues that they, separately from Bentham, reached the concept of less eligibility.

15 *The Poor Law Report of 1834*, ed. Checkland and Checkland, p. 378.

16 With reference to the report's view of discretion by the Justices as leading to a corruption of Poor Law principles, see *The Poor Law Report of 1834*, ed. Checkland and Checkland, 203 ff.

17 'Lunacy in seventeenth- and eighteenth-century England', Part II, *History of Psychiatry*, **3** (1992): 29 at 43 f. Brackets in original, footnotes omitted. Suzuki's quotation is drawn from *An Account of the Work-Houses in Great*

Britain, in the Year 1732, 3rd edn. (London, 1786), at p. 7. Suzuki notes that (apart from a child being nursed) it was only the two lunatics in this workhouse that were found by the governor of the workhouse to be completely unable to work.

18 *The Poor Law Report of 1834*, ed. Checkland and Checkland, p. 375.

19 M. A. Crowther, *The Workhouse System 1834–1929*, (1981; reprinted London: Methuen, 1983), p. 30.

20 Anne Digby, *The Poor Law in Nineteenth-Century England and Wales* (London: The Historical Association, 1982), p. 17.

21 Karel Williams, *From Pauperism to Poverty* (London: Routledge & Kegan Paul, 1981), p. 78. Most of the unions without workhouses in 1854 were in Wales. The ambiguity in the number of unions without post-1834 workhouses is the result of two different sources cited by Williams.

22 Digby, *Nineteenth-Century Poor Law in England and Wales*, p. 22.

23 Digby, *Nineteenth-Century Poor Law in England and Wales*, p. 21.

24 Poor Law Amendment Act, 4 & 5 Will. IV c. 76 ss. 21, 25.

25 See Appendix I.

26 Roberts, *Paternalism in Early Victorian England*, p. 208

27 'English rural society and the new Poor Law: Bedfordshire, 1834–47'. *Social History*, **10** (1985): 37.

28 *Pauper Palaces* (London: Routledge & Kegan Paul, 1978), esp. at pp. 100 ff. In her study, out-relief was provided for no less than 83 per cent of able-bodied paupers between the 1850s and 1870s: p. 112.

29 Ashby de la Zouch Minute Book, 1834–44, for 9 February 1842, LRO G/1/8a/1. This was not an isolated occurrence. The index to the correspondence of the Poor Law central authorities shows a peppering of enquiries as to what to do when a pauper refused to leave the workhouse, even though work was available: PRO MH 15.

30 See Appendix 1.

31 Report of Alfred Powers, Assistant Poor Law Commissioner, contained in Report of Poor Law Commissioners, PP 1834 (44) xxvii 1 at 249, Peter Wood, *Poverty and the Workhouse in Victorian Britain* (Stroud: Alan Sutton, 1991), p. 45.

32 Both quotations are from *The Poor Law Report of 1834*, ed. Checkland and Checkland, p. 115.

33 Both quotations are from *The Poor Law Report of 1834*, ed. Checkland and Checkland, p. 114.

34 Bentham, 'Expedients for satisfying indigence', in *Essay on Direct Legislation*, quoted in Charles Bahmueller, *The National Charity Company*, p. 15. Bahmueller accords Bentham's opposition to idleness in the poor an almost religious significance: *National Charity Company*, pp. 85 ff. Bentham's view must, of course, be read in context. As noted above, the eighteenth-century Poor Law was not itself sympathetic to those refusing work. Bentham's view is thus not inconsistent with old Poor Law orthodoxy in this regard.

35 Wood, *Poverty and the Workhouse in Victorian Britain*, p. 99.

36 See M. A. Crowther, *The Workhouse System 1834–1929*, p. 131.

37 See Pat Thane, 'Women and the Poor Law in Victorian and Edwardian England', *History Workshop*, **6** (1978): 29.

38 Dean, *Constitution of Poverty*, p. 85.

39 Thane, 'Women and the Poor Law, p. 32.

40 Wood, *Poverty and the Workhouse in Victorian Britain*, p. 99.

41 The emphasis placed on male pauperism by the Commissioners is not reflected in the statistics of people relieved. Women outnumbered men marginally in the workhouse, and by a considerable margin in the able-bodied category. This cannot be accounted for by the arbitrary categorization of married women, as only a tenth of the women in the workhouse appear to have been married. Less surprisingly, since the workhouse test was less stringently applied to women, they also represented the bulk of persons on outdoor relief.

Some scholars have speculated that this indicates the imposition of the new Poor Law with particular rigour on men. Karel Williams, for example, claims that '[i]n the twenty years after 1834, a line of exclusion was drawn against able-bodied men. Relief to unemployed and underemployed men was effectively abolished and this abolition was not a temporary or local phenomenon; it was national practice for sixty years from 1852 to 1912': *From Pauperism to Poverty*, pp. 73 f.

This argument is based on the low raw numbers of men relieved, and in that context it does suggest a consistency with the theory of the new Poor Law. It does not address the economic realities facing women relative to men. With lower incomes, women were likely to be more economically vulnerable, and more easily driven onto the Poor Law. Conversely, in periods of economic boom, such as the third quarter of the nineteenth century, men might reasonably be expected to share disproportionately in the spoils. It thus seems at least dubious whether the prevalence of women in workhouses and on poor relief generally is a result of differential application of the law between men and women, and a particular targeting of male pauperism.

42 William Cunningham Glen, *The Consolidated and Other Orders of the Poor Law Commissioners and the Poor Law Board*, 4th edn. (London: Butterworth, 1859), p. 59.

43 See, for example, *Fourth Annual Report of the Poor Law Commissioners*, PP 1837–8 [147] xxviii 145.

44 12 Anne c. 23 (1714). Similarly, in the 1732 account of the workhouse at St Andrew's Holborn cited by Suzuki, it was only the two lunatic inmates (apart from a child being nursed) who was found by the governor to be completely unable to work: 'Lunacy in seventeenth- and eighteenth-century England, part II', *History of Psychiatry*, **3** (1992): 29 at pp. 43 f.

45 See Bahmueller, *The National Charity Company*, p. 143, citing manuscript U.C. cli 238 from the Bentham Collection at University College London.

46 Concrete examinations into the practicability of developing a system of asylums under the jurisdiction of the Poor Law Commissioners continued to at least 1845: see Nicholas Hervey, 'The Lunacy Commission 1845–60', University of Bristol, 1987, dissertation, p. 31.

47 Bryan Green, *Knowing the Poor*, pp. 122 ff, and particularly p. 124.

48 Green's work is a textual analysis of the 1834 report, and his focus on that single text creates a sense of dialectical certainty which does not combine easily with a more historical approach, based on a variety of sources. The point here (and I think in Green's work as well) is not that matters such as lunacy were intentionally excluded by the Poor Law Commissioners because they realized it undercut their administrative structure. It is rather that, since lunacy could not be easily formulated in the terms of the Poor Law theory, it was excluded because the Commissioners could not articulate a consistent policy.

49 *The Poor Law Report of 1834*, ed. Checkland and Checkland (1834: reprinted Harmondsworth: Penguin Books, 1974), p. 430.

50 See for example 4 & 5 Will. IV c. 76 ss. 23, 25, which refer to unions having 'a Workhouse or Workhouses', suggesting that the possibility of categorization of paupers into separate buildings was still to be a possibility under the Act. The system of multiple workhouses was advocated briefly following the implementation of the new Poor Law by the Poor Law Commissioners themselves: see M. A. Crowther, *The Workhouse System 1834–1929*, pp. 37 ff.

51 *The Poor Law Report of 1834*, ed. Checkland and Checkland, p. 430.

52 *Eighth Annual Report of the Poor Law Commissioners*, PP 1842 [359] xix 1 at 111.

53 See Ruth Hodgkinson, *The Origins of the National Health Service* (London: Wellcome Historical Medical Library, 1967) p. 180.

54 See *Local Government Act 1888*, 51/52 Vict. c. 41, ss. 3(vi), 86, 111. The authority of Justices over asylum admissions is expressly retained by section 86(2) of that Act. That authority actually expands to include non-pauper admissions in 1889, and remains in effect until the Mental Health Act 1959, 7 & 8 Eliz. II c. 72, ss. 25, 26.

55 See Ch. 6.

56 Particular hiring criteria were introduced for medical officers by the Poor Law Commissioners, setting minimum professional qualifications and requiring the medical officer to live within his medical district. Involvement of the Poor Law Board became more influential, naturally, after Westminster began to pay half the salaries of medical officers. This system of contributions commenced as early as 1845: Ruth Hodgkinson, *The Origins of the National Health Service*, p. 376. It became more widespread as unions increasingly switched from a fee-for-service, which was not covered by the grants, to the salary model in the early 1850s.

57 25 & 26 Vict. c. 111 ss. 31, 32, 33. They also received authority to commission medical certificates for the admission of pauper lunatics at

this time, but this was a power used rarely, if at all.

58　16 & 17 Vict. c. 97 s. 87.

59　25 & 26 Vict. c. 111 s. 27.

60　From 1890, they could prompt a special report by the medical superintendent to the Visiting Justices on the condition of a pauper they believed appropriate for release on these grounds: see 53 Vict. c. 5 s. 38.

61　Thus when the City of London had not made provision for their pauper lunatics by the 1850s, the Commissioners in Lunacy did not litigate, but rather publicized the problem through their annual reports: see *Seventh Annual Report*, PP 1852–3 xlix 1, at 10; *Ninth Annual Report*, PP 1854–5 (240) xvii 533, at 9; *Thirteenth Annual Report*, PP 1859 2nd sess. (204) xiv 529, at 86 ff. The asylum for the City of London eventually opened in March 1866: see *Twentieth Annual Report of Commissioners in Lunacy*, PP 1866 (317) xxxii 1, at 6.

62　25 & 26 Vict. c. 111 s. 42.

63　16 & 17 Vict. c. 97 s. 126.

64　For the powers and involvements of the Lunacy Commissioners relating to county asylums, v. 8 & 9 Vict. c. 126 ss. 46, 47, 55, 56; 73, 75; 16 & 17 Vict. c. 97 ss. 19, 29, 30, 45, 56, 62–64, 66, 77, 82, 87, 89, 91–93, 126; and 25 & 26 Vict. c. 111 ss. 5, 8, 27, 31–33, 36, 37, 40, 42.

65　A minor exception is the Lunacy Laws Amendment Act, 1885, 48 & 49 Vict. c. 52, which gave explicit statutory authority for the temporary admission to workhouses in case of emergency of those lunatics not under proper care and control, pending admission to the asylum. Such emergency removals had long been used to remove dangerous paupers while asylum admission procedures were pursued. The 1885 statute expressly made this an option for the class noted, who were not necessarily paupers: see Chapter 5, below.

66　Respectively 16 & 17 Vict. c. 97 and 25 & 26 Vict. c. 111.

67　The relevant legislation for 1889 and 1890 is 52 & 53 Vict. c. 41 and 53 Vict. c. 5. The 1890 statute is historically important, as it survived with modifications until 1959, but its actual modifications of existing law were minimal. Previous to 1890, criminal lunacy, county asylums, private madhouses and inquisitions in lunacy (i.e., the law relating to Chancery Lunatics) were all under separate and unrelated statutes. The 1890 consolidated these four statutory categories, a matter which is perhaps conceptually significant. Its other major alteration subjected the admission of private patients to the authority of a Justice, and introduced expanded due process safeguards for these private patients. The 1889–90 revisions made minimal difference to the legal situation of pauper lunatics.

68　Roberts, *Paternalism in Early Victorian England*, p. 64.

69　See Peter Wood, *Poverty and the Workhouse in Victorian Britain*, p. 81, and Crowther, *The Workhouse System, 1834–1929*, p. 39.

70　Roberts, *Paternalism in Early Victorian England*, p. 245.

71 *Paternalism in Early Victorian England*, pp. 258 f.
72 In the late 1830s there had been as many as six Justices serving as Commissioners, about a third of the total number of Commissioners: Nicholas Hervey, 'The Lunacy Commission, 1845–60', p. 74.
73 9 Geo. IV c. 41 (1828).
74 The 1842 mandate of the Commissioners was established by statute: 5 & 6 Vict. c. 87. They were to visit madhouses outside the London area twice annually. Their mandate included reporting on conditions in those houses as well as the liberation of persons improperly confined: ss. 7–19. They were to visit county asylums annually and report on conditions therein, but for county asylums they were given no liberation powers: ss. 30–36. With reference to their visits to workhouses as without statutory authority, see also UK, *Report of the Metropolitan Commissioners in Lunacy to the Lord Chancellor* (London: Bradbury and Evans, 1844), p. 4. (This is a reprinting of PP [HL] 1844 xxvi 1.)
75 Samuel Tuke (1811), cited in Anne Digby, *Madness, Morality and Medicine* (Cambridge: Cambridge University Press, 1985), p. 29.
76 David Roberts, *Paternalism in Early Victorian England*, p. 205.
77 See Dunkley, 'Whigs and paupers', p. 144. This was particularly significant in the shires, where, as late as 1842, the traditionally paternalist squires and aristocracy accounted for over 85 per cent of the Justices: Carl H. E. Zangerl, 'The social composition of the county magistracy in England and Wales, 1831–1887', *Journal of British Studies*, **9** (1) (1971), 113, at 115.
78 *The Poor Law Report of 1834*, ed. Checkland and Checkland, pp. 203 ff. and 375 ff.
79 A. Brundage, D. Eastwood and P. Mandler, 'The making of the new Poor Law *redivivus*', *Past and Present*, **127** (1989): 183, at 196. But cf. their continued role in the administration of the Poor Law of lunacy, discussed below.
80 8 & 9 Vict. c. 126; 9 & 10 Vict. c. 84. See further discussion below.
81 The only breaks to this line of Whig administrations were a brief and unstable alliance formed under the 14th Earl of Derby, from February 1858 to June 1859, and brief ministries under Derby (June 1866 to February 1868) and under Disraeli to December 1868.
82 Actually, step-son-in-law, although it has been claimed that his wife actually was the natural daughter of Palmerston: Geoffrey Findlayson, *The Seventh Earl of Shaftesbury* (London: Eyre Methuen, 1981), p. 43. Palmerston was Home Secretary from 1852 to 1855, and thus at the time of the passage of the 1853 revisions to the lunacy statutes. With the exception of the brief Derby administration, he was Prime Minister, from 1855 to 1865, and so for the passage of the 1862 Act.
83 Anthony Brundage, *England's 'Prussian Minister'* (London and University Park: Pennsylvania State University Press, 1988), p. 62.

84 Such was the case in parts of Devon, for example: see Bill Forsythe, Joseph Melling and Richard Adair, 'The new Poor Law and the County Pauper Lunatic Asylum – the Devon experience 1834–1884', *Social History of Medicine*, **9** (1996): 335, at 345.

85 1869 figure from *Ninth Annual Report of the Local Government Board*, PP 1880 [2681] xxvi 1, at Appendix (D), no. 7; 1879 figure from *Twentieth Annual Report of the Local Government Board*, PP 1890–1 [6460] xxxiii 1, at Appendix (E).

86 Peter Wood, *Poverty and the Workhouse in Victorian Britain*, p. 148.

87 Figures in this paragraph are drawn from Appendix D, no. 71 to *Ninth Annual Report of the Local Government Board*, PP 1880 [2681] xxvi 1, at 356 f. The 1879 figure was an increase from mid-decade: indoor relief to able-bodied adults had fallen to 14,064 in 1875.

88 Private charity had of course always been active in the relief of the poor. While figures are bound to be unreliable, as there was no systematic collection mechanism for them at this time, David Owen claims that, in the 1860s, charitable donations in London totalled between £5.5 and £7 million annually: *English Philanthropy 1660–1960* (Cambridge: Harvard University Press, 1964), p. 218. This was roughly equivalent to the amount expended for the relief of the poor by the Poor Law, for all of England and Wales: see *Twentieth Annual Report of Local Government Board*, PP 1890–91 [6460] xxxiii 1, at Appendix (F) no. 119.

89 See Owen, *English Philanthropy, 1660–1960*, pp. 221 f.; Norman McCord, 'The Poor Law and philanthropy', in Derek Fraser (ed.), *The New Poor Law in the Nineteenth Century* (London: Macmillan, 1976), 87 at 101 f; Judith Fido, 'The Charity Organisation Society and social casework in London 1869–1900', in A. P. Donajgrodzki (ed.), *Social Control in Nineteenth Century Britain* (London: Croom Helm, 1977), p. 207.

90 This bears some similarity to Karel Williams' argument in *From Pauperism to Poverty*, pp. 73 f. Williams argues for a drastic restriction to outdoor relief for able-bodied men extending throughout the second half of the nineteenth century, based on the raw numbers of people relieved. Whatever the strength of this argument for the relatively long period he argues for, the raw numbers in the 1870s relating to the able-bodied do suggest a significantly higher eligibility requirement for the grant of relief. This cannot be seen as directed primarily against men, however. Women in fact were hit somewhat harder than men: the number of able-bodied women relieved dropped 35 per cent from 1 January 1869 to 1 January 1879, as compared to 28 per cent for men. Non-able-bodied women relieved fell 21 per cent due to the decrease in outdoor relief, whereas numbers of non-able-bodied men relieved fell only 14 per cent.

91 Hodgkinson, *The Origins of the National Health Service*, p. 269. Emphasis in original.

92 M. A. Crowther, *The Workhouse System 1834–1929*, p. 136.

93 30 Vict. c. 6.

94 30 Vict. c. 6 ss. 5–6. The Act also established the Metropolitan Poor
Fund, a common fund for the metropolis for most Poor Law expenses,
including expenses of maintaining lunatics in county asylums: ss. 61, 69.
This removed the worst of the inequities in funding of Poor Law in
London, and made the construction of Poor Law facilities a practical
possibility for the poorer unions, particularly in the East End of the city.

95 The statistics of the Commissioners in Lunacy show that 3,209 pauper
lunatics were contained in these institutions by 1 January 1872: *Thirty-
Sixth Report of the Commissioners in Lunacy*, PP 1882 (357) xxxii 1, at 6 ff.

96 Figures regarding the pauper insane are taken from the *Thirty-Sixth Annual
Report of the Commissioners in Lunacy*, PP 1882 (357) xxxii 1, at 6 ff. These
statistics, unlike those relating to able-bodied and non-able-bodied poor,
include children; however the number of children appears to have been
minimal. In the period at issue, county asylum admissions rose from 26,642
to 38,395 paupers (45 per cent increase). Pauper insane contained in all
other facilities (i.e., licensed madhouses, registered hospitals, Broadmoor,
etc.) fell from 2,103 to 1,477 (30 per cent): Appendix D, no. 71 to *Ninth
Annual Report of the Local Government Board*, PP 1880 [2681] xxvi 1, at 356
f. These latter figures include adults only.

97 See 30 & 31 Vict. c. 106 s. 22. Previous to this time, the insane could be
allowed to remain in workhouses if (in compliance with the 1834 Poor
Law statute) they were not dangerous, and if (after 1862, in compliance
with the statutory reforms to the county asylum legislation) they were
appropriately certified by the medical officer. These had not allowed
actual detention of an individual who wished to leave, however: that
step was taken by the above 1867 legislation.

98 8 & 9 Vict. c. 126 s. 50; 16 & 17 Vict. c. 97 s. 70.

99 See for example, *Thirteenth Annual Report of the Poor Law Commissioners*,
PP 1847 [816] xviii 1 at 21; and William Golden Lumley, *The New Lunacy
Acts* (London: Shaw, 1845), pp. xii, 160, 163. This appears to be a
defensible interpretation of the statute, the relevant portion of which
reads that 'if ... such Justice shall be satisfied that such Person is lunatic
... such Justice *shall*, by an Order under his Hand ... direct such Person
to be received into the Asylum ...': 8 & 9 Vict. c. 126 s. 48, emphasis
added.

100 See William Golden Lumley, *Manuals of the Duties of Poor Law Officers:
Medical Officer* (London: Knight, 1849).

101 See for example 9 Geo. IV c. 40 s. 38.

102 48 Geo. III c. 96 s. 17.

103 51 Geo. III c. 79 s. 1.

104 55 Geo. III c. 46 s. 8.

105 9 Geo. IV c. 40 ss. 36, 38.

106 Roy Porter, *Mind-Forg'd Manacles* (London: Athlone, 1987; reprinted
Harmondsworth: Penguin, 1990), p. 118. Re reluctance to place
individuals in institutions in this period, see also Peter Rushton,

'Lunatics and Idiots', *Medical History*, **32** (1988): 34; Akihito Suzuki, 'Lunacy in seventeenth- and eighteenth-century England, Part I', *History of Psychiatry*, **2** (1991): 437, at 452, for confinement of the dangerously insane in 'strong huts' into the early seventeenth century; and more generally 'Lunacy in seventeenth- and eighteenth-century England, Part II', *History of Psychiatry*, **3** (1992): 29 regarding Bethlem and houses of correction. Suzuki also argues that cure could be a factor in sending a pauper to a private madhouse, however [Part I, pp. 453 f.], and that the dangerous were not necessarily confined: Part II, p. 36. He also cites (albeit as atypical) the case of the North Riding of Yorkshire, where the Justices confined all poor lunatics in houses of correction, dangerous or not: Part II, pp. 31 f. This would suggest a significant degree of local variation, consistent with the old Poor Law.

107 Bentham also favoured a system of forcing beggars and those without honest means of livelihood into the panopticon: *Outline of a Work entitled Pauper Management Improved*, 1798, reprinted in *The Collected Works of Jeremy Bentham*, Vol. VIII, ed. John Bowring (Edinburgh: William Tait, 1843), pp. 401 and 403. These admission processes are discussed by Charles Bahmueller in *The National Charity Company* (Berkeley: University of California Press, 1981), p. 17. Bahmueller emphasizes the authoritarian aspects of Bentham's proposals. Where, in Bentham's plan, such persons would be surrendered to the institution by members of the public who would receive a reward, the asylum acts made it the province of professional Poor Law staff, arguably rendering the scheme more Foucauldean than its Benthamite counterpart.

108 9 & 10 Vict. c. 84 s. 1.

109 See 53 Vict. c. 5 s. 16.

110 16 & 17 Vict. c. 97 s. 67.

111 Ibid.

112 25 & 26 Vict. c. 111 s. 19.

113 16 & 17 Vict. c. 97 Sch. (F.), No. 3.

114 4 & 5 Will. IV c. 76 s. 45.

115 Instructional Letter to Boards of Guardians, dated 5 February 1842, and reproduced in *Eighth Annual Report of the Poor Law Commissioners*, PP 1842 [359] xix 1, at 111.

116 25 & 26 Vict. c. 111 ss. 8, 20, 21.

117 30 & 31 Vict. c. 106 s. 22. The 1834 prohibition against accommodation of the dangerously insane remained in effect, notwithstanding this enactment.

118 See for example, his evidence before the Select Committee on Lunatics, PP 1859 1st sess. (204) iii 75, at q. 590. The mandatory model of admissions has had its effect on modern historians as well: See for example, J. K. Walton, 'Casting out and bringing back in Victorian England: pauper lunatics, 1840–70', in *The Anatomy of Madness*, Vol. II, ed. William F. Bynum *et al.* (London: Tavistock, 1985), p. 132 at 137.

CHAPTER 4

The Pragmatics of Coexistence: Local Officials and Pauper Lunacy

The last chapter demonstrated that formal legal lines of authority were minimal and based on inconsistent administrative models. The responsibility for administering the new Poor Law was to rest with boards of guardians, who employed and supervised relieving officers, workhouse officers and medical staff. This line of authority was in conflict with the asylum acts, which gave these staff people independent authority in committals and in decisions as to choice of institutional care for the pauper insane. The Poor Law central authorities had broad regulatory powers but, apart from audit controls, little practical way to enforce their edicts. Justices of the Peace were subject to even less legal control in their management of the county asylums. Central authorities were not absent from local administration, but they tended to operate by alliance and persuasion rather than by fiat.[1] Their inspections were central to the establishment of these relationships, although voluminous correspondence between local and central authorities also ensued.

The administration of the Poor Law in general and the Poor Law of lunacy in particular is thus to be thought of in terms of webs of influence, alliance and distancing between the various persons involved. The statutes provided only a bare and inconsistent framework for the definition of these relations. The roles of the administrators were instead formed through participation in these relations. The administrators were not merely the constituent parts of these webs; their relative roles, functions and powers were also one part of the substance around which the alliances and divisions formed.

A local study is therefore necessary. The practical problems this poses for the researcher are summarized by M. A. Crowther:

The Poor Law also offers a striking example of central policy contending against local independence. Its history must avoid generalizations which give no idea of the great differences of practice in the localities, but also avoid the maze of colourful yet disconnected details in which this subject abounds. Source material is voluminous and confusing, and the thousands of volumes of correspondence between guardians and Poor Law authorities survive as memorials of these struggles. The huge bulk of documents, in the Public Record Office and in county archives, daunts the single researcher. No historian can consult more than a small number of them, and he will not know whether the area he selects is exceptional.[2]

Notwithstanding these difficulties, reference to a local jurisdiction is necessary to consider how the law was actually being implemented.

The local study here concerns Leicestershire and Rutland.[3] Given the importance of local administration, it is at best dubious whether a 'typical' area can exist. None the less, and with that caveat, there is little in the case of Leicestershire and Rutland to suggest that they were particularly atypical. Apart from local arrangements between the borough of Leicester and the counties regarding asylum care, discussed below, there were no relevant local acts affecting the implementation of Poor Law, and there were no Gilbert Unions. While manageable in size, the counties contained a good variety of urban and rural unions, and both manufacturing and agricultural industrial bases. The scale of the unions also provided variety. While Leicester workhouse grew to accommodate over 1,000 people by the late 1850s,[4] Billesdon workhouse in July 1864 contained only 21 inmates.[5] While the smaller workhouses did not have special accommodation for lunatics, Leicester Union began segregation of the insane within the workhouse in the early 1840s, and by the early to mid-1850s, paid nursing attendance had been provided for the roughly 40 insane persons in the wards.[6] There was nothing in the reports of the Lunacy Commissioners or the Poor Law inspectorate to suggest that the area was in any way notorious.[7]

The area was in general prosperous in the period from 1850 to 1870, so that various policy options were economically viable. The administration was further not centred around any single, pervasive and particularly politically active personality whose involvement would make the area atypical. The boards of guardians may have been cliques,[8] but that was not unusual. The head of the county asylum from 1853 was John Buck, the former Medical Officer of Health for Leicester. While he appears to have been a competent superintendent, he was not extraordinary in any respect. Thus, while he apparently read the *Journal of Mental Science,* he made only one relatively inconsequential contribution to it.[9]

The county asylum was constructed in Leicestershire in 1837. The 1845 Asylums Act put both Rutland County and the borough of Leicester under an obligation to make provision for their pauper lunatics in county asylums. Rather than construct asylums of their own, both made arrangements with the Leicestershire County Asylum, which took effect from the beginning of 1849.[10] These agreements remained in effect until the opening of a new asylum for the borough of Leicester in 1869. For this twenty-year period, therefore, the poor insane were admitted from across the entire area.

The asylum is atypical in that it continued to accept patients who were not paupers. The original asylum had been built as a joint venture between the County of Leicestershire and a private charity. Patients admitted through the charity were not technically paupers, although it is an open question how different they were from the class of paupers. Originally, the asylum also accepted private patients in addition to these charitable patients, but this ceased in the 1850s due to space restrictions.

The surviving asylum records are generally good, containing good runs of different sorts of document. This is particularly true after John Buck became superintendent in 1853.[11] There are, unfortunately, very few interesting documents relating to the charity until after 1870. The Poor Law documentation, both at the Public Record Office and the Leicestershire Record Office, is somewhat patchier. It is also much more voluminous, making reliance on indices a practical necessity.

The next three chapters will examine the interrelations of the administrators, focusing on Leicestershire and Rutland. This chapter will consider the roles of local officials in juxtaposition to each other. The next chapter will focus on the admission documents and casebooks of the Leicestershire and Rutland County Lunatic Asylum and such relevant records as remain regarding the insane in the workhouses of the unions in those counties, to determine how the local officers understood the decisions being made regarding the committals of individual insane people. Chapter 6 will examine the role of the Lunacy Commissioners.

JUSTICES OF THE PEACE

The legal position of the Justices of the Peace in administering the Poor Law of lunacy has already been discussed. They were in charge of overseeing the building and administration of county asylums, and their assent was required to send insane paupers to these asylums. In rural unions, they also served ex officio on boards of guardians, providing a point of contact between the Poor Law and lunacy administrations.

While the legislation concerning appointments of Justices remained unchanged from the mid-eighteenth to the twentieth century,[12] the composition of the bench did not remain constant even between the 1830s and the 1860s. The eighteenth-century bench had been composed primarily of local gentry. This resulted both from a property requirement contained in the statute and the fact that the post carried no remuneration, making it beyond the aspirations of those who were not of independent means. Particularly after 1780, clergy began to be appointed as gentry proved inadequate in numbers and inclination to fill the bench. By the early 1830s, these clergy accounted for roughly a quarter of England's Justices.[13] In 1835, this source of appointments came to an end. Sympathetic to pressures from dissenters and radicals, the Whig government made a policy at that time that clergy ought not generally to hold judicial appointment.[14] An increasing workload none the less meant the concurrent need to expand the benches. The Black Country, for example, just to the west of Leicestershire, had fewer than 40 Justices in 1833; by 1859, it had 104.[15] From the mid-1830s, the lack of local gentry to fill these positions was compensated for by the appointment of local industrialists. In the Black Country in 1860, only 11 per cent of those appointed were gentry, and over 50 per cent were masters of the local iron and coal industries.[16]

The Justices have been portrayed as stubborn opponents of centralization in government. In this regard, the following comments of Esther Moir are typical:

A large part of the countryside, with the magistracy frequently its strongest spokesmen, thought still in terms of a traditional pattern of duty. The ideal of the well-regulated village dominated and cared for both in body and mind by a patriarchal parson and squire died hard – and indeed in many places was still as vigorous as it had ever been.

* * *

The magistrates, as they watched this invasion of their empire by a central army of paid officials appointed by Whitehall, would however defend their position not in terms of mere self-interest but in terms of an abstract ideal of good government. For it was a widely held belief that too much central government would discourage local self-government and lessen individual self-reliance.[17]

While the change in composition of the Justices' benches suggests that the continuity of attitude suggested in Moir's work must be viewed sceptically, the Justices' disapproval of centralization is still not surprising. It was not merely that centralization attacked the traditional prerogatives of the county gentry and would thus have been unpopular with them. It was also that Justices who were local factory owners would have been unsympathetic to centralized government. The first major inspectorate established was the factory inspectorate in 1833, which worked in direct opposition to the financial interests of these Justices. Shaftesbury's involvement with the Lunacy Commission would further not have engendered trust, since his tireless efforts in the ten-hours movement, attempting to set maximum hours of work in factories, would have done little to endear him to those Justices who were factory owners.

The Justices can be seen as a reflection of the paternalist ideology which was recreated in the nineteenth century. Consistent with earlier paternalist notions, local prerogatives in government were seen as constitutional rights. Philips's study of the Black Country shows the use by the industrialist magistrates of their position to govern and control their workers. Thus a fifth of the cases before them involved the theft of small amounts of coal or iron, the industries in which they were involved. Troops were used by the magistrates to protect collieries against striking miners, and prosecution of workers under labour legislation numbered 10,000 between 1858 and 1875 in the Black Country.[18] Paternalism based on the values of the old gentry was giving way to a paternalism based on wage labour and employment, much as was seen in the discussion of Malthus and Poor Law theory, above. The paternalist hierarchy was becoming associated not merely with traditional social hierarchy, but also with the hierarchy of employment relations.

There were few practical methods available to challenge this exercise of local authority and antipathy to central control. Even when the Justices were acting in contravention of the law, enforcement mechanisms were cumbersome and beyond the practical reach of the central Poor Law and lunacy authorities, with their limited staffs and budgets. Publicity was not necessarily effective. Notwithstanding the persistent complaints of the Lunacy Commissioners in their annual reports, the City of London, largely through a policy of stubborn inactivity, did not open an asylum until 1866, more than twenty years after the legal obligation had been imposed.[19] In 1857 it was alleged that pauper lunatics in Birmingham and Nottingham were routinely admitted to the local workhouse, rather than being brought before Justices and admitted to the county asylum. This course was allegedly followed for reasons of expense. The matter was sent by the Lunacy Commissioners to the Solicitor General for a legal opinion. The resulting opinion held that to maintain pauper lunatics in workhouses who were proper persons for detention in asylums, for the purpose of lightening the poor rates, was an evasion of the legislation. The only remedy suggested was to apply for mandamus to require the Justices to hold proper hearings, a remedy which the opinion itself recognized was inadequate:

[W]e cannot disguise from ourselves that any proceedings for the purpose of putting a stop to these illegal practices are involved in a great difficulty, and that the aid of the legislature may be necessary to invest the Commissioners with larger powers in such cases.[20]

The granting of increased powers to the Commissioners had, of course, political problems of its own. Paternalism had its influence at Westminster as well as in the shires. Nicholas Hervey identifies two areas where otherwise good and sympathetic relations between the Home Office and the Lunacy Commission became strained: financial expenditures and the curtailment of Justices' authority.[21]

At the same time, the law of pauper lunacy could provoke a certain sympathy from Justices, as it provided authority for them in the Poor Law field, separate and distinct from the boards of guardians. The desire of the Justices for autonomy from central government and the Commissioners should not be taken as implying a unity between Justices and Poor Law authorities at the local level.

A particularly clear case of this protectionism concerned the Justices of the Hull Asylum, who, following complaints by the Sculcoates guardians regarding the quality of the food, refused to allow the guardians again onto the ward, arguing that the right of the guardians to 'visit and examine any or every pauper lunatic chargeable to such union'[22] referred only to the person of the lunatic, and not to the 'treatment, means of subsistence, and other comforts and requisites' offered in the asylum. The guardians complained to the Home Secretary, who asked for the opinion of the Commissioners in Lunacy. The Commissioners made a legalistic argument, which offered a compromise: the visitors had the right to view their insane paupers on their wards, but had no right to inquire into matters such as the food 'apart from such opportunity as a visit at the dinner hour might afford'. This view was forwarded to the asylum and the visiting Justices protested. The matter was then forwarded to the Law Officers of the Crown, whose opinion essentially upheld that of the Commissioners.[23] The tenacity of the Justices, in the face of both the guardians and the Commissioners, suggests a determination to guard their autonomy regarding the asylum.

Akihito Suzuki's work on Hanwell, the county asylum for Middlesex, would suggest that the role of the Justices was not merely protective of their turf, but also productive.[24] In Suzuki's view, the system of non-restraint, traditionally viewed as the project of medical superintendent John Conolly, was at least as much a project of the Middlesex Justices of the Peace. It was they who encouraged Conolly to visit Lincoln,[25] where the non-restraint system had been pioneered, to see if the system might work at Hanwell. The result, the well-ordered asylum with its focus on work and discipline, was as attractive to the Justices as to Conolly. This was not merely due to the paternalist ethic, although the system did allow for the care of the insane and the possibility of cure. It was also a matter of pride, protecting the space of the Justices against encroachment by central government:

Secondly and more importantly, they [the Justices] were in the middle of a race against the government, and particularly the Russells, to improve prisons. Adams [chairman of the Middlesex magistrates, 1836–44, during the introduction of non-restraint] implied that their modified silent system in the prison and the non-restraint system in the asylum had to be the most advanced, in order to win.[26]

The documents available for Leicestershire and Rutland are less forthcoming regarding local roles and relations, as the Justices as a group left very few relevant records. They signed documents authorizing paupers' admission to the asylum, but they did not comment on them, and key questions such as the frequency with which they refused to sign these admission documents cannot be answered in any systematic way. Such documents as there are suggest that the law of pauper lunacy was used by the Justices to reinforce their status as independent of both central authority and local Poor Law guardians.

The rules of the asylum were circulated to the Justices in 1849, along with a preface prepared by the visiting committee lauding praises of the asylum. The visitors were themselves primarily Justices.[27] This document was thus written by and for Justices of the Peace. The thrust of the preface was that the mid-nineteenth century county asylum was the first serious attempt to address the explosion of pauper lunacy. It provided a cursory history of lunacy law, marginalizing the importance of eighteenth-century legislation. The 1808 Act had been imperfectly implemented:

[I]t was not compulsory, however, and during the next twenty years only seven Asylums were erected, not capable of receiving in the whole more than 1457 Patients, although by Parliamentary Returns made in the year 1827 it appeared that there were at least between 9,000 and 10,000 Pauper Lunatics in England![28]

Early establishments for lunatics also suffered from improper supervision:

The condition of the insane poor was partially remedied by the establishment of these Asylums; but they were left to the unrestrained authority of attendants; there was no power to check the oppression and cruelty too frequently practised; madhouses became proverbially places of horror, and the patient received no other care from his keeper than that which was necessary for the confinement of his person.[29]

The rules of the Leicestershire and Rutland Lunatic Asylum provided a response to this problem, establishing the duties of the visiting committee regarding inspections.[30] The mid-century asylum was thus portrayed by the report as reflecting what would have been considered proper lines of authority, lines of authority headed by the Justices.

The preface emphasized lunacy as a social problem, exploding in its dimensions, a trend to which the county asylum provided a solution:

If, as will be shown hereafter, mental disorder be of a character peculiarly dependant for its cure upon early and judicious treatment, it may well be imagined that the reverse of this could have but one effect, and that the number of the insane must necessarily increase, from the few that were restored to reason; but few persons perhaps, except those who have seen the Parliamentary Return of 1847, are prepared to learn that on the first of

January in that year there were in County Asylums, Licensed Houses, Workhouses, and other places of confinement, upwards of 23,000 INSANE PERSONS IN ENGLAND AND WALES ALONE! that even these Returns were believed to be short of the truth, and that the number of Insane and of those engaged solely in their care, was not less than 30,000![31]

The preface went on to estimate national expenditures related to county asylums at close to a million pounds per year, emphasizing the importance of stemming the tide of lunacy sooner rather than later.[32]

If the county asylum was the solution to this dilemma, it was a solution which the visiting Justices juxtaposed to the principle of less eligibility of the new Poor Law. Consider the following description of the Leicester Asylum, contained in the preface:

Placed on an eminence, and commanding one of the most beautiful views in the County of Leicester, extending over the valley of the Soar, and bounded by the hills of Charnwood Forest, there is everything in its position to soothe and cheer the patient; the grounds belonging to the Asylum comprise in the whole twenty acres, part of which is laid out in walks and pleasure grounds, and the remainder, save such part as is occupied by the building and the yards for the exercise of the Patients, is cultivated as much as may be by the inmates themselves; labour in the open air being found of all employments the most conducive to health of the great majority of the insane; not, however, that the comforts of those who are necessarily debarred from this exercise, are neglected, no effort is left untried to cheer the melancholy, and soothe the excited, the great object being to make this Asylum a HOUSE OF CURE, and not a HOUSE OF DETENTION.[33]

Whether or not this was an accurate picture of asylum life is open to question; what is relevant here is the image presented, an image inconsistent with the hardness of the new Poor Law. This imagery continued throughout the period under study. When a separate asylum was being constructed for the borough of Leicester in the mid-1860s, the board of guardians for Leicester Union was moved to pass the following motion:

[T]hat this Board is gratified to find that at length accommodation is about to be provided for persons of unsound mind, in an Asylum for the borough.

This board however cannot conceal its regret, that in the Town Council there appears to be a desire for external ornament in the proposed building, which in the opinion of this board would be somewhat out of character in a Pauper Lunatic Asylum.

The chief object of such Institutions is the recovery of the Patients, and this Board would therefore, with all respect submit, that while every convenience and appliance that will further this object should be provided; it should ever be borne in mind that the inmates of such an Institution will for the most part, if not exclusively, be Paupers, and that to provide a building for their reception, with much external decoration, would be both impolitic and unwise' (A copy of the foregoing resolution to be sent to the Town Council).[34]

Lest the guardians be thought without justification, it might be noted that the capital costs for the construction of the new asylum eventually reached £50,000, almost three times its budgeted price of £17,300 and a sum criticized by the Lunacy Commission.[35]

Such documents as there are would suggest that the Leicester Justices viewed the admission of paupers to the asylum in a pragmatic way, as one would expect of local administrators. Here again, as on the larger issue of the construction and administration of county asylums, they appear to have guarded their independence, and felt free to make their own decisions as to appropriateness of admissions, notwithstanding pressure from medical officers or central authorities. The clearest documentation resulted from the report of Samuel Hitch on the workhouse and outdoor relief in Leicester, in 1844. Hitch, at that time the secretary and moving force of the Association of Medical Officers of Asylums and Hospitals for the Insane, stated that 14 people in the workhouse or on outdoor relief ought to be removed to the asylum. For seven of these people, the Justices refused to sign the admission documents. Five of the seven were held by the Justices to be not insane. To reach this conclusion, the Justices had to depart from the view both of Hitch, who had recommended them for removal to the asylum, and of the Poor Law medical officer, who had listed them as insane on the quarterly returns. The other two cases, those of Jane Abbott and Mary Bevan, the Justices did not consider proper for admission to the asylum. For them, unlike for the other five, reasons were given which warrant quotation:

[T]hough the said Jane Abbott is insane yet we are satisfied from the statement of her sister who has the charge of her and also from the [Poor Law] Surgeon that she is perfectly harmless and that she is well taken care of and no annoyance to any one. [I]t is also stated by the Surgeon that there is no probability of any improvement in her state of mind by removing her to the Lunatic Asylum; for these reasons we have declined making orders.

* * *

[T]hough the said Mary Bevan appears to be insane yet according to the evidence of the Matron and Surgeon she is perfectly harmless. It also appears that she is strongly attached to her mother who is with her in the Workhouse and is blind, and that they are a material comfort to each other;

for these reasons we do not think it a proper case to send to the Lunatic Asylum.[36]

These findings were completely at odds with Hitch's report. He had stated that Jane Abbott was allowed to wander for entire days at a time under essentially no control at all and was troublesome to her neighbours; and he referred to Mary Bevan's 'dangerous irascibility'.[37]

It is inappropriate to read too much into these few cases. This is particularly true since Hitch's inquiry was prompted by the visit of the Metropolitan Lunacy Commissioners to Leicester in preparation for their 1844 report. There was thus a politically charged atmosphere to the Justices' decisions. The decisions were none the less consistent with what would be expected. The Justices were guarding their own decision-making role regarding pauper lunatics and loath to relegate that role to either medical professionals or the central Commissioners. In general, it does not appear that the Justices were adverse to sending people to asylums, but they do seem to have insisted on the demonstration of a concrete reason to send each pauper; general praise of the institution does not appear to have been convincing.

BOARDS OF GUARDIANS

As indicated above, the Leicestershire and Rutland boards of guardians offered a variety of institutional responses to the problem of pauper lunacy, from little specialized treatment in small workhouses to dedicated wards in Leicester and Hinkley.[38] The problems of central authorities enforcing their edicts by litigation applied here as much as to the Justices, although audit controls gave the Poor Law central authorities some broad controls over local guardians, particularly in the enforcement of outdoor relief prohibition orders.

Local boards of guardians displayed a mixed response to the new Poor Law generally, and to the Poor Law central authorities in particular. There was general popular resistance to the introduction of the new Poor Law in the area. In both Leicester and Billesdon, workhouses were attacked. Troops were required to keep the peace in both Leicester and Hinkley in this period. This was associated with Chartist agitation, but the new Poor Law attack on outdoor relief was an important factor. The responses of the guardians to these problems varied. Thus it would appear that the guardians of Leicester Union, where conservatives held the majority until 1845, co-operated with the

Poor Law Commissioners in a vague alliance against the Chartists and radicals. In Hinkley, the outdoor relief prohibition order imposed on the union in the face of a trade depression at the end of the 1830s found the guardians unsympathetic to the Commissioners. They essentially refused to implement the new Poor Law. Their staff complained to the Commissioners that medical relief was used as a pretext for the grant of outdoor relief,[39] and it was only following the highly unusual step of the beginning of litigation by the Poor Law Commissioners that the Hinkley guardians agreed to build a workhouse.[40] Billesdon Union did build a workhouse, but refused to furnish the vagrant wards until after 1870. Throughout this period, vagrants were housed in local rooming houses and were not required to work,[41] a system reminiscent of the old Poor Law.

Approaches to Poor Law ideology were similarly varied. There were boards which adopted the new thinking relatively quickly. Other boards held to the old Poor Law thought patterns for some time after its replacement in 1834. Thus the correspondence of Billesdon Union with the Commissioners, particularly in the early years of the new Poor Law, emphasized the character of their paupers when they wished for a departure from the rigours of the new law, an approach which met with little success. Other boards wrote relatively freely to the Poor Law central authority asking for advice on the interpretation of the legislation. It would be overstating the case to imply that these boards saw themselves as administrative units of a centralized system, true to the Benthamite model; even these boards guarded a level of autonomy. Even so, they do seem to have had a relatively comfortable working relationship with the central Commissioners.

What should be emphasized at this point is the interest of at least some boards of guardians in matters of pauper lunacy. The minutes of the Leicester board of guardians, for example, show a legitimate attempt to ensure proper institutional care of their lunatics. When in the 1840s pauper lunatics had to be sent to private houses owing to the unavailability of the asylum, they sent members of the board to inspect the houses in advance.[42] Periodic inspections were made of these facilities while Leicester patients remained in them, and when a scandal broke about the Haydock Lodge madhouse, the borough acted promptly in removing its inmates.

Leicestershire and Rutland boards of guardians also appear to have taken their visitation duties to the county asylum relatively seriously, although unions farther from the asylum seem to have visited less. The minute book of visitors to the asylum lists 70 visits from Poor Law guardians between 1851 and 1865.[43] This should be seen as a minimum figure, as it is not clear how complete the record was.[44]

The guardians, like the Justices, were local administrators dealing with practical problems. Like the Justices, they needed to be convinced of the merits of asylum care for each individual to be sent. Without demonstrated merits, they could well be more hesitant. The following comment from the Hinkley Union does not appear atypical:

In reply to your letter of the 16th Inst 11743/43 relative to the cases of William Hill and Thomas Vernon and am directed by the Board of Guardians to state that after consulting with their Medical Officer they are of the opinion that the above are not fit cases for the Asylum, the paupers are not so dangerous as to require restraint, their habits being dirty, and their dispositions at times to tear their own clothes, from what we can learn from the friends of Hill he has been in an asylum, and Vernon has been imbecile for so many years that there is not the slightest chance of his recovery.[45]

This attitude conforms to the testimony of Poor Law Inspector H. B. Farnall before the Select Committee on Lunatics in 1859: 'if there was a prospect of their cure they would be removed [to an asylum]; if not, the guardians would object to paying more'.[46]

POOR LAW MEDICAL OFFICERS

The standard of Poor Law medicine and of Poor Law doctors was much criticized in the nineteenth century, as the rising medical profession found itself allied with the critics of the new Poor Law. Thus the Poor Law medical officers, even more explicitly than the guardians, Justices and central authorities, found themselves not merely participants in, but also subjects of, Poor Law debate. Increasingly, medical officers' duties, credentials, catchment areas and pay became the subject of legal regulation. By 1842, reasonably high professional standards were in place for Poor Law medical officers,[47] and all Poor Law medical officers were required to be registered under the Medical Act when it was introduced in 1858.[48] Increasingly over the 1840s and 1850s, medical officers were required to live within their districts and, by 1860, medical districts were not to exceed 15,000 acres, nor to extend more than six miles from the medical officer's residence. A problem in the South-West and the Midlands was lack of available candidates. This could be a problem in Leicestershire and Rutland.[49] The problem was aggravated by the relatively high medical certification required. Thus Peter Alfred Jackson of Leicester was appointed medical officer to a district in Barrow Union in 1857, as the only medical practitioner resident in the union did not have the required dual qualifications.[50] In 1861, 291 medical officers held 629 appointments in the South-West and Midlands.[51]

Standards of qualification do not necessarily translate directly to standards of practice. Both the nineteenth-century sources and much of the twentieth-century secondary literature suggest that Poor Law medical officers were held in low social esteem. Usually, they would practise privately in addition to their Poor Law duties. Crowther argues that the motivation to accept the position was essentially economic: to subsidize a private practice which was not paying well enough, or to keep a competing doctor from entering the territory.[52] Guardians were accused of paying more attention to economy than to an officer's calibre.[53] The Leicestershire documents provide some justification for the criticism of a low calibre of medical service: there were scandals in both Barrow and Blaby unions regarding medical officers failing to attend patients who later died.[54] In the Blaby case, the guardians were pressured by the Poor Law Commission into asking for the resignation of the medical officer concerned. In the Barrow case, the Poor Law Board, noting the medical officer's long and otherwise unblemished record, was content to 'express a hope that he [the medical officer] will be more careful in the discharge of his duties in the future'.[55]

Particularly in the early years of the new Poor Law, it would appear that guardians were able to keep a firm grip on their medical officers. Appointments were often by contract, subject to annual renewal. There was minimal organization within the medical profession, and the Poor Law Commissioners lacked an effective means to challenge the control of the guardians. It would be simplistic to suggest that this resulted in medical officers blindly following the will of their guardians, but it is certainly true that these structures of employment placed guardians in a relatively strong position over their medical officers.

As the new Poor Law developed, various influences increased the independence of the Poor Law medical officers. There was the increasingly specific regulation of duties, which in turn resulted in greater involvement of the central authorities. The county asylum acts, with their admission processes specifying the role of the medical officer of the union, are a part of this trend. Regulations of the Poor Law central authorities further defined specific duties for Poor Law medical officers, such as the inspection of paupers admitted to the workhouse, to identify those who ought to be sent to asylums.

Whether these duties were imposed by statute or by regulation of the central authority, medical officers might invoke the authority of the Poor Law Commissioners or Board against the guardians in the enforcement of the prescribed arrangements. Thus for example when the guardians of Barrow upon Soar Union failed to pay medical officer Downey for a visit to Jane Kettle in 1856, he enlisted the assistance of the Poor Law Board to enforce payment.[56] Such approaches were by no means always successful, but the Poor Law central authorities did treat the medical officers' concerns seriously. By arbitrating or deciding the issues between medical officers and the guardians as between distinct legal parties, the Board increased the image of the medical officer as an independent actor, having a role separate and distinct from following the orders of the guardians. This was further reinforced by the insistence of the central Poor Law authority on receiving the report of the medical officer regarding lunatics whom it thought ought to be in the asylum.

Early in the new Poor Law, the central authority had only the tools of persuasion and bureaucratic persistence to enforce these new relationships. From the 1840s, however, half of the salaries of permanent medical officers started to be paid by Westminster. The result relating to the relationships between guardians, medical officers and central authority was twofold. There was an economic inducement for boards of guardians to terminate arrangements based on annual contracts, thus minimizing the precarious nature of the employment of the medical officer and providing a certain autonomy from the guardians. This took effect gradually over the 1840s and 1850s to a point where permanent salaried positions became the norm. It also increased the persuasiveness of central involvement: when the central authority paid half the piper's costs, it began to enjoy a considerably expanded role in the choice of music. Details of proposed candidates' careers were increasingly scrutinized by the central board, and appointments of candidates deemed inappropriate were increasingly questioned. Again, this resulted not merely in the Board's increased control of the local situation, but also in increased independence of the medical officers from the guardians.

This independence was further reinforced by the increasing

organization of the medical profession. At the beginning of the nineteenth century, it was a diffuse and undifferentiated mass, but the growth of professional organizations, such as the British Medical Association, and legislative reforms, particularly the Medical Act of 1858, introduced the rudiments of professionalism. Disciplinary proceedings became a professional matter, not solely a matter between doctor and patient or, in the Poor Law context, between guardians, central authority and medical officer.

Connected with this were the lobbying efforts of the workhouse medical officers themselves. They formed a variety of professional organizations and interest groups over the course of the century, including the Provincial Medical and Surgical Association (founded in 1832 and active until the early 1840s), the annual Convention of Poor Law Medical Officers (commencing in 1846), the Poor Law Medical Relief Association (founded in 1855), the Association for the Improvement of Workhouse Infirmaries and the Poor Law Medical Officers' Association (both founded in 1866 and merging shortly thereafter). These gave some professional and collegial support to their members and also, of course, increased the profile of the medical officers. These organizations, along with the critical interest of the broader medical community, allied themselves with the humanitarians and those parts of the paternalists critical of the new Poor Law. Lord Shaftesbury presided at a number of meetings of the Poor Law Medical Relief Association and the Convention of Poor Law Medical Officers.[57]

Some indication of the relative importance accorded to medical officers as opposed to other Poor Law officials can be seen from their relative pay. Ruth Hodgkinson states that, in 1850, the average salary of a medical officer was £50 per annum, as compared to £268 for the district auditor, £110 for the union clerk, £82 for the relieving officers, £47 for the chaplain, £14 for the nurses, £37 for masters and matrons, £31 for schoolmasters and £21 for schoolmistresses.[58] This is misleading, in that atypically of those on the list, medical officers were almost exclusively part-time appointments.[59] A full-time medical officer of a sizeable workhouse might earn £250 to £350 per annum,[60] giving support to Crowther's contention that medical officers became the most important workhouse officials.[61]

The increasing independence of the medical officers did not necessarily mean a departure from the principles of the new Poor Law. Joseph Rogers was a central figure in the Poor Law Medical Officers' Association, and worked tirelessly to improve the professional position of medical officers in workhouses. His autobiography, published in 1889, portrays him as a humanitarian and crusading figure against the tyranny, corruption and ineptitude of the guardians.[62] Yet upon his appointment as medical officer of the Westminster Infirmary, his first act was to forbid much of the extra diet which was given to inmates, and to enforce the logic of the new Poor Law in the workhouse:

I learned afterwards that in the matter of diets an extensive system of exchange obtained throughout the House without any check or hindrance on the part of the officials. It took me the greater part of four days to see all the infirm people on extras, but the result was satisfactory, as it enabled me to put the establishment so far as the diets were concerned, on an economic basis. The clerk of the Board assured me at the time that I had caused a saving of some hundreds of pounds, a statement which I honestly believe was the truth.[63]

Rogers was in practice enforcing the workhouse test with a vigilance more forceful than the guardians, but in a way which supported his professional aims. Extra diet was to be given for health reasons and thus at his own discretion.[64] A similar dynamic can be seen in Leicester Union in 1862, when the Lunacy Commission argued for roast meat and beer to be a part of the diet for the insane in the workhouse and for a moderate allowance of tobacco to be offered. It was the medical officer who initially objected to the provision of beer and tobacco, and to the provision of roast meat unless it would be provided to all inmates.[65]

The medical officers could similarly be independently minded in their assessment of the insane. The following extract from the 1866 annual report of the Lunacy Commissioners would suggest that, in the 'few cases' where their removal powers under the 1862 Act had been used, it was as often to circumvent the medical officer as the guardians:

For while it will often happen, as we have seen in the case above-mentioned, that the opinion of the Medical Officer recommending such removal is successfully resisted by the guardians, it is also a not unusual occurrence that where the Guardians would sanction a removal the Medical Officer himself interposes difficulty.[66]

The independence of the medical officer in this area is perhaps not surprising. Certainly, medical officers had no formal training in lunacy-related matters and, in general, they were not chosen for an interest or expertise in matters of insanity.[67] On the other hand, they had as much expertise as anyone else in the admissions process and, as has been noted above, the statute gave them explicit authority to exercise their discretion in these matters. The independent judgement also takes on a somewhat different aspect regarding medical officers of workhouses with large lunatic wards. At a time when even superintendents of county asylums had no formal training in lunacy-related matters and where experience was the only teacher, it is not surprising that the medical officer would feel his experience as relevant as any to justify independent judgement.

The low status of the Poor Law medical officers and the poor reputation of Poor Law medical services has been noted above. It is possible to see this reputation as the result at least in part in terms of divergence within the profession. The Poor Law held a particular place in the development of medical professionalization. The level of services provided by the Poor Law was heavily criticized by the emerging medical profession, criticisms which struck a resounding chord with the forces opposed to the new Poor Law on paternalist or humanitarian grounds. The place of the Poor Law medical officers was ambiguous in this criticism. As medical men, they were part of the forces which were to reform this system; but as Poor Law officials, they were also the creators of the existing deficient system. Certainly there were Poor Law medical officers who were of a low standard. Some medical officers adopted and enforced the Poor Law system, such as those removing extra diet from inmates; but they might also be involved in more sympathetic activity, often reflecting public health initiatives which were also a part of the Poor Law. Thus George Greaves of the Chorlton Union published a guide for surgeons administering the Factory Acts in 1867 and a paper on pauper housing in 1861.[68] James Hawkings of Stepney Union wrote a work on the education of the deaf and dumb, and another on the tighter public control of charities for the poor.[69] These reflected the influence of the Poor Law, and would have endeared their writers neither to those in the medical profession whose concerns were the provision of services to individual patients, nor to those wishing to strengthen the humanitarian image of the profession by attacking the new Poor Law.

COUNTY ASYLUM MEDICAL SUPERINTENDENTS

The autonomous decision-making of the Poor Law medical officers appears more defensible when their background is compared with that of medical superintendents in county asylums and madhouses, the presumed medical specialists of the insanity business. They, like the Poor Law medical officers, were unlikely to have the benefit of formal training in lunacy-related matters. Academic courses were few and far between. Alexander Morison had instituted a course of lectures in 1823, John Conolly in 1842 and Thomas Laycock in the 1860s; but these had few students. Morison estimated that his course, over twenty years, attracted a total of little more than 100 students.[70] It was not until 1885 that a certificate course in psychological medicine was introduced by the General Medical Council, and no one applied for the first examination.[71] Training was by experience within asylums themselves.

The medical officers of county asylums and private madhouses developed their own professional organization, like their Poor Law counterparts. The Association of Medical Officers of Asylums and Hospitals for the Insane (AMOAHI) was formed in 1841, the name changing to the Medico-Psychological Association in 1865. The organization did induce some spirit of identity among its members. In 1852, it began to publish the *Journal of Mental Science*, edited by John Bucknill, the superintendent of the Devon County Asylum. The journal not only fostered a sense of community among the asylum doctors; as time passed it also increasingly provided the asylum doctors with a vision of their own professionalism. Richard Russell argues that, where the *Journal* had directed itself to a variety of asylum employees, its audience changed over time to exclude non-professional medical staff; and where its original orientation had been practical, including even cleaning tips, it grew into a theoretical journal oriented towards medicine.[72]

The effectiveness of the AMOAHI beyond its membership is much more questionable. Trevor Turner argues that in the nineteenth century, 'the most obvious feature of the psychiatric specialty, ... is the lack of any definite impact, in terms of seriously influencing public attitudes towards mental illness',[73] and that the first real lobbying success of the association was the superannuation campaign in 1910. Before that time, the asylum doctors had ridden on the coat-tails of the success of the British Medical Association and the broader profession. And the relationship of the mad doctors with the remainder of the profession was itself somewhat dubious, as Turner points out:

Overall, then, attitudes towards members of the MPA, echoing through that period, were those of suspicion and denigration. Alienists were corrupt or mad or incompetent or bureaucrats, or any combination thereof. They had 'failed to stay the progress of the disease by the exercise of their art' and had 'but partially succeeded in bringing their specialty within the pale of medical science'.[74]

One respected physician was quoted in the *Journal of Psychological Medicine*, the major competitor of the *Journal of Mental Science*, as saying 'that he should consider it less degrading to keep a public-house than an asylum'.[75]

Richard Russell shares this general assessment in his study of the West Riding county asylum in the second half of the nineteenth century:

In the face of this it needs to be asked how the medical profession operating in this area was able to survive. Certainly it could not be said to have flourished in the latter part of the century ...[76]

This is perhaps a little harsh, at least as far as Leicestershire is concerned. The superintendent of the Leicestershire and Rutland Asylum received salary and wages of £300 per annum in 1851,[77] suggesting a certain level of professional respect.

Relations between the asylum and the other administrative organs were a delicate balance. Regarding the workhouse, the asylum could be highly critical. In some cases, it was seen as a point on the slide from respectability, to vice, to lunacy. Throughout the 1850s, however, asylum inmates were released into the care of the workhouse authorities relatively cheerfully, as is shown by the case of John Finch in 1855:

This is a case of dementia arising most probably from the effects of poverty and old age. The dementia which is not complete appears to be the primary form of mental disorder. From the dirty + neglected state of his person + clothing there is every reason to imagine that he must have been destitute of the commonest necessaries of life. The case of this childish old man might probably be consigned to the authorities of the workhouse with advantage.[78]

The asylum visitors' book also contains messages of thanks from guardians to Superintendent Buck for his hospitality during their inspections.[79] Good relations with the guardians generally, and particularly on these visits when they might be accompanied by one of their medical officers, were a matter of practical necessity. At issue was not merely the desire to keep existing patients until they might appropriately be released, but also to ensure prompt removal of curable cases to the asylum. Given that the asylum was never able to care for all the insane of the counties, good relations also ensured the removal to the workhouse of cases such as Mr Finch, to allow the admission of a different and possibly curable case.

The members of the association did not form strong natural alliances with the central authorities. The Poor Law central authorities had little to do with county asylums and private madhouses, and thus little to do with the association. They did hire Dr Hitch, the association's president, to report on the Leicester workhouse and county asylum in 1844, however, suggesting they were not completely adverse to the association's perspective. The Lunacy Commission was ambiguous on the role of medical expertise in the asylum business. The Commission itself was composed of medical men, barristers and lay members, and visits were required to include one medical man and one barrister. Shaftesbury was not without his quirks where lunacy was concerned. Sometimes these opinions were in conflict with the interests of the medical profession. Thus Shaftesbury tended to view moral treatment, not in terms of scientific or medical theory, but more pragmatically, in terms of regimen.

The asylum doctors were not above challenging legal interpretations of the Commissioners. Thus John Bucknill in 1858 argued in the *Journal of Mental Science* against the view of the Commissioners that admission documents to the asylum ought to be sufficiently complete as to convince a subsequent reader of the insanity of the subject. He instead took the position that 'it would be difficult, in a court of law, to impugn on this ground, the validity of an admission paper, in which the medical man had stated *any two facts* observed by himself, as circumstances which had tended to produce in his mind the opinion that the patient was insane.'[80] Such a view would have considerably curtailed the powers of the Commissioners. Such challenges seem to have been relatively rare, but that may reflect the legal realities of the Commissioners's situation: as has been shown in the discussion of the legislative structures, the Commissioners possessed minimal power relating to county asylums, and thus posed a minimal threat to the asylum superintendents.

THE PAUPERS

This chapter closes with a brief discussion of the role of paupers in the administrative framework. The preceding analysis risks focusing too closely on the administrative authorities. F. M. L. Thompson rightly argues against such an approach:

In many ways this is a curious view, placing the working classes perpetually on the receiving end of outside forces and influences, and portraying them as so much putty in the hands of a masterful and scheming bourgeoisie, a remote and powerful state, and a set of technological imperatives. It allows little for the possibility that the working classes themselves generated their own values and attitudes suited to the requirements of life in an industrial society, and imposed their own forms on middle-class institutions.[81]

Consideration of the motives of the inmates and their families is difficult. The records of the Leicestershire and Rutland Asylum contain no letters or documents written by the lunatics or their families. The best that remains are comments in documents compiled and organized by the very administrators whose perceptions are already central to the historical account, and from which Thompson urges departure. The following remarks are therefore presented with considerable hesitancy. The patient histories contained in the asylum casebooks have been relied on most in what follows. In the next chapter, the specific administrative context of those documents will be discussed. It will be argued that facts are presented to show the asylum in the best possible light and to present a justification of the committal of the pauper. To wrench these facts from this structure, isolate them here and impute motives to the paupers they describe is methodologically highly dubious. The alternative in the instant context, however, is to say nothing about the motives of the paupers at all, to condemn the pauper to a passivity through silence. Such a response may be methodologically pure, but it is not intellectually satisfying.

The image of the insane poor as helpless is based in part in the nineteenth century itself. Andrew Scull cites a litany of such descriptions: the inmates were 'worn-out old dements, imbeciles and aged people', 'contorted harmless specimens of humanity ... senile dotards and hemiplegic wrecks'.[82] This may well have been true for many. The fact that only about half of those in the asylum appear to have been involved in any employment is consistent with such a view. The portrayal is also consistent with the paternalist justifications for the asylum, however: the asylum legislation was successful in part because of its image as a reform which 'vividly involved the helpless',[83] and asylum advocates would naturally emphasize that aspect. The county asylum legislation at best makes the pauper invisible. It was the

Poor Law officers and the Justices who were portrayed as the active parts of the admission system; the pauper lunatic was merely acted upon.

The case of David Perkins provides a countervailing image to that of the passive and inactive pauper: asylum admission procedures were commenced on him when he hurled a brick through the window of a local Justice's house. Perkins was at this time, according to the case book, suffering from melancholia caused 'chiefly from a want of Employment and its concomitant want of food'.[84]

The Perkins case provides an enticing image, but the documents provide insufficient evidence to make claims as to what exactly Perkins thought he was doing, or what if anything he wanted to induce the Justice to do. Was he seeking revenge on an unsympathetic local employer, who also had an appointment to the local magistracy? Was the detention perceived by Perkins as a punishment for the damage he caused with the brick, a confinement within the sole authority of the target of the property crime and an abuse of process? Or was the objective of throwing the brick to force the Justice to take a decision regarding Perkins's madness, a way to promote his admission to the asylum? The documents provide no clarification here.

The casebooks are more forthcoming about Frances Kirk, whose discharge note reads as follows:

There being no doubt but that this poor woman's symptoms of irritability were really assumed for the sake of getting into the asylum, she was this day discharged Relieved.[85]

It is rare that such documents were so clear; usually, the motivations of the patient are left to surmise. Thus Mary Matts apparently left the asylum with regret in 1845, 'having frequently expressed a wish to remain with us in the capacity of a household servant'.[86] Jane Roby 'returned home quite recovered, often expressing a wish to return and remain with us'.[87] William Burton was 'pleased to find himself once more under the protection of the asylum.'[88] Eliza Hardwick's readmission was triggered after she 'had been up to the asylum gates to beg a meal'.[89] In so far as these comments are representative, they suggest a perception in the inmate population of the asylum as a place of refuge, a place where, in exchange for moderate work, an individual might enjoy at least a basic standard of living.

Cases of this sort are not limited to persons living in the community.

The casebooks also show manipulation of the system by paupers wishing to be removed to the asylum from the workhouse. Robert Capenhurst, admitted to the asylum in 1868, provides a clear example:

He appears to have passed the greater portion of his life in the workhouse. It is stated in his certificate that he has attempted on several occasions to commit suicide. He says he tried it once in order to be removed from the workhouse.[90]

A similar speculation can be made of William Thompson, who in the workhouse was 'a refractory and troublesome pauper, but the officer who conveyed him from thence to Leicester informed me that when he knew his destination he became tranquil and quite cheerful. ... Within an hour of his admission he was usefully employed.'[91]

Thompson, Burton, Hardwick and Kirk were all readmissions and therefore knew precisely what to expect at the asylum.

There is much in asylum life which paupers might have found attractive. A brass band organized among patients and staff in 1854 survived through the 1860s.[92] Periodic excursions were made, to the Leicester Forest, to the Crystal Palace in London, to the circus and to agricultural fairs. The Leicester Dramatic Society presented occasional theatrical entertainment. There were weekly dances at which the sexes were permitted to mix, and in the summer, bowls and quoits were played on the asylum lawn. Employment, mainly gardening or farming for the men and laundry work and sewing for the women, was for six hours per day. Airing grounds were to be accessible to the patients at least six hours per day.[93] Anecdotal evidence would suggest a significant degree of freedom enjoyed by the inmates of the institution. In 1866, 45 men and 22 women were permitted to walk beyond the asylum unattended, being roughly 17 per cent of the asylum population at that time.[94] And when, in February 1864, an aged patient was assaulted on a road near the asylum and robbed of twenty-five shillings, the response of the asylum management was not to tighten supervision and further restrict patients' movement, but rather to improve the street lighting along the road.[95] Escape does not seem to have been an impossible proposition even for those patients relatively closely confined: one boy managed to escape simply by jumping over the wall of the airing court.[96] It is thus perhaps a measure of the satisfaction of the inmates that the superintendent's journal notes only 26 escapes or attempted escapes from 1853 to 1870.[97]

This image of desirability is reinforced by the life which was faced by some of the insane poor prior to their admission to the asylum. Consider Harriet Burbidge, for example, whose 'diminutive appearance has led to her being exhibited as a Talking Monkey about the country',[98] or Elizabeth Windram, who suffered from puerperal mania and whose 'recovery in the narrow confined yard in which she lived was jeopardized by the fact that the neighbours assembled in large numbers to hear the poor woman's cries',[99] or Richard Wright who prior to his admission was 'subjected to mechanical restraint of a severe character, and ha[d] abrasion of skin upon both wrists and ankles'.[100] Poverty was considered by the asylum staff to be one of the chief causes of madness, and striking numbers of patients admitted were shown in the casebooks as underfed and clad in little more than rags. To these people, a life of farm work, sewing, quoits on the lawn and dances every week coupled with steady food must have appeared almost idyllic.

This is consistent with the way in which the asylum chose to portray itself. In the 1862 medical report to the annual meeting of the asylum, Buck stated:

There is now but little reluctance felt by the poor in availing themselves of the advantages of your asylum; so that when, in the natural progress of organic disease, some mental disturbance is revealed, admission is more readily sought than heretofore; and we are bound to add, that this is a state of things which in our opinion seems not unlikely to increase.[101]

When patients were eventually transferred to the new borough asylum in 1869, Buck reported, 'Many of the older patients appeared to feel very much their removal from an Asylum which they had long considered their home'.[102]

An implied alliance can perhaps be seen between relatively able paupers actively pursuing admission and the asylum staff. An internal economy reduced asylum costs. From May 1845 to March 1846, George Harrison, a tailor committed as a pauper, had worked constructing clothing, and apparently saved the institution about ten pounds.[103] By the late 1860s, all clothing and shoes were made in the asylum.[104] The farm turned a profit of about £500 p.a. in 1870,[105] up from £211 in 1865. By comparison, in 1865, income from unions for maintenance charges totalled £7,284. Occasionally, some of this benefit reverted to the patients. Thus Thomas Bettoney, a pauper, was apparently paid £2 for the work he performed building the new workrooms,[106] and Buck encouraged the Committee of Visitors in 1866 to give 'some pecuniary acknowledgement' to Mr Hale, a charity patient, for the work he performed while a patient.[107] Consistent with the practice in other Poor Law institutions, payment was more usually in the form of increased rations, and the dietary approved refers specifically to increased rations for those employed.[108]

The idea of feigning lunacy was rarely discussed explicitly in the documents of either the Poor Law authorities or the Lunacy Commission. The concept was well known in the criminal context of the insanity defence, however, and it was discussed in the context of the building of Broadmoor, the asylum for criminal lunatics, by Dr Charles Hood, the resident physician at Bethlem:

[2424.] ... The atmosphere of a lunatic asylum, and the character of the treatment that must necessarily be adopted there, cannot possibly savour in any way of the discipline that is necessary in a convict prison. I therefore anticipate that the difficulties will be much increased when the asylum is opened; at any rate they must continue so long as the convicts are removed during their penal servitude to a place where everything is easy and comfortable.

2425. You think that they will feign lunacy to deceive the authorities? —Yes.

2426. Is it very easy to distinguish between feigned lunacy and real lunacy? — I think time is the best criterion.[109]

The Poor Law authorities had been aware under the old Poor Law of 'clever paupers', who used a variety of ruses to collect double rations. They were no doubt aware of the possibility of a pauper feigning madness. There is little reason to believe they would have been sympathetic to such tactics, and Poor Law medical officers may in some cases have delayed the commencement of the admission process on the basis that 'time is the best criterion'.

The argument that paupers were manipulating the system to obtain asylum admission views the asylum in its best light. A contrary image is equally defensible from the documents. The apparent openness of the asylum is not easily reconciled with the fact that the rules precluded anyone from taking letters to or from patients without the leave of the asylum superintendent.[110] The asylum was increasing in size, the average number of patients in the year increasing from 182 in 1849 to 484 in 1869, before falling back to 411 in 1870 with the opening of the borough asylum. In 1867 the asylum was housing about 70 more than the 342 it was designed for. A temporary building was constructed to house part of the increase, but crowded conditions remained. The superintendent's journal, particularly in the 1850s, contains periodic complaints about cesspools fouling the drinking water, and there also occurred bouts of diarrhoea, smallpox, influenza and typhoid.

In addition, the benefits of entertainment and the occupation of work in the asylum did not fall on all patients equally. On 28 March 1860, only 70 of the men and 104 of the women were employed, being roughly 41 per cent of the men and 55 per cent of the women.[111] One is left to wonder how the remainder filled their time.

It is difficult to compare conditions in the workhouse with those of the asylum. There was no attempt to portray the workhouses as attractive: quoits on the lawn were simply not a matter of discussion. Workhouses were supposed to be unpleasant; that was the whole point of the workhouse test. How much of this is a matter of competing mythologies is an interesting question. Certainly the workhouse was unlikely to enjoy the beautiful views and large airing grounds which were at least part of the asylum mythology, but as for the work required in the two institutions, particularly for women, it is difficult to see that the sewing and laundry required in the workhouse would be that much different a workload from that of the asylum. Certainly the workhouse might be overcrowded, as was the case in Leicester, particularly in the late 1840s, but so might the asylum be.

There is evidence that some people did not want to leave the workhouse. When an outbreak of fever in the workhouse induced the Ashby guardians to offer outdoor relief to 44 inmates in 1842, only 37 took up the offer. Although the outbreak was serious — at the time of the offer of outdoor relief, 40 inmates were ill, and five people eventually died — seven of the 44 preferred to remain in the workhouse rather than accept payment to live outside it.[112]

A comparison of the two quantifiable categories of dietary and visiting rights do not suggest that life in the asylum would have been significantly better than life in the Leicester workhouse.[113] The dietary of insane inmates of the workhouse was under the control of the medical officer. The discussion of workhouse dietaries in 1867 cites 'universal opinion' that the insane were to receive the enhanced diet of the aged and infirm,[114] and it seems likely that they were in general in receipt of this dietary well before this time. Neither workhouse nor asylum dietary is particularly appealing. Dinners at the asylum look by and large more palatable, but if it is the actual amount of food which is at issue, breakfasts and suppers were more generous in the workhouse.

As for visiting hours, the Leicester workhouse rules were clearly more lenient, again assuming that the insane received the same treatment as the old and infirm. These inmates could be visited on two afternoons per week and, if they wished to see anyone, the master or matron of the workhouse was under an obligation to send for the individual.[115] By comparison, asylum visits were limited to one per fortnight.[116] Visits might be much more practical for those living in the local workhouse than in the county asylum, simply by reason of distance. Some parts of Leicestershire were more than thirty miles from the asylum, a distance which would pose real practical problems for those wishing to visit persons confined.

Along with the evidence of highly unpleasant conditions of the poor living outside institutions, there are countervailing images. The lists of lunatic paupers outside the asylum, contained in the records of the Poor Law Commissioners,[117] tend to show few living alone. Thus of 46 pauper insane returned by Barrow upon Soar Union in January 1854, 20 were in the asylum, eight in the workhouse, 16 with family members, one with friends and only one living alone.[118] Those that were living alone generally elicited a request by these Commissioners for further detail, providing a mechanism to ensure that these individuals did not fall between the cracks of care. Sometimes, in these cases, neighbours appear to have kept an eye on things. While the abilities and inclination of these informal actors in providing care and support for the insane individual could no doubt be mixed, in some cases more than money appears to have been provided by the unions. Thus a number of persons categorized as paupers in the asylum had nurses prior to their admission.[119] It is difficult to believe that they all paid for these themselves. Instead, they were presumably provided by the unions, suggesting that any image of the insane pauper in the community starved and confined in squalid attics must be tempered.[120]

Consistent with this view, a number of patients clearly did not want to be admitted into the asylum. Prior to his admission, Francis Philpott apparently said to his father, 'I am the strongest man in Leicester. I will knock you and Mother down if you go to fetch anyone to me.'[121] Sarah Homes 'had taken a strong dislike to the person who brought her [to the asylum], and treated him with most unmitigated abuse'.[122] Catherine Conroy was 'very full of complaints at being kept here. She says she will bring actions against all the guardians for allowing her to be deprived of her liberty.'[123] And when Francis Garfoot discovered it was proposed that he would be sent to the asylum, he ran away from home.[124] Again, both Homes and Garfoot were readmissions, so they acted in the knowledge of what the asylum was actually about. Thus the manipulation of the system by the paupers could operate in favour of, or against, asylum admission.

Similarly, notwithstanding Buck's optimistic comment about the willingness of people to send their family members to the asylum, there are indications that the poor were loath to commit their relatives. The removal of Mary Carpenter from Westminster workhouse to the asylum in 1866 prompted a complaint to the Poor Law Board, reading in part as follows:

The order was made without any intimation to the board or Parish officers and without any inquiry or intimation to the friends or relatives of the pauper who were residing in the Parish and who would as the board is informed rather have taken her from the Workhouse than submit to her being sent to a Lunatic Asylum.[125]

Broader discontent can be seen in Leicester in 1867, when a relieving officer was prevented by a mob from executing an order removing a pauper to Birmingham Asylum. The pauper in question was eventually released into his wife's custody.[126]

The implication is that the poor were far from convinced of the benefits of the asylum. Scull asserts that changed economic circumstances made it increasingly difficult for families to care for their unemployed and unemployable relations at home.[127] This is a reasonable inference. Numbers of able-bodied men in the workhouse on 1 January, when there was little agricultural work to be had, tended to be roughly twice the numbers on 1 July.[128] This would suggest that poor people had little excess income to take care of themselves, let alone their incapacitated relations. A resort to the Poor Law of lunacy may well have been imposed by economic necessity.[129] In this situation, a finding of lunacy would have had particular attractions. Committal to the asylum did not involve committal of the entire family of the pauper, as regular admission to the workhouse might. Instead, if the lunatic were the father, the remainder of the family was eligible for outdoor relief.[130] If the lunatic were another family member, the asylum admission would at least not result in the institutionalization of the entire family, as indoor relief to the able-bodied would, at least in theory.

The involvement of paupers in the operation of the system is both tantalizing and frustrating. The Leicestershire paupers themselves left virtually no documents. The documents left by the officials admit of vastly divergent explanation. The following comment in the case book regarding Eliza Mosebey is typical of many asylum patients: 'she was most grateful for the kindness she had received, and as soon as she was strong enough to work employed the whole of her time for the benefit of the Institution.'[131] Was this report coloured by a desire to portray the asylum in a positive light? Was the desire for work motivated by a desire to make herself indispensable to the asylum, and thus extend her stay? Was it rather to provide self-respect to a woman admitted to a Poor Law institution? As work was a part of moral management, was it to show that she had been cured of her lunacy, and thus to promote her early release? Or was it simply because she was bored? The documents do not provide clear answers.

NOTES

1 The central authorities are discussed below in Chapter 6.

2 Crowther, *The Workhouse System 1834–1929*, (1981; reprinted London: Methuen, 1983), p. 6.

3 For a different local study with broadly similar emphasis, see Bill Forsythe, Joseph Melling and Richard Adair, 'The new Poor Law and the County Pauper Lunatic Asylum – the Devon Experience 1834–1884', *Social History of Medicine*, **9** (1996): 335.

4 Regarding the growth of the Leicester workhouse, see Kathryn Thompson, 'The Leicester Poor Law Union, 1836–71', University of Leicester dissertation, 1982, at Ch. 6.

5 Report of workhouse visit by R. Weale, Assistant Poor Law Commissioner, 11 July 1864. PRO MH 12/6415, 8115/65.

6 Correspondence, Leicester Guardians to Poor Law Board, 9 Dec. 1852, PRO MH 12/6476 at 47433/52, and report of the Lunacy Commissioners regarding Leicester Workhouse for 1854, contained in PRO MH 12/6477 at 10997/54. At the time of this report, there were 42 insane inmates in the workhouse, all in the specialized wards. Hinkley Union also had specialized workhouse wards for the insane, on a somewhat smaller scale.

7 Reports were in fact generally quite favourable, although it will be argued below that this may well be at least in part a result of a technique of alliance-building by the Commissioners: see Chapter 6, below.

8 Thus Kathryn Thompson details the connections between the Leicester Union guardians, showing family ties and business connections: see 'The

Leicester Poor Law Union, 1836–71', Ch. 4. Thompson sees this as related to the emergence of a new social élite in Leicester at this period. That in turn is consistent with the change in the composition of Quarter Sessions in the period: David Philips, 'The Black Country magistracy, 1835–60', *Midland History*, 3 (1976): 161, and further discussion below.

9 That was a letter in response to an article questioning what had become a standard practice of supervising incontinent patients at night. Buck's letter merely states that the practice of supervision at Leicester worked well: *Journal of Mental Science*, 4 (1858): 309.

10 The borough of Leicester had in fact been sending people to the asylum before this time. The decision of the Queen's Bench in *R. v. Justices of Cornwall* (1845), 14 LJ (NS) MC 46, held that borough Justices could not commit individuals to the county asylum, even when the borough had contributed to the asylum. This was solved by legislation in the case of Leicester, in 1849. The result can be seen as a restoration of the earlier status quo.

11 The high standard of the admission documents may in part at least be the result of Buck's personal influence. Admission documents exist for 1851–2, and they do not tend to be of such high standard except for the ones signed by Buck himself. The asylum under Buck's guidance, by comparison, actually occasionally refused admission when documentation was insufficiently completed: see Superintendent's Journal and Report Book, 10 Nov. 1869, LRO DE 3533/84.

12 The relevant legislation on the appointment procedure in this period is 18 Geo. II c. 20.

13 See Esther Moir, *The Justice of the Peace* (Harmondsworth: Penguin, 1969), p. 107. Moir indicates that in Hereford, Cornwall, Lincoln, Somerset and Norfolk, clergy represented more than half of the active Justices by 1833, and in Cambridgeshire represented almost the whole bench at that time.

14 See David Philips, 'The Black Country magistracy, 1835–60', p. 172.

15 See David Philips, 'The Black Country magistracy, 1835–60', p. 169. The Black Country, for Philips's purposes, comprised the area bounded by Wolverhampton, Stourbridge, West Bromwich and Walsall: Philips, p. 163. It was mainly in south Staffordshire, commencing roughly 15 miles to the west of Leicestershire.

16 See Philips, 'The Black Country magistracy, 1835–60', p. 164.

17 Moir, *The Justice of the Peace*, pp. 134–5.

18 See Philips, 'The Black Country magistracy, 1835–60', pp. 175 ff. The number of worker prosecutions is unusually high in this county. No other county had more than half this number of prosecutions in this period.

19 The asylum finally opened in March of 1866: see *Twentieth Annual Report of the Commissioners in Lunacy*, PP 1866 (317) xxxii 1, at 6. For previous complaints regarding the City of London's failure to provide

for its pauper lunatics, see *Seventh Annual Report*, PP 1852–3 xlix 1, at 10; *Ninth Annual Report*, PP 1854–5 (240) xvii 533, at 9; *Thirteenth Annual Report*, PP 1859 2nd sess. (204) xiv 529, at 86 ff.

20 PRO MH 51/749.

21 Hervey, 'The Lunacy Commission 1845–60', University of Bristol dissertation, 1987, p. 294.

22 16 & 17 Vict. c. 97 s. 65 (the 1853 County Asylums Act).

23 The account of this matter is drawn from the *Twentieth Annual Report of the Commissioners in Lunacy*, PP 1866 (317) xxxii 1, at 14–16.

24 Suzuki, 'The politics and ideology of non-restraint: the case of the Hanwell Asylum', *Medical History*, **39** (1995): 1.

25 Suzuki, 'Politics and ideology of non-restraint', p. 10..

26 Ibid., p. 11.

27 Since the asylum was formed in part as a charitable institution by public subscription, the charity appointed roughly one-third of the visiting committee. The distinction is of limited importance, given the overlap of personnel between the charity and the asylum. Thus of the eight trustees of the charity in 1849, all but the Duke of Rutland, Earl Howe and Lord Berners were also county visitors and thus Justices. Lord Berners became such a visitor two years later in 1851.

28 Leicestershire and Rutland Lunatic Asylum, 'Rules for the general management of the institution, with prefatory remarks by the Committee of Visitors' LRO DE 662/27, p. 11. The statement appears to refer to both county asylums and private madhouses which accepted paupers.

29 Leicestershire and Rutland Lunatic Asylum, 'Rules for General Management' 1849, p. 12.

30 Leicestershire and Rutland Lunatic Asylum, 'Rules for General Management' 1849, p. 4–8.

31 Leicestershire and Rutland Lunatic Asylum, 'Rules for General Management' 1849, p. 12. Emphasis in original.

32 Leicestershire and Rutland Lunatic Asylum, 'Rules for General Management' 1849, pp. 12f.

33 Leicestershire and Rutland Lunatic Asylum, 'Rules for General Management' 1849, p. 19.

34 Minutes of Leicester Board of Guardians, 3 April 1866, LRO G/12/8a/12.

35 *Twenty-Fifth Report of the Commissioners in Lunacy*, PP 1871 (351) xxvi 1, at 339.

36 Copies of these reasons are contained in the correspondence between the Leicester Guardians and the Poor Law Commissioners for 26 Dec. 1844, PRO MH 12/6470, 19730/44.

37 Hitch's report is dated 10 Dec. 1844. A copy is contained in the correspondence between the Leicester Guardians and the Poor Law Commissioners, PRO MH 12/6470, 18259/44. Unfortunately, Hitch did

not provide reasons for considering individuals insane, although he does provide diagnoses. His concern was with standard of facilities, appropriateness of care, the behaviour of the individuals and possibility of improvement or cure. Comparative assessment of the Justices' findings that the other five individuals were not insane is thus not possible.

38 Hinkley's wards appear to have been smaller than Leicester's, containing about 14 insane people in the early 1850s: correspondence with Poor Law Board, PRO MH 12/6447, #23734/52 (15 June 1852).

39 Correspondence between Hinkley Union and the Poor Law Commissioners, unsigned and undated [May 1838?], PRO MH 12/6443. See also Anne Digby, *Pauper Palaces* (London: Routledge and Kegan Paul, 1978), who remarks on the use of the same loophole in Norfolk in the same period.

40 Litigation was begun in June 1838: correspondence between Hinkley Union and the Poor Law Commissioners, PRO MH 12/6443, 6465C/38 (18 June 1838). The litigation was settled shortly thereafter on the undertaking that the union would build a workhouse. None the less, land was not purchased for another year: see 4889C/39 (15 June 1839).

41 See report of Assistant Commissioner Peel regarding his visit to the workhouse, 23 July 1868, contained in correspondence between Poor Law Board and Billesdon Union, PRO MH 12/6415, 49329, requesting the furnishing of the wards. The guardians refused to provide workhouse accommodation for vagrants: see subsequent report of Assistant Commissioner Peel, PRO MH 12/6415, 16349/69 (24 Mar. 1869).

42 See Leicester Guardians Minute Book, 8 Sept. 1846 and 29 Sept. 1846, LRO G/12/8a/3.

43 LRO DE 3533/8.

44 It is clear that later the record was not complete. Thus the guardians of Shardlow Union commented on 27 March 1882 that they were 'pleased to note that there have been many improvements in the sanitary arrangements of the institution since our last visit'. No previous visit was recorded. (Note that Shardlow Union was mainly in Derbyshire, so relatively infrequent visits are not a surprise.) There is furthermore not a single derogatory remark in the book, suggesting that comments may have been by invitation only, and the book used to portray the asylum in a positive light.

45 Correspondence with Poor Law Commissioners, 28 Sept. 1843, PRO MH 12/6446, #15392B/43.

46 *Minutes of Evidence of Select Committee on Lunatics*, PP 1859 1st sess. (204) iii 75, at q. 1624.

47 In order to be appointed as a Poor Law medical officer, a candidate had to possess the qualifications prescribed in one of the following categories:

1. A diploma or degree as surgeon from a Royal College or University in England, Scotland, or Ireland, together with a degree in medicine from a University in England, legally authorized to grant such degree, or together with a diploma or licence of the Royal College of Physicians of London.
2. A diploma or degree as surgeon from a Royal College or University in England, Scotland, or Ireland, together with a certificate to practise as an apothecary from the Society of Apothecaries of London.
3. A diploma or degree as a surgeon from a Royal College or University in England, Scotland, or Ireland, such person having been in actual practice as an Apothecary on the first day of August One thousand eight hundred and fifteen.
4. A warrant or commission as surgeon or assistant surgeon in Her Majesty's navy, or as surgeon or assistant-surgeon in Her Majesty's army, or as surgeon or assistant surgeon in the service of the Honourable East India Company, dated previous to the first day of August One thousand eight hundred and twenty-six. (William Cunningham Glen, *The Consolidated and other Orders of the Poor Law Commissioners and the Poor Law Board*, 4th edn., (London: Butterworth, 1859), at art 168)

48 21 & 22 Vict. c. 90. This Act created a formal register of medical practitioners, under the guardianship of the General Medical Council. The GMC had the power to remove individuals from the register for professional misconduct.

49 See James Wood (medical officer to districts in both Ashby and Loughborough Unions, for an uncertain period ending in 1865); Henry Nuttall (districts in both Barrow and Leicester Unions, 1865–70), Thomas Spencer (districts in both Market Bosworth and Hinkley Unions, 1868–74); Charles Crane (districts in both Market Harborough and Uppingham Unions, 1866–1878); Frank Fullagar (districts in both Blaby and Leicester Unions, 1846–63). Other medical officers worked in more than one medical district within one union.

50 See correspondence between Barrow Union and the Poor Law Board, 24 March 1857, PRO MH 12/6401, #14484/57.

51 See Ruth Hodgkinson, *The Origins of the National Health Service* (London: Wellcome, 1967), p. 371.

52 Crowther, *The Workhouse System 1834–1929*, p. 157.

53 One member of the 1859 Select Committee on Lunatics for example asked whether it was not 'notorious that the medical man appointed is one who will do the work for the lowest possible price': see PP 1859 1st sess. (204) iii 75, at question 1631. This allegation was denied by Assistant Commissioner Farnall, who stated that 'the guardians, when they advertise for a medical man, advertise the salary which they mean

to give him.... the amount is fixed in the advertisement': at question
1632.

54 See correspondence between Blaby Union and Poor Law Commissioners, 18 Nov. 1842, PRO MH 12/6422, #14546/42; correspondence
between Barrow Union and the Poor Law Board, 25 July 1859, PRO
MH 12/6401 #28559B/59. It would appear that such scandals were
common: see Crowther, *The Workhouse System 1834–1929*, pp. 160 ff.

55 Correspondence between Barrow Union and the Poor Law Board, 25
July 1859, PRO MH 12/6401 #28559B/59.

56 Correspondence between Barrow upon Soar Board of Guardians and
Poor Law Board, PRO MH 12/6400 #33838 (27 Aug. 1856). Joseph
Stallard of the Leicester Union adopted a similar tactic in 1853,
regarding the duty to visit quarterly and payment for such visits of
those pauper lunatics who were resident in workhouses: correspondence
between Leicester Union and the Poor Law Board, PRO MH 12/6476,
#38216 (26 October 1853).

57 Hodgkinson, *Origins of National Health Service*, p. 435.

58 Hodgkinson, *Origins of the National Health Service*, p. 386.

59 In 1857, only 27 of the 3,018 medical officers in England and Wales
were precluded from private practice in addition to their Poor Law
duties: Ruth Hodgkinson, *The Origins of the National Health Service*
(London: Wellcome, 1967), p. 371.

60 See for example, Charles Buncombe (City of London) who was paid
£275 p.a. in the 1850s and 1860s; Frederick Page (Portsea Island), paid
£315 p.a. in the late 1860s; and Edmund Robinson (Birmingham), paid
£250 p.a. from 1861 to 1865 and £350 p.a. from 1866 to 1869: Register
of Paid Officers, PRO MH 9.

61 Crowther, *The Workhouse System 1834–1929*, p. 156.

62 Thus his brother says in the introduction to the work,

In the eyes of the Strand Guardians, or rather a majority among them, his
offences on behalf of justice and humanity were unpardonable. He had to be got
rid of. In this the officials of the Poor Law Board, then under Lord Devon,
agreed with the Guardians. The guardians picked a quarrel with him, the Poor
Law Board instituted an inquiry, and apparently instructed their Inspector as to
what he should report, and the President gave solemnity to the farce by
removing him from his office. The ground on which he was dismissed was that
'he could not get on with the Board of Guardians.' Of course he could not. No
man of sense, honour, humanity, decency, and conscientiousness, could get on
with them, or, in those evil days, with the Poor Law Board either; for the
President and his officials, perhaps unconsciously, leagued with the guardians in
the maltreatment of the poor. (Thorold Rogers, Introduction to *Reminiscences of
a Workhouse Medical Officer*, by Joseph Rogers (London: T. Fisher Unwin,
1889), p. xix f.)

63 Joseph Rogers, *Reminiscences of a Workhouse Medical Officer* (London: T.
Fisher Unwin, 1889), p. 114 f.

64 Joseph Rogers, *Reminiscences*, p. 114. His approach is consistent with the

workhouse rules, which put the diet for sick and disabled paupers at the medical officers' discretion. This further illustrates how more regulation by the central authority resulted in greater independent authority for the medical officers.

65 See K. Thompson, 'The Leicester Poor Law Union, 1836–71', p. 226.
66 *Twenty-First Annual Report of the Commissioners in Lunacy*, PP 1867 (366) xviii 201, at 25.
67 See evidence of H. B. Farnall before the Select Committee on Lunatics, PP 1859 1st sess. (204) iii 75, at question 1627.
68 Greaves, *Hints to Certifying Surgeons under the Factory Acts* (1867); 'Homes for the working class', (Manchester [?]: n.p. 1861).
69 Hawkings, *On the Desirability of National Education for the Deaf and Dumb Poor* (London: Longmans, Green and Co., 1868); and *Are the Beneficent Uses of Public Institutions adequately Supported by their Present Organisation?* (London: Longmans, Green, 1872).
70 Regarding enrolments, see Andrew Scull, 'Mad-doctors and magistrates: English psychiatry's struggle for professional autonomy in the nineteenth century', *Archives Européen de Sociologie*, **17** (1976): 279.
71 Richard Russell, 'The lunacy profession and its staff in the second half of the nineteenth century', in *The Anatomy of Madness*, Vol. III, ed. Bynum, Porter and Shepherd (London: Tavistock, 1988), p. 302.
72 Russell, 'The lunacy profession and its staff', pp. 300 f.
73 Turner, ' "Not worth powder and shot': the public profile of the Medico-Psychological Association, *c.* 1851–1914', in *150 Years of British Psychiatry, 1841–1991*, ed. Berrios and Freeman (London: Gaskell, 1991), 3 at 14.
74 Turner, 'Not worth powder and shot', p. 8. The quotations are from J. B. Tuke, 'Lunatics as patients not prisoners', *Nineteenth Century*, **25** (1889): 595.
75 *Journal of Psychological Medicine*, **5** (1852): 160; quoted in Trevor Turner, 'Not worth powder and shot', p. 6.
76 Russell, 'The lunacy profession and its staff', p. 297.
77 *Third Annual Report of the United Committee of Visitors of the Leicestershire and Rutland Asylum* (1851), LRO DE 3533/13. By comparison, the matron received approximately £52, the chaplain £42, the keepers an average of about £13 and nurses an average of about £15. Subsequent annual reports reveal only total staffing costs, not the breakdown of salaries for each individual.
78 Adm. 16 May 1855. Casebook LRO DE 3533/187. The transfer was eventually completed, following the administration of a wholesome diet, on 18 July 1855:

This case appearing somewhat manageable by the care + attention of attendants in the Insane Ward at the Union Ho. he was removed to that institution today.

See also William Worrad (adm. 2 Sept. 1853, casebook LRO DE 3533/87); Eliza Woodcock (adm. 21 Feb. 1853, casebook LRO DE 3533/187); and Elizabeth Fowkes (adm. 15 Dec. 1849, casebook LRO DE 3533/186), also discharged into the care of the Poor Law authorities.

79 Minute Book of Visitors of Leicestershire and Rutland County Lunatic Asylum, 1851–94. LRO DE 3533/8. Note speculation above that this book may not record all visits.

80 Bucknill, 'The medical certificates of admission papers', *Journal of Mental Science*, 4 (1858): 312 at 312. Emphasis in original.

81 Thompson, 'Social control in Victorian Britain', *Economic History Review*, 2nd series, 34 (1981): 189 at 189. For a similar point, see Michael Ignatieff, 'Total institutions and working classes', *History Workshop Journal*, 15 (1983): 167 at 169 ff.

82 Scull, *The Most Solitary of Afflictions: Madness and Society in Britain, 1700–1900* (New Haven: Yale UP, 1993), pp. 370 ff., esp. in notes 99 to 114.

83 David Roberts, *Paternalism in Early Victorian England* (London: Croom Helm, 1979) p. 206.

84 See casebook, LRO DE 3533/186. Adm. 24 Oct. 1851.

85 Adm. 29 Nov. 1856. Casebook LRO DE 3533/188. See also the case of William Lord, admitted 25 Jan. 1864. Kirk's ruse, if ruse it was, was not unsuccessful, as the asylum kept her for two and a half months (thus through much of the winter), even though her counterfeit was suspected at the time of her admission.

86 Adm. 17 May 1845. Casebook LRO DE 3533/185.

87 Adm. 30 Jan. 1845. Casebook LRO DE 3533/185.

88 Adm. 27 July 1853. Casebook LRO DE 3533/187.

89 Adm. 22 Nov. 1854. Casebook LRO DE 3533/187.

90 Adm. 23 March 1868. Casebook LRO DE 3533/191.

91 Adm. 3 Sept. 1853. Casebook LRO DE 3533/187.

92 Reformation, see Superintendent's Journal, 9 May 1854, LRO DE 3533/83.

93 1849 rules, section 8. LRO DE 662/27.

94 See 1866 annual report. LRO DE 3533/13.

95 See Superintendent's Journal, 10 Feb. 1864, LRO DE 3533/84.

96 See Superintendent's Journal, Nov. 1853, LRO DE 3533/83.

97 See LRO DE 3533/83 and /84. Three of these were by the same person, in a one-month period in May 1859.

98 Casebook, adm. 20 Feb. 1864. LRO DE 3533/190.

99 Casebook, adm. 14 July 1866. LRO DE 3533/191.

100 See casebook, LRO DE 3533/191.

101 Superintendent's Journal, 20 Jan. 1862. LRO DE 3533/84.

102 See 1869 annual report. LRO DE 3533/14.

103 Adm. 10 May 1845. See comments in casebook, LRO DE 3533/185.

104 See 1866 annual report. LRO DE 3533/14.

105 See 1870 annual report. LRO DE 3533/14.

106 See casebook, LRO DE 3533/187. Adm. 28 Sept. 1855.

107 See Superintendent's Journal, 10 Jan. 1866, LRO DE 3533/84.

108 Regarding the reliance of workhouses on pauper labour, see M. A. Crowther, *The Workhouse System 1834–1929*, Ch. 8 and particularly pp. 196–201.

109 Testimony of Dr Charles Hood (resident physician, Bethlem Hospital) to the Select Committee on Lunatics, PP 1859 1st sess. (204) iii 75.

110 Leicestershire and Rutland Lunatic Asylum, 'Rules for the general management of the institution', 1849, section 85; Leicestershire and Rutland Lunatic Asylum, 'Rules for the General Management of the Institution', (1873), LRO DG 24/752/2, at section 102.

111 On 28 March 1860, 36 men were employed on the asylum farm (a number which peaked at 40 on 26 September, being harvest, and was as low as three on 26 December, during winter); 16 employed in the house and garden; 8 in workrooms; and 10 assisting on the wards. On that same day, 44 women were employed in workrooms and in sewing and mending; 37 in the laundry; 5 in housework and in the kitchen; and 18 on the wards. On 1 January that year, the asylum had contained 170 men and 188 women: *Twelfth Annual Report of the United Committee of Visitors of the Leicestershire and Rutland Lunatic Asylum* (1860), LRO DE 3533/13, Table 4.

112 Minute Book, Ashby de la Zouch Union, 9 Feb. 1842. LRO G/1/8a/1. This does not appear to be a situation unique to Ashby. The indices to the correspondence between the Poor Law central authorities and the local boards of guardians show a steady trickle of queries as to what to do when people refused to leave the workhouse, generally in cases where there was an offer of work: see PRO MH 15.

113 A copy of the dietaries for the two institutions is contained as Appendix 3.

114 *Twentieth Annual Report of the Poor Law Board*, PP 1867–8 [4039] xxxiii 1, at App. 2. The quoted material is on p. 60.

115 Minute Book, Leicester Union, 19 Jan. 1869. LRO G/12/8a/13.

116 Leicestershire and Rutland Lunatic Asylum, 'Rules for the general management of the institution', 1849, rule 13.

117 PRO MH 12.

118 PRO MH 12 6400. All but one living outside the asylum had been insane for many years and were shown as not dangerous; that one elicited a request for further particulars from the Poor Law central authorities: 5529/54. This was the case of an old man, William Cooper, in the care of his wife.

119 See for example Eliza Williams, adm. 14 July 1868, in admission documents, LRO DE 3533/229.

120 This is not necessarily to be understood as opposed to medical opinion. Thus one of the medical certificates relating to Caroline Barfoot in the

mid-1840s stated that she was a harmless idiot, and would be better under the care of her mother at home than in any establishment where numbers were congregated together: quoted in letter, Poor Law Commissioners to Leicester Guardians, 15 Dec. 1843. LRO G/12/57d/1.

121 Adm. 19 Dec. 1868. Adm. documents LRO DE 3533/229.

122 Adm. 25 Jan. 1853. Casebook LRO DE 3533/187.

123 Adm. 16 May 1868. Casebook LRO DE 3533/192.

124 Adm. 30 Aug. 1847. Casebook LRO DE 3533/185.

125 PRO MH/51/768.

126 Cited in Kathryn M. Thompson, 'The Leicester Poor Law Union, 1836–71', p. 232.

127 Scull, *Most Solitary of Afflictions*, pp. 332 f.

128 The figures for women are less extreme, January figures being close to 50 per cent higher than July figures. Out-relief also increased, although it is difficult to assess how much of those increases were caused by unemployment, as an 'able-bodied' person on outdoor relief might none the less be relieved on account of illness.

129 The quantitative figures in Appendix 1 may provide a counter-indication of a strict cause-and-effect relationship, however. The increase in pauper insane, both institutionalized and in total, bears no obvious correlation to the rate of pauperism in general.

130 Such relief was to be provided to the wife 'as if she were a widow': 7 & 8 Vict. c. 101 s. 25.

131 LRO DE/3533/186, adm. 7 May 1851.

CHAPTER 5

Local administration: the creation of coherence among misfits

In previous chapters, it has been argued that the focus of decision-making was at the local level, resting with local Justices of the Peace and local Poor Law officials. In this chapter, surviving documents regarding the processes of confinement of paupers in the Leicestershire and Rutland County Lunatic Asylum will be examined, to clarify how those decisions were made. In addition, such few documents as remain regarding categorization of the insane in the workhouse will be examined.

Inevitably, this study is confined by the documents available. There were essentially three options for the care of insane paupers: outdoor relief, the workhouse and the asylum.[1] For the first two of these, little documentation remains about individual decisions, although some general insights may be gained by implication of asylum admission documents, and through the occasional reference in minute books of guardians and correspondence with central authorities. Much better documentation exists for those admitted to the county asylum, in the form both of admission documents and casebooks.

Casebooks for the Leicestershire and Rutland Asylum survive from 1845 into the twentieth century. Those up to 1870 have been examined. The format of the casebooks changed in 1856. While much the same information was collected under both formats, the rephrasing is interesting. Both formats provided a series of short-answer questions.[2] Where the earlier book asked about specific physical conditions such as pregnancy, fits or accident and epilepsy, the later version asked for the assigned causes of the insanity, to be categorized as moral, physical and hereditary. Under the later version, staff were also required to assess the 'character' of the inmate.[3] Both versions allowed a large and full page for treatment notes.

The admission documents were prescribed by statute. For paupers and persons found wandering at large, they commenced with the certificate signed by the admitting Justice.[4] Next was a section with personal information compiled by the relieving officer: name, age and the like. Interestingly for this study, purported cause of insanity, how long insane and whether dangerous were among these questions.[5] Finally, there was the certificate signed by a medical practitioner — almost always the Poor Law medical officer of the union in which the pauper was resident, when it became legal for these officers to sign the forms in 1853.

The form of this certificate was amended under the 1853 Act explicitly to require the medical officer to identify those facts observed by himself indicating insanity, and also those facts communicated to him by others.[6] The source of these communicated facts was also identified, so this latter paragraph has been particularly useful in reconstructing where people were admitted from: a domestic setting, a workhouse or apprehended wandering at large. These parts of the Leicester Asylum documents were relatively completely filled out in the 1860s. This may have been due at least in part to the fastidiousness of Dr Buck, the asylum superintendent, who had included this information in detail when completing the forms prior to his appointment as medical superintendent in 1853, even though the older forms did not provide space for this information. At least four times in the 1860s, the asylum refused to admit persons on the basis of inadequate documentation.[7] Other indications are that the Lunacy Commissioners were becoming increasingly concerned at the incompleteness of these details.[8]

The form for the admission of an independent (including charity) patient was largely similar, except that no order of a Justice was required. The personal information was completed by the person admitting the patient, and there were two medical reports, not one. Up to the early 1860s, the contract between the asylum and the person admitting a private or charity patient was also included, allowing determination of who fell into which category, and just how much was charged to independent patients. After this time, these contracts were not routinely included, leaving it a matter of speculation which independent patients were admitted by the charity.

A reasonably good number of admission documents survive, although there are major gaps in their preservation. None exists prior to 1851; and 1856 to 1860 and 1871 to 1880 are missing.

Between 1861 and 1865, 406 people were admitted to the Leicester and Rutland County Lunatic Asylum. Of these, 336 (83 per cent) were classed as paupers, 64 (16 per cent) as private patients, including those admitted through the charity, and six (one per cent) were criminals.[9] Of the paupers, 181 (54 per cent) were women.[10]

Appendix 2 organizes the pauper admission documents into three categories, according to the admission route of the individual into the asylum. Persons admitted because they were found 'wandering at large' or 'not under proper care and control' or 'cruelly treated or neglected by any relative or other person having the care or charge' of them were admitted pursuant to a separate section of the Act.[11] Members of this class were not necessarily paupers, although classed as such in the asylum statistics. While admitted on pauper forms, these were amended to reflect their status, making them identifiable. The recording of facts communicated to the medical officer on the remaining forms record the source of the information. These have been categorized according to whether information was communicated by a family member or friend of the inmate, in which case admission directly to the asylum from a domestic setting has been assumed, or instead by a member of the workhouse staff, in which case admission is taken as being from the workhouse. In all, 293 people can be classed with reasonable certainty into one of these groups, being 37 wanderers, 177 persons from domestic settings and 79 from workhouses.[12]

Of the remaining 43 paupers, admission documents exist for 33. Of these, there was insufficient evidence to allow categorization in 31 cases. In two cases, patients were admitted from other institutions: the Leicester Infirmary and the Northampton Infirmary, both charitable hospitals. These 33 cases have been included in the statistical summary as 'miscellaneous'. In addition, no original admission documents of any sort were on file for ten paupers, transferred to the asylum from a private madhouse in 1865. As no information is available about them at all, they are excluded from the statistical survey.

To read the statute, one would expect Poor Law medical officers and relieving officers to be actively pursuing lunatics in their jurisdictions. This is a misleading picture: as regards the needs of individual paupers, the Poor Law was generally responsive rather than proactive. This was equally true of the Poor Law medical service: the sick person approached the Poor Law doctor for treatment, otherwise the Poor Law doctor would not generally intervene. This basic pattern carried over into the lunacy side of the Poor Law, and thus to domestic admissions. The admission documents to the asylum typically reflected only one examination of the individual by the medical officer. It would appear that the lunatic person lived in the community until the Poor Law medic was approached by someone in the community to become involved. This might go so far as to require that the apparently insane person be brought to the workhouse, town hall or police station for the required medical examination,[13] reinforcing the Poor Law associations of asylum care.

Usually, the approach was made by a family member of the lunatic, normally a spouse. This was not an inviolable rule. Thus Ann Woods was admitted because 'for some weeks past her conduct has been such as to raise much apprehension in the mind of her employers'.[14] Others were admitted by the intervention of friends and neighbours.[15] Alternatively, but atypically, the attention of the local Justice might be brought to the situation. As noted in the last chapter, for example, the attention of one Justice was drawn to the situation by the pauper heaving a brick through the window of the Justice's house.[16]

Admissions from the workhouse had a different character. The workhouse was an environment where much more intensive surveillance occurred. Admissions from the workhouse also appear to have been triggered by behaviour of the inmate, but the application for admission to the asylum was organized by staff. Of particular importance in this process appears to be the nurse or attendant of the insane wards of the workhouse, where they existed. The admission documents would suggest that the master of the workhouse was at least consulted in the decision as to whether to organize an asylum admission application for someone. The medical officer of the facility might also be involved, but this seems to have been contingent on the interest he showed in the insane persons. Often, the portion of the admission form detailing facts indicating insanity observed personally by the doctor is, as for domestic admissions, merely an account of one interview with the inmate.

The workhouse admissions may be placed in juxtaposition with the domestic admissions in this administrative context. Domestic admissions occurred in an environment of minimal administrative surveillance or control, workhouse admissions in an atmosphere of much more intensive observation and control. It is therefore appropriate to question the image of the workhouse as a place where lunatics were allowed to rot unnoticed and uncared for. Instead, it may well have been more likely that it was the person in the community, not sufficiently abhorrent in conduct to attract general attention and living alone or with persons either unaware of or unwilling to commence the committal processes, who would be left outside the structures of care. Part of this gap would have been filled by the quarterly returns of insane poor living outside asylums, which required the living arrangements to be specified. The Poor Law central authorities did inquire about individuals insane and living alone. None the less, even inclusion on this list presupposed that the attention of the Poor Law medical officer had been drawn to the situation in some way.

This juxtaposition applies to persons who were admitted to the workhouse well before being admitted to the asylum. The workhouse was also occasionally used as a brief holding area, where people might be held pending removal to the asylum.[17] This role of the workhouse was explicitly recognized in an 1846 policy decision in Leicester:

A misunderstanding existing between the Master of the Workhouse and the Relieving Officers as to the admission of Insane Persons previous to their removal to an Asylum it is ordered 'That the Master do receive every pauper presenting an order from a relieving Officer (and if such person is pronounced by the Medical Officer, or supposed to be of unsound mind) to take care of him until he can be removed, by placing some of the inmates with such person; and the Master is hereby empowered to allow paupers so acting as attendants such additional rations as he may consider necessary.'[18]

The Commissioners in Lunacy and the visiting committee of the asylum complained periodically that the Poor Law officials were avoiding their duties under the legislation.[19] In so far as this was an objection to the responsive nature of the Poor Law, the objection appears justified at least as regarded domestic admissions: the Poor Law officials had to be approached before they would intervene in a situation. Once they had been approached, however, there is little evidence that they avoided confinement of the individual.

The Commissioners also complained about the delay in sending people to the asylum, once they had been identified as insane. This objection was phrased in therapeutic terms, as in the following extract from the Metropolitan Commissioners' 1844 report:

At the Retreat, York, at the Asylums of Lincoln and Northampton, and at the asylum for the county of Suffolk, tables are published, exhibiting the large proportion of cures effected in cases where patients are admitted within three months of their attacks, the less proportion when admitted after three months, and the almost hopelessness of cure when persons are permitted to remain in Workhouses or elsewhere, and not sent into proper Asylums until after the lapse of a year from the period when they have been first subject to insanity.[20]

This complaint was specifically made about the Leicester workhouse in the Commissioners' 1844 report.[21] Whatever the situation in 1844, the admission documents for the early 1860s do not suggest that a large number of people were delayed in their admission to the asylum. The admission documents for the 1861 to 1865 period indicate that almost three-quarters of those admitted from domestic settings were admitted to the asylum within three months of the commencement of their attack of lunacy, a markedly higher figure than was the case for private patients, whose admission was out of the hands of the Poor Law authorities. The figure for workhouse admissions is somewhat lower, with roughly 60 per cent of admissions occurring within the three-month period. This is skewed, however, by a relatively large proportion of persons admitted from the workhouse after a number of years insane, often from birth, and often from what were understood as hereditary or congenital causes. For these people, cure would not have been understood as a reasonable probability.[22] If curability was understood to be compromised mainly in the period from three months to one year from the onset of the attack, only 9 per cent of workhouse admissions occurred in this period, and 8 per cent from domestic settings.[23] The admission documents taken at face value thus do not support a view that people were generally held back in the workhouse while curable and then sent to the asylum at a later time.[24]

Conspicuous by their absence in the accounts of both the casebooks and the admission documents are references to sexuality, and factors associated with gender. Concerns about promiscuity, inappropriate sexual behaviour or the conception of illegitimate children are not referred to specifically in the documents. More common, particularly in the admission documents and especially with regard to the admission of men from the workhouse, was scandalous conduct, in particular exposing one's person in inappropriate circumstances.

The documents similarly do not support a finding of general differential treatment of women. Women represented roughly 55 per cent of admissions to the Leicester asylum from 1861 to 1865, a proportion typical of pauper admissions to county asylums, at a time when women were roughly 52 per cent of the population. Apart from women confined following childbirth, to be discussed below, the material in their reports does not differ notably from pauper men confined.

The class of wanderers and persons not under proper care and control presents rather different issues. The statutory provision descended from the eighteenth-century lunacy statutes, where protection of the public from dangerous people and protection of the lunatic from wanton cruelty were the legislative aims. The people committed under this section fell into two categories, reflecting the distinction in the statute. Some people were apprehended wandering at large, such as Thomas Proudman, 'found wandering abroad doing purposeless and insane things'[25] or John Baskin, committed in 1865:

John Iliffe, Superintendent of Police, [stated Baskin was] Wandering in the street with a crowd of persons about him, saying he had given a man money to buy a Rifle to shoot persons who were after him to kill him, saying he expected to be killed every minute, said he had been shut up in a room by his Father, he escaped + they have been following him about ever since to kill him, + he would shoot the first devil I can meet with.[26]

Many people admitted under the above section of the Act are indistinguishable on the facts provided in their admission documents from domestic admissions, however. Most appeared to be dangerous on the admission documents, but then again, so did most people admitted from domestic situations. There were also exceptions. All that was said of William Lord's admission as a wanderer on 23 March 1863, was as follows:

The said William Lord the Elder is afraid of persons and unable to give instructions respecting his Trade. He is fearful lest he should destroy himself and his opinion with respect to the relations of things is vague.[27]

In some cases, the choice of this admission route was not based on grounds of insanity, but rather on economic grounds. This section of the Act did not require the individual to be a pauper, yet allowed admission to the asylum at the pauper rate. It thus seems to have been used to some degree by people with some money, for admission at a price they could afford. This was clear for example with Lord, who had previously been both a private and a charity patient in the asylum, and would be readmitted as a wanderer the following year. Occasionally this is made quite specific on the admission documents, which identify the individual as 'not chargeable'.

It could be argued that this calls into question the status of the asylum as a Poor Law institution. Is this after all not a case where the Poor Law is being manipulated to ensure the admission of a wider category of patient? The scale of these admissions must be recognized, however. Inmates not chargeable to the Poor Law can be identified relatively easily through 1862, as the signature of two justices was required for their admission, rather than one if the individual was a pauper. Only nine of the 148 pauper admissions in 1861 and 1862 were so admitted. An additional 12 persons of the 178 admitted between 1863 and 1865 were either admitted by two Justices, or specifically shown as not chargeable on their admission documents. The numbers thus appear small.

ISSUES OF INTERPRETATION

Inconsistencies render the interpretation of the local documents problematic. This is true, not merely between the casebooks and the admission documents, but even within these sets of documents. The recording of the causes of insanity provides an illustration. Causes listed by relieving officers on admission documents were admittedly rare, but in order of frequency the first five causes of insanity of paupers admitted from 1861 to 1865 were religion (11 cases), business or employment disappointment (eight cases), puerperal mania or childbirth (seven cases), heredity or congenital (seven cases) and grief and bereavement (six cases). In the casebooks, they were heredity (50 cases), intemperance (26 cases), grief and bereavement (14 cases), poverty (13 cases) and puerperal mania or childbirth (12 cases). In the patient register, compiled by the clerk of the asylum on the instruction of the medical superintendent,[28] they were heredity or congenital (53 cases), poverty (38 cases), intemperance (30 cases), puerperal and childbirth (15 cases) and old age (14 cases).[29] Poverty was never cited as a cause in the admission documents. Reference to an individual case shows the breadth of the inconsistency. The insanity of Roger Dalby was shown as caused by intemperance in the patient register compiled by the asylum clerk. In the admission notes in the casebook, the cause of Dalby's insanity was shown as a fall from a ladder. The entry in the casebook relating to his death nine months later referred to 'disease of the brain and paralysis'.[30]

At the same time, the casebooks and the admission documents are the most direct sources available to understand the relations between individual paupers and the system. Both sets of document purport to record factual information. It would be simplistic to dismiss some or all of the documents as simply 'inaccurate'. Instead, the nature of the documents themselves requires examination, including this process of fact recording. At issue are two interrelated problems.

The first is that the document itself does not stand outside the historical or sociological endeavour. The document itself has a place and a status. It is an administrative product, with a place in the administrative system; it is not an abstract arbiter of facts. In his essay, ' "Good" organizational reasons for "bad" clinical records',[31] Garfinkel distinguished between 'actuarial' and 'contractual' functions of documents. The former was a relatively conventional view where the document described a list of events which occurred. The paradigm for this might be an account book, where all credits and debits are described: the actuarial function of the document in this example would be the describing of the financial transactions which occurred.

Contractual functions of documents did not merely describe events or facts which had occurred; they rather affirmed the fulfilment of certain norms in the behaviour of the individual constructing the record. The records in Garfinkel's example did not merely provide a list of treatments given (the actuarial function); they were constructed in addition with the intent of showing that the doctor who had made the record had behaved in a way appropriate to a patient–doctor relationship. At issue was not just documenting that certain treatments had been given, but also demonstrating that the medic concerned had been a 'good doctor'. Nelken's study of harassment crime by landlords provides an additional example. Investigation reports of official Harassment Officers served at least in part an administrative function divorced from the crime described, that was, the demonstration that the case had been handled in accordance with the relevant administrative procedures.[32] Focusing on that contractual process, it becomes possible to use the documents to describe those procedural norms, not merely to describe the actual events listed in the document.

The examples given tend to analyse in terms of a pre-existing paradigm of the role of the person making the record. The issue in the medical record example was not defining what the appropriate behaviour for a doctor was, but rather the doctor demonstrating that the predefined role had been fulfilled. A similar but more creative function of the document would occur where the norm had not already been settled: the recording of the administrative action would not merely show that the appropriate administrative standard had been met; it would also implicitly define what that standard was. In a parallel situation to that described by Garfinkel, this would not be explicit, through reflexive analysis in the document of the procedures being followed, but would instead be implied in the facts which were reported.

This leads directly to the second issue, which concerns the process of fact-finding itself. Recent textual criticism has focused on the 'creation' of facts, raw actuality being drawn through administrative processes and restructured in a particular context. Descriptions of this process by sociologists, such as the following one by Dorothy Smith, can border on impenetrability:

The fact is not what actually happened in its raw form. It is that actuality as it has been worked up so that it intends its own description. That actuality has been assigned descriptive categories and a conceptual structure. The structure incorporates a temporal organization which both marks the boundaries of what actually happened so that it comes to have the form of an 'event,' 'episode,' 'state of affairs,' etc. It will be accorded an internal temporal structure. These categorial and conceptual procedures which name, analyse and assemble what actually happens become (as it were) inserted into the actuality as an interpretive schema which organizes that for us as it is or was. Using that interpretive schema to organize the actuality does not appear as imposing an organization upon it but rather as a discovery of how it is.[33]

The 'fact' is created in a specific context, and its content is structured by that context; but it is taken as 'true' and in some sense presumably is 'true'.

The nature of the resulting conundrum may perhaps be clarified by examining a specific case. In his work on the Glasgow Royal Infirmary, Jonathan Andrews cites the difficulties of relying on the questionnaires completed by relatives of patients, questionnaires remarkably similar to the admission documents to English county asylums:

Perhaps the foremost difficulty in using case notes and questionnaires is that they often convey more about the preoccupations of the Asylum's medical regime than about patients and their histories. Far from representing patients' impressions, case notes pre-eminently constitute the impressions of the medical officers who wrote them. Inevitably prejudiced by the interests of medical men in portraying a favourable record of their own practice, case notes are also limited by the criteria governing the selection of what (and what not) to record.[34]

This recognizes half of the problem: the recording of the fact is affected by the particular context of the recording. Perhaps because Andrews's interest is explicitly in the use of these documents to discover the patients' experiences in the asylum, he does not highlight the second part of the problem: the documents at issue recorded 'facts' which were in some sense 'true'. The statements were made in good faith as descriptions of the individuals and their situations, or to use the sociological jargon, the statements intended the truth of their content. As a result, they had social effects: the documents to be discussed below were viewed by the Commissioners in Lunacy, and were presumably important in shaping their attitudes to social policy. They also structured the administrative processes for the committal of individuals.

The complication of the fact-finding process is particularly interesting when combined with the first issue discussed above. In the case of an extreme contractual functioning, the text not merely describes that the appropriate processes have been followed, but also defines what those processes are. That does not necessarily imply a consideration of those processes apart from the situations in which they are implemented, and, when these occur together, the process of fact-finding becomes indistinguishable from the process of the creation of administrative norms.[35] The result is that textual production is a creative administrative process. As Dorothy Smith says, 'The text itself is to be seen as organizing a course of concerted social action. As an operative part of a social relation it is activated, of course, by the reader but its structuring effect is its own.'[36]

CASEBOOKS AND FACTUAL REPORTING

The keeping of case notes by doctors is, of course, an old phenomenon, but the intended nature and purpose of these notes appears to undergo a change in the first half of the nineteenth century. Where previously they had been understood as aides-mémoires for physicians, or ways to highlight particularly interesting individual cases, in the nineteenth century they came to be seen as mechanisms to view entire classes of patients suffering from specific maladies. It was Thomas Percival who made the first English plea for such standardized recording of insanity cases, in 1803.[37] Leading English institutions began to keep casebooks in the second decade of the nineteenth century, but they did not become compulsory until 1845 in English and Welsh county asylums.[38] This was, again, a new departure: an attempt to standardize practices of record-keeping across an entire system of asylums, and the considerable number of doctors they contained.

The attempt to introduce a standardized format for casebooks into asylums can therefore be seen as a novelty. The requirement for the casebook in the statute referred to the contents only generally, requiring that 'as soon as may be after the Admission of any Patient, the mental State and bodily Condition of every Patient at the Time of his Admission, and also the History from Time to Time of his case whilst he shall continue in the Asylum' be recorded for the periodic inspection of the visiting committee.[39] The administrative order of the Lunacy Commissioners provided much more detailed guidance.[40] First, basic personal information was to be recorded. The order continued:

SECONDLY – An accurate description of the external appearance of the Patient, when first seen after admission; – of his habit of body, and temperament; – of the appearance of his eyes, the expression of his countenance, and any peculiarity in the form of his head; – of the physical state of the vascular and respiratory organs, and of the abdominal viscera, and their respective functions; – of the state of the pulse, tongue, skin, &c.

THIRDLY – A description of the phenomena of mental disorder which characterize the case; – the manner and period of the attack; – with a minute account of the symptoms, and the changes produced in the Patient's temper or disposition; – specifying whether the malady displays itself by any, and what, illusions, or by irrational conduct, or morbid or dangerous habits or propensities; whether it has occasioned any failure of memory or understanding; or is connected with epilepsy, hemiplegia, or symptoms of general paralysis, such as tremulous movements of the tongue, defect of articulation, or weakness or unsteadiness of gait.

FOURTHLY – Every particular which can be obtained respecting the previous history of the Patient: – what are believed to have been the predisposing and exciting causes of the attack; – what have been his habits, whether active or sedentary, temperate or otherwise; – whether he has experienced any former attacks; and, if so, at what periods; – whether any of his Relatives have been subject to Insanity, or any other cerebral disorder; and whether his present attack has been preceded by any premonitory symptoms, such as restlessness, unusual elevation or depression of spirits, or any remarkable deviation from his ordinary habits and conduct; – and whether he has undergone any, and what, previous treatment, or has been subjected to personal restraint.

The Lunacy Commission instruction suggests that the casebook was to be a form of examination, the sense that Foucault uses the term in

Discipline and Punish. In Foucault's disciplinary institutions, specific techniques were used to subjugate the body: hierarchical observation, through which the individual was under constant and minute surveillance; and normalizing judgement, where departure from the precise institutional rules was subject to correction. In examination, these themes met:

It is a normalizing gaze, a surveillance that makes it possible to qualify, to classify, and to punish. It establishes over individuals a visibility through which one differentiates them and judges them.... The superimposition of the power relations and knowledge relations assumes in the examination all its visible brilliance.[41]

The professional gaze, the 'economy of visibility'[42] was transformed into a power relationship; the individual inmate was organized into documentary structures; and the inmate became a 'case':

[T]he child, the patient, the madman, the prisoner, were to become, with increasing ease from the eighteenth century and according to a curve which is that of the mechanics of discipline, the object of individual descriptions and biographical accounts. This turning of real lives into writing is no longer a process of heroization; it functions as a procedure of objectification and subjection.[43]

The Commissioners' order suggests some consistency with Foucault's model. The order invited an objective, somewhat sanitized and professional description, based largely on physical symptoms. The patient was to become a 'case', establishing both a hierarchical treatment relationship and the individual patient as a base of knowledge. Consistent with the interests of the Lunacy Commissioners in systemically compiling and promulgating knowledge about effective care and treatment of the insane,[44] the order required that particulars be recorded 'in a manner so clear and distinct, that they may admit of being easily referred to, and extracted, whenever the Commissioners shall so require'. The order was in this respect consistent with Percival's original plea for the keeping of casebooks, explained by Roy Porter as follows:

To counter the regrettable fact 'that the various diseases which are classed under the title of insanity, remain less understood than any others with which mankind are visited', Percival recommended that full particulars of each patient be recorded, including 'age, sex, occupation, mode of life, and if possible hereditary constitution'.[45]

The Leicester casebooks departed from this order in various interesting ways. What is initially striking is their lack of the sanitized professional gaze suggested by the Commissioners' order. They were not detached and objective accounts suitable for tabular presentation, but torrid tales of woe, often with overtones of moralization. Particularly in the 1840s and 1850s, the description of the physical appearance of the patient could verge on the poetic. Tongues were furry or, rarely, clean. Eyes were described by colour, darkness, expression, fullness, prominence and expressiveness. Temperaments might be nervous, angry, restless, phlegmatic or sanguine, and heads might be round or bullet-shaped. Countenance might be bloated, melancholic or 'peculiar', this last indicating lack of intellect or idiocy. The description of John Healey admitted in 1851, provides a particularly clear example of such metaphoric language:

The Patient's temper is very vindictive, and his disposition bad, his conduct has been very irrational, and his propensities dangerous to others ... The habits of this Patient, for years past have been very irregular, he has had no home, or settled abiding place, but has been a wanderer and a vagabond, he had a similar attack four years ago [for which he was apparently not confined] his life has been one of intemperance, idleness, and vice, his conduct to his mother has been most unnatural, and cruel, ... he is very restless, taciturn, and cunning, and his countenance bears the stamp of undisguised villainy.

His case note regarding his readmission the following year was even more extreme:

He was more disreputable in appearance, more diabolical in aspect, and certainly in worse health. There was not so much mental excitement, but in its place was a large amount of animal cunning, low trickery, and all the paltry, and petty devices of an abandoned character, his habits had become those of a confirmed drunkard, idle, dissolute, and intemperate, his conduct most irrational, his propensities violent and, toward his Mother, dangerous and most unnatural.[46]

The description of the mental malady itself tended to focus on the symptoms and behaviour of the individual upon his or her admission to the facility. The entry regarding Joseph Johnson, admitted in June of 1861, was typical:

This is a case of Mental Imbecility of some degree, the patient never speaks intelligibly but is frequently uttering unmeaning sound. He eats his food ravenously, is threatening + sometimes violent to those around him. He fights + kicks those near him without any apparent cause. [H]e walks out daily in the airing Court. He sometimes breaks + destroys furniture, but not to any great extent.[47]

The history, as well, typically centred less on medical matters, as implied in the Commissioners' order, and more on the circumstances of the individual's life. Thus of John Kettle it was stated:

This man's business has lately left him in consequence of a competitor springing up in his village who charged more moderately. The effect on the poor man was soon seen, he became negligent, intemperate, and idle, when before this disappointment he was remarkable for his steady, industrious and sober habits, his spirits at first were dreadfully depressed, now, however they are elevated, he is very restless, and destructive in his habits, he has been under medical treatment but not subjected to personal restraint.[48]

It is difficult to see in these accounts the 'ritual and "scientific"'[49] enrolment of individual difference of the Foucauldean examination and as implied in the Lunacy Commission's order. There is no reason to doubt Foucault's more fundamental claim, that the construction of individuals' lives in the casebooks subjected the individual inmate to a power relationship, but the imagery of the casebooks suggests that this was less through a sanitized professional gaze than through a process of marginalization and, often, moralization, the tools of the Poor Law.

Little information was added to the casebooks prior to the departure of the patient. In the 1840s and early 1850s, the initial treatment accorded to the patient would be noted, and a summary paragraph would be added regarding the outcome, completing the morality tale. Thus after recording the medicines and leeching undergone by Harriet Dakin, admitted in 1846, the casebook concluded:

[S]he gradually regained her health and strength, and for several weeks previous to her leaving the asylum was industriously employed in working for the benefit of the Institution.
She left quite recovered, and with many expressions of gratitude [sic] for the benefit she had derived.[50]

By the 1860s, however, it was more frequent that the discharge note would indicate merely whether discharged (cured, improved or, rarely, not improved), transferred or died, and the date. As a result, it is not possible to establish with any certainty how it was decided when a patient should leave.

These cannot have been intended as complete accounts of the

inmates' lives or treatment in the asylum in the sense of a modern clinical record. Frequently, there would be no indication of what happened to the individual between admission and discharge, some months, years or decades later. It is more reasonable to see them as recording both the appropriateness of the admission (the actuarial function) and that proper care had been taken to ensure the appropriateness of the admission (the contractual function). Consistent with this, there was a concerted attempt to paint the asylum in the best possible light. In the early years, when a significant entry might be included regarding the outcome of the case, this might involve alteration of attitudes during the construction of the record. Thus, upon John Dalley's admission in 1845, the casebook states:

This Man appears to be suffering more from poverty and want than from any other cause, and does not, as far as I can judge, appear to be labouring under any particular delusions, he is quiet in his manner, amounting to reserve, cleanly in his habits and disposed to be industrious, but destitution has for the present incapacitated him from laborious employment.[51]

The prognosis for this patient ought to have been good. Standard asylum practice was to provide a 'liberal diet' to all patients upon admission, a programme which would have been expected to result in speedy and marked improvement in Dalley's condition. Perhaps for this reason, there is an extended, albeit inconsistent, note five weeks later, blaming his death on medical treatment received prior to admission to the asylum:

This poor man when admitted into the Asylum was in a very low, and desponding condition, his health, too, was much disordered and it was with extreme difficulty he could be kept alive for a length of time previous to his admission he had been in a most excited state labouring under one of the most violent forms of mania, for which he was bled, blistered, leeched and physicked and reduced to such a state of exhaustion that his system never recovered from the shock. For a length of time he was kept up by the administration of a most generous diet, meat, eggs, wine and ale, but he gradually sunk and died from the effects of maniacal exhaustion.

It is much to be regretted that in cases of maniacal excitement the system is so generally, and so extensively depleted thereby rendering the subsequent state so extremely hazardous to the Patient, when exhaustion suddenly supervenes, and the vital energy having been previously completely prostrated, is unable to rally, and all hope is excluded of a favourable termination to the case.[52]

Similarly it is not easy to reconcile the note upon Jane Chadbourne's readmission, that she was 'discharged contrary to Mr. Buck's advice, her friends being anxious to try her at home' with the note upon that discharge, 'Jane Chadbourne was discharged Jan. 12th 1867 as recovered',[53] except that each portrayed the asylum in favourable terms at the time the record was constructed. Such discursive jumps become somewhat less frequent as the period progresses. Perhaps owing to increasing numbers of readmissions,[54] the casebooks became increasingly guarded about the prognosis of individual patients. This hesitancy in itself minimized inconsistency in the event of a subsequent admission.

It is not clear how promptly the casebooks were completed. The wording of the following entry for William Bradshaw, admitted in November 1865, would suggest that it may not have been completed until after his death in March 1866, thus allowing the asylum the opportunity to present a favourable account:

This is a case of Chronic Mania the result of old age + poverty. The patient altho' in a very helpless + infirm state is very irritable, jumping up + catching hats of anyone or anything which was in his reach, and his filthy habits made his case a very wretched one.

But little remains to be done for such a case he was speedily cleansed of the filth + vermin with which he was covered, and altho his appearance was improved in appearance, he soon succumbed to the influences of increasing age + decay.[55]

The asylum's practices suggest a different administrative agenda from that implied by the Commissioners' order; yet there was no other obvious source for the asylum staff to receive guidance on the completion of case records. The casebooks can therefore be understood not merely as recording the fulfilment of a predefined relationship, but also as creating the definition of what appropriate fulfilment of that relationship entailed. They not merely demonstrated that the patients got the 'treatment they deserved', as Garfinkel's records did, but also defined, through the facts they contained, what was relevant to determine whether the patients got the 'treatment they deserved'.

According to the statute, the prime readers of the casebook were to be the visiting committee of the asylum,[56] a group primarily composed of Justices, who had a particular interest in and sympathy with the asylum. The Leicester casebooks were also read by the Lunacy Commissioners, who signed them and who commented upon them in their reports on the asylum. The Poor Law guardians and medical officers who visited the asylum had no statutory right to read or examine the casebooks,[57] and there is no indication for the Leicestershire and Rutland Lunatic Asylum whether or not they did so. It was thus the visiting committee and the Commissioners who were to be convinced of the appropriateness of the asylum's conduct. The casebooks were completed by the medical superintendent, whose views as to relevance would be reflected, and, in addition, while the Lunacy Commission's guideline was departed from in spirit, it was influential in form. Despite these implied influences, the formation of an orthodoxy was unlikely to have been by conscious political compromise or negotiation. It is to be assumed that the medical superintendent was merely trying to be persuasive both of his readers and of himself, and through this process created an orthodoxy of relevance and standards in the casebooks.

In this context, the focus upon the admission of the individual to the asylum is interesting. On the one hand, this can be seen as reflecting the broad social concern that people were being wrongfully committed. The Lunacy Commission presented itself as a protection against such wrongful confinement, and the fact that there were no protections to prevent wrongful confinement of persons in workhouses had been important in their criticism of workhouse care of the insane in the late 1850s.[58] It is thus not surprising that it was addressed in the case reports.

What is surprising is the focus on admission to the near exclusion of all other aspects of asylum care and treatment. Various consequences flow from this. First, the absence of comments regarding individual treatment and progress would effectively preclude treatment which required knowledge of the individual patient to be developed over time. There were in the early 1860s almost 400 patients at a time in the asylum. It is inconceivable that the medical superintendent was able to remember significant information about each case without the aid of notes, and there is no suggestion that he kept notes apart from the casebook. It must be that the treatment offered did not require this information to be kept. Consistent with this, minimal medical treatment was offered, or at least minimal medical treatment that cost money. In 1865, when there were an average 397 patients in the asylum, the dispensary spent £63/7/2 on drugs, or just over 3 shillings per patient. An additional £56/17 was spent on wine and spirits for the dispensary, or just under 3 shillings per patient. At least in the decade after 1845, some medicinal treatment seems to have occurred upon admission; given minimal costs overall, this would suggest little such treatment later in the individual's stay. While people were often leeched, blistered, and physicked upon admission, it must have been the case that the average patient received little from the dispensary after that.

This is perhaps not a surprise. By the 1850s, the treatment of preference was moral management, which was based not on drugs but on organization of the behaviour of the patient. This too was not comprehensive. Even allowing that the work performed by the patients was intended as therapeutic, a minority of patients was engaged in such work, even at high season. The records offer no insight as to whether this was due to a lack of work, or an inability of patients to engage in such work; but it does suggest limitations on the moral management which was being offered. The development of individual characteristics of the patient in the mid to long term must have been irrelevant for the understanding of the moral treatment, since those individual characteristics were not recorded. System seems to have succeeded individual status.

This is consistent with the move from eighteenth to nineteenth-century moral treatment. The small, eighteenth and early nineteenth-century facilities forced the mad person to confront his or her unreason, to use Foucault's image, and for those treated by Fox at Ticehurst or Tuke at York, the scale of the institution allowed moral treatment with an individual focus.[59] The failure to record the personal details which are the preconditions of such individual treatment is indicative of the move away from individual care toward reliance on the system. The inmate may have been a 'case' at the point of admission to the asylum, but not thereafter.

The exclusion of personal information relating to the progress of the inmate also suggests that neither the readers of the casebooks nor their author believed it sufficiently important to insist on their inclusion – not the Justices of the Peace, not the Lunacy Commission and not even the medical superintendent. General peace and good order may have been an important objective for the asylum,[60] but the improvement of individuals, at least until their discharge, was not.

Even at the point of admission, the casebooks are striking in their focus on the individual, not on diagnosis or the characteristics of the mental disease of the patient. With the exception of heredity, a factor which the medical superintendent was specifically instructed to watch for by the Commissioners' direction, all other major causes of insanity listed by the casebooks reflect social conditions of the individual. Insanity was caused by grief, intemperance, childbirth,[61] religion or poverty, according to the casebooks. Brain disease was cited in only eight of 167 cases where causes were shown between 1861 and 1865, and all other diseases in only an additional nine. There was no clear distinction made between the insanity and the behaviour of the individual. Consider the following account of Marianne MacHale's fall from sanity:

[She was] placed in a respectable situation as soon as she left the Asylum on the 5th of August 1845 where she might have gained a decent livelihood had she conducted herself with propriety. She soon, however, left it; frequented her old haunts of vice and profligacy, took to drinking and soon beggared herself. She was subsequently sent to the Union where she addicted herself to theft and became the terror of all the inmates, and in consequence of her excessive violence she was soon removed to this establishment.[62]

While the casebook does normally provide a diagnosis, the focus was on the behaviour which justified the committal; in this, the casebooks resemble the admission documents, to be discussed below.

The imagery in these descriptions is highly reminiscent of the judgemental language of the new Poor Law. Poverty itself appeared as a cause of insanity 13 times between 1861 and 1865 in the casebooks. The emphasis on character in the descriptions has already been noted. The treatment accorded by the asylum upon the arrival of the inmate was portrayed as humanitarian and beneficial, consistent with the placement of the asylum as in opposition to the hardness of the new Poor Law. Thus in Marianne MacHale's case note quoted above, the workhouse was portrayed as one step on her slide into madness. The asylum inmates themselves were portrayed particularly in early years in extremely moralizing terms, as can be seen in the examples from the casebooks above. With the introduction of the new casebook format in 1856, the medical superintendent was explicitly required to assess 'character'.

This moralization appears to be a change between the eighteenth and the nineteenth century. Suzuki notes precisely the opposite trend among the eighteenth-century poor confined to houses of correction, where morally judgemental language ceased when the pauper was identified as a lunatic.[63] Thus while the nineteenth-century asylum may have been in part created as a paternalist challenge to the Poor Law, the lunatic became described in new Poor Law imagery.

The use of Poor Law imagery frequently imported a moral condemnation on the insane pauper, but occasionally the judgement was critical of social factors instead, factors which drove the pauper to madness. Thus it was said of Elizabeth Spawton,

This patient has worked, for many years, as a factory hand in a crowded and vitiated atmosphere, where, no doubt, she contracted her disposition to pulmonary disease, and the predisposing one of her Insanity.[64]

The criticism of the persons insane due to poverty could be tempered by an implied criticism of poverty itself. When the new format of casebook distinguishes between moral and physical causes of insanity, poverty is normally considered a physical cause. Some of the people who were insane due to poverty were not blameworthy in the eyes of the asylum as they were perceived as poor for reasons beyond their control. This imagery is reminiscent of another side of the Poor Law, that concerned with public health. The 1842 Sanitary Report, upon which Chadwick and Shaftesbury collaborated, blamed the mental decay of the poor on public health factors. Himmelfarb summarizes:

[It was] the foul odors of open cesspools, the garbage, excrement, and dead rats rotting in the streets, the filth and scum floating in the river, the sewage that passed as drinking water ... the 'miasma' emanating from all that decaying matter, the 'fetid effluvia,' 'poisonous exhalations,' and 'reking atmosphere' which were the source of the physical, moral, and mental deterioration of the poor.[65]

The public health connections are particularly apparent in the appointment of John Buck, Leicester's first medical officer of health, as the asylum's second medical superintendent in 1854.

The use of the various strands of Poor Law imagery in the casebooks reflected and reinforced the ideals of the asylum. If the care offered by the asylum involved relatively little chemical treatment, what it did pride itself on offering was food and respite, a regimen from which those suffering from the physical effects of poverty might hope to benefit. And the point of moral management, in so far as it was actually practised in the asylum, was reformation of character. The adoption of the Poor Law is consistent with the asylum's attempt to portray itself in the best light, justifying committals as cases where its treatment would be reasonably expected to be effective.

The admission of women following childbirth was a special case of this. Almost one-tenth of the women admitted from a domestic setting, and one-fifth of those for whom a cause was recorded in the casebooks, were shown as suffering from insanity caused by childbirth, or puerperal mania. The description of Mary Ann Wood was typical:

[T]he patient has been delusive + restless for some days + nights previous to her admission. It appears that she had some excessive discharge upon her before admission, that her appetite suddenly failed her, and that becoming restless and delirious + even threatening in her language + conduct her friends have moved to place her in the asylum. She expresses absurd fancies about rules and prison. She is constantly crying and is very restless at times.[66]

Restlessness, exhaustion and crying without cause were typical of the descriptions of these women. They often had a large number of small children at the time of their admission. Interestingly, these women were not generally described in terms of fallen characters, or sexual immoderates. In essence, the justification for committal seems implicitly to have been admission of the woman to allow her some recovery time away from the poverty of her ordinary life.[67] These women were, almost without exception, discharged cured within a few months.

ADMISSION DOCUMENTS

In practice, the admission documents were required to have a relatively strong actuarial character: it was these documents which convinced the Lunacy Commissioners and the local Justices of the propriety of a committal. It would be naive to think that these documents did not have a contractual function as well. The scale of operations would have required the Lunacy Commissioners to rely on Poor Law medical officers doing their jobs with relative efficacy, and the admission documents must have demonstrated that standard. Similarly, in a system of local administration where reputation of individual officers might be expected to be important, the medical man and the relieving officer would want the admission document to demonstrate that they had done a good job. None the less, Justices and Commissioners could be independently minded in their decision-making, and the admission documents thus had to contain sufficient detail to convince of the appropriateness of the committal.

The selection of facts in the documents therefore had an instrumental function. They were not merely descriptive. The 'situated reality' of the individual was turned into a textual account, which in turn became the definitive version of the original event, and a justification for the subsequent committal. This issue arises in any factual reporting, but it may be particularly acute regarding insanity where, as Dorothy Smith argues in a modern context, the structuring of the concept of mental illness is intended to impose an order onto a situated reality, a patient's life, which is chaotic:

The institution of mental illness, its conceptual organization, forms of social action, authorized actors and sites, and so forth, are concerned precisely with creating an order, a coherence, at those points where members of a community have been unable or unwilling to find it in the behaviour of a particular individual.[68]

The process of fact-finding in this context thus involves the creation of a coherence in the actions of the mad individual. With the coherence comes significance, a realization that the individual is mad, and with that, certain social consequences, most importantly in the instant context, admission to the asylum.

The theoretical discussion of this process belongs to the twentieth century, but its practical implications were articulated in the nineteenth. John Bucknill's 1861 article, 'On medical certificates of insanity', was a user's manual of how raw observations were to be worked up to form justifications for committal. The character of this piece may be gleaned from the following excerpt:

The imperfections of medical certificates arise perhaps more frequently from the form in which the facts are stated, than from any deficiency in the facts themselves. Allow me to illustrate this by a few examples. The following was a statement of facts sent with an idiot, 'He puts stones in his pockets and will not talk.' This, of course, was not sufficient although it applied to an idiot boy found wandering, of whom nothing was known. But if the medical man had thrown almost the same observation into the following form, his certificate would have been unimpeachable.

'His appearance is idiotic, —

[']He picks up stones, and puts them in his pockets as if he attached value to them.

[']When interrogated, he does not speak.'

Here are the facts which, taken together, afford good grounds for the opinion that the individual is an idiot.

* * *

Here is another example in which no language, and therefore no expression of delusion could be observed, 'Her general demeanour, preserving a sullen silence, and the expression of her countenance, and her restless movements.' This was a case of sullen and dangerous mania; and the fault of the certificate is not that of defective observation, but of defect of form; since there is nothing in this language to shew that the general demeanour, the sullen silence, the expression of countenance, and the restless movements were not the indications of reasonable fear, or reasonable anger, or some other state of sound mind. Let us try to recast these observations thus, 'The expression of her countenance is wild; she is in a state of restless movement without object. When questioned, she preserves a sullen silence.'[69]

Bucknill's comments here are consistent with the contents of the admission documents to the Leicestershire and Rutland asylum, although the Leicester documents also detailed facts communicated by others, matters considered by Bucknill to be mere surplusage. The comments on the documents of Sarah Smith, admitted in 1864, are typical:

[Facts observed:] Restless, roving manner, calling upon neighbours and people without any apparent object, incoherent, sleepless, rises very early in the morning and wanders about the house.

[Facts communicated by others:] Threatened to stab Elizabeth Hunt with a large knife and when she made her escape threw it with violence at her, and in the presence of another women said she would kill her, communicated by Mrs. Hunt, Mother of Elizabeth Hunt.[70]

The reporting of the facts imports a significance to the lives of the individuals and creates an order in them. For sociologists such as Dorothy Smith, the academic interest is looking at the persuasive function of texts in this process. In the present context, the persuasiveness is accepted. What is of greater interest is the clarification of the structure of the ordering within the documents, to elucidate how the role of the asylum was understood.

In general, the admission documents identified domestic admissions as dangerous to others or suicidal. Only 12 of the 177 domestic admissions appeared to be otherwise. The remarks regarding Elizabeth Tarry are typical:

[Facts observed:] Very incoherent in her manner and conversation. appears very low and melancholic.

[Facts communicated by others:] The patient's Sister Mary Neale informed me that the patient had refused to take her food or to get out of bed and sometimes locks herself in her room for two or three days together, and that on thursday last, she attempted to strangle herself with a piece of Cord which she placed around her neck and tied to the side of her bed, and would have accomplished her purpose but for the interference of her sister and a neighbour.[71]

This determination of dangerousness appears to have been central to the decision to send an individual to the asylum from a domestic setting. It applied, for example, to the pregnant women suffering from mania related to childbirth and exhaustion. The admission document of Mary Ann Wood, whose case note was quoted above, reads as follows:

[Facts observed:] Incoherent + hesitating manner of answering questions; delusions with regard to the state of her house, Expressing her belief that everyone entering it brings filth + bad smells into it. Violent prejudice against the child of her husband by a former wife + her neighbours all of whom she believes wish to do her harm.

[Facts communicated by others:] The neighbours report that she constantly makes use of very gross language. On tuesday last was very violent to her daughter, Has threatened to burn her house, and has said that she feels that she must chop her childs head off. Has had previous attacks, and there is a clear history of hereditary predisposition. Leah Chamberlin of Gilmorton communicated the above facts to me.[72]

In this reliance on dangerousness, the admission documents can be seen as reflecting the broader legal agenda. As discussed above, the eighteenth-century introduction of consideration of lunacy into the Poor Law had concerned persons who were 'furiously Mad, and dangerous to be permitted to go Abroad'.[73] Under the nineteenth-century Poor Law, it was only dangerously insane people who were precluded from workhouse accommodation, and if one of the functions of the admission document was to justify asylum admission as distinct from workhouse admission, dangerousness would be the obvious criterion to cite.

There were also common law roots regarding confinement which continued to resound, even though the committal criteria of the asylum acts did not explicitly require dangerousness to be shown. Comyn's *Digest* recorded the following plea in defence of an action for false imprisonment:

So, the defendant may plead that he did it to prevent apparent mischief, which might ensue: as, to restrain the plaintiff, non sane, from killing himself, or others, burning a house, or other mischief.[74]

A similar statement is found in Bacon's *Abridgment*.[75] This defence would appear to have been well-established by the eighteenth century. Brook's *Abridgement* from the sixteenth century contains another similar statement referring specifically, as in Comyn, to restraining the lunatic from killing, or doing mischief such as setting fire to a house.[76]

These roots continued to be influential in the nineteenth century. In *In Re Fell* (1845), Patteson J commented that 'These [i.e. the 1828 and 1845 madhouse] statutes were passed for the protection of the public ...'.[77] In *Nottidge* v. *Ripley* (1849),[78] Sir Frederick Pollock C B stated in his charge to the jury, 'It is my opinion that you ought to liberate every person who is not dangerous to himself or others ... and I desire to impress that opinion with as much force as I can.'[79] In *R.* v. *Pinder* (1855), Coleridge J made the following similar remarks:

This is a general observation; but I cannot help perceiving, in reference to this and preceding statutes upon the same subject, that the legislature has proceeded in them with the double object of protecting the public and lunatics, real or supposed; facilitating in many respects the reception of persons dangerous to themselves or others or of unsound mind into asylums, where they will be properly restrained and treated, yet guarding both their reception and continuance there with great, and it cannot be denied with proper, jealousy, to secure persons placed there from being improperly treated there with harshness or inconsiderateness, or detained there unnecessarily.[80]

Treatment was mentioned, but not as the *raison d'être* of the confinement. The reason for the confinement is the protection of the public and the 'real or supposed' lunatic. These attitudes continued until well after the 1870 termination of the current study. In *R.* v. *Whitfield, ex parte Hillman* (1885), for example, Lord Coleridge, then Chief Justice, found that the alleged lunatic was 'neither epileptic nor dangerous to himself or others',[81] and continued as follows:

Mr. Hillman is not alleged to have been a raging and dangerous lunatic. The common law always allowed the restraint of the liberty of such persons. The statute authorizes, and most properly, interference with the liberty of those who, though not dangerous as regards life or limb to themselves or others, are yet the subjects of 'proper care and control.' But their liberty is to be interfered with only as the statute directs.[82]

Lord Coleridge was in dissent on the outcome in this case, but Lindley LJ, in the majority, comments as follows:

The object of the statute is not to enable justices to adjudicate a person to be non compos mentis, but to enable them to place under proper care and control persons whom they are satisfied are lunatic and require to be so placed. They have to act in cases of emergency and of great danger, as well as in other cases; their measures are precautionary measures only; if they make a mistake, it can soon be corrected.[83]

The court did appear to find that the dangerousness criterion had been loosened as a result of the statute, but it does not appear to have been discarded completely.

Of these, only *Whitfield* involved a county asylum, the rest referring to committals to private madhouses. Even *Whitfield* involved the admission of an individual under the provisions regarding insane persons wandering at large, and so, as discussed above, his pauper status was somewhat ambiguous. As such, the effect of the cases on perceptions of pauper committals is not clear-cut. Perhaps because of the concern with dangerousness in eighteenth-century Poor Law statutes, there does seem to have been some influence on the standards understood to be applicable to the insane poor. The charge to the jury in *Nottidge*, for example, provoked the Lunacy Commission into publishing an open letter of objection in 1849.[84] This letter referred equally to admissions to county asylums and private madhouses.

The concern about dangerousness is to be considered in the context of a strain of modern scholarship which has portrayed the asylum as accumulating social casualties of the nineteenth century. Andrew Scull is most frequently quoted on this point:

And yet, if asylums, and the activities of those running them, did not transform their inmates into upright citizens, they did at least get rid of troublesome people for the rest of us. By not inquiring too deeply into what went on behind asylum walls, and by not being too sceptical of the officially constructed reality, people were (are) rewarded with a comforting reassurance about the essentially benign character of their society and the way it dealt (deals) with its deviants and misfits. Granting a few individuals the status and perquisites ordinarily thought to be reserved for those with genuine expertise and esoteric knowledge was a small price to pay for the satisfaction of knowing that crazy people were getting the best treatment science could provide, and for the comfortable feelings which could be aroused by contemplating the contrast between the present 'humane' and 'civilized' approach to the 'mentally ill' with the barbarism of the past.[85]

A similar point is made by David Mellett:

[T]he asylum, originally designed for aberrant members of the middling ranks of society, gradually became a public house of detention for people who acted oddly, or who had no place to go: alcoholics, geriatrics, depressives, paranoids. In other words, NOT the stereotyped lunatics of earlier periods, but pathetic victims of daily life in a brutalising society filled the wards of Victorian asylums.[86]

There is a point of contact here with the passage from Dorothy Smith, cited above. For Smith, the documents involved 'creating an order, a coherence, at those points where members of a community have been unable or unwilling to find it in the behaviour of a particular individual',[87] a vision not necessarily inconsistent with the social casualties and misfits of Scull's and Mellett's work. This transfer is problematic, however. Where Nelken was able to examine the behaviour of Harassment Officers, landlords and tenants to assess what transformations were made during the keeping of documents, the historian does not have this luxury: the situated reality of the subjects of historical documents is gone forever.

The attribution of characteristics to this situated reality creates the risk of warping understanding of social policy. In the case at hand, it becomes much too easy to portray the behaviour of the nineteenth-century actors in a simplistic and judgemental way, as for example imposing an 'out of sight, out of mind' policy on the unattractive of society. An element of this can be seen in the quotation from Scull, above. The situation is more complicated, however, for the nineteenth century had other institutions in which the unattractive could have been hidden, the workhouse being the most obvious. More to the point, the understanding of lunacy created by the admission documents is not congruent with the category of 'pathetic victims of daily life in a brutalising society': where the casebooks might sometimes perceive the insane person in the context of a social casualty, the admission documents focused on the inmate as a problem of order. Those admitted to the asylum were not merely mad; they were people whose behaviour required the intensive surveillance and disciplinary structures of the asylum.

Asylum admissions from the workhouse are administratively distinguishable from admissions from a domestic setting. The work-house was already an environment of relatively intensive supervision by Poor Law staff, where conduct did not go unnoticed. Admissions from the workhouse also appear to have been triggered by behaviour of the inmate, but the application for admission to the asylum was organized by staff, not family as had been the case with domestic admissions. Of particular importance in this process appears to be the nurse or attendant of the insane wards of the workhouse, where they existed (particularly at Leicester), since much of the conduct which formed the basis of the application occurred at night, when other staff were not present. The admission documents would suggest that the master of the workhouse was at least consulted in the decision as to whether to organize an asylum admission application for someone. The medical officer of the facility might also be involved in the decision as to whether an application should be commenced, but this seems to have been contingent on the interest he showed in the insane persons. Often, the portion of the admission form detailing facts indicating insanity observed personally by the doctor is, as for domestic admissions, merely an account of one interview with the inmate.

These documents, like those for domestic admissions, focus on the insane as a problem of order. Dangerousness was still a common factor, with over 70 per cent identifiably dangerous to others or suicidal from their admission documents. The documents for Sarah Shaw, admitted in 1862 from Barrow upon Soar workhouse, are typical:

[Facts observed:] Restless wandering, incoherent and obscene conversation, she imagines that she is going to marry an inmate of the workhouse who is an idiot.

[Facts communicated by others:] Hannah Osborne and other inmates of the Workhouse. S. Shaw constantly uses very bad language, frequently pulls up her clothes in the presence of others, if remonstrated with for so doing, she becomes very violent, strikes or throws anything she can lay her hands on at the person and is with great difficulty restrained from breaking the windows of the ward.[88]

None the less, where less than 7 per cent of domestic admissions could not be identified as dangerous or suicidal, 23 of the 77 workhouse admissions, or almost 30 per cent, could be so identified. Of these, 19 could be identified as unmanageable. William Chamberlain provides an example of this:

[Facts observed:] Very childish desires and pursuits, vacant countenance with receding forehead, vague unsteady wandering eye.

[Facts communicated by others:] Very dirty in his habits, noisy, exposes his person, undresses himself and walks about quite naked, communicated by Mr. Gillespie the Master of the Union.[89]

The litany of night wandering, exposure of person, restlessness, swearing and shouting in a disruptive manner and violent conduct run throughout the cases. Issues such as wandering and violent conduct were by no means absent from the domestic admission documents, but in that context, the issue seems to have been whether the individual was safe or adequately cared for in the domestic setting. In the workhouse cases, the issue seems at least in part to have been the efficient management of the house. When the Hitch report in 1844 recommended the removal of a number of paupers from the workhouse to the asylum, the Poor Law medical officer provided the following response:

Reynolds, Homer, Levin, Barfoot, Hobill, Robinson, and Harris have been removed to the Lunatic Asylum

Henry Killingsworth is quiet, harmless and manageable

Derry is a case of Melancholia, he is quite manageable

Gurden has much improved and is quiet and manageable

Brown is still ill tempered and sullen and will not work, + he is however manageable

Wright, Sarah, is more knave than fool and though ill tempered is manageable

Sandford is still irritable and when aroused dangerous, + he had been managed without difficulty or accident

Hand Susannah. Is harmless quiet and industrious, she appears very comfortable.[90]

Once again, it is tempting to speculate in the mould of Scull and Mellett that the asylum was being used as a 'dump for the awkward and inconvenient of all descriptions';[91] but once again, this overstates the case. The admission documents did include facts to demonstrate the madness of the individuals; and most were understood to be actually dangerous. The argument can certainly be no stronger than the following comment of Janet Saunders regarding the weak-minded in prisons:

It is tempting to speculate whether the label of weak-minded was not in some cases merely a label for individuals who doggedly refused to give in and accept their role as repentant sinners quietly working out their punishment. The sources, however, allow only the conclusion that people labelled as weak-minded represented a perpetual problem for the prison authorities, and were viewed as a distinct category of deviant, requiring new institutional provisions.[92]

The focus on manageability is not surprising. The essential concern of the workhouse staff was the good administration of the workhouse, and in so far as the insane compromised that order, the workhouse staff would have viewed them as problematic. What is more interesting is that this criterion was adopted by the Lunacy Commissioners in their local dealings with Poor Law officials. Consider the following report from Commissioner Wilkes about two inmates of the Barrow upon Soar workhouse in 1858:

Thomas Ferne is insane, and is very restless and troublesome, and I recommend him to be removed to the Asylum. Robert Jarrett is very noisy and greatly disrupts the other inmates of the ward, and on this account I think he is unfit to be kept here. This workhouse is not at all adapted for patients who are at all troublesome or excited, and only the most quiet class of weak minded persons should be allowed to be sent to, or detained in it.[93]

In this case, it was the response of the guardians which referred to possibility of cure, albeit along with criteria of manageability:

In reply to which I have been directed to state that in consequence of the entry made in the Visitors Book above referred to the Board of Guardians directed the Medical officer of the Workhouse to pay strict attention to the two cases for some time and report on the result to the Board with his opinion whether they are proper persons to be sent to the Lunatic Asylum or not and he has done so and his opinion is that they are not[;] they are neither dangerous to themselves or to others. Thomas Fern is suffering from softening of the Brain and is paralysed and bedridden and is unable to help himself or harm himself or others and Robert Jarratt is a person of rather weak intellect and has been so from infancy[;] he is 48 years of age he is not always observant in his language to his fellow inmates which is a complaint against him. The Medical Officer considers that no Medical or other treatment than that which they now receive in the Workhouse could improve their condition he therefore does not recommend their removal therefrom.[94]

Conspicuous by its absence from the admission documents was the Poor Law imagery which characterized the asylum casebooks. In the casebook context, it was argued that this imagery was used because of its ability to make the pauper appear appropriately placed in the asylum: the moral and physical effects of poverty were what the asylum was to address. The focus in the admission documents is instead on the problem of order. Certainly, it was this which justified the choice of the asylum as the institutional response to the pauper, but it did not merely define the institutional response, but also was a defining characteristic of lunacy itself, or at least lunacy as the term was to be understood for purposes of the asylum acts. It was the onset of dangerousness, an impulse to commit suicide or, occasionally, unmanageable tendencies which were the relevant criteria to identify the individual as insane: that was when the 'length of time insane' was calculated from on the admission form. Occasionally, the failure of the relieving officer to make a complete identification between the problematic behaviour and the insanity reveals the association explicitly. Thus regarding the length of time Robert Woodcock was said to be insane, it was said, 'It has been coming on him for months but has not been dangerous till now'.[95] For Sarah Homes, it was said, 'Melancholy about a year, violent five days'.[96] For most of the documents, however, the association seems to have been complete and implicit.[97]

There is no reason to believe that this was a convenient or cynical realignment of legal categories, creating a legal fiction of 'length of time insane' being equated to 'length of time violent'. Rather, consistent with the sociological discussion of fact reporting above, it seems more convincing to argue that the people creating the documents believed what they were writing down. This is consistent with the legal and historical associations between insanity and violent, suicidal or unmanageable behaviour, discussed above. It is also consistent with some of the discourses from the asylum and Lunacy Commissioners themselves, discourses which emphasized how those requiring restraint in the workhouse could be managed without it in the asylum.

Lines between behaviour and insanity were thus not clear. It would be misleading to perceive the committal process as two separate decisions, first whether the individual was insane and, second, what was to be done with him or her. They were co-mingled and indistinguishable issues. The image is not of the psychiatric professional, assessing and diagnosing according to abstract criteria, but of local officials, without special training in insanity-related issues, making the best of the entirety of the situation before them.

WORKHOUSE AND OUTDOOR RELIEF OF THE INSANE

The documentation for the care of the insane under the remainder of the Poor Law system in Leicestershire and Rutland does not allow for the same systematic analysis as the asylum casebooks or admission documents. The workhouse kept no helpful records as to how classifications were made, and the annual returns of insane paupers, some of which survive at the Public Record Office, contain little useful information. Assessment must rely on the patchier documents which remain in either correspondence files or minute books of local guardians, as well as what may be inferred from the asylum documents. As a result, little is known about workhouse inmates and outdoor relief from local sources.

The situations which did generate some existing documents tended to involve disputes as to whether an individual on outdoor relief or in the workhouse ought to have been in the asylum. This is not surprising, as the asylum acts provided a structure for such discussion, and the Lunacy Commissioners and Poor Law central authorities made it their business to ensure that these statutes were followed. There was once again an administrative context for such discussions. Much has already been said about the images of workhouse confinement in particular which is contained in the asylum casebooks and admission documents, but the limitations of sources which juxtapose the asylum with other Poor Law relief must be acknowledged. Such documents tend to be more revealing about asylum admission criteria and structures than about the remainder of the Poor Law care of the insane. It was argued above that the process of asylum admission did not distinguish clearly between the insanity of individuals and their dangerous, suicidal or unmanageable behaviour. Paupers were assessed instead according to their entire situation as an undifferentiated whole. The best which can be gleaned from this about the remainder of the Poor Law is that for those on out-relief, this nexus of factors justifying asylum admission was not perceived to exist. This is, however, definition through negation: it says nothing about the nexus of factors which defined the understanding of other poor relief of the insane.

Regarding out-relief, for example, these documents place an emphasis on the family situation of the insane person and on their own abilities, to show that they were not dangerous and therefore did not require asylum admission. Thus Hannah Mills and Hannah Johnson, both of Barrow upon Soar Union, were assessed by the guardians to be appropriate to leave on out-relief, not because of the degree of their illness, but because of their behaviour:

In order to shew the opinion of the Medical Officer respecting their cases I have enclosed a copy of the last return to the Commissioners in Lunacy &c made by him which shews that he Mr. Wood visited them on the 29th March last (he resides in the same village where they live) and he describes them both as being 'harmless, cleanly and never required restraint'. They are each of them competent to manage their own domestic and other affairs and require neither restraint nor control and in the opinion of the guardians may with propriety continue to live as they have heretofore done in which opinion the Medical Officer coincides.[98]

Similar comments were made regarding Ann Bull, aged 77 and living alone on outdoor relief, by the medical officer of Billesdon Union:

In answer to the Poor Law Boards enquiries respecting Ann Bull of Newton Harcourt I beg to say that I consider her to be as safe living by herself as most persons of her age. She though an imbecile has the instincts of self-preservation pretty well developed. Indeed it can scarcely be said that she lives alone strictly speaking as a neighbour, a respectable woman, frequently goes into her house and looks after her wants.[99]

The point was that these people were receiving adequate care, without the necessity of asylum admission. The asylum was perceived as an extreme option, for those unable to cope outside it.

Consideration of the insane in other branches of the Poor Law ought instead to review the culture and administration of those other branches. The paucity of documents at the local level means that this enterprise is of necessity speculative.

Determination of insanity would become necessary for persons living in the community only when there was an application for relief. The 1834 Poor Law Report had divided paupers into able-bodied and 'impotent', the latter being defined as everybody except the able-bodied.[100] The instructions to the Assistant Poor Law Commissioners for the purposes of their investigations were marginally more forthcoming:

Under this head are comprised all those who are prevented, by disease of body or mind, by old age, or by infancy, from earning a part or the whole of their subsistence.[101]

Anne Digby explained the situation as follows:

Paradoxically, although the able-bodied had been a prime target for the reformers of 1834 in their policy of preventing the pauperization of the labouring class, the Poor Law administrators who implemented their policies never succeeded in defining who the able-bodied actually were. Like so much else in Poor Law history, the practice is more revealing than the policy and this suggests that the able-bodied were those aged 15 years or more who could support themselves by their own labour.[102]

The Leicestershire documents support that ability to work was taken into account as an indicator of insanity. Sarah Rodwell was a widow on outdoor relief identified as a lunatic by Dr Hitch in his 1844 report. She had not been included in the lunacy return of that year, as the medical officer explained: 'this woman is not deemed insane or an idiot, being capable of managing the house for her father and she also goes out washing.'[103] The question is whether this is paradoxical, as Digby suggests. The new Poor Law was to encourage employment in those able to work, and the use of this criterion to determine the able-bodied from the infirm thus seems unsurprising. It was only when the relief to be provided needed to be decided that distinctions between able-bodied and infirm, and within the various categories of infirm, became relevant; and it is not surprising that internalist Poor Law criteria such as the ability to work would have informed those distinctions.

Identifying the occasions for assessment in the workhouse is more problematic. It was argued in Chapters 2 and 3 that the workhouse was increasingly composed of those who were unable to survive outside it: the sick, the old, the feeble and the infirm, as well as the insane. There was general agreement that in practical terms, it might be difficult to tell the insane from some of these other groups. The practical differences between being identified as old or sick and identified as insane would be minimal: in either case, the more liberal dietary would be available, and the somewhat softened accommodation rules accorded to the non-able-bodied. Apart from visitation by the Commissioners in Lunacy little practical distinction would have been made in administrative terms between the insane and these other groups. It would not have been obvious to those running the house why the insane ought to be specially identified, as a distinct category from these other groups, and the Poor Law central authorities made no requirement of such separate identification.[104]

The powers of the Lunacy Commissioners extended only to the insane in workhouses, and the Commissioners therefore had to develop a working definition as to who these people were. In their investigations prior to their 1847 report on workhouses, they discovered that there were generally a number of people in the workhouse who were not permitted by the master to leave at their own will, but who could be released only with the agreement of the guardians.[105] The Commissioners turned this practice into the defining characteristic of lunacy in the workhouse:

With respect to the persons coming within the meaning of the term Lunatic ... [the Commissioners were of the opinion that] the term was to be construed in its largest sense, as applying to all persons kept in workhouses, who, by reason of deficiency, infirmity, derangement, or other unsoundness of mind (whatever form it might assume, and whether they were violent, or harmless, curable or incurable), were not deemed competent to take care of themselves, or proper to be left entirely under their own guidance and control, without supervision of any kind; and of course as including all those who, in consequence of their mental condition, stood practically on a different footing, in respect to their personal liberty, from the ordinary paupers in a workhouse, and were not allowed to quit the house at their own sole discretion, upon an ordinary notice to the Master.[106]

Their 1859 report on workhouses contained the essentially identical test.[107] These insane were not 'proper persons to be *confined*, in the narrow and technical sense of the term, that is to say, as patients in a Lunatic Asylum' but equally not 'fit to be left entirely at large'.[108] This reinforces the image of the insane as the old, the feeble, the harmless and the helpless.

In 1867, a practical reason for identification of the insane did arise, as unlike other paupers, their right to leave the facility could from that date be formally curtailed. In the first half of October 1867, immediately upon the Act taking effect, 72 persons were ordered to be detained in the Leicester workhouse.[109] Unfortunately, while the record of these committals stated that these individuals were 'certified by the Medical Officer ... as suffering from mental and bodily disease as renders them unfit to leave the workhouse', thus containing an implied reference to the Commissioners' test, the actual medical certificates do not survive. The form of the certificate was not prescribed by statute or regulation, so that the amount and nature of information these certificates would have contained is a matter of speculation.

There was no way legally to force an individual into the workhouse. Insane persons presumably entered the workhouse when they felt unable to survive on their own, or when in practice forced by families unwilling or unable to care for them any longer. Also contained in the workhouse were persons transferred out of the asylum. It is difficult to identify a number here. From 1853 to 1867, 182 people were discharged either 'not improved' or 'relieved' (as distinct from 'cured') from the Leicestershire and Rutland asylum, and it is a fair speculation that many of these may have entered the workhouse either directly from the asylum, or at some subsequent time. Even for those discharged 'cured', the cure was frequently not permanent, and a workhouse admission might be the eventual result. The Leicester guardians specifically justified keeping people in the workhouse on the basis that they had been discharged from the asylum.[110]

The process of categorization of the insane in workhouses appears to have had a somewhat fluid structure. At issue seems to have been matching the behaviour of the individuals with the behaviour on the various workhouse wards. Thus the minute of the creation of the first segregated area for the insane in the Leicester workhouse reads as follows:

Read the Report of the Visiting Committee, that complaints had been made of the indecent practice of the aged Idiots it is recommended that a room be prepared for them apart from the Old Men which was ordered.[111]

This approach is again consistent with general administrative precepts of the new Poor Law. At issue would have been whether the individual fitted into the workhouse culture. Thus the comment of the medical officer regarding pauper lunatics identified in the Leicester workhouse by Dr Hitch in 1844, but not included in the return of insane paupers of that date, is not surprising: 'Mary Freer, Augusta Cowell, Mary Jarratt, John Price: Inmates of the Workhouse have never been classed as Lunatics or idiots, being orderly and quiet in their habits'.[112]

The categorization within the workhouse was part of a protection against moral contagion. The construction of separate wards for the various moral categories of pauper, including the insane, was mandated by Article 99 of the Consolidated Orders of the Poor Law Board:

The Guardians shall from time to time, after consulting the Medical officer, make such arrangements as they deem necessary with regard to persons labouring under any disease of body or mind.

Secondly. The Guardians shall, so far as circumstances will permit, further subdivide any of the classes enumerated in Article 98, with reference to the moral character or behaviour, or the previous habits of the inmates, or to such other grounds as may seem expedient.[113]

The editorial footnote to these comments made it clear that this was to be a protection from moral contagion:

This is an important provision, enabling the Guardians to place persons of bad character in classes by themselves, so that they may not contaminate the virtuous and well-conducted inmates of the house.

Other categories which were given as cases where special wards were justified included 'females of dissolute and disorderly habits' and vagrants, further emphasizing the purposes based in morality. The inclusion of the insane as a group requiring such a specialized ward may suggest that they were viewed as a part of this moral risk.

In Leicester, it was not so clear whether the insane were to be protected from immoral influences, or were themselves the immoral influences from which others were to be protected. The argument for a new workhouse in 1845 relied in part on the possibility of providing better facilities for the insane. There was also to be better classification generally, through which the moral were to be segregated from evil influences:

As a matter of course many of the inmates of a Workhouse are of a notoriously profligate character, the very refuse and dregs of society, and of whose reformation there is perhaps little to be hoped; but there are others who from misfortune, sickness, or accident, may have become inmates, and to whom the Workhouse instead of being a place of rest, is one of continual torment; compelled as they of necessity are, to occupy the same rooms, to associate with, and to be witnesses of the blasphemy, obscenity, and profaneness, of those whose only aim seems to be to annoy their more orderly companions, and set at nought the common decencies of life. With persons of weak minds need it be a matter of surprize if amid such associations they become corrupted, sinking to the level of their more depraved companions, and whether remaining in the Workhouse or returning to their friends, spreading the moral pestilence with which they are infected.[114]

On this basis, it would be reasonable to expect that moral assessment would form a part of the decision as to whether an individual was to be placed in an insane ward, as well, perhaps, as an assessment of the risk that they be morally influenced. Unfortunately, documents do not survive to provide further illumination on this evaluation.

This assessment has been of necessity speculative, but it is all that can be done, given the documents available. It may well be that the decisions themselves were idiosyncratic and largely arbitrary. To carry the sociological views of fact-finding cited above to their ultimate conclusion, it is at least open to be argued that since the officials involved never went through the exercise of identifying what facts were relevant to the categorizations of people as insane in the workhouse and on outdoor relief, and writing them down, canons of interpretation never developed. This may overstate the case. The insane under out-relief and in the workhouse were subject to the decision-making structures of the new Poor Law. It seems excessive to suggest that since these structures left no records on the decisions of interest, that therefore the decisions were made in some sense arbitrarily. None the less, as discussed above, it is consistent with the administrative practices which would be expected in the workhouse and on outdoor relief that these decisions would be ad hoc and relatively fluid in character. The fact that the decisions were not recorded in a fixed form would do nothing to restrict this fluidity.

NOTES

1 Pauper lunatics could also be sent to private madhouses, in the event that the county asylum was full. This was particularly significant in the borough of Leicester, which by statute had a right to only 25 places in the county asylum. In practice, for most of the period, the asylum held considerably more for an increased per capita fee, but Leicester also sent some insane paupers to private madhouses. It would appear from the documents that the criteria for the sending of an individual to a private madhouse were similar to those for sending to the county asylum. Mary King was to be 'sent to the County Asylum if there be room, and if not to the Camberwell Asylum [a private madhouse]': Minutes of Leicester Board of Guardians, 15 Dec. 1846, LRO G/12/8a/4. See similar comments at, e.g., 29 May 1849 and 21 Aug. 1849, LRO G/12/8a/5; 8 June 1858 and 12 April 1859, LRO G/12/8a/9; 2 July 1861, 7 Oct. 1862 and 18 June 1867, LRO G/12/8a/10. County asylums in Derby and Lincoln were also used to accommodate this overflow: Minutes of Leicester Board of Guardians, 19 Nov. 1861 and 21 Oct. 1862, LRO G/12/8a/10.

2 A list of these questions is contained in Appendix 4.

3 See Casebook, LRO DE 3533/188 and subsequent casebooks.

4 Or until 1863, two Justices, if the individual was admitted as wandering or not under proper care and control. The statutory admission procedures allowed admission to the asylum directly by the relieving officer and an officiating clergyman in exceptional cases. In such cases, which constituted roughly a quarter of the admissions in the 1860s, the

documents would be signed by these officers instead of Justices.

5 A copy of the printed questions to which the relieving officer was to respond are attached as Appendix 4.

6 16 & 17 Vict. c. 97 sch. F(3).

7 William Hunter was refused admission in October 1869: see Superintendent's Journal, 10 Nov. 1869, LRO DE 3533/84. Robert Bayfield and a Mr Jackson were also refused in July 1865: see Superintendent's Journal, 12 July 1865, LRO DE 3533/84. John Harris was discharged three days following admission because of inadequate certificates in 1865: see Casebook, LRO DE 3533/191, adm. 22 Nov. 1865. Unfortunately, none of these entries details the specific deficiencies in the documents.

8 See, for example, the comments of John Bucknill, head of the Devon County Asylum, in 'The medical certificates of admission papers', *Journal of Mental Science*, 4 (1858): 312, at 312–13.

9 Basic statistical information regarding these cases is contained in Appendix 2. The cases studied were cases 2237 to 2642 in the asylum casebooks, LRO DE 3533/189–191. The annual reports show 409 admissions in this period, presumably including the three persons discharged immediately owing to insufficient documentation, noted above.

10 This is marginally higher than for the country as a whole. The annual reports of the Lunacy Commission indicate that of 32,693 admissions from 1861 to 1865 inclusive, 16,406 (50 per cent) were women.

11 16 & 17 Vict. c. 97 s. 68.

12 A small number of these people were transferred to the Leicester asylum from other asylums. Generally, their admission documents to that original asylum have been included with their transfer documents to Leicester, and they have been classified according to these earlier admission documents, even though these documents may have been signed prior to the 1861 commencement of my statistics. In ten cases, copies of these original admission documents were not on file: see below.

13 Examinations were held at the town hall in Leicester, workhouses in Melton Mowbray, Lutterworth and Loughborough, and the police station in Loughborough. Examinations at the police station do not appear to have been limited to persons found by police officers wandering abroad; see, for example, the case of Sarah Roworth, LRO DE 3533/227, adm. 7 Sept. 1861, examined at the police station but admitted apparently from the workhouse.

14 Adm. 30 Jan. 1861. Casebook, LRO DE 3533/189.

15 See, for example, Ann Kilby, adm. 1 Sept. 1853. Casebook LRO DE 3533/187. See also Thomas Bettoney, where both spousal and neighbour involvement seem to have been factors:

Lately he has been in a state of almost constant intoxication + chronic Mania. He has beaten his wife frequently, spent his earnings most foolishly, he has kept his neighbours in a state of constant alarm by his outrageous conduct. (adm. 28 Sept. 55. Casebook LRO DE 3533/187.)

16 See case of David Perkins, adm. 24 Oct. 1851. Casebook, LRO DE 3533/186.

17 This appears to have been a relatively common use for the workhouse: see the testimony of A. Doyle, Assistant Poor Law Commissioner, before the Select Committee on Lunatics, PP 1859 2nd sess. (156) vii 501, at qq. 1762 ff.

18 Leicester Guardians, Minute book, 26 June 1846, LRO G/12/8a/3. The minute book shows Robert Hewitt as being admitted to the workhouse on this basis in August of that year.

19 For visiting committee, see their introduction to 'Rules for General Management of the Institution', 1849, LRO DE 662/27 at 20, and their 1869 Annual report LRO DE 3533/14. For Lunacy Commission, see *Fourth Annual Report*, PP 1850 (291) xxiii 363, at 13, 16; *Eleventh Annual Report*, PP 1857 2nd sess. (157) xvi 351, at 16; *Supplement to the Twelfth Annual Report*, PP 1859 1st sess. (228) ix 1, at 32 f.

20 UK, *Report of the Metropolitan Commissioners in Lunacy to the Lord Chancellor*, (London: Bradbury and Evans, 1844), pp. 80 f. Reprinting PP [HL] 1844 xxvi 1.

21 UK, *Report of the Metropolitan Commissioners in Lunacy to the Lord Chancellor*, Appendix (C).

22 See comments contained in *Twenty-First Annual Report of the United Committee of Visitors of the Leicestershire and Rutland Lunatic Asylum* (1869), LRO DE 3533/14, that a third of asylum admissions for 1868–9 were incurable because their case was caused by congenital defects.

23 These figures are based on the relieving officer's response to the question 'Duration of existing attack'. The analysis is reliant on the dubious assumption that the commencement of the attack was a clear point, allowing for accurate measurement of the duration.

24 This was a specific complaint made about Leicester Union in 1847 by the visiting committee of the asylum: see correspondence between Lunacy Commissioners and Poor Law Commissioners, 8 April 1847, PRO MH 12/6471. Whatever the situation in 1847, the complaint does not appear justified for the early 1860s.

25 Adm. 28 March 1862, admission documents, LRO DE 3533/228.

26 Adm. 16 Sept. 1865, admission notes, LRO DE 3533/228.

27 Admission documents, LRO DE 3533/228.

28 LRO DE 3533/187. The patient register was a list of patients compiled by the asylum clerk, chronologically by the date of admission. Its form was established by statute: see 8 & 9 Vict. c. 126 sch. G(1); 16 & 17 Vict. c. 97 sch. G(1), which provided that the cause listed was to be as

determined by the medical superintendent. As the medical superintendent also kept the casebook, these sources might reasonably be
expected to match.

29 A complete breakdown of these causes is contained in Appendix 2.
30 LRO DE 3533/190. Adm. 21 May 64.
31 Contained in Harold Garfinkel, *Studies in Ethnomethodology* (1967;
    reprinted Cambridge: Polity, 1987), p. 186.
32 David Nelken, *The Limits of Legal Process* (London: Academic Press,
    1983), pp. 132 f.
33 Smith, 'The social construction of documentary reality', *Sociological
    Inquiry*, **44**(4) (1974): 257–68, at 258.
34 Jonathan Andrews, 'Case Notes, Case Histories, and the Patient's
    Experience of Insanity at Gartnavel Royal Asylum, Glasgow, in the
    Nineteenth Century'. *Social History of Medicine* 11(2) (1998): 255.
35 As an example of this, see Bryan Green, *Knowing the Poor* (London:
    Routledge & Kegan Paul, 1983), which is a study of the 1834 and 1909
    Poor Law reports. Part of Green's argument is that the process of
    writing a Royal Commission Report had not been standardized by 1834.
    Through its fact-finding processes, the 1834 report was therefore not
    merely recording, but also justifying its own approach to the process of
    writing a report.
36 D. Smith, *Texts, Facts, and Femininity* (London: Routledge, 1990) p. 121.
37 See Jonathan Andrews, 'Case Notes, Case Histories' p. 256; Roy Porter,
    Mind-Forg'd Manacles (1987; reprinted Harmondsworth: Penguin, 1990),
    p. 211; Richard Hunter and Ida MacAlpine, *Three Hundred Years of
    Psychiatry* (London: Oxford University Press, 1963), p. 585.
38 According to Andrews, the Glasgow Royal commenced to keep case
    notes in 1816; the Royal Edinburgh Infirmary did not do so until 1840.
39 8 & 9 Vict. c. 126 s. 74; 16 & 17 Vict. c. 97 s. 90.
40 See order of Commissioners in Lunacy dated January 1846. A copy of
    this order is contained in LRO DE 3533/216.
41 Foucault, *Discipline and Punish*, trans. Alan Sheridan (New York: Random
    House, 1977), pp. 184 f.
42 Foucault, *Discipline and Punish*, p. 187.
43 Foucault, *Discipline and Punish*, p. 192.
44 The Lunacy Commissioners had, for example, included summaries by
    asylum of treatment techniques and efficacy as an appendix to the
    Supplementary Report, PP 1847 [858]; *in octavo* 1847–8 xxxii 371.
45 Porter, *Mind-Forg'd Manacles*, p. 211. The quotations are from Percival,
    Medical Ethics (Manchester: Johnson & Bickerstaff, 1803).
46 LRO DE 3533/186; admissions on 16 June 1851 and 5 April 1852.
47 LRO DE 3533/190; adm. 10 June 1861.
48 Adm. 19 April 1849. LRO DE 3533/186.
49 Foucault, *Discipline and Punish*, p. 192.
50 LRO DE 3533/185; adm. 17 June 1846.

51 LRO DE 3533/185; adm. 28 March 1845.

52 Ibid.

53 LRO DE 3533/191; adm. 28 Jan. 68. See also the case of Mary Farndon, whose discharge followed the cure of a uterine problem not mentioned at all in the relevant question in the pre-printed section of the admission notes: LRO DE 3533/185.

54 The annual reports and casebooks of the asylum indicate that between 1853 and 1868, 340 of the 1,641 admissions were readmissions. By comparison, 846 persons were discharged alive from the asylum in this period.

55 Adm. 4 Nov. 1865. LRO DE 3533/191. Bradshaw was aged 82 at the time of his admission.

56 8 & 9 Vict. c. 126 s. 74; 16 & 17 Vict. c. 97 s. 90.

57 Their rights on visitation were limited by 8 & 9 Vict. c. 126 s. 69; and 16 & 17 Vict. c. 97 s. 65.

58 See *Supplement to the Twelfth Annual Report of the Commissioners in Lunacy*, PP 1859 1st sess. (228) ix 1, for example at 11.

59 See Porter, *Mind-forg'd Manacles*, pp. 226 f. Regarding moral therapy and treatment at the York Retreat, see Anne Digby, *Madness, Morality and Medicine* (Cambridge: Cambridge University Press, 1985), Chs 3 and 4.

60 Andrew Scull has argued that the asylum superintendents defined their role in terms of management of the insane, as the nineteenth century wore on: Scull, *Museums of Madness* (1979; reprinted Harmondsworth: Penguin, 1982), particularly at Ch. 6; *Most Solitary of Afflictions* (New Haven: Yale University Press, 1993), at Ch. 6, esp. pp. 284 ff.

61 Regarding childbirth in this context, see further below.

62 Adm. 2 May 1846. Casebook LRO DE 3533/184.

63 Suzuki, 'Lunacy in seventeenth- and eighteenth-century England, Part II', *History of Psychiatry*, 3 (1992): 29, at 34.

64 Adm. 14 March 1851. Casebook LRO DE 3533/186.

65 Himmelfarb, *The Idea of Poverty* (London: Faber, 1984), p. 357.

66 LRO DE 3533/190; adm. 30 May 1863.

67 A similar argument has been made regarding eighteenth-century hysteria at the Edinburgh Infirmary: see Roy Porter, 'Divided selves and psychiatric violence', *Cycnos*, 6 (1990): 95, at 98.

68 Smith, 'K is mentally ill: the anatomy of a factual account', in *Texts, Facts, and Femininity* (London: Routledge, 1990), 12 at 44.

69 *Journal of Mental Science*, 7 (1861): 79, at 83 f.

70 LRO DE 3533/228; adm. 16 Aug. 1864.

71 LRO DE 3533/227; adm. 22 June 1861.

72 LRO DE 3533/228; adm. 30 May 1863.

73 12 Anne c. 23 (1714).

74 Sir John Comyn, *Digest of the Laws of England*, 5th edn., 8 vols, ed. Anthony Hammond (London: Strachan, 1822), Vol. 6, p. 544, pl. 3.M.22.

75 Sir Matthew Brook, *A New Abridgement of the Law*, 7th edn., 8 vols, ed. H. Gwillim (Vols 2–4) and C. Dodd (Vols 1, 5–8) (London: Strachan, 1828), Vol. 7, p. 664.

76 Robert Brook, *La Grande Abridgement*, 2 vols (n.p., 1573), 'Faux Imprisonment', pl. 28, Vol. 1, p. 330.

77 (1845), 3 Dowl & L. 373, 15 LJ (NS) MC 25 at 29 (QB).

78 Court of the Exchequer, June 1849. Quotation taken from Andrew Scull, 'The theory and practice of civil commitment', in *Social Order/Mental Disorder: Anglo-American Psychiatry in Historical Perspective* (London: Routledge, 1989), p. 280 at 283 f. Scull cites *The Times* (London), 27 June 1849, p. 7, column 5 as the source of the quotation.

79 Quoted in Andrew Scull, 'The theory and practice of civil commitment', pp. 283 f.

80 *R. v. Pinder; In re Greenwood* (1855), 24 LJ (NS) QB 148, at 151.

81 15 QB 122 (CA), at 131.

82 15 QB 122 (CA), at 132.

83 15 QB 122 (CA) at 149 f. Some mention should be made of *R. v. Ellis* (1844), 14 LJ (NS) MC 1 (QB) where Coleridge J indicates that the purpose of the asylum act was to 'provide a proper place of confinement for pauper lunatics and ... to get rid of the nuisance of the miserable parochial care to which such paupers were before left in many instances' [at 3]. This does not appear to be inconsistent with his other pronouncements, although it admittedly puts rather a different cast on them. This was not a committal case, however, and should thus not be read as defining standards of committal.

84 PP 1849 (620) xlvi 381.

85 Scull, 'Mad-doctors and magistrates: English psychiatry's struggle for professional autonomy in the nineteenth century', *Arch. Europ. Sociol.*, **17** (1976): 279, at 303 f.

86 Mellett, *The Prerogative of Asylumdom* (New York: Garland, 1982), p. 11.

87 Smith, 'K is mentally ill: the anatomy of a factual account', in *Texts, Facts, and Femininity*, p. 44. This is not an extension of the argument which would be made by Smith, who refuses to make any statement about K, her subject, beyond that which is contained in the factual account, and certainly makes no claim as to K's mental state.

88 LRO DE 3533/228; adm. 4 Sept. 1862. Hannah Osborne was apparently in charge of insane paupers at this workhouse: see admission documents of Mary Greenwood, adm. 17 Oct. 1862, where she was also quoted.

89 LRO DE 3533/228; adm. 2 Aug. 1864. 'Dirty habits' was a reference to incontinence.

90 Contained in letter from Leicester Guardians to the Poor Law Commissioners, LRO G/12/57d/1, 17 Aug. 1844.

91 Scull, *Museums of Madness*, p. 250.

92 'Quarantining the weak-minded: psychiatric definitions of degeneracy and the late-Victorian asylum', in Bynum, Porter and Shepherd (eds), *The*

Anatomy of Madness, Vol. III (London: Routledge, 1988), pp. 280 f.

93 Contained in correspondence between Barrow upon Soar Union and the Poor Law Board, PRO MH 12/6401, 28 Oct. 1858.

94 PRO MH 12/6401, #4292/59; 27 Jan. 1859.

95 LRO DE 3533/230; adm. 27 Nov. 1869.

96 LRO DE 3533/225; adm. 31 July 1852.

97 For the sceptics, it should be pointed out that there are only two other theoretically possible explanations. First, either the lengths of time insane or the dangerousness could be simply wrong, either through negligence or fraud on the part of the persons completing the documents. Negligence is unlikely, given the uniformity of both standards' appearance in the documents; and it is simply not convincing that all medical officers or relieving officers were party to a conspiracy. Alternatively, it is possible that very few people became dangerous after two or three months insane. This conflicts with the version of the Lunacy Commissioners, however, discussed below.

98 Correspondence between Barrow upon Soar Union and the Poor Law Board, PRO MH 12/6401, #16178/59, 23 April 1858.

99 Correspondence of Billesdon Union with Poor Law Board, PRO MH 12/6416, #10777/65, 24 March 1865. See also comparable comments regarding Hannah Wade, in the same place.

100 PP 1834 (44) xxvii 1, at 24.

101 PP 1834 (44) xxvii 1, at 249. The following paragraph directed the assistants as to specific matters for their investigations of treatment of the impotent, and specifically enjoined them to report on the provision made for lunatics and idiots. This use of ability to work as a reference point lasted into the twentieth century: see *Report of the Royal Commission on the Poor Laws and Relief of Distress* (majority report), PP 1909 [4499], 1 at 272.

102 Digby, *Pauper Palaces* (London: Routledge and Kegan Paul, 1978), p. 144.

103 Correspondence between Leicester Guardians and Poor Law Commissioners, LRO G/12/57b/1, 31 Oct. 1844.

104 This was the topic of a protracted correspondence between the Lunacy Commissioners and the Poor Law Commissioners, commencing with PRO MH 19/168, #1480R/47 (17 May 1847), 4748R/47 (29 May 1847), 12295/47 (28 Aug. 1847). The Poor Law Commissioners did not insist on separate identification of the insane, except as an accounting entry. The Lunacy Commissioners complained that the insane were often not distinguished from the old and infirm, or children. The Poor Law authorities did not appear to see that as problematic.

105 PP 1847 [858]; *in octavo*, 1847–48 xxxii 371, at 285.

106 PP 1847 [858]; *in octavo*, 1847–48 xxxii 371, at 239.

107 *Supplement to the Twelfth Annual Report of the Commissioners in Lunacy*, PP 1859 1st sess. (228) ix 1, at 14.

108 PP 1847 [858]; *in octavo*, 1847–48 xxxii 371, at 249n.

109 Minutes of Leicester Union Board of Guardians, LRO G/12/8a/12, for 1 and 10 Oct. 1867. Committals do not appear to have been routinely recorded in the guardians' minute book after this time.

110 See comments relating to Sarah Berrington and Samuel Bulls, correspondence between Leicester Guardians and Poor Law Commissioners, LRO G/12/57b/1 (31 Oct. 1844).

111 Leicester Board of Guardians, LRO G/12/8a/2 (13 July 1841).

112 Correspondence between Leicester Guardians and Poor Law Commissioners, LRO G/12/57b/1, 31 Oct. 1844.

113 William Cunningham Glen, *The Consolidated and other Orders of the Poor Law Commissioners and the Poor Law Board*, 4th edn., (London: Butterworth, 1859), pp. 58 ff.

114 Pamphlet contained in correspondence between Leicester Union Guardians and Poor Law Commissioners, PRO MH 12/2471, at 9 f. (30 March 1845).

CHAPTER 6

The Lunacy Commissioners and the soft centre of reform

The 1845 legislation created the Commissioners in Lunacy as a permanent central authority, with a national mandate. While this body provides the modern historian with a wealth of printed and manuscript sources, it was in a position of administrative and political weakness regarding the Poor Law of lunacy. It received minimal formal enforcement powers for county asylums or other Poor Law institutions. Politically, the Commission was threatened by the same resentment of centralization as the Poor Law Commissioners, and the same ideological conflicts between Benthamite utilitarianism, evangelicalism and paternalism. Unlike the Poor Law central authorities, it never developed a new orthodoxy as its guiding principle: there was nothing which corresponded to the 'principles of 1834' for the Lunacy Commission. Instead, it adopted a variety of bureaucratic responses: gentle persuasion of local officials, alliance and coexistence with the Poor Law central authorities and the provision of masses of statistical and other information in their annual reports. It does not follow that they were ineffectual; instead, they were strong on pragmatics and weak on broad policy objectives.

Reflecting its origins as the Metropolitan Commissioners in Lunacy, the Commission's prime function lay in inspecting, regulating and licensing private madhouses in the London area. The 1845 mandate also included such inspection and regulation (but not licensing) of private facilities nationally.[1] The Commissioners' powers regarding county asylums were much more limited. They were to receive the building plans for capital projects, but could merely comment on them; approval lay with the Home Secretary.[2] Similarly, they could inspect and comment on any contracts between the Justices and private

197

madhouse keepers for the care of pauper lunatics; but intervention lay with the Home Secretary.[3] They never had any formal power to approve or amend the rules for the government of county asylums, nor employment of staff, although they were required from 1853 onwards to be informed of the circumstances surrounding any dismissals of nurses or attendants.[4] Commencing in 1853, they received all asylum annual accounts, but this appears to be not primarily for scrutiny, but merely for tabulation and presentation to Parliament.[5] They also, beginning in 1853, had a formal power to prosecute offences under the County Asylums Act,[6] but the expense of such prosecutions and the limited financial and personal resources of the Commissioners made such prosecutions a rarity. They also, of course, inspected county asylums annually, generally in pairs. They published reports of these visits in their annual reports, but otherwise lacked any practical mechanism to enforce any improvements they believed necessary.

With regard to admissions and discharges, the Commissioners were in a similarly weak position. The statutes required that they receive copies of a variety of documents: lists of county asylum inmates, lists of pauper insane inside and outside asylums and admission documents,[7] yet these were coupled with minimal powers of intervention. In 1853, they did receive statutory authority to allow the amendment of inadequate admission documents,[8] but it was only in 1862 that they received explicit statutory power to discharge persons confined in county asylums on inadequate forms.[9] Otherwise, they never had authority to discharge a pauper from a county asylum, and it was only in 1862 that the Commissioners received the power themselves to obtain a medical certificate and admit a pauper lunatic to a county lunatic asylum.[10] When this latter power was obtained, it was rarely, if indeed ever, used, due both to limited personal resources at the Commission, and the generally conciliatory approach they followed.

The Commissioners' involvement in the other aspects of the Poor Law of lunacy was even more tenuous. Their official mandate in 1842 had been to examine only county asylums, hospitals containing insane persons and private madhouses; they had added union workhouses to their task at their own initiative. While they did receive inspection powers for workhouses from in 1845, they received no formal authority over them. It was not until 1862 that they could remove paupers from a workhouse to the asylum and even then their order was subject to appeal by the guardians to the Home Secretary.[11]

It was not merely a lack of legal authority that limited the

Commissioners' influence. It was also a lack of staff, and while the Commissioners professed a particular concern for the care of pauper lunatics, institutions for them occupied by no means all of their time. The madhouse statutes required charitable hospitals to be visited by two Commissioners, twice annually. These statutes also required two Commissioners to visit provincial madhouses twice annually, and metropolitan madhouses four times per year.[12] Between the 1830s and 1870, the number of provincial madhouses varied between 64 and 100, and the number of metropolitan houses from 39 to 47. For these private and charitable facilities, the Lunacy Commission did not have a mere inspection function; they actually had enforcement powers. They had the authority to liberate patients, a power they were cautious about exercising, but which carried significant symbolic weight. They were also the licensing authority for metropolitan madhouses.[13] By comparison, county asylums were to be visited annually, by two Commissioners. At Leicester, these visits normally lasted two days. Workhouses were normally visited by one Commissioner only, and while those with large lunatic populations might be visited annually, the usual routine involved a visit once every three years.

The Commission contained six paid Commissioners, being three medical professionals and three barristers, who did the bulk of the inspections. For these six, the workload was considerable. In the six months ending 4 February 1858, for example, the six professional Commissioners each made an average of 115 visits, seeing 5,717 patients and travelling 3,394 miles.[14] The remaining Commissioners seem to have had no more than mixed enthusiasm for the day-to-day grind of inspections. Even Lord Shaftesbury, their chairman and most visible advocate, cannot be considered a zealot in his lunacy duties. He apparently ceased completely to perform inspections himself in the 1860s,[15] some 20 years before he ceased to chair the Commission. His mammoth biography by Findlayson does not suggest an obsession with lunacy issues. For the critical period between 1842 and 1845, Findlayson portrays Shaftesbury as interested in the ten-hours movement to the near exclusion of everything else; the Commissioners' 1844 report and the 1845 Acts merit only a brief mention. His involvement otherwise seems to have been limited primarily to weekly meetings on Monday afternoons, appointments he seems to have been relatively faithful at keeping, but a time commitment he at least occasionally resented.[16]

The temptation is therefore to discount the Commission completely regarding administration of the Poor Law of lunacy. In a sense, the case is stronger than Bartrip makes out for the factories and mines inspectorates.[17] Bartrip's argument is based on these inspectors having minimal efficacy due to their small scale. Here, the issue is not merely a relatively small inspectorate, but minimal legal powers as well.

Certainly, it would be inappropriate to focus on the Lunacy Commission as central to the operation of the Poor Law of lunacy. In terms of the actual functioning of the system, they were largely an administrative sideshow. They did do their best to influence matters, however, and in this regard a basic division of techniques can be identified. In their routine administrative operations, both with the Poor Law central authorities and local administrators, they attempted to build alliances. This is in contrast to their annual and special reports, which were directed first and foremost to their funder, the government, in an attempt not merely to further the reform of the institutions for the insane, but also to consolidate, or at least maintain, their own involvement in the administration of the system. In addition, these reports provided something of a public face for the Commission, again resulting in different discursive pressures.

As important was the fact that the Commission was a part of a process of reconceptualizing county asylums from essentially local institutions, to a national system. Their function in this context was consistent with developments in other quarters, such as the establishment of an organization of asylum superintendents in 1841. The Commission's work was a further step in the same direction. The simple fact of national inspections, and annual reports in which the various institutions were described together, gave the asylums an identity as a system. Individual institutions could be compared, and one set of standards could apply. That step away from a conception of the asylum as a distinctly local institution does represent a change.

STRUCTURAL DIFFICULTIES AND RESPONSES

The structure and composition of the Lunacy Commission itself did not promote a united front. Unlike the Poor Law central authorities, where a staff of inspectors reported to a board of three Commissioners who were responsible for policy-making, the Lunacy Commission included the inspectors on the board itself. This brought the policy-making into the hands of the people actually seeing conditions in local facilities, a system defended by Shaftesbury on the basis that it provided the inspectors with increased respect and authority at the local level. It also meant a much larger board, with consequently increased possibilities of internal conflict. Eighteen men signed the 1844 report. The 1845 Act appointed 11 Commissioners,[18] and the possibility for divergent attitudes to policy formulation corresponded to these larger numbers. Hervey details the diversity of the group, from former asylum superintendents (such as Gaskell and Wilkes); to private medical men with little knowledge or interest in lunacy but great evangelical zeal (Nairne); to those concerned about civil rights and wrongful committal (Pritchard); to those favouring centralized control (Shaftesbury and Gordon); to those favouring local control (Myle).[19]

This degree of diversity did not promote a uniform approach to issues. There does not even appear to have been a consensus on how insanity was to be understood. Shaftesbury had what Hervey describes as a 'loose and popular perspective' of madness. Much of it he related to intemperance, but at other times he apparently ascribed it to commercial speculation or railway travel.[20] At issue here is not a simple division between medical and non-medical views, for part of the prevailing medical thought was also that the pressures of civilization caused insanity.[21] Instead there were a spectrum of opinions about contextualization both within and outside the medical community. Thus there was no doubt in Shaftesbury's mind that alcohol was a cause of insanity among the poor: 'one half, and perhaps more, of the cases of insanity that prevail among the poorer classes arise from their habit of intoxication.'[22] In this view medical opinion concurred,[23] but while there is nothing to suggest that the evangelical Shaftesbury saw this in other than moral terms, there was apparently not a consensus within the Medico-Psychological Association as to whether intemperance was a moral vice or a medical illness.[24]

As a result, the Lunacy Commission, unlike the Poor Law central authority, never had a coherent ideological base. The tensions lay at the base of the Lunacy Commissioners' view of the asylum itself. At times, it adopted a medical approach: the asylum was about cure, or at least professional medical care. At other times, it was an institution to control the behaviour of the inmate. The basic dichotomy is identified by Peter McCandless:

The Victorians never clearly established what they meant by 'wrongful' confinement. At times they seemed to mean the confinement of the sane; at other times they seemed to include those who were insane but were not manifestly dangerous.[25]

In the county asylum system, the division was still more complicated. Even where the appropriate criterion for admission to the asylum was acknowledged to be other than dangerousness, there was no consensus as to whether the asylum was for all the insane, for the curable only or for the unmanageable. Thus the 1844 report had encouraged the removal of incurable insane people from asylums, to make way for the curable cases.[26] This approach occurred sporadically throughout the period under study. This focus on curability placed insanity squarely within the medical context, as is clear from the following quotation from the 1844 report:

The clause which is supposed to sanction the confinement in Workhouses of lunatics, without adverting to the probability of their being curable or not, provided they be not dangerous, is, in our opinion, impolitic, and open to serious objection. Although a patient may not be violent or raving, he may require medical treatment, and it is at the beginning of attacks of insanity, when the causes of the disease are in most powerful operation, and the symptoms are developing themselves, that the skill of a medical officer experienced in this disease is most required.[27]

The criterion of cure fell at the intersection of a variety of themes. It was not merely humanitarian, although it certainly had that appeal, but was also appealing to the utilitarian and economic desires to reduce rates and eliminate pauperism, for an insane person who recovered might cease to be a burden on the rates.[28] The focus on medical concepts is also consistent with the Commissioners' policy of alliance-building, and it reflected the medical component of their own membership. Hervey, who emphasizes the importance of the asylum as a curative facility in his study of the Lunacy Commission, also identifies a paternalist element:

Shaftesbury knew Southey and Coleridge personally, as did Prichard and Procter, and all these men believed fervently in a Tory paternalism which carried with it social obligations to provide for the poor and disadvantaged. Shaftesbury and a number of other Commissioners saw the provision of a nationwide system of public asylums very much in this light, but also social reforms were perceived as a medium for diffusing or pre-empting civil unrest. In 1831 Southey wrote to Shaftesbury saying that whatever government was in office, it must endeavour to better the condition of the people: 'this must be amended or we perish'.[29]

The focus on cure and care rather than confinement of dangerousness certainly reflected this paternalist element, while the comment regarding perishing is reminiscent of Benthamite concerns about security.

It is an open question how convincing all this language of cure was. There was also the inescapable sense in the Commission's annual reports that people were not being cured. Notwithstanding optimistic language, these reports were from the beginning justifications for failure. The 1844 report began the litany, emphasizing that the reason people were not being cured in asylums was that they were full of incurable cases, precluding curable cases from admission.[30] This complaint would continue for decades. Recent scholarship has argued that this vision of the asylum as a therapeutic failure is inaccurate,[31] but this misses the point: contemporary observers, including the Commissioners themselves, saw little cure happening.

At the same time, the Lunacy Commission portrayed itself as a guardian against wrongful committal, and of the civil rights of the inmates. This was one of the factors which distinguished workhouse from asylum accommodation, for in the former the Commissioners claimed that the inmate became 'a prisoner for life, incapable of asserting his rights, often of signifying his wants, yet amenable to as much punishment as if he were perfectly sane, and a willing offender against the laws and regulations of the place'.[32] When portraying the asylum in a medical context, the civil libertarian role was downplayed: the asylum was about cure, not civil rights. The Commissioners went so far as to publish an open letter objecting to the dangerousness standard of confinement, following the Nottidge case in 1849.[33] There was none the less considerable concern regarding wrongful committal in Victorian times. The 1859 Select Committee on Lunacy heard four witnesses from the Alleged Lunatics' Friend Society, a society devoted to publicizing cases of wrongful confinement and amending the laws of lunacy.

Yet the Commissioners can hardly be understood as steadfast in their policy. Their exercise of their authority to release individuals from private facilities did not at all resemble their repudiation of the dangerousness standard, noted above. Instead, they exercised this authority on the following terms:

Without laying down any precise rule on the subject, we have assumed, as a general principle for our guidance, that wherever a man of ordinary intellect is able so to conduct himself, that he is not likely to do injury in person or property, to himself or others, he is unfit to continue as the inmate of a Lunatic Asylum.[34]

There is no obvious way to reconcile this comment with the statement emphasizing the medical nature of the asylum also drawn from the 1844 report, except for context: in the first statement, advocacy of asylum care was at issue; in the second one, it was civil rights.[35]

THE LUNACY COMMISSION AND THE POOR LAW OF LUNACY

Similar contradictions pervaded the views of the Commissioners as they encountered their work in Poor Law terms. On one hand, they were keen to expand the application of county asylums to include a class who were not strictly paupers, suggesting a relatively egalitarian framework; on the other, they favoured the construction of simple buildings because it was paupers who would live in them, and they favoured the segregation of private from pauper patients.

At times, consistent with humanitarian paternalist influences, the Lunacy Commissioners appear to have portrayed the asylum as a place of gentility, removed from the hard strictures of the Poor Law. They did not approve of a restrictive interpretation being placed on the definition of 'pauper' under the County Asylum Acts. In their *Ninth Annual Report*, they comment on the practice of admitting to the asylum persons not previously in receipt of parish relief, who were 'not infrequently tradesmen, or thriving artisans', upon their families reimbursing the parish. They spoke favourably of the practice, and argued for its legality, so long as the entire cost of maintenance was not reimbursed:

It should, however, be borne in mind, that the language of the statute, the interpretation clause of which defines the term 'pauper' to mean 'every person maintained wholly or in part by, or chargeable to any parish, union, or county,' seems to countenance, if it does not actually justify the practice; and that to insist upon a rigid observance of a different rule would, in most cases, either compel the party interposing, if legally liable for the maintenance of the lunatic, to throw himself as well as the patient on the parish for support, or where he was not so liable, would induce him to decline undertaking any portion of the burden.[36]

They also spoke of the middle classes reduced to poverty by the lunacy of the family breadwinner. In these situations, the family was seen to pay for care until their assets were depleted, at which point the insane person would be transferred to the county asylum: 'This is the main reason why, in our Pauper Lunatic Asylums, many inmates are to be met with who have formerly held a respectable station in society, and who, in point of education and manners, are greatly superior to the inmates of a workhouse.'[37] This class in turn was used to justify a higher standard of accommodation in the asylum than for ordinary paupers in the workhouse.[38]

At the same time, an institution was not to include both private and pauper patients. The Metropolitan Commissioners had been sceptical of this system as practised in some county asylums in their 1844 report, on the basis that such mixed asylums compromised care of paupers by restricting access to much of the buildings and airing grounds.[39] By the late 1850s, the rationale had changed: paupers were to be housed separately from private patients for reasons of order, the paupers posing a threat to the good behaviour of the private patient.[40]

Even the 1849 letter responding to *Nottidge*, with its emphasis on broad confinement on medical models, understood the consequences of inadequate asylum provision differently as between paupers and private patients. For private patients, the issues were not merely annoyance to the families and the lack of cure, but also the exposure of the family of the insane person to violent conduct. This was particularly lamentable 'where there are children, whose minds might receive a shock, and perhaps be incurably injured, by continually witnessing the paroxysms or maniacal extravagances of a lunatic'.[41] The patient, also, deserved protection from the prying eyes of the household and the neighbourhood, and for all concerned, the immoral habits of the women patients and the filthy habits of all these insane people ought to be shielded from general observation. The concerns regarding pauper patients are quite different:

In respect to pauper lunatics, it has already been the subject of almost universal complaint, that the number of such lunatics has been multiplied, and the country burthened to a prodigious amount, because the poorer class of lunatics have been allowed to remain at large, or kept in workhouses, deprived of that medical treatment which a lunatic establishment properly managed is best calculated to afford, until their malady has become incurable.

The misery to the lunatics' families, and the great cost to the various parishes and counties consequent on this course, it would be difficult to exaggerate.[42]

For the private patients, the concern was the emotional burden on the family, and the protection of private morality; for the pauper patients, the concern was the public threat of increasing numbers and expense.

The Lunacy Commissioners were perceived as a check on extravagant construction, and to that end they emphasized the pauper clientele of the asylum. In their 1844 report, for example, they argue that no unnecessary cost ought to be spent on decoration, 'especially as these Asylums are erected for persons who, when in health, are accustomed to dwell in cottages'.[43] Dormitories were to be substituted for single sleeping rooms in part because they 'better accord with the pauper's previous habits' than sleeping alone. Single rooms were to be used only for the violent, noisy and mischievous, and for those in the throes of paroxysm.[44] The construction of buildings considered lavish might result in criticism for extravagance, as did the Leicester Borough Asylum in 1870.[45]

The Commissioners also favoured the removal of pauper patients from private madhouses.[46] This movement did occur; smaller proportions of pauper insane were sent to private facilities as the century progressed, although it is difficult to tell how much of this was the result of the Commissioners' involvement, since if Leicester provides a typical example, the private madhouse became more expensive than county asylum care in the period under study.[47]

The belief in the opposition of the Lunacy Commissioners to the care of the insane in workhouses is almost dogmatic in the history of madness. The following comment of David Mellett is typical:

The singlemindedness of the Commissioners, closely linked to their unshakable faith in the asylum, and circumscribed by the letter of the law, was nowhere more in evidence than in their campaign against workhouse detention of the insane.[48]

The image is of the crusaders for humanitarian care battling against parsimonious local authorities for the removal of the poor insane to places where decent accommodation and treatment might be offered. In prior accounts, here were the Commissioners at their reforming best.

The documents would suggest that their position was not nearly so simple. Certainly, there were times when the Commissioners could be critical. Chief among these was their special report in 1859, discussed at some length below. Other indications are that the Commissioners were broadly supportive of workhouse care. In the 1840s, they had recommended large-scale transfers to workhouses from asylums,[49] and their 1847 special report to the Poor Law Commissioners was in no way critical of such accommodation. The bulk of the inmates at that time were described as 'those who from birth or from an early period of life have exhibited a marked deficiency of intellect as compared with the ordinary measure of understanding among persons of the same age and station', and they were held to be rightly kept in the workhouse:

For the most part they are harmless, tractable, and readily disposed to work; and with a little encouragement and superintendence from the Master or Matron often become extremely industrious and useful.... So long as persons of this kind are kept within the precincts and subject to the discipline of the Workhouse, they conduct themselves well, and require slight degree of supervision. But when that supervision is withdrawn, and they are left at large to mix freely with their fellows in the ordinary intercourse of life, they are unable to resist the temptations that beset them; advantage is often taken of their weakness by the knavish and the profligate; and they are exposed to, and many commit, very serious mischief.[50]

They estimated there to be 6,000 insane people in workhouses, 'not more than a few hundreds – probably not a tenth of the whole, [being] proper persons to be *confined*, in the narrow and technical sense of the term, that is to say, as patients in a Lunatic Asylum',[51] and a much smaller number suitable to be left at large. Specialized wards for lunatics were spoken of not unfavourably:

[T]he patients are placed under attendants of their own, and have a more liberal dietary allowed to them, and where, except that they cannot have the benefit of much outdoor exercise or occupation, they receive all the advantages, as well as all the medical care, which could be usefully bestowed on them in a chronic lunatic hospital.[52]

While refusing to approve of such wards explicitly, given their status as appended to workhouses and the consequent legal difficulties of confining persons therein, the Commissioners did allow that such wards had 'undoubtedly in some instances afforded a seasonable and salutary relief to County Asylums, as well as to the Workhouses themselves'.[53]

At other points, the Lunacy Commission was admittedly much more critical, as in the following passage, from Lord Shaftesbury's testimony before the 1859 Select Committee:

[I]n every instance of a chronic patient going back to the workhouse, he has declined in health and appearance, for in fact they require to be placed in a totally different position, to undergo different kinds of treatment, and to be put upon different sorts of diet; in every instance of a chronic patient being sent back to the workhouse, he has declined.[54]

Indeed, the workhouse was sometimes perceived as itself a cause of madness in the poor:

The result is, that detention in Workhouses not only deteriorates the more harmless and imbecile cases to which they are not unsuited, but has the tendency to render chronic and permanent such as might have yielded to early care. The one class, no longer associating with the other inmates but congregated in separate wards, rapidly degenerate into a condition requiring all the attendance and treatment to be obtained only in a well-regulated Asylum; and the others, presenting originally every chance of recovery, but finding none of its appliances or means, rapidly sink into that almost hopeless state which leaves them generally for life a burden on their parishes. Nor can a remedy be suggested so long as this Workhouse system continues.[55]

At the same time, the Commissioners complained of paupers being sent from workhouses to the asylums, as in the following extract from their *Eleventh Annual Report* regarding Hanwell and Colney Hatch, the two Middlesex county asylums:

Making allowance for the actual spread of the disorder, and also for the advantage not unlikely to have been taken of such Asylums to find room therein for Patients not absolutely Paupers, it does not admit of any reasonable doubt that both buildings have been too much crowded with inmates who ought not to have been sent to either; and that, instead of continuing to be used as hospitals for the treatment, these expensive structures are in danger of being turned into mere houses for the safe custody of the Insane. Hardly had they been built, when into each the Workhouses sent such large numbers of chronic cases, as at once necessarily excluded the more immediately curable until the stage of cure was almost passed; and the doors of both these Establishments became virtually closed, not long after they were opened, to the very inmates for whom only it was needful to have made such costly provision.[56]

Here again, there was no consistency. Unlike the Poor Law central authorities, who by and large attempted to formulate coherent and consistent policy, the Lunacy Commissioners were reactive. Their responses were often determined by pragmatic considerations, tending to be based on the specifics of situations rather than general policy. It does not follow that they were ineffectual; but their successes were through a process of incrementalism at the local level, brought on through the quiet techniques of persuasion in individual circumstances, rather than the hard selling of broad ideology.

THE LUNACY COMMISSIONERS AND LOCAL RELATIONS

As Nicholas Hervey has argued, the Lunacy Commission pursued a conciliatory style with the local officials.[57] In their role as a local inspectorate, the Commissioners should be understood less as enforcers than as attempting to establish working relationships with local officials. Perhaps of necessity, as they had minimal legal power, their efforts were not through legal fiat, but persuasion. In this, the Commissioners' approach resembled the techniques used by other inspectorates. Esther Moir explains:

It was most important for the development of happy relations between central and local governments that the inspectors were the sort of men who could generally command the respect of the magistrates. They were very far from bureaucratic civil servants; in fact they formed almost a new intelligentsia. The great majority of them (the total was 140) came from the upper ranks of the middle class: mostly the sons of country gentry or professional men. Among the assistant Poor Law Commissioners, for example, eight were magistrates themselves, and many others owned or managed landed property. They upheld the same orthodoxies as the body of men who formed the Bench of Justices, not least a sturdy Christianity and a deeply rooted moral code which emphasized 'character', and which would scorn to use its powers for unworthy ends.[58]

Roberts speaks of this as a foundation of the revitalized nineteenth-century paternalism: 'One of the greatest forces within the politics of paternalism that led to a stronger paternal government was ... the actual existence of a paternal government and of men in that paternal government who wanted it to grow stronger.'[59] The strategy was to form a moral partnership between local administrators and central government. The image is not one of confrontation, but of alliance; of players not manipulated by autocracy, but through diplomatic approaches. The development and implementation of policy was not through legal strong-arm tactics, but through webs of influence.

The success and effectiveness of this approach is difficult to assess. In Leicestershire and Rutland, both the asylum and the workhouses received generally favourable reports, and perhaps as a result there is no indication of antagonism between the local authorities and the Commissioners. These inspection reports may be perceived as part of the alliance-building objective of the Commissioners, however. The approach appears to have been one of incremental improvement. The reports offered general praise, followed up by a suggestion to make the institution just that little bit better. The asylum reports, for example, usually began with general praise, typically that the inmates were 'remarkably quiet and orderly'. Numbers attending church were cited with approval. The 1854 report went on to praise increased employment offered to the patients, but lamented the need for a better chapel and wash-house. In 1855, particular praise was accorded the number of inmates taking exercise, but an increase in furnishings was suggested. In 1856, it was a few too many women in seclusion. In 1858, the introduction of washstands was particularly praised, and insufficient bathwater criticized.[60]

Surviving documents do not provide direct insight into how local officials viewed these reports, although their inclusion in the asylum annual reports starting in 1854 may suggest some pride, and consequent success of the Commissioners at the establishment of a working relationship. Various suggestions of the Commissioners were carried into effect: wooden floors replaced stone ones, additional employment was provided for inmates, furnishings were upgraded. The Commissioners were not always successful, however. Perhaps consistent with the asylum being a Poor Law institution, their recommendation that a house for the patients be acquired at the seaside fell on deaf ears.[61] Complaints about more than one individual using the same bathwater were raised in 1858; the problem remained in 1867.[62]

The events surrounding the appointment of an assistant medical officer suggests that it may not have been the Justices on the visiting committee, but rather the medical superintendent who was blocking the recommendations. The appointment of such an individual had been recommended by the Lunacy Commissioners in their reports of 1864 and 1865. The visiting committee noted that no reason had been given for the request, and in fact that the Commissioners had been firm in their praise of the running of the asylum. The medical superintendent, John Buck, had been clear in 1858 that he wanted no assistant,[63] and his mind had not been changed since that time. He specifically did not complain of the onerousness of his duties, and indicated that it was some of the duties of the head attendant which he would transfer to an assistant superintendent, if one were hired. What is particularly astonishing is that Buck stated he would only recommend the appointment of an assistant, if he (Buck) were given a new house separate from the asylum building, an expense which, not surprisingly, the visiting committee did not think it could justify.[64] It seems a reasonable surmise that Buck saw the appointment of an assistant as a threat to his authority or prestige in the institution. It is fair to wonder whether the Commissioners' statement the following year, that 'the duties imposed upon the Medical Superintendent in this large Asylum cannot be fully performed with justice to himself, and due regard to the medical treatment of the patients, by any one individual however zealous and efficient'[65] was to convince the Justices or the medical superintendent himself.[66]

The incrementalist approach can also be seen in the Commissioners' dealings with workhouses in Leicestershire. A couple of examples will demonstrate the similarity between the Commissioners' asylum and workhouse reports, and of the responses of the local officials. The following are the comments regarding the Leicester workhouse wards, the largest in the county, contained in the report of the visit of the Lunacy Commissioner in 1854:

There are at present 42 patients in this Workhouse, all of whom are kept separate from the other inhabitants of the establishment. Each sex has a separate day room + bed rooms and are under the care of Attendants (a man and his Wife) who receive regular pay. The rooms were clean, at the time of our visit, the clothing of the patients good, and the bedding clean and sufficient.

We learned, on enquiry, that a large proportion of the patients of each sex are taken out, once or twice a week, for a walk into the Country adjoining the Town of Leicester. With the exception of a few Women, who are occupied in needlework, none of the patients appear to be employed. We strongly recommend that all who are capable of work, men as well as Women, should have the means of employment placed before them, and be induced to occupy themselves as much as possible. No patient is subjected to mechanical restraint, but two of them (hereinafter mentioned) are fastened in their rooms at night. The Attendants have each some hand-straps in their possession, which we have desired to be given up to the custody of the Master of the Workhouse.[67]

The straps were promptly removed from the attendants, and work was introduced for the insane inmates. Women were given sewing and household work; men were to pick worsted or cotton waste:

This employment is simple without being too monotonous, and as the patients are capable the Guardians propose to employ them in other work, care being taken that it shall be of as an agreeable character as possible.[68]

The following report of Commissioner Campbell's visit to the Billesdon workhouse was typical of reports of smaller Leicestershire workhouses:

I have examined the insane and idiotic inmates. There are 5 men and 2 women. They are all quiet, harmless cases, and seem to be kindly treated. Thomas Jordan is very feeble from repeated attacks of epilepsy, and I recommend that a proper leaning arm-chair should be provided for his use.[69]

The report of Assistant Poor Law Commissioner Robert Weale's visit to the workhouse on 15 February the following year indicates that the chair had been provided.[70]

Even when the Commissioners were more proactive, their approach might reflect the categorical structures of the local officials. Thus in assessing the appropriateness of the retention of insane individuals in workhouses, the issue reduced to behaviour. According to his testimony before the 1859 Select Committee, Lunacy Commissioner Robert Lutwidge stated that he had found the records at Barnstaple Union sufficiently bad that he had interviewed everyone in the workhouse.

[2227.] ... I found there eight persons who were decidedly of unsound mind, and incapable of taking care of themselves; one a decided lunatic, labouring under delusions, who was digging for the bones of her brother; she fancied she had a great number of children, and that she was pursued and persecuted, and she had been so insane for upwards of six months; upon my representation, she was removed to an asylum.

* * *

2229. With regard to the other seven cases, what was done? – They were left there, because they were a perfectly harmless and quiet class; and because there is really not adequate accommodation in an asylum for a great number who we think would be better in asylums than in workhouses. I did not recommend, under the circumstances, that they should be sent to an asylum, because they were associated with the other paupers in the workhouse, and they might, in one sense, be properly retained there.[71]

Conspicuous by its absence was any discussion of the prospect of cure. The claim that the seven were not removed to the asylum for reasons of space must be viewed somewhat critically. Barnstaple Union was in Devon, where John Bucknill superintended the county asylum. Bucknill had testified two weeks earlier that 'we never shut our gates; we have always admitted all patients who have been brought there with proper admission papers'.[72] Bucknill's comment should not be taken

212

completely uncritically either: given that he was advocating the virtues of asylum care, the philanthropic image of placing care above convenience may have had a propaganda effect. More relevant is that Lutwidge's justification for choosing which paupers to send involved an assessment of which were disruptive and which were harmless and quiet, manageable in the sense sometimes criticized by the Commission, in their more public discourses.

This is consistent with the justifications offered when the Lunacy Commissioners on rare occasions did exercise the power granted to them in 1862 to remove an individual from the workhouse to the asylum, as the following example contained in their *Seventeenth Annual Report* shows:

It appeared from the correspondence which took place that the idiot was so destructive, dirty, and troublesome, that the Guardians had applied to the Justices in Petty Sessions for an order for his removal to an Asylum, but the Bench had refused the order, on the ground that he was not a dangerous lunatic, although it was shown that his habits were most filthy, that he was quite unmanageable, and that he greatly disturbed the other inmates of the house.[73]

The practices of the Lunacy Commission therefore suggest that dangerousness and manageability were significant factors in their administrative policy. There is a congruence here with the practices identified in the last chapter, where the decision as to whether or not the individual was insane was not distinguishable from the assessment of the behaviour of the individual. This further reinforces the image of the Commissioners in their local dealings as working largely within the framework of the local views.

THE LUNACY COMMISSION AND THE POOR LAW CENTRAL AUTHORITIES

The circumstances of the development of the Poor Law left the Poor Law of lunacy as a jurisdiction split between central authorities. The Poor Law central authorities were to oversee the Poor Law staff, and thus those responsible for much of the admission process. The Poor Law central authority and the Lunacy Commission each had inspection powers over workhouses, while the Lunacy Commission had exclusive inspection powers over county asylums and those lunatics, including paupers, lodged in private madhouses. The Lunacy Commissioners and the central Poor Law authorities thus had to make working arrangements with each other. Hervey portrays the relations between the two central authorities as unproductive, if not antagonistic: 'In a classic case of divided responsibility, it proved easy for the Poor Law authorities at central and local level to collude in obstructing the Commission.'[74]

This portrays the Poor Law administration and the local authorities too much in the role of villains. There were certainly tensions between the two central authorities; this was perhaps inevitable given their overlapping jurisdictions. The involvement of the Lunacy Commission in asylum inspection in the mid-1840s was in part a political challenge to the new Poor Law. The Metropolitan Commissioners had expressed a particular interest in pauper lunacy, an interest reflected in their 1844 report, and in their work after they received their national mandate. It is thus not unreasonable to expect a certain friction. The result was not simple antagonism, however, but a development of routine bureaucratic relations, threatened only briefly in the late 1850s.[75]

As discussed in Chapter 3, the Poor Law central authorities were not generally antagonistic to county asylum ideals. They had been aware of problems regarding pauper lunacy well before the Lunacy Commission received its national mandate in the 1840s. In 1835, Assistant Poor Law Commissioner William Gilbert wrote to the Poor Law Commission advocating an extended county asylum system in the strongest terms. His advocacy for the large-scale removal of mechanical restraint, which he had seen at Hanwell and Lincoln asylums, was in terms at least as favourable as the Lunacy Commission would use nine years later:

Of late years the subject of lunatic treatment has attracted great public attention and some humane and intelligent men have brought all their energies, talents and humanity to the task of relieving the calamities of that large portion of the human race. Amongst these stands pre-eminently the name of the great 'Pinel', who threw open the doors of the 'Bicêtre' to the unfortunate inmates and with one bold stroke removed from their limbs the chains + fetters which they had borne for years, and which in many cases had worn through the flesh to the very bones. Since that period his example has been followed in France, and gentle treatment and kind management substituted for fetters, whips and dungeons.[76]

He cited France, Germany and Prussia, where nationwide systems of asylums were said to be in place. He himself proposed to organize unions to this end.[77] His scheme did not proceed, but the Poor Law central authorities continued to recommend the removal of pauper lunatics to county asylums on a regular basis.

The Poor Law Commission and Board were similarly not blind to the issues surrounding lunatics in workhouses. They perused the returns of lunatics forwarded to their office from the local authorities, and in dubious cases sought further information from the clerk of the board of guardians to ensure that the individual ought not properly be in an asylum. The number of cases where they acted in this manner was small. In 1842, 115 inquiries were addressed to the guardians, with 11 persons eventually removed to the asylum; in 1843, 137 inquiries resulted in 24 removals. In their *Tenth Annual Report* (1844), they commented:

We are aware that such inquiries by letter are far from being sufficient in themselves or satisfactory in all their results; and we feel, moreover, that the number of county asylums in England is still so small in proportion to the wants of the country, that the necessary facilities for affording the best treatment to the lunatic poor are not given. We have, in our former Reports adverted to this state of things, and we have expressed our regret at the deficiency.[78]

Nor did this practice cease when the Lunacy Commission achieved its national mandate. The Leicestershire and Rutland examples show continued and persistent inquiries regarding people believed by the central Poor Law authority to be better placed in the asylum.[79] A point of contact can be seen here with the Poor Law local authorities in the documents discussed above: inquiries were sent regarding those listed on returns as dangerous but not in the asylum, and those living alone on outdoor relief. While their success at obtaining removals to the asylum remained limited, there is no reason to doubt the good faith of their attempts.

The Poor Law Commissioners were instead generally supportive of county asylums. Their instructional letter to the boards of guardians in 1842 stated that dangerous lunatics ought to be detained in workhouses only for such time as was 'necessary for taking the steps preparatory to his removal to a county Lunatic Asylum, or Licensed house',[80] presumably well under the 14 days the lunatic could be held in the workhouse by law. Consistent with the opinion of the Law Officers of the Crown, the instructional letter noted that insane paupers who were not dangerous could legally be kept in the workhouse, but it was sceptical of this practice.[81]

Bureaucratic sibling rivalry was perhaps inevitable with the introduction of the national mandate of the Lunacy Commission in 1845. In general, however, there were greater pressures for bureaucratic accommodation and co-operation. This flowed not merely from the general nature of bureaucracies, but also from the precariousness of centralized administration itself. Centralized government was by no means a foregone conclusion in the mid-nineteenth century, and a row between central authorities ran the risk of causing the collapse of both in a triumph of regionalism. The Poor Law and lunacy central authorities were influenced by similar collections of utilitarians, evangelicals and paternalists, suggesting affinities in political outlook. Thus Chadwick and Shaftesbury were apparently able to work together quite effectively on public health issues.[82] Tensions between the two bodies there may have been, but there were no irreconcilable differences.

Rather than covert challenges, relations between the two central authorities were marked generally by mutual support and administrative etiquette. The Poor Law Commissioners adopted strong interpretations of the 1845 lunacy legislation and instructed medical officers and boards of guardians accordingly. They rather tersely drew the attention of the medical officers to the punitive clauses for failing to report paupers as soon as they became lunatic:

And if any medical officer shall return any *such pauper* in any list as fit to be at large, or shall knowingly sign any such list, *untruly* setting forth any of the particulars required by this Act, he shall, for every such offence, forfeit any sum not less than *ten*, and not exceeding *fifty* pounds.[83]

The admission processes were portrayed in the letter to boards of guardians as permitting no discretion, from the medical officer to the Justice, as it related to pauper lunatics settled in the union. The duties of the medical officer regarding returns of insane persons, and the penalties accruing to the medical officers for making false statements, were detailed clearly.[84] Circular letters were dispatched to the guardians following all significant changes in the law in this period,[85] and the manuals prepared by Poor Law Assistant Secretary William Golden Lumley similarly provided a clear exposition of the duties of the various officers.[86]

For their part, the Lunacy Commissioners relied on the Poor Law central authorities for much of the enforcement of the county asylum legislation. Poor Law Assistant Commissioners in their inspections of workhouses routinely examined the report of inspections by the Lunacy Commissioners, and checked whether any recommendations or concerns had been addressed. A routine administrative relationship developed regarding the removal of insane paupers from the workhouse to the asylum: the Lunacy Commissioners not only made their views known in the workhouse visitors' book, but also notified the Poor Law central authorities, who in turn followed up on the matter with the local board of guardians. The Assistant Commissioner would then do a final check during his next inspection. How successful this system was is open to some question. The Poor Law Board, in an understandable attempt to portray itself in a good light, suggested a relatively high success rate, commenting for example in 1848 that 'for the most part the recommendations of those [i.e., the Lunacy] Commissioners have been promptly carried out, on the [Poor Law] Board communicating with the proper authorities'.[87] The Lunacy Commissioners were not necessarily so positive, sometimes complaining of the limited powers of the Poor Law Board. Thus Shaftesbury in his testimony before the 1859 Select Committee on Lunatics stated:

We are constantly applying to the Poor Law Board to give us assistance; the Poor Law Board, I must say, have always from the very beginning shown the Commissioners the greatest kindness, and have given us assistance upon all occasions to the full extent of their means; but they constantly say, 'It is very well, but we have no power to do what you wish.'[88]

Notwithstanding these reservations regarding efficacy, the Lunacy Commission preferred to act through the Poor Law central authorities. For example, when the Commissioners believed that clerks to boards of guardians were failing to send on the returns of insane paupers, they turned to the Poor Law Board to intervene with the local authorities.[89] And their references to the goodwill and assistance of the Poor Law central authorities were almost routine in their annual reports.[90]

The Lunacy Commissioners' respect of the administrative balance created with the Poor Law central authorities went so far as to preclude the use of relatively easy techniques which would have jeopardized these relations, a position apparent in the following excerpt from Lord Shaftesbury's testimony before the 1859 Select Committee, under the questioning of Sir George Grey:

[612:] ... If the Commissioners in Lunacy have the lists of all these pauper lunatics, and ascertain that many of them are in the workhouses, have they not the power of bringing that fact to the knowledge of the justices, and cannot the justices upon their information, take all the necessary steps prescribed by this clause [i.e., the procedures for admission to the asylum] to place those lunatics under proper care? – We have never considered that we had power to interfere to such an extent as that.

613. My question is, whether they have not the power of communicating the fact to the justices of the county? – Yes; but we generally communicate with the Poor Law Board.[91]

Shaftesbury continued that such intervention was not made because the Justices resented their interference. It is thus open to question whether the approach through the Poor Law Board resulted from a belief that it was more effective in its dealings at the local level, or from a concern about bureaucratic politesse. Whatever the reason, the Lunacy Commissioners relied heavily on the Poor Law central authorities.

1859 AND ITS AFTERMATH

It was not until the late 1850s that the overall tone of the Commissioners' public pronouncements altered. Most significant was the publication in 1859 of a special report on workhouse care, the tone of which might fairly be described as blistering.[92] They moved from a position either ambivalent to or even supportive of workhouse care, to the .offensive.

Yet this was an unusual time. The broad range of lunacy statutes were coming in for criticism. William Tite, Whig Member of Parliament for Bath, had been pressing since his election in 1854 for a broad review of lunacy policy in England and Wales. He was eventually successful in 1859, when a select committee of the House of Commons was established to consider all aspects of the legal regulation of lunacy. This review was thus not to be restricted to pauper insane, and, especially as it would concern the private madhouse sector, would place the Lunacy Commission under particular scrutiny. The 1859 report can, perhaps, be seen as a mechanism to draw the fire into the Poor Law arena, where the Lunacy Commission role would no longer be central.

There can be little doubt that the Lunacy Commission was threatened by the prospect of change. Walpole, the Home Secretary, had been hesitant to allow a broad enquiry into that area. Instead he promoted greater regulation of county asylums by Poor Law medical officers to protect against wrongful confinements.[93] While they were to be under the direction of the Lunacy Commissioners, the Commissioners saw even this plan as a threat to their power and authority.[94] The scepticism of asylum committal perhaps reached its zenith with the remarks of the Bolton board of guardians, who were quoted as saying that long-term detention in asylums was 'virtually a species of imprisonment not contemplated or intended by any of the acts relating to lunatics' and that once shown to be incurable in the asylum, 'the responsibility regarding future treatment is cast upon the guardians'.[95]

The Poor Law itself was applying its own pressures, particularly in the metropolitan area. Funding inequities were creating pressures for unions of unions, jurisdictions which might support Poor Law asylums, as eventually became the case under the Metropolitan Poor Act 1867.[96]

The 1859 report was thus not simply a question of humanitarian reform. It was also a justification by the Commission of its own existence in the Poor Law of lunacy. Workhouse wards became 'practically, ... Lunatic Asylums without any of their advantages for treatment, or safeguards against their abuse'.[97] The report went on to complain of lack of legal protection of the patients, lack of qualified attendants, lack of medical treatment, prevalence of restraint, inadequacy of diet, filth, lack of exercise space and amusements and lack of proper records.

Where previously the Commissioners had tended to see those who were incurable and who could mix with the general workhouse population as appropriately confined there, a strain of imagery now appeared which focused on the workhouse as a punitive institution, and thus not appropriate for the insane by the very nature of its design. An example of this rhetoric is contained in the following testimony of Shaftesbury to the 1859 Select Committee regarding the maintenance of the chronically insane in workhouses:

No; just consider for a moment the confinement to which they are exposed in the workhouse. Many of the pauper lunatics, who would pine away in a workhouse, would flourish even upon inferior diet, if they were living under the care of their relatives. The discipline of the workhouse was intended for a totally different order of beings; it was intended for able-bodied paupers, and it was contrived for the purpose of making the workhouse disagreeable, and painful to a man who ought to be earning his livelihood; and, therefore, there is every kind of restraint imposed, and the discipline itself is very severe. And then, again, particularly in large towns, look at the airing courts; see how they are divided, and sub-divided into small spaces, with high walls, into which these wretched lunatics who ought to enjoy fresh air and exercise, are allowed to go once or twice in the course of the day, and where they go round and round like so many wild beasts – the poor creatures pine under it.[98]

Similar comments appeared almost annually in the annual reports of the Lunacy Commissioners throughout the late 1850s and into the 1860s.

The result was a clash with their own local reports, discussed above. Predictably, given the relationships that the Lunacy Commission had been fostering both with the Poor Law Board and with local authorities, the new tone came in for heavy criticism. In this testimony before the 1859 Select Committee, Poor Law Inspector Andrew Doyle cited the local inspection reports of the Lunacy Commission to challenge the criticisms in the 1859 report point by point. He claimed that the report was a 'one-sided and scarcely ingenuous representation' of the Commissioners' observations regarding individual workhouses.[99] Where the Commissioners had implied that excessive mechanical restraint was common in workhouses, Doyle pointed out that in only three of the 600 workhouses visited by the Lunacy Commissioners in preparation of the 1859 report had chaining been found. Restraint was found in only 19 workhouses, and there were only about three cases where this restraint had not been considered justified.[100] He also pointed out that the Lunacy Commissioners claimed to have been vigilant in recommending the removal of all workhouse paupers who were proper to be admitted to the asylum, noting that in the unions he inspected, these totalled 20 of the 628 insane persons in workhouses; in the country as a whole, they were only 153 of the 7,000 insane people contained in workhouses.[101]

Doyle spoke highly of the fairness of the individual workhouse reports compiled by the Lunacy Commissioners, but complained that their 1859 report did not accurately reflect those individual reports:

1983. You do not intend to state that there is any exaggeration in that Report of the 3rd November 1858 [i.e., a report of an individual workhouse visit] which I have read? – As I stated before, I have not found, so far as I can judge, one word of exaggeration from the beginning to the end of the Reports of the Commissioners. Accidental mistakes I have found. But I have found exaggeration, misstatements, and incorrect quotations of the Reports of the Commissioners in this Supplemental Report. Of the separate Reports of the Commissioners, as to their impartiality and general fairness, I cannot speak too highly. It is impossible that any document can contrast in those qualities more remarkably with them than this Supplemental Report which professes to be founded upon them.[102]

Here, the Commissioners were trapped by their own policy of gentle local persuasion. The reports regarding the Leicestershire workhouses are examples of the generally positive reports. While this may have been a successful technique to improve conditions in individual workhouses, it threatened the Commission's credibility in the broader complaints of workhouse conditions contained in the 1859 report.

Claiming the reason for the detentions in the workhouse to be financial, the solution proposed by the Lunacy Commission involved the establishment of a system of new and less expensive asylums for chronic patients. The description of the buildings in the 1856 annual report reflected this context:

Our last Report directed attention to the fact, that in providing, not merely for the harmless and demented, but for the more orderly and convalescing, the most suitable was also the least expensive mode; that they might satisfactorily be placed in buildings more simple in character, and far more economically constructed; ... And whether the mode adopted may be, for the convalescing, by simple and cheery apartments detached from the main building, and with opportunity for association with individuals engaged in industrial pursuits; or, for harmless and chronic cases, by auxiliary rooms near the outbuildings, of plain or ordinary structure, without wide corridors or extensive airing-court walls, and simply warmed and ventilated; it is, we think, become manifest that some changes of structure must be substituted for the system now pursued, if it be desired to retain the present buildings in their efficiency, and to justify the outlay upon them by their employment as really curative establishments. In this way only, as it seems to us, can justice be done to the rate-payer as well as to the pauper.[103]

The previous annual report had argued that these buildings should be located near to the patients' workshops, apparently to limit the time necessary to take the inmates to and from their employment.[104]

These facilities were never built on a national scale, although the construction of asylums under the 1867 Metropolitan Poor Act can be seen in part as resulting from this strand of argument. This proposed institution had obvious similarities to workhouse wards. Gone was the objective of cure. What was advocated by both the Lunacy Commissioners and the advocates of workhouse wards was inexpensive, decent accommodation, particularly for chronic or long-term cases. The Commissioners claimed that the standard of care would be far superior to that in workhouse wards, but this was never demonstrated particularly convincingly.

Predictably, therefore, the Select Committee did not recommend the removal of all insane people from workhouses. Instead, the 1862 Act gave the Lunacy Commissioners greater involvement in workhouses. This occurred in part through the authority to remove inmates from workhouses to asylums, a power which they almost never used. In addition, the following provision was enacted:

8. It shall be lawful for the Visitors of any Asylum and the Guardians of any Parish or Union within the District for which the Asylum has been provided, if they shall see fit, to make Arrangements, subject to the Approval of the Commissioners [in Lunacy] and the President of the Poor Law Board, for the Reception and Care of a limited Number of chronic Lunatics in the Workhouse of the Parish or Union, to be selected by the Superintendent of the Asylum, and certified by him to be fit and proper so to be removed.[105]

Rather than introduce a third type of institution, it was expected that transfers would be made to workhouses. The Lunacy Commission's political position was buttressed by its authority over such transfers. A legal opinion of the Law Officers of the Crown in 1867 further consolidated this authority in the workhouse, by holding that persons transferred according to these provisions remained legally in the asylum, not in the workhouse,[106] and that position was given statutory force later that year.[107]

Local authorities increasingly constructed insane wards in work-houses. Notwithstanding their increased authority over these wards, the Lunacy Commission at times remained highly critical.[108] At other times, the Commissioners were much more positive, as in the following passage from the 1866 annual report:

On the other hand, there has also been frequent favourable report from houses under quite different conditions, where, as in many of the larger towns throughout the kingdom, the inmates of unsound mind collected in the workhouses have become so very numerous as to require special arrangements for their accommodation; and, the principle being admitted of their claim to a kind of treatment other than that extended to the ordinary pauper, though the law admits of no such claim, the result of the visitation by Members of this Commission, and of the support given by the Poor Law Board to suggestions made by us which we have ourselves no power to enforce, has been to obtain from the respective Boards of guardians more liberal arrangements, better dietaries, improved airing-courts, in some few instances careful medical records, and proper paid attendants.[109]

The result, consistent with the Commissioners' alliance-building at the local level, was at least occasional co-operation with local unions in the construction of specialized workhouse accommodation, and the transfer of insane people to it. The following case of Mile End Union in 1862 provides an example:

In the case of Mile End Old Town, however, the proposal embraced the sanctioning of an entirely new detached building, constructed expressly for lunatic wards upon ground within the Workhouse precincts, and intended for the reception of 26 Male and 50 Female Patients. Two members of our Board, who inspected the wards, having reported favourably as to their general construction and arrangements, we in this case intimated to the guardians that, before granting our approval of their proposal for the reception therein of chronic Lunatics under the provisions of the 8th section, we should require compliance with certain specified conditions. To this they readily assented.[110]

The way was once again clear for the Commissioners to advocate the transfer of chronic and manageable cases from asylums to the workhouse, to ensure treatment of recent cases in the asylum. This they did, for example, in their 1866 annual report:

In our last (as in the present) Report we have adverted to the creditable condition of the Lunatic Inmates in some of the larger Workhouses, and we have stated that where such proper provision is made a larger proportion of Imbeciles and chronic cases may, without impropriety, be retained in them, and the pressure for increased accommodation in Asylums be proportionably reduced.[111]

In addition, workhouses continued to care for people without the intervention of the asylum, as they always had. The Commissioners had objected to accommodation of the insane in such wards in the 1859 report largely on the basis of inappropriate classification and inappropriate regulatory systems. For chronic cases who could mix freely with others in the house, and particularly for those 'capable of being usefully employed' or found to be 'trustworthy servants', they had always acknowledged workhouse accommodation as not inappropriate.[112] It was those who required special care or facilities whom the Lunacy Commissioners insisted ought to be removed to the asylum.

The Lunacy Commissioners even went so far as to press for the regularization of detention of the insane in workhouses. Far from objecting to the 1867 provisions which allowed formal detention of the insane in workhouses, the Commissioners' *Twenty-Second Annual*

Report claimed it as one of their successes. The report stated that the amendment was implemented following an approach by the Lunacy Commission to the Poor Law Board suggesting that existing powers required clarification.[113]

The workhouse issue was thus not obviously about humanitarian reform. This is not a case, to use Fraser's phrase, of reform 'geared to meet real and pressing problems', where '[i]t was the pressure of facts, and unpalatable ones at that, which produced unexpected and (by most) undesired administrative growth'.[114] Certainly unpalatable facts were cited by the Commissioners in their annual and special reports; but the facts became known in a particular political climate, and the resulting reforms owed less to the creation of 'that real state of equal opportunity in which meaningful natural liberty could flourish'[115] than to bureaucratic accommodation.

CENTRAL DOCUMENTS AND DISCOURSES

With the exception of the 1859 report and its aftermath, relations with the Poor Law central authorities and the local Poor Law officials and magistrates occurred largely out of the public perception. The Lunacy Commission also submitted annual and special reports which were published as part of the Parliamentary Papers. These were first and foremost reports to legislature, their funder and the source of their powers. At a time when central authorities were still controversial, this is more than a trivial statement of the obvious. The reports were an overt justification of the Commission's existence.[116] They were also more public than the local reports, and as such were important to the Commission's broader credibility.[117] This public nature also created a situation where issues relating to the care of the insane could be brought to light, pressure created for reform and the agenda for the care of the insane affected. In addition, of course, the reports had to satisfy the diversity of individuals on the Lunacy Commission itself. It is within this political network that the reports are to be understood: certainly, they were intended to ensure the continued visibility of issues regarding care of the insane, but, consistent with that and perhaps more immediately important, they were also to justify the continued mandate of the Lunacy Commission.

The annual reports developed a relatively pro-forma character quite quickly. The Lunacy Commission was portrayed as vigilant and effective, priding itself in its accomplishments, and making clear how much more needed to be done. Reports of private madhouses requiring correction and workhouses with lunatics in substandard care pepper the reports, along with recommendations for reform and the seemingly obligatory deluge of statistics. The annual reports by and large centred on private madhouses. In so far as bulk is indicative, their annual report for 1861 for example included 44 pages devoted to private establishments, eight pages to county asylums and fewer than two pages to workhouses. In part, this can be seen as reflecting the numbers of institutions: that year, there were 41 county asylums and 127 private institutions. This broad hierarchy is consistent with the priorities of the Lunacy Commission as established in the legislative history. They had first and foremost been inspectors of private facilities, and secondarily of county asylums. Their powers were greater regarding private madhouses, again suggesting that these occupied a more central place in their mandate.

The minimal attention to workhouses is notable, however. This relative lack of attention may have resulted from a variety of factors. As noted above, the Commission acquired jurisdiction to inspect workhouses almost by accident. The lack of attention may reflect that historical marginalization of workhouses in the Commissioners' role. It may also indicate that the legislators, whom the reports were primarily intended to convince, were more interested in private madhouses than in the insane in workhouses. Finally, it may be that the Commissioners themselves did not wish to emphasize their role in workhouse inspection. As we have seen, the Commissioners were contradictory in their annual and special reports as to the role of workhouses in the care of the insane, and a result may have been a de-emphasis in their reports.

A sense of what the parliamentarians expected may perhaps be gleaned from the following comment of Thomas Wakley, Member of Parliament for Finchley and editor of the *Lancet*, in his opposition to a permanent mandate for the Metropolitan Commissioners in 1841:

Though he admitted the existing commission had done essential service to the public and to the cause of humanity, it had fallen short in its effects of what the public had a right to expect. He had yet to learn whether they had furnished all the information that was looked for in the shape of reports, and whether the public had received any great information from their labours.[118]

Information was what was wanted; information was provided, and in increasing quantities. The *Fifth Annual Report* of the Commissioners had contained 13 pages.[119] The *Fourteenth Annual Report* had grown to 101 pages, with an additional 157 pages of appendices.[120] This explosion of information is noted by David Mellett:

The Board was quick to become figure-conscious and the gathering and assembling of information was dangerously near to becoming an end in itself in the Commissioners' urgency to maintain a complete registry of all the lunatics in the kingdom, and of all persons having charge of them.[121]

The emphasis in the annual reports was on the results of inspections. A variety of particular cases would be reported, generally with a summary comment as to how important the Lunacy Commission had been in ensuring standards of care, such as the following comment from their *Fifth Annual Report*:

On reviewing the several entries made by the Commissioners who have during the preceding 12 months visited the various asylums, hospitals, and licensed houses subjected to our inspection, we have to report that they are generally in a very satisfactory condition. It has been thought expedient, indeed, in the course of these visits, to make numerous suggestions, having for their object the improvement of the various establishments, or the increase of the patients' comforts; but defects of a serious character have rarely been discovered, and when discovered have been, for the most part, remedied without delay. Upon the whole we have to report, that the character of the various institutions for the insane is in an improved and still advancing state; and the treatment of lunatic patients appears to us to be, for the most part, humane and judicious.[122]

Reflecting the local relations of the Lunacy Commission, the image was of institutions improving incrementally, and of the Commission at the centre of that process.

The 'character of the various institutions' was assessed largely in terms of physical surroundings, order and regimen. Andrew Scull is cynical about this focus:

To judge by the space and emphasis allotted each topic, by the mid-1850s the question of curing asylum inmates ranked considerably below the urgent issue of the composition of the inmates' soup.[123]

Scull sees this as a departure from an earlier emphasis on cure, and thus as part of the broader failure of reform. Whatever the merits of that view, it is also true that the reports had a productive function in creating an image for their readers of what the 'good' asylum was. The focus of the reports on the standards of the facility was not inconsistent with a concern about cure. The 1844 report did not draw a distinction between physical standards and the recovery of inmates. Instead, diet, exercise yards and heating systems were seen as necessary features to aid the inmate's recovery of sanity. Physical standards in this context fell at the intersection of humanitarianism and cure. At the same time, the asylum was to be a place of order, where the nature of the regimen, supported by the very architecture of the building itself, was to render the uncontrollable docile.

This focus reflects the interest of the Home Office in the late 1840s. The Lunacy Commission had been reluctant to attempt a uniform set of rules for county asylums in 1846, but had acceded under pressure from the Home Office.[124] While the Commission actually reported to the Lord Chancellor after 1845, the Home Office had responsibility for county asylum construction, and it was keen to establish minimum standards in these facilities. The continued focus on asylum standards can thus be seen as reflecting these political priorities.

Issues of physical standards did not emphasize the inconsistencies of the Commissioners' ideologies. We have already seen contradictions regarding the medical nature of insanity, the purpose of the asylum and the role of the workhouse in the care of the insane. These flowed from the make-up of the Commission itself, in its mixture of Benthamite, paternalist, evangelical, medical and legal ideologies. They were further in part imposed by the administrative purpose of the reports, justifying the position of the Commission to both Westminster and the public. While the attempt to impose nationwide standards was apparently resisted by the medical Commissioners,[125] the discussion of the standards of institutions did not otherwise emphasize the doctrinal disagreements and inconsistencies of the Lunacy Commission.

The differing discourses of local reports of county asylums and the centralized annual and special reports of the Lunacy Commission could generally coexist in the network of practical administrative relations established by the Lunacy Commission. As discussed above, the Lunacy Commission operated through the Poor Law central authority when the asylum admission system was perceived to break down: the Justices of the Peace were not confronted directly by the Lunacy Commission regarding admissions. Similarly, while the Lunacy Commission could be critical of the high capital costs expended by the Justices on asylums, both the Commission and at least most of the Justices were partisans of the county asylum system. At the same time, the Commissioners did not generally criticize the continuation of workhouse care, adopting instead the same soft-sell approach that they used for county asylums.

Where, in all this, is reform? The Lunacy Commission in some sense was at the centre of the care of the insane, in that they saw all the institutionalized, and were able, albeit usually indirectly, to effect incremental change. Their focus on the physical standard of institutions did not imply a radical theoretical agenda. Instead, it lay at the intersection of themes regarding humanitarianism, control of the dangerous, medical interests and cure. The technique of persuasion implied in their local reports did nothing to challenge the authority of local officials. The existence of the Lunacy Commission no doubt furthered the change in perception of the asylums as individual and local institutions, to asylums as forming a national system, but this involved no obvious change in the perception of the social role of the asylum. In so far as it makes sense beyond this to see the role of the Commissioners in terms of 'reform', the reform should be considered in terms of incrementalism, gradually increased physical standards and a more pervasive regimen, not in terms of theoretical changes.

NOTES

1 Consistent with this mandate, the Commissioners had some real power regarding transfers to and from these private sector facilities, even if the transfer also involved a county asylum: see 8 & 9 Vic. c. 126 ss. 29, 56; 16 & 17 Vic. c. 97 ss. 45, 77, 82.

2 See 8 & 9 Vic. c. 126 s. 28; 16 & 17 Vic. c. 97 ss. 29, 30.

3 8 & 9 Vic. c. 126 s. 29; 16 & 17 Vic. c. 97 s. 45.

4 16 & 17 Vic. c. 97 s. 56.

5 16 & 17 Vic. c. 97 s. 58.

6 16 & 17 Vic. c. 97 s. 126.

7 8 & 9 Vic. c. 126 ss. 46, 47, 55, 73;

8 16 & 17 Vic. c. 97 s. 87.

9 25 & 26 Vic. c. 111 s. 27.

10 25 & 26 Vic. c. 111 s. 32.

11 25 & 26 Vic. c. 111 s. 31. The same statute allowed the Commissioners, along with the Chairman of the Poor Law Board, to approve transfer of chronic insane paupers from asylums to workhouses: s. 8.

12 8 & 9 Vict. c. 100 s. 61. When two Commissioners were to visit, one was to be medically trained, and the other a barrister.

13 8 & 9 Vict. c. 100 s. 14.

14 PP 1859 1st sess. xxii 175, at 4 ff.

15 N. Hervey, 'The Lunacy Commission, 1845–60', University of Bristol dissertation, 1987, p. 120.

16 *The Seventh Early of Shaftesbury, 1801–1885* (London: Eyre Methuen, 1981), p. 253. Consistent with this, it was the Commissioners' secretary, not Shaftesbury, who wrote the reports of the Commission.

17 Bartrip, 'State intervention in mid-nineteenth-century Britain: fact or fiction', *Journal of British Studies*, **23** (1983): 63.

18 8 & 9 Vict. c. 100 s. 3.

19 Hervey, 'The Lunacy Commission, 1845–60', pp. 32 and 140 ff.

20 N. Hervey, 'A slavish bowing down: the Lunacy Commission and the psychiatric profession 1845–60', in *The Anatomy of Madness*, Vol. II, ed. William F. Bynum *et al.*, (London: Tavistock, 1985), p. 98 at 105.

21 See, for example, Daniel Hack Tuke, 'Does civilization favour the generation of mental disease?', *Journal of Mental Science*, **4** (1858): 94.

22 Testimony to the Select Committee (1859), PP 1859 1st sess. (204) iii 75, at q. 52.

23 See D. Mellett, *The Prerogative of Asylumdom* (New York, London: Garland, 1982), pp. 72 ff.

24 Trevor Turner, 'Not worth the powder and shot', in Berrios and Freeman, *150 Years of British Psychiatry* (London: Gaskell, 1991), p. 3 at 13.

25 McCandless, 'Dangerous to themselves and others', *Journal of British Studies*, **23**(1) (1983): 84 at 84.

26 UK, *Report of the Metropolitan Commissioners in Lunacy to the Lord Chancellor* (London: Bradbury and Evans, 1844), at Ch. 2.

27 UK, *Report of the Metropolitan Commissioners in Lunacy to the Lord Chancellor* (London: Bradbury and Evans, 1844), p. 99.

28 The Commissioners themselves used this argument, for example in Shaftesbury's 1859 testimony, PP 1859 1st sess. (204) iii 75, at question 672.

29 Hervey, 'The Lunacy Commission 1845–60', p. 94.

30 See UK, *Report of the Metropolitan Commissioners in Lunacy* (London: Bradbury and Evans, 1844), pp. 6f, 79 ff.

31 Laurence Ray, 'Models of madness in Victorian asylum practice', *European Journal of Sociology*, **22** (1981): 229; David Wright, 'Getting out of the asylum: understanding the confinement of the insane in the nineteenth century', *Social History of Madness*, **10** (1997): 137, at 143.

32 *Supplement to the Twelfth Annual Report of the Commissioners in Lunacy*, PP 1859 1st sess. (228) ix 1, at 7.

33 *Copy of Letter to the Lord Chancellor from the Commissioners in Lunacy, with reference to their Duties and Practice, under the Act 8 & 9 Vict., c. 100*, PP 1849 (620) xlvi 381. In *Nottidge* v. *Ripley* (1849), a society heiress successfully sued her family for wrongful confinement in a private madhouse. The family had instituted this course of action following her

defection to an obscure religious cult. In his charge to the jury, the Chief Baron Sir Frederick Pollock advanced a dangerousness standard of confinement in no uncertain terms.

34 UK, *Report of the Metropolitan Commissioners in Lunacy*, (London: Bradbury and Evans, 1844), p. 170.

35 The two frameworks were actually placed in adjoining sentences in the discussion of the clause purporting to allow harmless lunatics to be kept in the workhouse, in the 1844 report:

> Our objection to the clause of the Act to which we have referred is, that it has a tendency to impress upon those who have the care of the poor, the belief that there is no harm in keeping lunatics away from Asylums so long as they are not dangerous, and thus to combine with the other causes which we have pointed out in producing that incurable condition in which pauper lunatics are so often sent to Asylums. The clause seems, moreover open to this observation, – if it really sanctions the detention of harmless lunatics, – namely that the Parish Authorities may take advantage of it to deprive persons of their liberty, although they would do no harm if at large. (p. 99)

There was no acknowledgement that the objection made in the second sentence applies equally to those confined in asylums under the terms of the first sentence.

36 PP 1854–5 (240) xvii 533, at 34 f.

37 PP 1854–5 (240) xvii 533, at 35.

38 See, e.g., *Supplement to the Twelfth Annual Report of the Commissioners in Lunacy*, PP 1859, 1st sess. (228) ix 1, at 6.

39 UK, *Report of Metropolitan Commissioners in Lunacy* (London: Bradbury and Evans, 1844), pp. 30 f.

40 Regarding class-based rationales for, and implementation of, the policy of segregation, see L. D. Smith, ' "Levelled to the same common standard"? Social class in the lunatic asylum, 1780–1860', in *The Duty of Discontent*, ed. O. Ashton, R. Fyson and S. Roberts (London: Mansell, 1995), p. 142.

41 PP 1849 (620) xlvi 381, at 11.

42 PP 1849 (620) xlvi 381, at 10.

43 UK, *Report of Metropolitan Commissioners in Lunacy* (London: Bradbury and Evans, 1844), p. 12.

44 UK, *Report of Metropolitan Commissioners in Lunacy* (London: Bradbury and Evans, 1844), p. 13.

45 *Twenty-Fifth Annual Report of the Commissioners in Lunacy*, PP 1871 (351) xxvi 1, at 339.

46 See, for example, *Fourteenth Annual Report of the Lunacy Commissioners*, PP 1860 (338) xxxiv 231, at 19.

47 Charges rose from seven to nine shillings per week at the county asylum in Leicester in the period under study. In 1868, Fisherton House and Peckham House, private madhouses containing some insane paupers from Leicester Union, charged fifteen shillings and sixteen shillings and four pence per week respectively.

48 Mellett, *The Prerogative of Asylumdom*, p. 134. Elsewhere, Mellett claims the Commissioners were 'understandably hostile to the principle, as well as the realities of workhouse confinement': *The Prerogative of Asylumdom*, p. 141. See also Scull, *The Most Solitary of Afflictions* (New Haven: Yale University Press, 1993), p. 133.

49 UK, *Report of the Metropolitan Commissioners in Lunacy to the Lord Chancellor* (London: Bradbury and Evans, 1844), p. 92, reprinting PP [HL] 1844 xxvi 1; *Supplementary Report to the Home Secretary*, PP 1847 [858]; *in octavo* 1847–8 xxxii 371, at 36.

50 Appendix (A) to *Supplementary Report to the Home Secretary*, PP 1847 [858]; *in octavo* 1847–8 xxxii 371, at 257–9.

51 Appendix (A) to *Supplementary Report to the Home Secretary*, PP 1847 [858]; *in octavo* 1847–8 xxxii 371, at 249.

52 Appendix (A) to *Supplementary Report to the Home Secretary*, PP 1847 [858]; *in octavo* 1847–8 xxxii 371, at 281.

53 Appendix (A) to *Supplementary Report to the Home Secretary*, PP 1847 [858]; *in octavo* 1847–8 xxxii 371, at 281.

54 PP 1859 1st sess. (204) iii 75, at question 671.

55 *Eleventh Annual Report of the Lunacy Commissioners*, PP 1857 2nd sess. (157) xvi 351, at 16.

56 PP 1857 2nd sess. (157) xvi 351, at 13.

57 'The Lunacy Commission, 1845–60', pp. 94 f. and Chs. 5 and 6.

58 Moir, *The Justice of the Peace* (Harmondsworth: Penguin, 1969), p. 149. The same point is made by Roberts in *Paternalism in Early Victorian England* (London: Croom Helm, 1979), p. 207.

59 Roberts, *Paternalism in Victorian England*, p. 207.

60 Copies of all these reports are contained in LRO DE 3533/13.

61 Report of the Lunacy Commissioners dated 5 and 6 Aug. 1859, contained as appendix to *Annual Report of the United Committee of Visitors of the Leicestershire and Rutland Lunatic Asylum* (1860), LRO DE 3533/13.

62 Report of Lunacy Commission dated 27 Oct. 1858; contained in *Tenth Annual Report of the United Committee of Visitors of the Leicstershire and Rutland Lunatic Asylum* (1858), and Report of Lunacy Commission, 23 April 1867, contained in *Nineteenth Annual Report of the United Committee of Visitors of the Leicestershire and Rutland Lunatic Asylum* (1867). Both asylum annual reports contained in LRO DE 3533/13.

63 See *Twenty-Second Annual Report of the United Committee of Visitors to the Leicestershire and Rutland Lunatic Asylum* (1858), LRO DE 3533/13.

64 See *Eighteenth Annual Report of the United Committee of Visitors of the Leicestershire and Rutland Lunatic Asylum* (1866), LRO DE 3533/13.

65 Report of Lunacy Commissioners, dated 27 Nov. 1866, contained as appendix to *Eighteenth Annual Report* of the asylum (1866), LRO DE 3533/13. The assistant superintendent was not hired until after the Lunacy Commission's 1867 report. The appointment was justified by

construction in the asylum resulting in capacity of the asylum rising by 80 patients. By 1872, Buck had his house, complete with covered portico attaching it to the remainder of the asylum.

66 A similar dynamic is suggested by the concern about pauper and non-pauper mixing in the asylum. The Commissioners in Lunacy had advised the removal of non-pauper patients from the asylum, without success, in 1859 and 1860 in their reports on the asylum. At this point, Buck favoured the same regulations for private and pauper patients and a system of segregation was not followed: see Superintendent's Journal and Report Book, 11 Oct. 1859, LRO DE 3533/83. By 1869, he had changed his mind, and no longer favoured such a mixture: 'the private patient, when intelligent, is always discontented; and the pauper patient readily becomes his equal in this respect': see Medical Superintendent's Report, 25 Jan. 1869, contained in *Twentieth Annual Report* of asylum (1868), LRO DE 3533/14. The complete segregation of private and pauper had been effected by 1874: see *Twenty-Sixth Annual Report* of the asylum, contained in LRO DE 3533/14.

67 A copy of this report is contained in the correspondence between the Leicester Union Guardians and the Poor Law Board, PRO MH 12/6477, #10997/54.

68 Correspondence between the Leicester Union Guardians and the Poor Law Board, PRO MH 12/6477, #15204/54.

69 Contained in correspondence between Billesdon Union and the Poor Law Board, PRO MH 12/6415, #30972/63 (27 July 1863).

70 A copy of this report is contained in correspondence between Billesdon Union and the Poor Law Board, PRO MH 12/6415, #5948/64.

71 PP 1859 2nd sess. (156) vii 501, at questions 2227 sq.

72 PP 1859 2nd sess. (156) vii 501, at question 1111.

73 PP 1863 xx (331) 437, at 25.

74 Hervey, 'The Lunacy Commission, 1845–60', pp. 309 f. Other scholars have portrayed relations as less antagonistic, but do not deal with the matter in depth: Mellett, 'Bureaucracy and mental illness', *Medical History*, **25** (1981): 221, at 236; Hodgkinson, 'Provision for pauper lunatics, 1834–71', *Medical History*, **10** (1966): 138.

75 The Lunacy Commission in 1858 published a supplemental report to its *Twelfth Annual Report*, which dealt specifically with workhouse care of the insane: PP 1859 1st sess. (228) ix 1. In this report, discussed in detail below, the Commissioners were highly critical of workhouse care. This theme was carried over into their testimony before the Select Committee on Lunatics, 1859. The Poor Law Board was not directly attacked by the report; in fact they were acknowledged by Shaftesbury as co-operative. Whether or not the central Poor Law authorities were intended as a target, they seem to have been highly offended at what they perceived as an unfair attack. The Commissioners were relatively quick to repair the damage. In February 1860, following the report from

the Select Committee, Foster, the secretary of the Lunacy Commission, arranged a meeting between the Commission and the Poor Law Board. Hervey describes the situation as follows:

He felt it was vital they should clearly understand each others views, so that the powers vested in each should be exercised in aid of the other, to produce the greatest benefit for the lunatic paupers. ('The Lunacy Commission 1845–60', p. 319)

While the events of the late 1850s may have resulted in a cooling of relations, at least in the short term, it does not appear to have destroyed the bureaucratic relations between the authorities.

76 Correspondence between William Gilbert and the Poor Law Commissioners, undated [approx. 1 Jan. 1835], PRO MH 32/26.

77 Correspondence between William Gilbert and the Poor Law Commissioners, 7 Aug. 1835, PRO MH 32/26.

78 *Tenth Annual Report of the Poor Law Commissioners*, PP 1844 [560] xix 9, at 19 f.

79 See for example, the inquiry to Barrow upon Soar Union, 17 Feb. 1854, regarding William Cooper, PRO MH 12/6400 5529, 7342/54; correspondence with Barrow upon Soar Union, re Hannah Wills and Hannah Johnsen, commencing February 1859, PRO MH 12/6401 5887, 16178, 22303/59, 11531/60.

80 *Eighth Annual Report of the Poor Law Commissioners*, PP 1842 [359] xix 1, at 111, quoting Theobald, *Treatise on the Poor Laws*.

81 *Eighth Annual Report of the Poor Law Commissioners*, PP 1842 [359] xix 1, at 111. This letter was discussed in greater detail above in Chapter 3.

82 Findlayson comments that they 'began the active cooperation that was later to be a marked feature of the public health movement': see *The Seventh Earl of Shaftesbury, 1801–1885*, p. 250. Chadwick's most recent biographer similarly appeared to see no conflict between the two men: see Anthony Brundage, *England's 'Prussian Minister'* (London and University Park: Pennsylvania State University Press, 1988), Ch. 8. Their work together in this field commenced in 1848, immediately after the demise of the Poor Law Commission of which Chadwick was the secretary, suggesting that any personal animosities from Chadwick's Poor Law days would not have dissipated by the time of their co-operation on the Board of Health.

83 *Twelfth Annual Report of the Poor Law Commissioners*, PP 1846 [704] xix 1, at Appendix A(6), p. 51. Emphases in original.

84 *Twelfth Annual Report of the Poor Law Commissioners*, PP 1846 [704] xix 1, at Appendix A(6), pp. 52–5. Similar positions are taken by William Golden Lumley, the Assistant Secretary to the Poor Law Commissioners, in his treatise *The New Lunacy Acts* (London: Shaw, 1845), pp. xii, 160, 163. Both took the position that admission of lunatics not chargeable to the union was discretionary on the Justices: p. 54 of Poor

Law Commission Report, and p. 163 of Lumley. The Commissioners and Lumley both envisaged a problem of insufficient space in county asylums to allow proper implementation of the Act. The Poor Law Commissioners thus took the position that the duty of medical officers to report insane persons took effect only 'after an asylum shall be established for any county or borough under the provisions of this Act': p. 51. Lumley commented merely, 'It is manifest from the provisions of this bill, that this provision cannot at present be carried into force. There are not sufficient asylums for all the paupers who are lunatic and at large, nor can there be for a long time to come': p. 160. He did not attempt to resolve this apparent contradiction.

85 See, for example, Appendix 14 to *Sixth Annual Report of the Poor Law Board*, PP 1854 [1797] xxix 333, and *Fifteenth Annual Report of the Poor Law Board*, PP 1863 [3197] xxii 1, at 22.

86 See, for example, *Manuals of the Duties of Poor Law Officers: Master and Matron of the Workhouse* (London: Knight, 1869), pp. 51–2; *Manuals of the Duties of Poor Law Officers: Medical Officer*, (London: Knight, 1849), pp. 23, 28, 36–7, 50, 53; *Manuals of the Duties of Poor Law Officers: Medical Officer* 3rd edn. (London: Knight, 1871), pp. 31–3, 58–60, 67–70.

87 *First Annual Report of the Poor Law Board*, PP 1849 [1024] xxv 1, at 8.

88 17 March 1859, PP 1859 1st sess. (204) iii 75, q. 619.

89 *Thirteenth Annual Report of the Lunacy Commissioners*, PP 1859 2nd sess. (204) xiv 529, at 75.

90 See, for example, *Supplementary Report of the Lunacy Commissioners*, PP 1847 [858]; *in octavo* 1847–8 xxxii 371, at 262; *Third Annual Report*, PP 1849 [1028] xxii 381, at 7; *Fourth Annual Report*, PP 1850 (291) xxiii 363, at 14; *Fifth Annual Report*, PP 1850 (735) xxiii 393, at 12; *Ninth Annual Report*, PP 1854–5 (240) xvii 533, at 34; testimony of Shaftesbury before the Select Committee on Lunatics, 17 March 1859, PP 1859 1st sess. (204) iii 75, at question 688; testimony of Robert Lutwidge (Secretary to Commissioners in Lunacy, 1845 to 1855; Commissioner in Lunacy thereafter) to Select Committee on Lunatics, 4 Aug. 1859, PP 1859 2nd sess. (156) vii 501, at question 2231, and *Twentieth Annual Report*, PP 1866 (317) xxxii 1, at 18. These compliments must be taken somewhat critically, as the annual reports were to place the Commission in a good light with the government, its funder. None the less, the pressure to avoid the appearance of conflict for funding purposes cannot be entirely separate from the pressure to avoid conflict in working relations between the bodies.

Nicholas Hervey argues that the Lunacy Commission's compliments of the central Poor Law authority were largely disingenuous. 'Almost without exception, its [i.e., the Lunacy Commission's] attempts to get support for wider policy changes were opposed': 'The Lunacy Commission 1845–60', p. 319. This conclusion is based on several factors. The central Poor Law authority failed to advocate administrative and legal pressures on medical officers who neglected to turn in the returns required by law, instead pointing out that such matters were within the legal authority of the Lunacy Commission: p. 314. Hervey argues that placing this responsibility on the Lunacy Commission was impractical; it is not obvious why it would have been more practical had it been performed by the Poor Law central authority. The Poor Law central authorities also apparently did not necessarily implement changes in workhouse administration, regulation and record-keeping as recommended by the Commissioners in Lunacy: pp. 315 ff. The Commissioners' request in this regard did not merely extend to lunatics in the workhouse. They were instead arguing as to how records for the workhouse as a whole ought to be kept, along with greater involvement in classification of all workhouse inmates: see letter from Lunacy Commissioners to Poor Law Commissioners, PRO MH/19 168, #2295/ 47 (22 July 1847). A note from Assistant Commissioner Lumley on this document suggests that it was not practically possible to require the workhouse masters to vary their practice in this way. As will be discussed further below, the Poor Law central authorities favoured a relatively clear demarcation between their responsibilities and those of the Lunacy Commission. The Lunacy Commission's suggestions would have involved the Commissioners in Lunacy in advising regarding the running of workhouses generally, and it is thus little wonder that the Poor Law authorities were unenthusiastic. While the result may have been frustrating to the Commissioners, it is not obvious that the central Poor Law authority had much other option, if the focus and control of their board was to be maintained.

91 PP 1859 1st sess. (204) iii 75.
92 *Supplement to the Twelfth Annual Report of the Commissioners in Lunacy*, PP 1859 1st sess. (228) ix 1.
93 *Hansard*, Vol. 152 (1859), 405.
94 Testimony of Shaftesbury to Select Committee on Lunatics, PP 1860 (495) xxii 349, at q. 282.
95 J. C. Bucknill, 'The custody of the insane poor', *Journal of Mental Science*, 4 (1858): 460, at 463.
96 30 Vict. c. 6. Re establishment of district asylums, see ss. 5 ff.; re establishment of metropolitan common poor fund, see ss. 60 ff.
97 See *Supplement to the Twelfth Annual Report of the Commissioners in Lunacy*, PP 1859 1st sess. (228) ix 1, at 11. This may be compared to the following description of workhouse wards in the supplement to their 1847 annual report, quoted above.
98 PP 1859 1st sess. (204) iii 75, at q. 676.
99 PP 1859 2nd sess. (156) vii 501, at q. 2079.
100 PP 1859 2nd sess. (156) vii 501, at qq. 1871, 2015.
101 PP 1859 2nd sess. (156) vii 501, at qq. 1708 ff. and qq. 2018 ff.

102 PP 1859 2nd sess. (156) vii 501, at q. 1983.

103 *Eleventh Annual Report of the Lunacy Commissioners*, PP 1857 2nd sess.
(157) xvi 351, at 21. The call for such institutions is a recurrent theme in
the writings of the Lunacy Commission at the end of the 1850s: see also,
for example, *Tenth Annual Report of the Commissioners in Lunacy*, PP
1856 (258) xviii 495, at 26 ff.; *Supplement to the Twelfth Annual Report of
the Commissioners in Lunacy*, PP 1859 1st sess. (228) ix 1, at 36;
Thirteenth Annual Report of the Commissioners in Lunacy, PP 1859 2nd
sess. (204) xiv 529, at 2f.

104 *Tenth Annual Report of the Commissioners in Lunacy*, PP 1856 (258) xviii
495, at 26 ff.

105 25 & 26 Vict. c. 111 s. 8. A clarifying statute the following year made it
clear that the workhouse under this scheme could accept paupers from
unions other than that in which it was located: 26 & 27 Vict. c. 110 s. 2.

106 PRO MH 51/760.

107 Poor Law Amendment Act 1867, 31 & 32 Vict. c. 106 s. 23.

108 See, for example, *Nineteenth Annual Report of the Commissioners in
Lunacy*, PP 1865 (387) xxi 1, at 36 f.

109 *Twenty-First Annual Report of the Commissioners in Lunacy*, PP 1867 (366)
xviii 201, at 21.

110 *Seventeenth Annual Report of the Commissioners in Lunacy*, PP 1863 xx
(331) 437, at 24.

111 PP 1867 (366) xviii 201, at 70.

112 PP 1859 1st sess. (228) ix 1, at 12.

113 PP 1867–8 (332) xxxi 1, at 89.

114 Fraser, *Evolution of the British Welfare State*, 2nd edn. (London:
Macmillan, 1984), p. 117.

115 Fraser, *Evolution of the British Welfare State*, p. 122.

116 Their use in this regard appears quite explicitly in the parliamentary
debates surrounding the continuation of the Metropolitan Commissioners in 1841: *Hansard*, Vol. 59 (3rd ser.), 694, 697 (21 Sept. 1841).

117 They were, for example, discussed in the *Journal of Mental Science*. The
1844 Report of the Metropolitan Commissioners was also published
separately by Bradbury and Evans in 1844.

118 *Hansard*, Vol. 59 (3rd ser.), 694 (21 Sept. 1841). The desire for
information is consistent with Fraser's view of the nineteenth-century
fetish for facts:

The whole spirit of the age was geared to the accumulation of facts, for society
had an insatiable appetite for knowledge of itself, with the mushrooming of
statistical societies and surveys both by Government and private agency.
(*Evolution of the British Welfare State*, 2nd edn. (London: Macmillan, 1984), p.
117)

119 PP 1850 (735) xxiii 393.

120 PP 1860 (338) xxxiv 231.

121 Mellett, 'Bureaucracy and mental illness', p. 235.
122 PP 1850 (735) xxiii 393, at 5.
123 Scull, *The Most Solitary of Afflictions* (New Haven and London: Yale University Press, 1993), p. 303.
124 See Hervey, 'A slavish bowing down', p. 108.
125 Hervey, 'A slavish bowing down', p. 108.

CHAPTER 7

Conclusion: asylums, Poor Law and modernity

The argument has been that county asylums are to be understood in the context of nineteenth-century Poor Law. The issue has been how the Poor Law of lunacy developed, how it was administered and how decisions were made regarding its occupants. It has not primarily been a study of nineteenth-century professionalization, and certainly not of professionalization of the medical specialists who served as super-intendents of asylums. It has not been the study of a total institution in its splendid isolation. It has instead been about the administration of pauper lunacy. It has been about nineteenth-century governance.

Those familiar with the literature in this area will already have remarked on the relative absence of reference to the work of Michel Foucault in the previous chapters. That has been intentional. Foucault's creativity is inspiring, his originality astonishing, his vision captivating and his breadth of insight enthralling. Roy Porter has referred to *Madness and Civilization* as 'by far the most penetrating work ever written on the history of madness',[1] and a host of Foucault's other works have proven similarly important. Each is self-contained; yet each expounds fundamental concepts which overlap with other works. A creative scholar, his ideas and interests changed and developed over time, making matters of comparison between works complex. Each has a sense of refreshing iconoclasm about it, forcing fundamental re-assessment of what had previously been considered obvious. The oeuvre has thus predictably been both influential and controversial, defenders and detractors staking out positions and trading barbs, often in not entirely respectful tones. The literature is now legion. The risk in previous chapters has been that a detailed discussion of Foucault's views would have moved the focus from the nineteenth-century insane to Foucault and his ideas.

That was to be avoided. This is a book about the Poor Law of lunacy; this is not a book about Foucault. At the same time, Foucault cannot be avoided. It is not merely that he wrote at length on madness and the roots of psychiatry, on the creation of asylums and other institutions and on the nature of nineteenth-century social reform. His vision of the practices of power has also been influential in the methodology of the preceding chapters, almost a ghost in the machine. At the same time, the foregoing chapters raise questions about Foucault's work, and it seems appropriate to address at least some of those. The complexity of Foucault's work and the literature surrounding it does not allow of a full treatment in one chapter. In particular, I am not going to address the perennial issue among historians, whether Foucault 'got his facts right'.[2] Certainly, historians must take appropriate care as they apply Foucault's general visions to specific situations; but that cannot be an argument for ignoring the vision when it is helpful and meaningful. Similarly, I will not be engaging with the collection of debates which occupy internalist Foucauldean scholarship. Thus while I am happy to acknowledge that Foucault's thought develops over time, and in particular in the late 1970s, for present purposes I will instead be focusing on various continuities in the work of Foucault and related scholarship. These are intended to draw together some of the issues in the preceding chapters, by way of conclusion.

QUESTIONS OF SUBJECT MATTER AND APPROACH

Foucault was not an historian. His interest was in modernity more generally. He used the past as a way to account for and explain the present, to create 'philosophical fragments in historical building sites',[3] as he once explained. Understanding the roots of the present is a different project from describing the past. The two are related — historians will obviously balk at any suggestion that our work is irrelevant to understanding the present — but they are different, with consequences relating to relevance and significance of subject matter and appropriate forms of argument.

And what are these philosophical fragments? At the core of Foucault's theory is the question of power. Between roughly the eighteenth and the nineteenth centuries, he sees a change in the way power was manifest. *Discipline and Punish*, Foucault's study of the birth of the prison, begins by juxtaposing an account of an *amende honorable* in 1757 with the timetable of a prisoner's day from 1838.[4] Where the eighteenth century had seen social control through public spectacle and terror, the nineteenth hid punishment away, and saw the criminal as malleable, docile. The nineteenth century sought to control the soul. Control of the body became a technique of that intervention, rather than an end in itself. Correction through the body became more specialized, more specific. The body was to be governed, not broken, and precise mechanisms were devised to that end. The individual became the object of study.

Particularly in Foucault's later work, this was extended beyond deviant populations. Individual bodies were perceived as governable on a large scale. Where the eighteenth century had structured power in the command that individuals not transgress certain rules, the nineteenth had individuals conform to behavioural norms. Central to this new technique of power was the development of knowledge of human behaviour and how to amend it. Professions such as psychiatry, criminology and social work began to occupy increasingly important places in the maintenance of social order. As their truths were disseminated through the pedagogues of society, such as teachers, parents, priests, husbands and employers, so they become social norms of general currency. Social policy integrated into personal ethics.

It is the development of these knowledge bases which is pivotal for Foucault's method. He largely ignores the traditional landmark events of history. Despite the time-span of *Discipline and Punish*, he barely mentions the French Revolution. His focus is instead on the developing discourses of punishment, the institutions which grew out of them and the power implied in that dialectic.

Several corollaries follow. Foucault's fascination with power and its exercise suggests a parallel with the literature of social control. His theory provides an interesting response to the criticism of Thompson[5] and others that social control theory does not allow any clear answer as to who is doing the control, and who is being controlled. Foucault's use of discourse theory solves this problem of agency by positing control everywhere and nowhere. Ignatieff comments:

In place of these accounts [Marxist, functionalist], he [Foucault] argues that punitive power is dispersed throughout the social system: it is literally everywhere, in the sense that the disciplinary ideology, the *savoir* which directs and legitimizes power, permeates all social groups (with the exception of the marginal and deviant), ordering the self-repression of the repressors themselves.... Given that all social relations were inscribed within relations of domination and subordination, ordered, so Foucault says, by a continuous disciplinary discourse, it is impossible to identify the privileged sites or actors that controlled all the others. The disciplinary ideology of modern society *can* be identified as the work of specified social actors, but once such an ideology was institutionalized, once its rationality came to be taken for granted, a fully exterior challenge to its logic became impossible.[6]

As Foucault himself says, power is 'a machine in which everyone is caught, those who exercise power just as much as those over whom it is exercised.... [I]t becomes a machinery that no one owns.'[7]

Power thus resides throughout the social machine, in the mundane as well as the spectacular, in daily interactions between people and in individuals' self-governance.

Even this brief summary demonstrates the degree to which my work relies upon and presupposes the work of Foucault. His discussion of power provides a nuanced alternative to a traditionally directional view of history, where the asylum is viewed in terms of progressive improvement in care of the insane, failed reform, or class oppression based in economic determinism. Foucault's focus on the structures and applications of power instead allows a considerably increased range of factors to be considered. The motives, understandings and practices of the individuals administering or otherwise involved in the system, self-styled reformers or otherwise, remain relevant; they form the truth of the system. These are not read uncritically, however. The issue ceases to be one of 'success' or 'failure' of reform. The issue is instead the more open-ended and less judgemental one, to describe and understand what was created. There is an obvious parallel to my methodology. Using the legal structure as a starting point, the chapters above examine the practices and understandings of those administering the Poor Law of lunacy. The question has not been one of 'success' or 'failure'; the question has been how they understood what they were doing, and why the system developed the way it did. The motivations may be different. Foucault wishes to examine the roots of the present in a critical but non-Marxist framework; I wish to examine the past, escaping a similar theoretical straitjacket based on the 'success' or 'failure' of reform. None the less, the techniques overlap, and I am clearly in Foucault's debt in this regard.

At the same time, there are sufficient departures from Foucault's work and theory to warrant discussion.

FOUCAULT AND THE POOR LAW OF LUNACY

As noted above, Foucault was not doing history. While the work in the previous chapters owes much to Foucault in methodological terms, it does make a historical claim of describing the past. Where Foucault examines the pedigree of a modern way of thinking of power, this book describes a specific set of administrative relations.

As a result, this project has situated discourses back with political actors, primarily Justices of the Peace, Poor Law officers, insane paupers and central authorities. The discourses have been shown to be not merely related to broad questions of political ideology and the new, very Foucauldean vision of the state's role as police, but also to much more specific discourses: the threat to the power of Justices of the Peace, the tension between central and local administration in the nineteenth century and the pragmatics of running a Poor Law system. The result is a portrait of a specific set of administrative relations.

This is not necessarily inconsistent with Foucault's view. He favoured analysis of the practices of power at the point of their application, which is in essence what the study above does. It does have some different effects, however. Unlike Foucault, a historical work must account for the multiplicity of discourses, some of which may have faded from modern consciousness. Thus the interplay between discourses, and the specific influences of particular political, practical and social factors upon the discourses, has been significant above. As a result, I hope I have put to rest some of the stereotypical visions of the Poor Law staff in their administration of lunacy: few in the system were either ogres or saints. Most were presumably trying to do a vaguely good job; the interest has been in what 'a vaguely good job' meant to them, and how those understandings affected each other.

The specific results do provide some challenges for Foucauldean scholarship. There has, in this scholarship, been a tendency to view Foucault as juxtaposing law with discipline.[8] Law is associated with the old, classical forms of government, and with centralized power. In so far as we continue to embrace law in modern culture, it is a relic of an earlier ideology: 'In political thought and analysis, we still have not cut off the head of the king.'[9] Discipline, by comparison, is the modern way, involving close surveillance, self-government and minute manipulations. It occurred at local levels, of individuals more than the global world of legislatures and courts.

As Hunt and Wickham point out, this juxtaposition is taken on relatively scant Foucauldean material: a few pages of the introductory volume of the *History of Sexuality*, a couple of lectures[10] and, by implication more than by direct reference, some aspects of *Discipline and Punish*. It is difficult to see that such an analysis of law is in any way central to Foucault's thought; indeed, as Hunt and Wickham point out, at times he himself even hints at the possibility of other forms of legal model, if we could only escape the old, repressive conception.[11]

My work challenges the neatness of the division between discipline and law. Poor Law in England never fits comfortably into the mould of a centralized, authoritarian and repressive power structure which is the apparent Foucauldean classical paradigm of law. The old Poor Law had been significant since at least the sixteenth century, and was always administered locally. Indeed, the classical constitution in England did not centralize power. In English political theory, the king was not a totalitarian ruler of the continental style. Criminal law, with its jury system, was as much about reinforcing the power of localized élites as it was about centralized repression, for example.

Certainly, ideologies of government changed during the nineteenth century, but as we have seen, this local locus of power continued. This could be read as indicating that England developed a disciplinary society earlier than the continent, but that misses the point. It is not simply that the Justices of the Peace were understood in their lunacy work to be engaged in a judicial function, not mere local administration, although the case of *Hodson* v. *Pare* in 1899 makes that point explicitly.[12] As significantly, it was not until 1899 that the question was asked. The distinction between law and administration, between law and discipline, was not clear in nineteenth-century England, and it is not clear that it assists to attempt to impose that division retrospectively.

Equally challenging is the movement away from a univocal focus on alienists in the care of the insane. Much profitable scholarship has developed Foucault's view of the professionalization of power in examining the relationships of doctor–patient and therapist–patient.[13] Yet whatever the twentieth-century situation, a study of the Poor Law of lunacy of the nineteenth century would suggest quite a different set of relevant discourses. Poor law discourses were key. The medical discourses were peripheral, and in so far as they were relevant, it was the knowledge of the Poor Law medical officers, not that of the specialists in the asylums, which were most significant in operating the system.

That is, perhaps, a peculiarity of the English administrative system which Foucault could accept. He himself seems to have had few illusions generally about the professionalization of alienists and scientific medicine. In *Madness and Civilization*, he writes:

It is thought that Tuke and Pinel opened the asylum to medical knowledge. They did not introduce science, but a personality, whose powers borrowed from science only their disguise, or at most their justification. These powers, by their nature, were of a moral and social order; they took root in the madman's minority status, in the insanity of his person, not of his mind.... The physician could exercise his absolute authority in the world of the asylum only insofar as, from the beginning, he was Father and Judge, Family and Law — his medical practice being for a long time no more than a complement to the old rites of Order, Authority, and Punishment.[14]

It is difficult to see, given the administrative structure in England, that Foucault would find it surprising that these same themes were contained in the non-alienist decision-makers, albeit without the specifically medical cloak. Colin Gordon has argued that Foucault's interest in Tuke and Pinel was not in literal truth, but in their status as 'legend of foundation for the profession and institution which produced and used it'.[15] That suggests incorporation of the legend into the profession at a later period, a process which clearly occurred in England as in France. It was not evident in mid-nineteenth-century English practice, but on this reading, that would not be fatal to Foucault's interest. Instead, it raises a question for future research: how and when did the myth become consolidated into English practice?

This allows Foucault to escape too easily, however, for in later work, in particular *Discipline and Punish*, he is interested in the broader question of social policing, a question which implies a specialist professional knowledge. His emphasis is on a new mentality of state control, where entire populations could be managed, through the mechanism of the disciplinary society. Subject populations became understood as docile. Through a process of perpetual examination, knowledge was developed about the individuals in this system. They became cases.

It is worth discussing that progression at greater length, because the research above is relevant for each stage.

Foucault's paradigm for the change in perception of subject populations is the soldier:

To begin with [in the seventeenth century], the soldier was someone who could be recognized from afar; he bore certain signs: the natural signs of his strength and his courage, the marks, too, of his pride; his body was the blazon of his strength and valour; and although it is true that he had to learn the profession of arms little by little – generally in actual fighting – movements like marching and attitudes like the bearing of the head belonged for the most part to a bodily rhetoric of honour.... By the late eighteenth century, the soldier has become something that can be made; out of a formless clay, an inapt body, the machine required can be constructed; posture is gradually corrected; a calculated constraint runs slowly through each part of the body, mastering it, making it pliable, ready at all times, turning silently into the automatism of habit; in short, one has 'got rid of the peasant' and given him 'the air of a soldier'.[16]

This docility was indeed at the base of much of nineteenth-century theory of social police. Its imposition can be seen in the silent system of the prisons, the principle of less eligibility of the Poor Law and the moral management of the asylum:

The keeper intervenes, without weapons, without instruments of constraint, with observation and language only; he advances upon madness, deprived of all that could protect him or make him seem threatening, risking an immediate confrontation without recourse. In fact, though, it is not as a concrete person that he confronts madness, but as a reasonable being, invested by that very fact, and before any combat takes place, with the authority that is his for not being mad. Reason's victory over unreason was once assured only by material force, and in a sort of real combat. Now the combat was always decided beforehand, unreason's defeat inscribed in advance in the concrete situation where madman and man of reason meet. The absense of constraint in the nineteenth-century asylum is not unreason liberated, but madness long since mastered.[17]

This docility was the prerequisite of moral treatment, the productive power of the asylum:

We see that at the Retreat the partial suppression of physical constraint was part of a system whose essential element was the constitution of a 'self-restraint' in which the patient's freedom, engaged by work and the observation of others, was ceaselessly threatened by the recognition of guilt. Instead of submitting to a simple negative operation that loosened bonds and delivered one's deepest nature from madness, it must be recognized that one was in the grip of a positive operation that confined madness in a system of rewards and punishments, and included it in the movement of moral consciousness. A passage from a world of Censure to a universe of Judgment.[18]

Historians of madness may object to a perceived anti-Utopian vision in this line of writing; but as Roy Porter suggests, it is harder to fault Foucault's fundamental point:

Foucault's judgement seems wilful, not least in view of the fact that the Retreat clearly succeeded in restoring so many of its patients to normal social life. Yet his comment rightly draws attention to one point: the Retreat's concern with self-mastery. The Retreat was opening up a new psychiatric space.[19]

Indeed; and the nineteenth-century asylum can in this context be seen as a success. It is not merely that the asylum tried to instil the ethics of work and morality into its charges. It is also that the poor in asylums appear to have been generally docile and well-behaved. As we have seen, by 1890, the *average* county asylum contained over 800 inmates. Staffing levels were minimal; yet when the Lunacy Commission visited, the number of persons under restraint could generally be counted on the fingers of one hand.

Porter's point is further reflective of the Foucauldean vision of modernity, however, in that for Porter, as for virtually all modern history and theorization of patienthood, the objective is normalization. The lunatic is not to be left in his or her madness. That would somehow be ethically wrong. The lunatic is instead to be returned to our world. The 'restoration' to a 'normal social life' suggests the processes of internalization of norms which is central to Foucault's theory of power: if that is the aim, Foucault has a point. The point appears trivial, almost mundane, but it contains so much to suggest just how perceptive Foucault's position is.

All this accepted, Foucault does seem to present a very 'top-down' vision for a theorist purporting to be opposed to that sort of analysis. Foucault scholars sometimes see acceptance of the new régimes, and the complicity of the population, as unproblematic, as in the following passage by Randall McGowen:

The prison and its experts produce the reality of the offender who in turn anchors both the knowledge and the institution. Eventually all society is swept up in these changed relations as the discourse of criminality spawns a welfare apparatus dedicated to surveying the community for the slightest traces of incipient deviancy.[20]

Yet the indications are that the population was not particularly passive. The riots of the poor prior to the establishment of the Poor Law Commission of 1832 present an appropriate countervailing image. The question remains for the Foucauldean, how did the new logic actually take hold?

The research above is relevant to that analysis, both regarding the individuals we have traditionally thought of as the powerful and the marginalized. Regarding the former, the new discourse of pauper insanity lay at the intersection of Benthamite, paternalist and economic discourses otherwise prevalent in mid-nineteenth-century England. While the reasons the formalized Poor Law of lunacy was accepted differed between adherents to those theories, it could be articulated in an appealing fashion in each.

My work similarly suggests how the logic took hold with the poor. The various characterizations of the asylum and the workhouse can be seen as providing discursive structures for the Poor Law officers to entice or threaten, coerce or control the pauper into submission either in the workhouse, with the threat of a transfer to the asylum when portrayed in a punitive light, or in the asylum with the assurance that this was a beneficent gift of the paternalist authority. Often faced with few if any alternatives outside the Poor Law structure, the creation of alternatives in the Poor Law system itself can be seen as providing an economy of choices, an incentive to compliance in one institution or another. The documents relating to admissions to workhouses and county asylums do not record how these arguments were used in the relations between relieving officers, workhouse attendants, pauper insane and their families; but the criteria on the asylum admission forms would suggest that these discourses were not far from the actors' minds. If, as Foucault claims, the prison administers an economy of illegalities,[21] the Poor Law of lunacy administers an economy of pauper madness.

In Foucault's system of discipline, the docile body is subjected to continuing examination.

The examination combines the techniques of an observing hierarchy and those of a normalizing judgement. It is a normalizing gaze, a surveillance that makes it possible to qualify, to classify and to punish. It establishes over individuals a visibility through which one differentiates and judges them.[22]

Paradigmatically, examination is ongoing and continuous. It provides both the rationale for reclassification of individuals within the system, and also the fodder for an overview, often through statistics, of the administration of the system, 'the constitution of a comparative system that made possible the measurement of overall phenomena, the description of groups, the characterization of collective facts, the calculation of gaps between individuals, their distribution in a given "population" '.[23]

Examination also made possible knowledge of the individual subject.

The consitution of the individual as a describable, analysable object, not in order to reduce him to 'specific' features, as did the naturalists in relation to living beings, but in order to maintain him in his individual features, in his particular evolution, in his own aptitudes or abilities, under the gaze of a permanent corpus of knowledge.[24]

The individual became a 'case'. That in turn was to open up a new form of intervention. The individual became identified with the specifics of 'the features, the measurements, the gaps, the "marks" that characterize him and make him a "case" '.[25] Much more specific and tailored intervention became possible, by the new professions engaged in constructing and treating the cases.

Points of connection can be seen between this model and the Poor Law of lunacy. Certainly, as shown in the chapters which precede and the appendices which follow, there was the examination necessary to create the statistical overviews of admissions, discharges, diagnoses and cure rates. As discussed in Chapter 6, the creation, compilation, tabulation and distribution of this information was understood by the Lunacy Commission as an important part of its role. Such examinations exist not merely for the county asylums, but in a somewhat abbreviated form, for workhouses as well. Similarly, basic information was collected and circulated regarding the insane poor on outdoor relief.

For the development of a 'case', however, more was required. Examination was about methods of identifying, signalling or describing of subjects. Thus the military had to keep track of its soldiers in order to identify deserters, pay the troops and establish a proper register of the dead. Hospitals had 'to recognize patients, expel shammers, follow the evolution of diseases, study the effectiveness of treatments, map similar cases and the beginnings of epidemics'.[26] The development of the case, as we have seen, was also to allow the use of this intervention in personalized interventions regarding the individual.

Here, it is much more dubious whether there can be said to be examination in the Poor Law of lunacy. Certainly, individuals were moved between wards in asylum and workhouse, although the absence of documentation makes it not obvious what information or examination was conducted prior to such transfers. If the Poor Law of lunacy is conceived as an administrative whole, the admission documentation to the asylum may be perceived as an examination leading to the construction of a case, in that it was explaining why asylum admission was appropriate, as opposed to other forms of Poor Law provision. Similar assessments were to occur for the admission of lunatics to workhouses by the workhouse medical officer, although I have not located records of such examinations.

It is difficult to see these as creating the insane pauper as a case in any sort of treatment sense, however, for as Chapter 5 argued, it is not at all clear that the casebooks were used in that way. They generally contained minimal information between the patient's admission and discharge. They were not about specialized, professional intervention during the detention. They charted the fall to madness, but not its treatment. This is in a way unsurprising; the Victorians believed in the curative powers of systems, of institutions themselves. One side of the Poor Law ideology was about a self-administering system. Foucault himself alludes to that aspect, as part of the nature of the system of discipline.[27] The Poor Law was to structure choice in the pauper, not to create an information-intensive bureaucracy. In so far as the asylum is to be understood as a Poor Law institution, a spillover effect is unsurprising. Just as detailed case notes were not kept for individual paupers in the workhouse, so it is perhaps unsurprising that minimal notes were kept of the pauper's stay in the asylum: once they were in, the system was to take over.

If the focus is altered from the asylum itself to the Poor Law of lunacy as a whole, however, the case notes and admission documents take on a different relevance. They present a framework understanding the world outside the asylum, where people were not yet mad and had a hope of avoiding the same fate, rather than in the provision of treatment for the apparent subject of the record. Here, there is sufficient relevant detail to consider the individuals 'cases', but the area of concern involves people becoming insane paupers, not people becoming cured. Again, this makes some sense in a Poor Law structure. The case notes and admission documents can be seen as chronicling the causes of this form of pauperism, creating a field of knowledge through which the creation of pauper lunacy in society could be understood.

The admission documents and case notes also articulate the criteria by which the economy of madness was administered within the Poor

Law. Here, the pauper becomes a case in a different sense. At issue was which institutional response would be employed in the broader Poor Law. As such, they are about classification of paupers. Here again, they fit well into a Poor Law context. As we saw in Chapter 3, and despite the apparent intent of its founders, the Poor Law never acted as a self-acting system. It always relied on the discretion of the Poor Law authorities and, in the case of pauper lunacy, the magistracy. The records can be seen as providing the knowledge necessary for exercise of that discretion, an essential factor in the Poor Law administration.

The view of the records as creating the pauper lunatic as a 'case' makes sense only if the context is understood as Poor Law administration, rather than the internal requirements of the county asylum itself. The resulting discourses did have another, related function divorced from the individuals, however: they articulated broader social rules for how the care of the insane poor was to be understood. This is consistent with a different strand of Foucault scholarship. Particularly in his later work, Foucault envisaged disciplinary structures as extending into the population at large. The system never did, in fact, self-administer, and the records provide articulation of administrative rules. Here again, there is some tension between the records and Foucault's vision. The latter tends to describe a movement towards mass population governance, in particular through the use of quantification and statistics. Certainly, this approach can be seen in the way the Lunacy Commissioners instructed that forms would be completed. As noted in Chapter 5, their intent was to develop a statistical model of the causes of insanity. Notwithstanding an attempt in their 1847 special report, however, the forms as actually completed did not lend themselves to this approach. Instead, they contained the morality tales of Poor Law discourse. If the statistical side of the argument failed in practice, however, the broader issue remains: the casebooks and the admission documents can be seen as creating a local discourse, relevant to administration. In part, this reinforces the basic argument of this book. The criteria of the Lunacy Commission would have been relevant to an understanding of insanity per se; what in the end was produced instead reflected, not so much a scientific vision of madness and its causes, but a sketch of the administration of lunacy in a Poor Law context.

CONCLUSION

The use of Foucault to bring together various themes in conclusion has its risks as well as its advantages. This is not a book 'about' Foucault. While his work is insightful and helpful, it should not blind the reader to the broader themes of the present work, relating to the administrative structure of the nineteenth-century state as it applied to pauper lunacy. None the less, there is a final point which can be made with reference to Foucault, upon which it is appropriate to finish.

As noted above, Foucault's work traces the origins of specific discursive structures. Discourses collateral to those structures are justifiably marginalized in his discussion. History takes a different approach. In the chapters above, I have attempted an account of the variety of administrative practices and discursive frameworks which created the care of the insane pauper in the mid-nineteenth century. It is appropriate, then, to ask the Foucauldean question: what happened to these other discourses? Foucault himself, as we have seen, recognizes the possibility that medical science was a shell in which a variety of other ideas of policing were contained. Changes in the legal structures of insanity have been significant on paper, but it remains the poor who are confined, overwhelmingly, in psychiatric facilities. Is it not fair to ask the degree to which twentieth-century mental health and its administration remain the Poor Law of lunacy?

NOTES

1   Roy Porter, 'Foucault's great confinement', in *Rewriting the History of Madness: Studies in Foucault's* Histoire de la folie, ed. Still and Velody (London and New York: Routledge, 1992), p. 119.

2   With reference to Foucault and insanity, this debate is developed in Still and Velody (eds), *Rewriting the History of Madness*, (London: Routledge, 1992).

3   Quoted in Felix Driver, 'Bodies in space', in *Reassessing Foucault: Power, Medicine and the Body*, ed. C. Jones and R. Porter (New York and London: Routledge, 1994), p. 113 at 114.

4   Foucault, *Discipline and Punish*, trans. Alan Sheridan (New York: Random House, 1977) pp. 3 ff.

5   F. M.L. Thompson, 'Social control in Victorian Britain', *Economic History Review*, **34** 2nd ser. (1981): 180.

6   M. Ignatieff, 'State, civil society and total institutions', in *Social Control and the State*, ed. Cohen and Scull (1983; reprinted Oxford: Blackwell, 1985), p. 75 at 93.

7   C. Gordon (ed.), *Power/Knowledge: Selected Interviews and other Writings 1972–1977 by Michel Foucault* (New York, London: Harvester Wheatsheaf, 1980), p. 156.

8   See, for example, Alan Hunt and Gary Wickham, *Foucault and Law: Towards a Sociology of Law as Governance* (London: Pluto, 1994), Chs. 1, 2; Laura Engelstein, 'Combined underdevelopment: discipline and the law in imperial and Soviet Russia', *American Historical Review*, **98** (1993): 344; Jan Goldstein, 'Framing discipline with law: problems and promises of the liberal state', *American Historical Review*, **98** (1993): 364.

9   Foucault, *History of Sexuality: An Introduction* (1976); trans. Robert Hurley (New York: Random House, 1978), pp. 88–9.

10   The most significant of these is the second of Foucault's 'Two lectures' (1976), reprinted in Colin Gordon (ed.), *Michel Foucault: Power/Knowledge* (Hemel Hempstead: Harvester Wheatsheaf, 1980) pp. 92 ff. Jan Goldstein also relies on Foucault's 'The dangerous individual', *International Journal of Law and Psychiatry*, **1** (1978): 1; reprinted Lawrence Kritzman (ed.), *Michel Foucault: Politics, Philosophy, Culture* (London: Routledge, 1988), p. 125.

11   Hunt and Wickham, *Foucault and Law*, pp. 63–4.

12   68 LJ QB 309; [1899] 1 QB 455, 80 LT 13, 47 WR 241, 15 LTR 171 (CA). Thus statements made in applications to confine individuals were protected by privilege in an action for defamation.

13   See, for example, Nikolas Rose, *The Psychological Complex* (London: Routledge, 1985), where the history of psychology in the twentieth century is given a Foucauldean twist.

14   Foucault, *Madness and Civilization*, pp. 271–2.

15   Gordon, *'Histoire de la folie*: an unknown book by Michel Foucault', in *Rewriting the History of Madness*, ed. A. Still and I. Velody (London: Routledge, 1992), p. 19 at 32.

16   *Discipline and Punish* p. 135.

17   *Madness and Civilization*, pp. 251 f.

18   *Madness and Civilization*, p. 250.

19   Porter, *Mind-Forg'd Manacles* (1987; reprinted Harmondsworth: Penguin, 1990), p. 225, endnotes omitted.

20   McGowen, 'Power and humanity, or Foucault among the historians', in *Reassessing Foucault*, ed. C. Jones and R. Porter, (London: Routledge, 1994), p. 91 at 97.

21   *Discipline and Punish*, p. 272.

22   *Discipline and Punish*, p. 184.

23   *Discipline and Punish*, p. 190.

24   *Discipline and Punish*, p. 190.

25   *Discipline and Punish*, p. 192.

26   *Discipline and Punish*, p. 189.

27   *Discipline and Punish*, at, for example, p. 201.

APPENDIX 1

Quantitative indicators

This appendix presents an overview of relevant statistical information drawn from the annual reports of the Lunacy Commission, the Poor Law Board and the Local Government Board. The use of this material poses both practical and theoretical difficulties.

There are to begin with the usual anomalies of data, where categorical structures were changed over time. This is particularly problematic with the Poor Law statistics. Up to 1848, the statistics listed the number of people relieved in the quarter ending on Lady Day (25 March); after that time, they showed the number of persons actually on relief on 1 January and 1 July of the given year. That transition is of assistance, in that it brought the Poor Law statistics into closer conformity with those of the Lunacy Commission, which from 1849 published an annual table as to where pauper lunatics were relieved on 1 January. It also means that the information contained in earlier reports from the Poor Law Commissioners is virtually useless for comparison purposes, and it has been ignored in this appendix.

Returns of apparently the same information completed by the same people for the same days routinely did not match. The thirty-sixth and forty-fifth annual reports of the Commissioners in Lunacy listed the number of insane persons contained in workhouses on 1 January from 1859 to 1891. The ninth and twentieth annual reports of the Local Government Board listed what appears to be the same information. The numbers do not agree. By the end of the period, the differences were statistically minimal, about half a percentage. In the 1860s the difference was generally less than 2½ percent, but in 1859, it was 6 per cent. The reports themselves do not account for this differential, although part may be due to the inclusion of Gilbert Unions and parishes under local Poor Law acts within the statistics of the Lunacy Commission.

The central authorities were not even necessarily consistent within their own series of reports. Thus Appendix D (71) to the *Ninth Annual Report of the Local Government Board* purported to be a continuation of Appendix 33 to the *Eleventh Annual Report of the Poor Law Board*. The tables overlapped, each providing data for 1 January 1858, 1 July 1858 and 1 January 1859. For each of these dates, the later report showed 7 per cent more individuals in workhouses, and 3 per cent more on outdoor relief, than the earlier table. No explanation was provided for the differential.

There were also anomalies in the collection of the information, particularly in the early years, which do not inspire confidence in the quality of the statistics. For both the able-bodied and non-able-bodied categories, Appendix 33 of the *Eleventh Annual Report of the Poor Law Board* distinguished married couples receiving indoor relief from other adults receiving similar relief. The married couples are divided by sex. Obviously, one would expect the number of married men to equal the number of married women, and commencing with the figures for 1 January 1858, they do so.[1] For the period from 1849 to July 1857, the figures are not the same, and are occasionally radically different. In the extreme, in their able-bodied married category for 1 July 1857, Cumberland Union listed 26 women and one man. The total able-bodied married class routinely seems to number one and a half times the number of married women to married men in July returns. The consistency is interesting, suggesting that carelessness may not have been the only issue, although the equalization of the numbers starting in 1858 would suggest that, at least in the view of the Poor Law Board, the expectation was that husbands would equal wives. At issue here is not the reason for the differential, but rather that the statistics cannot necessarily be taken simply at their face value.[2]

The Poor Law statistics regarding lunacy are particularly problematic. An increase of the insane on outdoor relief by 60 per cent in 1859, from 13,420 to 21,501, was explained by the following note:

The increase in the number of Insane Paupers, recorded in the Out-door portion of this Summary on the 1st January 1859, arises from the circumstance of those persons chargeable to the Poor Rates and maintained in Lunatic Asylums being then fully returned for the first time.[3]

It would thus appear that, prior to 1859, there was no consistent practice for the recording of lunatics on the general return of pauperism. The 1859 increase of 8,081 was close to half the number of paupers in asylums, registered hospitals and private madhouses at that time, suggesting that the bulk of the returns before 1858 were also insane paupers kept in these institutions. There is no way of assessing that with any accuracy, however, making this column essentially useless to determine the number of people on outdoor relief and not contained in an institution, a figure not readily available elsewhere.[4]

Some unions were said prior to 1859 to have returned paupers in asylums as on indoor relief.[5] The degree to which this was the case cannot be assessed with any accuracy, but it cannot account for a large proportion of those not accounted for in the outdoor category. The total insane on indoor relief was listed as 7,555 for 1 January 1858 and 8,451 for 1 January 1859.[6] The *Fifteenth Annual Report of the Lunacy Commission* showed 6,800 insane paupers actually in workhouses for 1857, suggesting that the reporting of those in asylums in this category may have been minimal.

Even after 1859, the figure for outdoor relief of the insane remains questionable. If the practice outlined above was routinely followed, the return ought to equal the sum of those paupers in asylums, registered hospitals, private madhouses and on outdoor relief. In comparison with Lunacy Commission statistics for these categories, it still underreports. Once again, the degree of this underreporting decreases over the period, from about 8 per cent in 1859 to about 4 per cent in 1890. As before, this may in part be accounted for by the inclusion of Gilbert Unions and parishes under local acts in the Lunacy Commission statistic; however, the differential is considerably greater here than in the workhouse case noted above, suggesting the presence of other factors.

The statistics were also affected by quirks in the legal structure of the Poor Law. This is particularly significant for married couples on indoor relief, where the expectation seems to have been that both members of the couple receiving indoor relief would be categorized in the same way for statistical purposes.[7] The question arises as to how a couple composed, for example, of an able-bodied man and a non-able-bodied woman would be categorized. The returns for outdoor relief contained in the *Eleventh Annual Report of the Poor Law Board* were explicit that able-bodied status was determined in these circumstances with reference to the male.[8] This is consistent with the patriarchal structure of the Poor Law, discussed in the body of this book. The reasonable assumption is that the same policy was used to determine the wife's status on indoor relief. As such, the statistics bear no relationship to the actual physical condition of the wife, and are of limited application in this regard. There was no indication that this reporting policy changed in the period in question.[9] The importance of this for the overall understanding of the statistics is important, but should not be overestimated. The percentage of women married to men in the workhouse, according to the *Eleventh Annual Report* where this is calculable, is generally between roughly 5 and 10 per cent of the adult women in the relevant class.

The second place where Poor Law policy renders the recording of the statistics ambiguous concerns those people transferred to workhouses pursuant to section 8 of the 1862 Act, discussed above. Under a legal opinion of the Law Officers of the Crown, persons transferred under these provisions remained legally in the asylum, even though they were physically in the workhouse.[10] The statistics do not indicate how these people were categorized in the tables, but given the explicit direction in the legal opinion that they be retained on the books of the asylum, it seems likely that they were categorized as asylum inmates, not workhouse inmates.

As a result, the statistics which follow must be approached with considerable caution. They may indicate broad trends, but should not in any way be taken as reflecting twentieth-century statistical standards.

The theoretical difficulties regarding the statistics concern what they are and how they are to be understood. On the one hand, they were a part of the discourse constructed by the central authorities about the insane in the nineteenth century. Just as the content of local and central reports of the Lunacy Commission regarding workhouses and asylums were shown to be at least in part determined by bureaucratic factors, the content of the statistics must presumably be viewed with the same reservations: just how much can they be taken to say about 'situated reality', and just what do they measure?

At the very least, they may be understood as part of the material available to policy-makers in the nineteenth century. The apparently increasing incidence of lunacy, particularly in the pauper class, was the topic of debate and concern, and it was on these statistics that the arguments were based. They are relevant in that context, if none other. The question is whether they may be used for any assessment of what was 'really' happening.

It is clear that the compilation of the statistics did occur in an administrative context. The focus of that context has already been misrepresented here, in that no reference has been made to the considerable interest of financial issues in the statistical material compiled by the central authorities. Concerning the enumeration of individuals, the policies regarding married women and paupers removed under section 8 of the 1862 Act provide examples of situations where administrative factors place a specific structure and interpretation onto the statistics.

At a more basic level, the individual only became a statistic when it was necessary to approach the Poor Law authorities for relief, either by way of the usual poor relief or for admission to the asylum. If, following Scull, it is allowed that this was in part a function of economic forces which increasingly left the poor little option but to resort to relief rather than supporting their incapacitated family members out of their own income, occasions for categorization may in fact be related to market forces.[11]

It is also the case that what are counted are acts of categorization, and the relationship between these categorizations and situated reality can be problematic. Thus there is no reliable indication as to how much the rise in persons kept in the workhouse was the result of a change in classificatory procedures within the workhouse, and how much it represented the introduction into the workhouse of people who otherwise would have been left outside it. This means that it is highly dubious to use the statistics even as a measure of how many of the people cared for by the Poor Law were 'insane', in any objective sense (if, indeed, an objective meaning of insanity is itself a coherent concept).

What the statistics measure is the growth of insanity as an administrative category within the Poor Law. With that caveat (and the practical ones noted above), it does seem reasonable to accept them as 'true' within their administrative context. It seems merely stubborn, for example, on the basis of there being 'nothing outside the text' to suggest that the recording of the returns of the numbers contained in county asylums have nothing to say about asylum growth.

The statistics are presented in the following pages in the form of graphs. This perhaps presents a theoretical issue of its own. The originals are in long and sometimes complicated tables, rendering interpretation difficult. The organization in graphic format can be seen as a restructuring away from the original text: it was, after all, the impenetrable tables which confronted the nineteenth-century policy-maker. The graphic interpretation loses the precision of the individual numbers of the tables, but, given the practical difficulties of those numbers noted above, the concession to easier interpretation seemed a justifiable compromise.

NOTES

1   For example, the number of men in the male, married, able-bodied, indoor relief class matches the number of women in the corresponding female class.

2   The difference prior to 1858 cannot be explained by categorizing the wife as able-bodied or non-able-bodied according to her own physical health. If this were the case, the sums of able-bodied and non-able-bodied men would equal the sum of able-bodied and non-able-bodied women, and they do not.

3   *Ninth Annual Report of Local Government Board*, PP 1880 [2681] xxvi 1, App. (D), no. 71.

4   The Poor Law Board did publish occasional tables relating to lunacy which included information as to where the insane were kept, distinguishing those in county asylums, private madhouses, workhouses and on outdoor relief: see *Seventh Annual Report of the Poor Law Board*, PP 1854–5 [1921] xxiv 1, at Appendix 40 for 1 January 1854; *Fifth Annual Report of the Poor Law Board*, PP 1852–3 [1625] l 1, at App. 33 for 1 January 1852; and a separate return not contained in an annual report, at PP 1847–8 xxxii 371, for 1 January 1847. A similar table was included in the *Eleventh Annual Report of the Lunacy Commissioners*, PP 1857, 2nd sess. (157) xvi 351, at Appendix E for 1 January 1857. These give a more specific division of outdoor relief, and have been relied upon when a figure is required. They are problematic, however, in that they do not distinguish lunatics contained in registered hospitals, leaving it a matter of speculation as to where, if anywhere, these paupers were included in the table. The number of paupers in these charitable facilities appears to have been small, however. The figures contained in the reports of the Lunacy Commission starting in 1859 show only 354 paupers in these facilities.

5   *Twelfth Annual Report of Poor Law Board*, PP 1860 [2675] xxxvii 1, at App. 22, Table II, note.

6   *Ninth Annual Report of the Local Government Board*, PP 1880 [2681] xxvi 1, at App. (D), no. 71. Cf. *Eleventh Annual Report of the Poor Law Board*, PP 1859 1st sess. [2500] ix 741, at App. 33, where the increase was from 6,947 to 7,672.

7   This point is clearest after 1858, when the figures for men and women in married couples started to agree within able-bodied and non-able-bodied categories. As noted above, problems of the returns themselves make it difficult to assess recording practices prior to that time regarding these

numbers, but there is no indication of a change in attitude to statistical practices relating to women at this time.

8   These returns were contained on the same table as the problematic indoor returns, viz. Appendix 33.

9   Appendix (D), no. 71 to the *Ninth Annual Report of the Local Government Board*, PP 1880 [2681] xxvi 1, regarding 1858 to 1879, states:

> The corresponding table to this, but with a more detailed classification, will be found at page 196 of the Eleventh Annual Report of the Poor Law Board, where the particulars are given in reference to twenty-one periods commencing with January 1849.

This later report does not include the separate classification of married paupers, but this note would suggest that the classification structure did not change between these reports.

Different practices regarding married paupers cannot account solely for the inconsistencies between the Lunacy Commission and Poor Law statistics, although it does appear that those statistics categorized married women without reference to their husbands. In fact, the Poor Law and Lunacy Commission outdoor relief statistics after 1859 were marginally more different for men than for women. As noted above, the overall difference was about 8 per cent in 1860, reducing to about 4 per cent by 1890; for men, the corresponding figures are 10 and 5 per cent.

10 PRO MH 51/760.

11 Interestingly, there does not appear to be any correlation between the grant of relief generally and the relief accorded to the pauper insane. On Scull's hypothesis, one might expect such a correlation, given that the same pressures which would force individuals onto relief might reasonably be expected to force them to give up their insane relatives to the care of the Poor Law. Positing such a correlation implies a variety of assumptions, the most notable being the increase in poor relief being an indicator of diminishing flexible income on the part of the remainder of the poor, but the case none the less appears strong enough to warrant further consideration.

FIGURES, SOURCES AND ANNOTATIONS

1   *Institutionalization of the insane, private versus pauper, 1 January 1849–90*
This graph shows the number of paupers and private patients in institutions. Both children and adults are included. Figures for 1859 through 1882 are drawn from Table I in the *Thirty-Sixth Annual Report of the Commissioners in Lunacy*, PP 1882 (357) xxxii 1, at 6 ff. The figures for 1883 to 1890 are drawn from Table I of the *Forty-Fifth Annual Report of the Commissioners in Lunacy*, PP 1890–91 (286) xxxvi 1, at 6 ff. The figures on the graph do not include either paupers on outdoor relief or private patients living 'with friends or elsewhere'. The figures for private

patients for 1849 to 1858 are drawn from the annual reports of the Commissioners in Lunacy. The figures for paupers in this period are the sum of the returns of pauper lunatics in asylums, charitable hospitals and private madhouses contained in the annual reports of the Commissioners in Lunacy for the respective years, plus the return of the number contained in workhouses, as reported in the *Eleventh Annual Report of the Poor Law Board*, PP 1859 1st sess. [2500] ix 741, at 196 ff., being Appendix 33. This mixture of reports of Lunacy Commission and Poor Law Board is regrettable for the reasons indicated above, but it is unavoidable since the reports of the Lunacy Commission do not provide statistics for workhouses for this period.

2   *Inmates of county asylums, private versus pauper, 1 January 1849–1890*
This graph shows the number of people in county lunatic asylums, distinguishing between private and pauper patients. The source of the figures from 1859 through 1882 are drawn from Table I in the *Thirty-Sixth Annual Report of the Commissioners in Lunacy*, PP 1882 (357) xxxii 1, at 6 ff. The figures for 1883 to 1890 are drawn from Table I of the *Forty-Fifth Annual Report of the Commissioners in Lunacy*, PP 1890–91 (286) xxxvi 1, at 6 ff. Figures for 1849 through 1858 are drawn from the annual reports of the Commissioners in Lunacy for the year in question.

3   *Relief of pauper insane in various institutions, 1 January 1849–1890*
This graph shows the number of paupers relieved on 1 January 1849 to 1890 in county asylums, registered hospitals, licensed madhouses and workhouses. The sources of these statistics are as in Figure 1. Outdoor relief statistics are also shown commencing in 1859. These figures are also drawn from the *Thirty-Sixth* and *Forty-Fifth Annual Reports* of the Commissioners in Lunacy. Regarding the inadequacy of statistics relating to outdoor relief, see introduction to this appendix, above. Figures for outdoor relief prior to 1858 have been drawn from the *Eleventh Annual Report of the Lunacy Commissioners*, PP 1857, 2nd sess. (157) xvi 351, at Appendix E for 1 January 1857; the *Seventh Annual Report of the Poor Law Board*, PP 1854–5 [1921] xxiv 1, at Appendix 40 for 1 January 1854; the *Fifth Annual Report of the Poor Law Board*, PP 1852–3 [1625] l 1, at App. 33 for 1 January 1852; and a separate return not contained in an annual report, at PP 1847–8 xxxii 371, for 1 January 1847. The assumption has been made that trends were steady between these points.

4   *Relief of pauper insane in various institutions, 1 January 1849–90, by percentage*
This graph shows the percentage of insane paupers relieved on 1 January 1849 in workhouses, licensed madhouses, registered hospitals, county asylums and on outdoor relief. The sources of statistics is the same as those for Figure 3, and are subject to the same limitations on reliability regarding outdoor relief prior to 1859.

5   *Adult paupers in workhouses, 1 January 1849–90*
This graph shows the number of paupers contained in workhouses from

1 January 1849 to 1890, distinguishing those categorized as insane, able-bodied non-able-bodied, and vagrant. The statistics from 1849 to 1857 are drawn from the *Eleventh Annual Report of the Poor Law Board*, PP 1859 1st sess. [2500] ix 741, at 196 ff., being Appendix 33. Those for 1858 through 1874 are drawn from the *Ninth Annual Report of the Local Government Board*, PP 1879–80 [2681] xxvi 1, at Appendix (D) 71. Those for 1875 through 1890 are drawn from the *Twentieth Annual Report of the Local Government Board*, PP 1890–91 [6460] xxxiii 1, at 480, App. (E).

6   *Adult paupers in workhouses, 1 January 1849–90, by percentage*
This graph shows the percentage of paupers in workhouses from 1 January 1849 to 1890 who were respectively insane, able-bodied, non-able-bodied and vagrants. Sources are as for Figure 5.

7   *Outdoor relief of adults, 1 January 1859–90*
This graph shows the number of persons on outdoor relief on 1 January from 1859 to 1890, distinguishing the able-bodied, the non-able-bodied, and the insane. The sources for able-bodied and non-able bodied are those indicated in Figure 5. The source for outdoor relief of the insane for 1859 through 1882 is drawn from Table I in the *Thirty-Sixth Annual Report of the Commissioners in Lunacy*, PP 1882 (357) xxxii 1, at 6 ff. The figures for 1883 to 1890 are drawn from Table I of the *Forty-Fifth Annual Report of the Commissioners in Lunacy*, PP 1890–91 (286) xxxvi 1, at 6 ff. These figures regarding the insane are not strictly comparable, as the Lunacy Commission figures include children, who are excluded from the Poor Law statistics used here. The number of children appears to have been minimal, however.

8   *Outdoor relief of adults, 1 January 1859–90, by percentage*
Percentage of those receiving outdoor relief on 1 January 1859 through 1890 who were able-bodied, non-able-bodied or insane. Sources as in Figure 7.

9   *Adult insane paupers, 1 January 1859–90, by sex and as a percentage of total adult paupers*
This graph shows in absolute numbers and by percentage the adult paupers who were insane, by sex. The source of the statistics from 1859 to 1882 is the *Thirty-Sixth Annual Report of the Commissioners in Lunacy*, PP 1882 (357) xxxii 1, at Table iv, pp. 14 f., and for 1882 to 1890, the *Forty-Fifth Annual Report of the Lunacy Commissioners*, PP 1890–1 (286) xxxvi 1, at Table iv, pp. 14 f.

10   *Costs of pauper lunatics in county asylums, as percentage of total expenditure on relief of the poor, 1857–1890*
Shows the maintenance costs for pauper lunatics in asylums and licensed houses, and the percentage this comprises of the total costs expended for the relief of the poor. The asylum costs do not include outdoor relief or costs associated with workhouse care. On the face of it, they appear to be only maintenance costs, with costs associated with removal contained under a residual category for miscellaneous expenses associated with

relief. Total poor relief figure (forming the basis of the percentage comparison) includes costs of indoor and outdoor relief, care of the insane (as above), principal and interest expenditures for workhouse loans, salaries of officers and other costs 'immediately connected with relief'. It does not include costs of other services which the poor rate was used as a mechanism to fund, e.g., policing, highway expenses, expenses associated with proceedings before Justices, vaccination fees and the costs of maintaining jury lists, which increased the poor rate in total by roughly one-third. Source of statistics: *Twentieth Annual Report of the Local Government Board*, PP 1890–1 [6460] xxxiii 1, at Appendix 118.

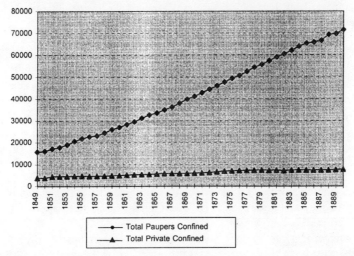

Figure 1 *Institutionalization of the insane, private versus pauper, 1 January 1849–90*

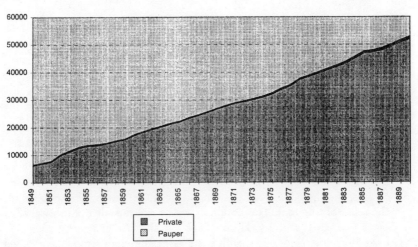

Figure 2 *Inmates of county asylums, private versus pauper, 1 January 1849–90*

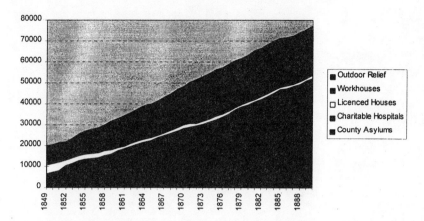

Figure 3 *Relief of pauper insane in various institutions, 1 January 1849–90*

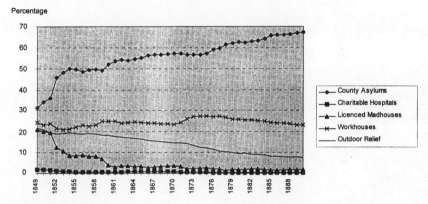

Figure 4 *Relief of pauper insane in various institutions, 1 January 1849–90, by percentage*

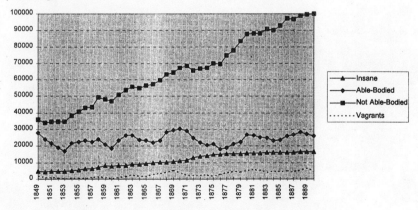

Figure 5 *Adult paupers in workhouses, 1 January 1849–90*

263

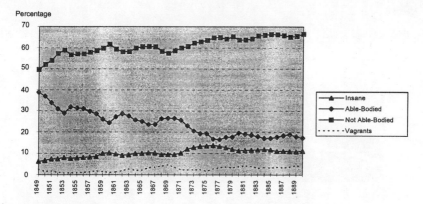

Figure 6 *Adult paupers in workhouses, 1 January 1849–90, by percentage*

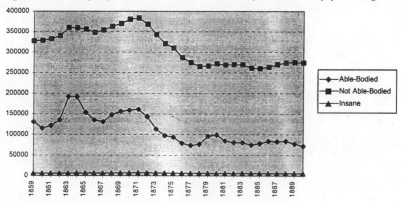

Figure 7 *Outdoor relief of adults, 1 January 1859–90*

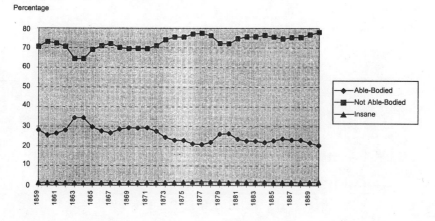

Figure 8 *Outdoor relief of adults, 1 January 1859–90, by percentage*

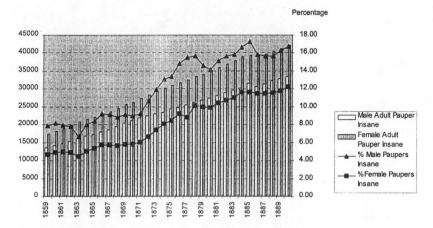

Figure 9 *Adult insane paupers, 1 January 1859–1890, by Sex, and as a percentage of total adult paupers*

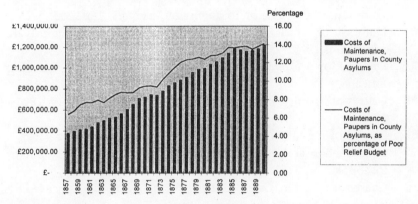

Figure 10 *Cost of pauper lunatics in county asylums, as percentage of total expenditure on relief of the poor, 1857–1890*

APPENDIX 2

Leicestershire records: statistical overview

Table 1 Overview of persons in Leicestershire and Rutland Lunatic Asylum, 1 January 1849–70

Year	Paupers			Criminals			Private/Charity			Total		
	M	W	Tot	M	W	Tot	M	W	Tot	M	W	Tot
49												175
50			155						51			206
51			171						48			219
52			186						47			233
53	90	93	183				24	26	50	114	119	233
54	79	91	170	14	5	19	22	23	45	115	119	234
55	89	111	200	14	3	17	24	30	54	127	141	271
56	101	127	228	13	3	16	21	30	51	135	160	295
57	104	128	232	13	3	16	24	32	56	141	163	304
58	117	134	251	13	2	15	26	27	53	156	163	319
59	115	131	246	14	2	16	22	29	51	151	162	313
60	131	158	289	15	2	17	24	28	52	170	188	358
61	175	142	317	15	2	17	24	30	54	181	207	388
62	150	176	326	14	2	16	20	36	56	184	214	398
63	147	167	314	14	2	16	22	34	56	183	203	386
64	142	178	320	15	2	17	29	27	56	186	207	393
65	151	178	329	13	2	15	23	23	46	187	203	390
66	154	172	326	11	2	13	24	28	52	189	202	391
67	159	182	341	11	1	12	22	25	47	192	208	400
68	158	194	352	12	1	13	21	25	46	191	220	411
69	201	228	429	7	1	8	21	29	50	229	258	487
70	167	184	351	7	0	7	22	27	49	196	211	407

Source: Annual reports of the Leicestershire and Rutland Lunatic Asylum

Table 2 Admissions and discharges, 1849–70

Year	Admitted	DISCHARGES				Died
		Cured	Relieved	Not Relieved	Total	
1849	121	51	6	0	57	33
1850	101	49	13	0	62	26
1851	95	46	15	0	61	20
1852	85	50	16	0	66	19
1853	120	65	18	0	83	36
1854	131	47	23	0	70	24
1855	105	39	17	0	56	25
1856	107	53	11	3	69[1]	29
1857	116	52	12	0	64	35
1858	96	56	14	0	70	30
1859	132	37	7	1	47[2]	40
1860	111	43	11	0	55[3]	26
1861	107	45	3	3	51	46
1862	72	32	5	1	38	46
1863	74	33	8	5	46	21
1864	78	28	2	3	34[4]	47
1865	78	27	7	7	41	36
1866	78	27	12	0	39	30
1867	73	24	9	0	34[5]	28
1868	163	42	6	0	49[6]	38
1869	130	40	90[7]	27	157	53
1870	90	32	9	0	41	39

Source: Annual reports of the Leicestershire and Rutland Lunatic Asylum
Notes: 1. Includes two escapees.
2. Includes two escapees.
3. Includes one escapee.
4. Includes one escapee.
5. Includes one escapee.
6. Includes one escapee.
7. The bulk of these patients and the 27 'relieved' patients were transferred to the new Leicester Borough Asylum.

Table 3 Chronic pauper patients versus total pauper patients, 1857–69

Year	Paupers in asylum more than 2 years on 31 December	Total paupers in asylum, 31 December	Percentage paupers in asylum over 2 Years
1857	168	251	67
1858	185	246	75
1859	190	289	66
1860	207	317	65
1861	195	326	60
1862	246	314	78
1863	275	320	86
1864	266	329	81
1865	266	326	82
1866	274	341	80
1867	274	352	78
1868	298	429	69
1869	267	351	76

Source: Annual reports of the Leicestershire and Rutland Lunatic Asylum

Table 4: Basic breakdown of pauper admissions, 1861–65

	Men	Women	Total
Domestic admissions	77	100	177
Workhouse admissions	37	42	79
'Wanderers'	21	16	37
Miscellaneous	16	17	33
Total	**151**	**175**	**326**

Source: Abstracted from admission documents, Leicestershire and Rutland Lunatic Asylum

Table 5 Duration of attack prior to admission, paupers, 1861–65

Duration of attack prior to confinement	Domestic admissions			Workhouse admissions			Wan	Misc	Total Paupers Admitted		
	M	W	Total	M	W	Total	Total	Total	M	W	Total
1 week or less	16	25	41	7	4	11	13	3	31	37	68
1 week to 1 month	27	28	55	9	9	18	9	14	50	46	96
1 to 3 months	18	24	42	4	14	18	3	8	27	44	71
3 to 12 months	4	11	15	3	4	7	5	5	12	20	32
Over 1 Year	10	10	20	9	11	20	3	3	22	24	46
Unknown/Not Given	2	2	4	5	0	5	4	0	9	4	13
Totals	77	100	177	37	42	79	37	33	151	175	326

Source: Statements of relieving officers, admission documents, Leicestershire and Rutland Lunatic Asylum

Table 6 Duration of attack prior to confinement, pauper versus private admissions, 1861–65

Duration of attack prior to confinement	Paupers			Private patients			Total		
	M [%]	W [%]	Tot [%]	M	W	Tot [%]	M [%]	W [%]	Tot [%]
1 week or less	31[1] [21]	37 [21]	**68** **[21]**	5	5	**10** **[16]**	36 [20]	42 [20]	**78** **[20]**
1 week to 1 month[2]	50 [33]	46 [26]	**96** **[29]**	8	7	**15** **[23]**	58 [32]	53 [25]	**111** **[28]**
1 to 3 months	27 [18]	44 [25]	**71** **[22]**	7	7	**14** **[22]**	34 [19]	51 [25]	**85** **[22]**
3 to 12 months	12 [8]	20 [11]	**32** **[10]**	5	4	**9** **[14]**	17 [9]	24 [12]	**41** **[11]**
Over 1 Year	22 [15]	24 [14]	**46** **[14]**	5	7	**12** **[19]**	27 [15]	31 [15]	**58** **[15]**
Unknown/Not Given	9 [6]	4 [2]	**13** **[4]**	1	3	**4** **[6]**	10 [5]	7 [3]	**17** **[4]**
Totals Inmates	151	175	**326**	31	33	**64**	182	208	**390**

Source: Statements of relieving officers (for paupers) and persons signing committal orders (for private patients), contained in admission documents to Leicestershire and Rutland Lunatic Asylum

Notes: 1. The percentages in brackets represent the proportion of the figure at the bottom of the column; e.g., in this case [21] means that 21 per cent of pauper men were certified within one week of the commencement of their attack.

2. Admissions falling on the boundary line have been included in the shorter time category; e.g., persons whose attack had lasted precisely one month were categorized in this category, not the next one.

Table 7A Distribution of paupers for whom causes shown by relieving officer

Paupers where causes shown	Domestics			Workhouse			Wan	Misc	Total		
	M	W	Tot	M	W	Tot	Tot	Tot	M	W	Tot
Number	19	22	41	6	3	9	10	4	34	30	64

Table 7B Causes of insanity shown on pauper admission certificates, 1861–65

Cause	Frequency of occurrence
Religion	11
Business/Employment	9
Puerperal mania/Childbirth	7
Heredity/Congenital factors	7
Grief	6
Intemperance	5
Head injury	4
Other injury	4
Idiocy/Imbecility/etc.	3
Epilepsy/Fits	3
Desertion by spouse	2
Brain disease	2
Other disease/fever	2
Fear of poverty	2
Drugs	2
Old age	2
Bad habits	1
Family trouble	1
Fright	1
Ill-treatment by spouse	1
Trouble over settlement	1
TOTAL	76

Source: Admission documents, Leicestershire and Rutland Lunatic Asylum

Table 8 Causes of insanity of paupers, as found in patient register

	Domestics			Workhouses			Wan	Misf	Total		
	M	W	Tot	M	W	Tot	Tot	Tot	M	W	Tot
Paupers where causes shown	53	56	109	26	22	48	22	20	103	96	199
Causes											
Hereditary/Congenital	11	9	**20**	15	10	**25**	3	5	32	21	**53**
Poverty	11	15	**26**	3	3	**6**	3	3	16	22	**38**
Intemperance	12	2	**14**	2	3	**5**	8	3	24	6	**30**
Puerp. mania/Childbirth		10	**10**		3	**3**	1	1		15	**15**
Old age	4	4	**8**	2	2	**4**		2	6	8	**14**
Other disease/Fever	4	3	**7**		1	**1**	3	1	7	5	**12**
Grief/Anxiety	3	4	**7**				1	1	4	5	**9**
Hysteria		7	**7**				1	1		9	**9**
Brain disease	5		**5**	1		**1**	1	1	6	2	**8**
Debility		1	**1**	2	2	**4**		1	2	4	**6**
Catoxia	2	1	**3**				2		3	2	**5**
Head injury				3		**3**			3		**3**
Epilepsy/Fits	1		**1**						1		**1**
Other injury	1		**1**						1		**1**
Drugs		1	**1**							1	**1**
Family trouble								1	1		**1**
Fright		1	**1**							1	**1**
Total Causes	54	58	112	28	24	52	23	20	106	101	207

Source: Patient register, Leicestershire and Rutland Lunatic Asylum, LRO DE 3533/147

Table 9 Causes of insanity of paupers as found in 'Cause' column of casebooks

	Domestics			Workhouses			Wan	Misc	Total		
	M	W	Tot	M	W	Tot			M	W	Tot
Paupers where causes shown	48	48	96	22	14	36	23	12	94	73	167
Causes											
Hereditary/ Congenital	11	14	25	14	3	17	3	5	31	19	50
Intemperance	12	3	15	2		2	7	2	22	4	26
Grief	4	5	9		1	1	4		5	9	14
Poverty	4	4	8		3	3	1	1	5	8	13
Puerp. mania/ Childbirth		9	9				2	1		12	12
Religion	6	4	10				1		7	4	11
Other disease/ Fever	1	2	3		1	1	1	4	6	3	9
Brain disease	2	1	3	4	1	5			6	2	8
Epilepsy/Fits	3		3		3	3			3	3	6
Old age	1	1	2	1	3	4			2	4	6
Business/ Employment	3		3		1	1	2		4	2	6
Other injury	3		3				2		5		5
Head injury				2	1	3			2	1	3
Desertion		3	3							3	3
Idiocy/imb./etc				1		1	1		1	1	2
Family trouble	2		2						2		2
Hysteria		1	1		1	1				2	2
Fear of poverty							1			1	1
Disappointed love		1	1							1	1
Bad habits	1		1						1		1
Fright		1	1							1	1
Albresiamania		1	1							1	1
Debility		1	1							1	1
Birth of illegit. child		1	1							1	1
Totals	53	52	105	24	18	42	25	13	102	83	185

Source: Casebooks of Leicestershire and Rutland Lunatic Asylum, 1861–65

Table 10 Causes as found in 'Cause' column of casebooks, supplemented by comments in treatment notes (paupers)

	Domestics			Workhouses			Wan	Misc	Total		
	M	W	Tot	M	W	Tot			M	W	Tot
Paupers where causes shown	58	66	124	29	27	56	26	22	114	114	228
Causes											
Hereditary/ Congenital	11	14	25	14	3	17	2	5	31	18	49
Intemperance	18	4	22	4	1	5	10	3	32	8	40
Poverty	10	12	22	2	6	8	1	3	13	21	34
Idiocy/imb/etc.	3	4	7	9	6	15	1	4	14	13	27
Grief	5	6	11		1	1	4	2	6	12	18
Epilepsy/Fits	5	2	7	2	7	9		1	7	10	17
Puerp. mania/ Childbirth		12	12				2	2		16	16
Religion	6	7	13				1	1	7	8	15
Other disease/ fever	3	4	7	1	1	2	3	2	9	5	14
Brain disease	4	1	5	4	2	6			8	3	11
Hysteria		6	6		2	2				8	8
Old age	1	2	3	1	4	5			2	6	8
Business/Emp.	2	1	3		1	1	2	1	4	3	7
Head injury				2	1	3		1	3	1	4
Other injury	3		3					1	4		4
Bad habits	2		2	1	1	2			3	1	4
Family trouble	2	1	3		1	1			2	2	4
Desertion		3	3							3	3
Neglect		1	1					2		3	3
Debility	1	1	2						1	1	2
Fear of poverty							1			1	1
Disapp. love		1	1							1	1
Drugs		1	1							1	1
Fright		1	1							1	1
Birth illeg. child		1	1							1	1
Blindness					1	1				1	1
Total	76	85	161	40	38	78	27	28	146	148	294

Source: Casebooks of Leicestershire and Rutland Lunatic Asylum, 1861–65.

Dietaries, Leicester Asylum and Leicester Workhouse

LEICESTER WORKHOUSE DIETARY[1]

The following was the original dietary of the workhouse, instituted in November 1837:

Breakfast and supper

milk, porridge and bread – 1½ pt. porridge and 7 oz. bread for men, 1¼ pt. porridge and 6 oz. bread for women, and tea and coffee with raw sugar for the aged and infirm.

Dinner

two days: beef broth (made with 5 stone of beef without bone to make enough for 100 persons), as much as the inmates wanted, and bread – 8 oz. for men and 7 oz. for women;
two further days: cold meat and potatoes – 7 oz. meat for men and 6 oz. for women and potatoes without stint;
two further days: meat soup thickened with peas and potatoes (made from the bones of the meat cooked on the two meat days);
seventh day: suet pudding with a sauce made of treacle, flour, water and vinegar. The pudding was made from 1½ lb. of suet to a stone of flour, lightened with bread; 16 oz. was the men's allowance and 14 oz. for the women, but in fact unstinted.

In addition, each pauper was to be allowed ½pt. 'small beer' on the cold meat dinner days.

Commencing in February 1838, suppers were changed to bread and cheese, unless paupers preferred porridge. Otherwise, the dietary remained essentially unaltered until 1870.

ASYLUM DIETARY[2]

Breakfast

Coffee or cocoa, 1 pt. Bread 6 oz. (men) or 5 oz. (women). $\frac{1}{3}$ oz. butter.

Dinner

Meat days [Sunday, Mon, Wed, Thurs]: 6 oz. (men); 5 oz. (women) cooked, free from bone, with 3 oz. of bread; 12 oz. veg. in season.
Tuesdays: Irish stew, 16 oz., with 3 oz of bread. Irish stew, per lb., contained 2 oz. meat and 10 oz. potatoes.
Friday: Soup day. 1 oz. cheese. Males: 1½ pt. soup with 6 oz. bread; females: 1 pt. soup with 4 oz. bread. 1 gal. soup: 1½ lb. legs and shins; 2 oz. oatmeal, 2 oz. peas with carrots, onions and herbs.
Saturday: Meat pie: 1 lb., 3 oz. bread, 1 oz. cheese.

½ pint beer daily, excepting Fridays.

Supper

Tea, 1 pint, $\frac{1}{3}$ oz butter, 6 oz. (men) or 5 oz (women) of bread.

Patients employed in the Wards and Laundry are allowed for Luncheon, 4 oz. bread, 1 oz. cheese and ½ pt. Beer, extra. Those employed in the workshops and farm, 4 oz bread, 1 oz. cheese and 1 pt. beer, extra.

Extra diet at discretion of Medical Superintendent.

NOTES

1. Source: K. Thompson, 'The Leicester Poor Law Union, 1836–71, University of Leicester, dissertation (1982), pp. 119 f.
2. Source: *Twelfth Annual Report of United Committee of Visitors of Leicester and Rutland Lunatic Asylum* (1860). LRO DE 3533/13.

Forms of admission documents and casebooks

CASEBOOKS, 1845 FORMAT

The record for each patient is on two facing pages of the book, each page being roughly 10 inches by 18 inches. The information given is as follows.

In a band across the top of the two pages:

Number. [The accession number to the institution]

Name. [Both given name and surname]

Age.

Place of Abode. [Usually an address. Occasionally refers to a union house]

Class or parish. [Class numbers refer to the standard classification in the asylum: first class being county paupers, second class being out-county paupers, third class being subscription patients, fourth class being private patients. This appears to be for purposes of chargeability. Thus a soldier found wandering (#590) was listed as 'County of Leicester' in this category, even though there is nothing obvious in his background (which appears largely unknown) to associate him with the county. Note that he would be chargeable to Leicestershire, however, given his admission docs in this circumstance.]

Occupation or profession.

Married, single or widowed.

Number of children.

Date of admission.

Date of discharge.

The left-hand page is a list of set questions, with spaces for answers to be written in. The questions are as follows:

When did this attack commence?

Was it preceded by any severe or long-continued mental emotion or exertion?

Did it succeed any serious illness or accident affecting the nervous system?

Is it consequent on pregnancy, parturition, or lactation?

Has it risen or been accompanied by any irregularity of the uterine functions?

Has the patient suffered from former attacks of the disease? and, if so, how long were the intervals of sanity?

What is the supposed cause of the malady?

Has the Patient attempted self-destruction or violence towards others?

Is the Patient prone to tear clothes or break furniture?

Has the Patient refused to take food?

Are the Habits of the Patient cleanly?

Is the Patient subject to Fits or Palsy?

Does the Patient labour under any other Disease?

What is the state of the general health?

Has any Relative of the Patient been insane?

What are the deranged ideas or mental hallucinations under which the Patient has laboured?

By whose authority sent? Medical Certificate. [i.e., this box was to include both the persons who signed any warrants, and the name of the doctor signing the medical certificate. The dates of the documents were also given.]

The right-hand page is given over to treatment and observations of the patient.

CASEBOOKS: 1856 FORMAT

The two-page format is maintained in the new version. The entire right-hand page, and the bottom fifth of the left-hand page, are free for treatment notes. The top four-fifths of the left-hand page are pre-printed on a format as follows:

In a band across the top are patient number and name, date of admission, height and weight, [marital] state and age, number of children, duration of attack, whether first attack and residence.

There is a series of categories in a band down the left-hand side of the page, with spaces for the following information provided to their

279

right: by whose order sent; name, abode and relationship of nearest known relative; occupation; character; education [entries include whether pauper was literate]; religion; assigned causes, with spaces for moral, physical and hereditary causes; physical state; and symptoms of mental disorder.

ADMISSION DOCUMENTS

The admission documents for 1860 to 1865 were prescribed by the 1853 Act.[1] While this Act did make minor modifications from the prescribed forms under the 1845 Act,[2] no alterations to these documents were made by the 1862 legislation. The statement signed by the Justice was relatively pro forma:

I *C.D.*, the undersigned, having called to my assistance a physician [*or* surgeon *or* apothecary], and having personally examined *A.B.*, a pauper, and being satisfied that the said *A.B.* is a lunatic [*or* an idiot, *or* a person of unsound mind], and a proper person to be taken charge of and detained under care and treatment, hereby direct you to receive the said *A.B.* as a patient into your Asylum. Subjoined is a Statement respecting the said *A.B.*[3]

The form instructed the Justices signing a form for a person detained as not under proper care and control, as distinct from a pauper from within the parish, to so indicate on the form by deletion of the words 'a pauper', and insertion of an indication as to whether the person was found wandering at large or was instead not under proper care or cruelly treated. The statement was substantially similar to that under the 1845 Act, with the exception of the phrase 'a proper person to be taken charge of and detained under care and treatment', which replaced 'a proper Person to be confined' in the 1845 statute.[4]

The statement of the relieving officer consisted in short answers to the following questions:

Name of patient, and christian name, at length.
Sex and age.
Married, single, or widowed.
Condition of life, and previous occupation (if any).
The religious persuasion, as far as known.
Previous place of abode.
Whether first attack.
Age (if known) on first attack.

When and where previously under care and treatment.
Duration of existing attack.
Supposed cause.*
Whether subject to epilepsy.
Whether suicidal.
Whether dangerous to others.
Parish or union to which lunatic is chargeable (if a pauper or destitute lunatic).*
Name and christian name and place of abode of the nearest known relative of the patient, and degree of relationship (if known).*[5]

Questions marked with an asterisk were introduced in the 1853 Act. Apart from minor wording differences, the other questions had appeared in the 1845 Act as well.[6]

The statement to be signed by the medical officer read as follows:

I, the undersigned, [*qualifications for practice to be set forth, e.g., 'being a Fellow of the Royal College of Physicians in London'*] and being in actual practice as a physician [or surgeon or apothecary] hereby certify, that I, on the   day of   , [*here insert the street and number of the house (if any) or other like particulars,*] in the county of   , ... personally examined A.B., of
[*insert residence and profession or occupation, if any,*] and that the said A.B. is a [lunatic, *or* an idiot, *or* a person of unsound mind,] and a proper person to be taken charge of and detained under care and treatment, and that I have formed this opinion upon the following grounds; viz.:

1.   Facts indicating insanity observed by myself [*here state the facts*].

2.   Other facts (*if any*) indicating insanity communicated to me by others [*here state the information, and from whom*].[7]

Once again, this essentially reflected the requirements of the 1845 Act, although consistent with the change to the statement of the Justices, the 1845 statement of the medical officer had referred merely to 'a proper Person to be confined', rather than to 'a proper person to be taken charge of and detained under care and treatment'.[8] Also, the 1845 forms did not provide a space for the medical man to detail the facts observed and communicated. As a result, at least in Leicester, the admission documents prior to the 1853 Act generally do not contain this information.[9]

APPENDIX 4

NOTES

1   16 & 17 Vict. c. 97 sch. (F) no. 1 (Justice's order and statement of relieving officer) and 3 (medical certificate).
2   8 & 9 Vict. c. 126 sch. (E) no. 1.
3   16 & 17 Vict. c. 97 sch. (F) no. 1. Italics in original. Parenthetical statements in original, but irrelevant parenthetical comments deleted here to aid readability.
4   8 & 9 Vict. c. 126 sch. (E) no. 1.
5   16 & 17 Vict. c. 97 sch. (F) no. 1.
6   8 & 9 Vict. c. 126 sch. (E) no. 1.
7   16 & 17 Vict. c. 97 sch. (F) no. 3. Italics in original.
8   8 & 9 Vict. c. 126 sch. (E) no. 1.
9   Admission documents for 1851 and 1852 are contained in LRO DE 3533/225.

Bibliography

MANUSCRIPT AND ARCHIVAL SOURCES

Public Record Office (PRO)

MH/9	Register of Paid Officers compiled by the Poor Law Commissioners
MH/10 92	Index to circulars of the Poor Law Commissioners
MH/12	Correspondence between Poor Law Commissioners and Boards of Guardians
MH/15	Index to correspondence between Poor Law Commissioners and Boards of Guardians
MH/19 168–170	Correspondence between Poor Law Commissioners and Lunacy Commission
MH/32	Poor Law Commissioners' correspondence
MH/51 747–772	Opinions of Law Officers of the Crown relating to Lunacy

County Record Office, Leicestershire (LRO)

DE 662/27	Leicestershire and Rutland Lunatic Asylum, 'Rules for the General Management of the Institution, with Prefatory Remarks by the Committee of Visitors', 1849
DE 3120/1	Burbage Parish Receipt and Disbursement Book, 1838–74
DE 3533/1	Leicestershire and Rutland Lunatic Asylum, Land and Building Subcommittee Minutes, 1858–68
DE 3533/8	Leicestershire and Rutland Lunatic Asylum, Minute Book of Visitors, 1851–94
DE 3533/13–14	Leicestershire and Rutland Lunatic Asylum, annual reports, 1849–80
DE 3533/83–84	Leicestershire and Rutland Lunatic Asylum, Superintendent's Journal and Report Book, 1853–1870

DE 3533/145 Leicestershire and Rutland Lunatic Asylum, Admission and Discharge Register [all classes of patient], 1837–1896

DE 3533/147 Leicestershire and Rutland Lunatic Asylum, Register of Pauper Patients, 1837–79

DE 3533/148 Leicestershire and Rutland Lunatic Asylum, Register of Private Patients, 1847–1906

DE 3533/149 Leicestershire and Rutland Lunatic Asylum, Register of Subscribers Sponsoring Charity Admissions, 1836–1855

DE 3533/150 Leicestershire and Rutland Lunatic Asylum, Register of Discharges, Removals and Deaths of Private Patients, 1855–85

DE 3533/175 Leicestershire and Rutland Lunatic Asylum, Letters recommending admission of Patients, 1863 and 1870

DE 3533/185–192 Leicestershire and Rutland Lunatic Asylum, Casebooks, 1845–1870

DE 3533/216 Leicestershire and Rutland Lunatic Asylum, Continuation Casebook, 1856–1858.

DE 3533/217 Leicestershire and Rutland Lunatic Asylum, Casebook, Charity Patients, 1839–1888.

DE 3533/225–230 Leicestershire and Rutland Lunatic Asylum, Receiving orders, medical certificates and statements of Relieving Officers, 1851–1870 [incomplete]

DE 3533/415 Leicestershire and Rutland Lunatic Asylum, 'The Charity of the Leicestershire and Rutland Lunatic Asylum', pamphlet outlining the nature of the charity

DG 24/752/2 Leicestershire and Rutland Lunatic Asylum, 'Rules for the General Management of the Institution', 1873

DG 24/752/3 Leicestershire and Rutland Lunatic Asylum, 'Memorandum concerning the Leicestershire and Rutland Lunatic Asylum', being a report of the Metropolitan Fire Chief, Captain Shaw, dated 23 Feb. 1874

DG 24/752/4 Leicestershire and Rutland Lunatic Asylum, Report evaluating the value of the Asylum, for purposes of deciding the Charity's share [1869]

DG 24/752/5 Leicestershire and Rutland Lunatic Asylum, 'Report as to Capital' (1869) by Freer and Reeve, Leicester

DG 24/752/6 Leicestershire and Rutland Lunatic Asylum, Rules of the Asylum, n.d. [c. 1851?]

G–1–57 Ashby de la Zouch Union, correspondence, 1840–43

G–1–60 Ashby de la Zouch Union, Workhouse Admission and Discharge Registers

G–1–8a/1 Ashby de la Zouch Union, Board of Guardians Minute books, 1838–1864

G–2–28/1 Barrow upon Soar Union, Index of Paupers Relieved

G–8–85/1	Lutterworth Union, Workhouse Master's Report and Journal, 1855–1859
G–12–23c/1	Leicester Union, Workhouse Form A Returns, 1848–53
G–12–57b/1	Leicester Union, Correspondence with Poor Law Commissioners, 1843–49
G–12–57d/1	Leicester Union, Letters from Poor Law Commissioners, 1844–5
G–12–57d/65	Leicester Union, Local Government Orders, 1841–71
G–12–75a/1	Leicester Union, List of Lunatics, Borough of Leicester, 1851–96
G–12–8a/1–13	Leicester Union, Board of Guardians Minute Books, 1836–70
QS/107/1	Leicestershire Quarter Sessions. Letter Book re Leicestershire and Rutland County Lunatic Asylum. 1854–1875
QS/84/3/1	Leicestershire Quarter Sessions. Register of Pauper Lunatics in the County and Town of Leicester, 1867–72
QS/89/83	Order from Poor Law Commissioners regarding Powers and Duties of Justices in the Administration of Poor Relief, dated 6 October 1834 [printed source]

Statutes

1324	De Prerogativa Regis, 17 Edw. II stat. I
1597	An Act for Punishment of Rogues, Vagabonds and sturdy Beggars, 39 Eliz. c. 4
1597	An Act for erecting Hospitals, or Abiding and Working Houses for the Poor, 39 Eliz. c. 5
1601	An Act for the Relief of the Poor, 43 Eliz. c. 2
1662	An Act for the better Relief of the Poor of this Kingdom, 13 & 14 Car. II c. 12.
1714	An Act for reducing the laws relating to Rogues, Vagabonds, Sturdy Beggars and Vagrants into one Act of Parliament, 12 Anne c. 23
1722	Knatchbull's Act, 9 George I c. 7
1744	An Act to amend and make more effectual the Laws relating to Rogues, Vagabonds, and other idle and disorderly Persons, and to Houses of Correction, 17 Geo. II c. 5
1745	An Act to amend and render more effectual on Act passed in the Fifth Year of his present Majesty's Reign, intituled, *An Act for the futher Qualification of Justices of the Peace*, 18 George II c. 20.
1774	An Act for regulating Madhouses, 14 Geo. III c. 49
1782	Gilbert's Act, 22 George III c. 83
1795	An Act to amend so much of an Act, made in the Ninth Year of the Reign of King George I intituled *An Act for amending the Laws*

relating to the Settlement, Employment, and Relief of the Poor, as prevents the distributing occasional Relief to Poor Persons in their own Houses, under certain Circumstances and in certain Cases, 36 George III c. 23

1800   An Act for the safe Custody of Insane Persons charged with Offences, 39 & 40 Geo. III c. 94

1808   An Act for the better Care and Maintenance of Lunatics, being Paupers or Criminals in England, 48 Geo. III c. 96

1811   An Act to amend an Act of the Forty eighth Year of His present Majesty, for the better Care and Maintenance of Lunatics, being Paupers or Criminals, in England, 51 Geo. III c. 79

1815   An Act to amend an Act passed in the Forty eighth year of the Reign of His present Majesty entitled An Act for the better Care and Maintenance of Lunatics, being Paupers or Criminals, in England, 55 Geo. III c. 46

1816   An Act to amend an Act passed in the Thirty ninth and Fortieth Year of the Reign of His present Majesty for the safe Custody of Insane Persons charged with Offences, 56 Geo. III c. 117

1819   An Act for making Provision for the better Care of Pauper Lunatics in England, 59 Geo. III c. 127

1824   An Act to amend several Acts passed for the better Care and Maintenance of Lunatics, being Paupers or Criminals, in England, 5 Geo. IV c. 70

1828   An Act to amend the Laws for the Erection and Regulation of County Lunatic Asylums, and more effectually to provide for the Care and Maintenance of Pauper and Criminal Lunatics, in England, 9 Geo. IV c. 40

1828   An Act to regulate the Care and Treatment of Insane Persons in England, 9 Geo. IV c. 41

1829   An Act to explain, amend, and alter the Act of the Ninth Year of the Reign of His present Majesty, for regulating the Care and Treatment of Insane Persons in England, 10 Geo. IV c. 18

1830   An Act for consolidating and amending the Law relating to Property belonging to Infants, Femes Covert, Idiots, Lunatics, and Persons of Unsound Mind, 11 Geo. IV & 1 Will. IV c. 65

1832   An Act for regulating for Three Years, and from thence until the End of the then next Session of Parliament, the Care and Treatment of Insane Persons in England, 2 & 3 Will. IV c. 107

1833   An Act to amend an Act of the Second and Third Year of His present Majesty, for regulating the Care and Treatment of Insane Persons in England, 3 & 4 Will. IV c. 64

1834   An Act for the Amendment and better Administration of the Laws relating to the Poor in England and Wales, 4 & 5 Will. IV c. 76

1835   An Act to Continue for Three Years, and from thence to the End of the then next Session of Parliament, Two Acts of the Second and Third and the Third and Fourth Year of His present Majesty, relating to the Care and Treatment of Insane Persons in England, 5 & 6 Will. IV c. 22

1838   An Act to continue for Three Years, and from thence to the End of the then next Session of Parliament, Two Acts relating to the Care and Treatment of Insane Persons in England, 1 & 2 Vict. c. 73

1838   Act to Repeal 39 George III c. 94, 1 Vict. c. 14

1840   An Act for making further Provision for the Confinement and Maintenance of Insane Prisoners, 3 & 4 Vict. c. 54

1841   An Act to continue for Three Years, and from thence to the End of the then next Session of Parliament, Two Acts relating to the Care and Treatment of Insane Persons in England, 5 Vict. c. 4.

1842   An Act to amend and continue for Three Years, and from thence to the End of the next Session of Parliament, the Laws relating to Houses licensed by the Metropolitan Commissioners and Justices of the Peace for the Reception of Insane Persons, and for the Inspection of County Asylums and Public Hospitals for the Reception of Insane Persons, 5 & 6 Vict. c. 87

1844   An Act for the further Amendment of the Laws relating to the Poor in England, 7 & 8 Vict. c. 101

1845   An Act for the Regulation of the Care and Treatment of Lunatics, 8 & 9 Vict. c. 100

1845   An Act to amend the Laws for the Provision and Regulation of Lunatic Asylums for Counties and Boroughs, and for the Maintenance and Care of Pauper Lunatics, in England, 8 & 9 Vict. c. 126

1846   An Act to amend the Law concerning Lunatic Asylums and the Care of Pauper Lunatics in England, 9 & 10 Vict. c. 84

1847   An Act for the Amendment of the Laws relating to the Provision and Regulation of Lunatic Asylums for Counties and Boroughs of England, 10 & 11 Vict. c. 43

1849   An Act to continue an Act of the last Session of Parliament, for charging the Maintenance of certain Poor Persons in Unions upon the Common Fund; and to make certain Amendments in the Laws for the Relief of the Poor, 12 & 13 Vict. c. 103

1850   An Act to continue two Acts passed in the twelfth and thirteenth years of the Reign of Her Majesty, for charging the Maintenance of certain Poor Persons in Unions in England and Wales upon the Common Fund; and to make certain Amendments in the Laws for the Relief of the Poor, 13 & 14 Vict. c. 101

1853   An Act to amend an Act passed in the Ninth Year of Her Majesty, 'for the Regulation of the Care and Treatment of Lunatics', 16 & 17 Vict. c. 96

287

1853   The Lunatic Asylums Act, 1853, 16 & 17 Vict. c. 97
1855   An Act to amend the Lunatic Asylums Act, 1853, and the Acts passed in the Ninth and Seventeenth Years of Her Majesty, for the Regulation of the Care and Treatment of Lunatics, 18 & 19 Vict. c. 105
1856   An Act to amend the Lunatic Asylums Act, 1853, 19 & 20 Vict. c. 87
1858   The Medical Act, 21 & 22 Vict. c. 90
1860   An Act to make better Provision for the Custody and Care of Criminal Lunatics, 23 & 24 Vict. c. 75
1861   An Act to amend the Laws regarding the Removal of the Poor and the Contribution of Parishes to the Common Fund in Unions, 24 & 25 Vict. c. 55
1862   An Act to amend the Law relating to Lunatics, 25 & 26 Vict. c. 111
1863   An Act to amend the Lunacy Acts in relation to the building of Asylums for Pauper Lunatics, 26 & 27 Vict. c. 110
1865   An Act to provide for the better Distribution of the Charge for the Relief of the Poor in Unions, 28 & 29 Vict. c. 79
1865   An Act to explain and amend 'The Lunatic Asylum Act, 1853', and 'The Lunacy Act Amendment Act, 1862', with reference to Counties of Towns which have Courts of Quarter Sessions, but no Recorder, 28 & 29 Vict. c. 80
1867   The Metropolitan Poor Act, 1867, 30 Vict. c. 6
1867   An Act to make the Poor Law Board permanent, and to provide sundry Amendments in the Laws for the Relief of the Poor, 30 & 31 Vict. c. 106
1868   An Act to make further Amendments in the Laws for the Relief of the Poor in England and Wales, 31 & 32 Vict. c. 122
1884   Criminal Lunatics Act, 1884, 47 & 48 Vict. c. 64
1885   Lunacy Acts Amendment Act 1885, 48 & 49 Vict. c. 52
1886   Idiots Act 1886, 49 Vict. c. 25
1888   Local Government Act 1888, 51 & 52 Vict. c. 41
1889   Lunacy Acts Amendment Act 1889, 52 & 53 Vict. c. 41
1890   Lunacy Act, 1890, 53 Vict. c. 5
1891   Lunacy Act, 1891, 54 & 55 Vict. c. 65
1959   Mental Health Act 1959, 7 & 8 Eliz. II c. 72
1983   Mental Health Act, 1983, c. 20

PARLIAMENTARY PAPERS (Listed Chronologically)

Report of the Select Committee on the State of Criminal and Pauper Lunatics and the Laws Relating thereto, 1807. PP 1807 (39) ii 69
Report together with the Minutes of Evidence taken before the Select Committee

appointed to consider the provision being made for the better regulation of *Madhouses in England, 1815*. PP 1814–15 (296) iv 801

Return of the Number of Houses in Each County ... Licenced for the reception of Lunatics ... 1819. PP 1819 (271) xvii 131

A Return of the Number of Lunatics confined in the Different Gaols, Hospitals and Lunatic Asylums. PP 1819 (272) xvii 131

Return of Lunatic Asylums erected under the provisions of 48 George III c. 96, 1824. PP 1824 (329) xviii 171

Report of the Metropolitan Commissioners in Lunacy, 1830. PP 1830 (541) xxx 275

Returns ... specifying the number of Lunatics and idiots ... confined and in regular asylums and of those not confined, 1830. PP 1830 (542) xxx 283

Report from His Majesty's Commissioners for Inquiring into the Administration and Practical Consequences of the Poor Laws. PP 1834 (44) xxvii 1.

First Annual Report of the Poor Law Commission for England and Wales. PP 1835 (500) xxxv 107

Second Annual Report of the Poor Law Commissioners. PP 1836 (595) xxix 1

Third Annual Report of the Poor Law Commissioners. PP 1837 (546) xxxi 127

Fourth Annual Report of the Poor Law Commissioners. PP 1837–8 [147] xxviii 145.

Fifth Annual Report of the Poor Law Commissioners. PP 1839 (239) xx 1

Sixth Annual Report of the Poor Law Commissioners. PP 1840 [245] xvii 397

Report with Table showing the Relief afforded to Lunatics and Idiots by the Unions and Parishes comprised in the Metropolitan District ... PP 1840 (394) xxxix 305

Seventh Annual Report of the Poor Law Commissioners. PP 1841 [327] xi 291

Annual Reports of the Metropolitan Commissioners in Lunacy, 1835–1841 inclusive. PP 1841 2nd sess. (56) vi 235

Eighth Annual Report of the Poor Law Commissioners. PP 1842 [359] xix 1

Ninth Annual Report of the Poor Law Commissioners. PP 1843 [468] xxi 1

Report of the Metropolitan Commissioners in Lunacy. PP [HL] 1844 xxvi 1

A Return of the Number of Pauper Lunatics and Idiots chargeable to each of the Unions in England and Wales, in the months of August 1842 and 1843 respectively ... PP 1844 (172) xl 189

Tenth Annual Report of the Poor Law Commissioners. PP 1844 [560] xix 9

Eleventh Annual Report of the Poor Law Commissioners. PP 1845 [624] xxvii 247

A Return of the Number of Pauper Lunatics and Idiots chargeable to each of the Unions in England and Wales, and also to those places under Local Acts, in the month of August 1844 ... PP 1845 (333) xxxviii 133

Return of payments to Lunacy Commissioners ... PP 1846 (48) xxxiii 409

Returns respecting County Lunatic Asylums. PP 1846 (90) xxxiii 409

Return of Lunacy Commissioners, showing number of visits made ... PP 1846 (104) xxxiii 407

Twelfth Annual Report of the Poor Law Commissioners. PP 1846 [704] xix 1

Report of the Poor Law Commissioners upon the Relief of the Poor in the Parishes of St. Marylebone and St. Pancras, with Appendix. PP 1847 [802] xxviii 275

Thirteenth Annual Report of the Poor Law Commissioners. PP 1847 [816] xviii 1

First Annual Report of the Lunacy Commissioners. PP 1847 (471) xxxiii 339

Second Annual Report of the Lunacy Commissioners. PP 1847–8 (34) xxvi 225

Supplementary Report to the Home Secretary. PP 1847 [858]; *in octavo* PP 1847–48 xxxii 371

Fourteenth Report of the Poor Law Commissioners. PP 1847–8 [960] xxxiii 1

Copy of Letter from the Commissioners in Lunacy, with reference to their Duties and Practice, under the Act 8 & 9 Vict. c. 100. PP 1849 (620) xlvi 381

Third Annual Report of the Commissioners in Lunacy. PP 1849 [1028] xxii 381

Report of the Commissoners for Administering the Laws For Relief of the Poor in England [and Wales]. PP 1849 [1024] xxv 1

Fourth Annual Report of the Commissioners in Lunacy. PP 1850 (291) xxiii 363

Fifth Annual Report of the Commissioners in Lunacy. PP 1850 (735) xxiii 393

Second Annual Report of the Poor Law Board. PP 1850 [1142] xxvii 1

Sixth Annual Report of the Commissioners in Lunacy. PP 1851 (668) xxiii 353

Third Annual Report of the Poor Law Board. PP 1851 [1340] xxvi 1

Fourth Annual Report of the Poor Law Board. PP 1852 [1461] xxiii 1

Seventh Annual Report of the Lunacy Commissioners. PP 1852/3 xlix 1

Fifth Annual Report of the Poor Law Board. PP 1852–3 [1625] l 1

Eighth Annual Report of the Commissioners in Lunacy. PP 1854 (339) xxix 1

Sixth Annual Report of the Poor Law Board. PP 1854 [1797] xxix 333

Ninth Annual Report of the Lunacy Commissioners. PP 1854–5 (240) xvii 533

Seventh Annual Report of the Poor Law Board. PP 1854–5 [1921] xxiv 1

Tenth Annual Report of the Commissioners in Lunacy. PP 1856 (258) xviii 495

Letter from Guardians of St. Marylebone answering the Report of the Commissioners in Lunacy in regard to the Treatment of Pauper Lunatics in Marylebone Workhouse. PP 1857 2nd (111) xxxii (2) 533

Eleventh Annual Report of the Lunacy Commissioners. PP 1857. 2nd sess. (157) xvi 351

Twelfth Annual Report of the Lunacy Commissioners. PP 1857–8 (340) xxiii 583

Tenth Annual Report of the Poor Law Board. PP 1857–8 [2402] xxviii 1

Report of the Select Committee on Lunatics; Together with the Proceedings of the Committee, Minutes of Evidence, Appendix, and Index. PP 1859 1st sess. (204) iii 75

Returns relating to Lunatics. PP 1859 1st sess. (19) xxii 175

Supplement to the Twelfth Annual Report of the Commissioners in Lunacy. PP 1859 1st sess. (228) ix 1

Eleventh Annual Report of the Poor Law Board. PP 1859 1st sess. [2500] ix 741

Report from the Select Committee on Lunatics; Together with the Proceedings of the Committee, Minutes of Evidence, Appendix, and Index. PP 1859 2nd sess. (156) vii 501

Thirteenth Annual Report of the Lunacy Commissioners. PP 1859 2nd sess. (204) xiv 529

Report of the Select Committee on Lunatics, together with the Proceedings of the Committee, Minutes of Evidence, and Appendix. PP 1860 (495) xxii 349

Fourteenth Annual Report of the Lunacy Commissioners. PP 1860 (338) xxxiv 231

Twelfth Annual Report of the Poor Law Board. 1859–60. PP 1860 [2675] xxxvii 1

Fifteenth Annual Report of the Lunacy Commissioners. PP 1861 (314) xxvii 1

Thirteenth Annual Report of the Poor Law Board. PP 1861 [2820] xxviii 1

Second Report of the Select Committee on Poor Relief, together with the Minutes of Evidence and Appendix. PP 1862 x (321) 183

Sixteenth Report of the Commissioners in Lunacy. PP 1862 (417) xxiii 1

Return stating the Number of Unions in England and Wales in which the sane are not intermixed with the Insane, and where Lunatic Wards have been established; the number of Lunatics in each separate ward; together with the Number of Lunatics received into all Union Workhouses from January 1861 to January 1862. PP 1863 (477) lii 85

Fourteenth Annual Report of the Poor Law Board. PP 1862 [3037] xxiv 1

Seventeenth Annual Report of the Commissioners in Lunacy. PP 1863 xx (331) 437

Fifteenth Annual Report of the Poor Law Board. PP 1863 [3197] xxii 1

Eighteenth Annual Report of the Commissioners in Lunacy. PP 1864 (389) xxiii 1

Sixteenth Annual Report of the Poor Law Board. PP 1864 [3379] xxv 1

Nineteenth Annual Report of the Commissioners in Lunacy. PP 1865 (387) xxi 1

Seventeenth Annual Report of the Poor Law Board. PP 1865 [3549] xxii 1

Twentieth Annual Report of the Commissioners in Lunacy. PP 1866 (317) xxxii 1

Eighteenth Annual Report of the Poor Law Board. PP 1866 [3700] xxxv 1

Twenty-First Annual Report of the Commissioners in Lunacy. PP 1867 (366) xviii 201

Nineteenth Annual Report of the Poor Law Board. PP 1867 [3870] xxxiv 1

Twenty-Second Annual Report of the Commissioners in Lunacy. PP 1867–8 (332) xxxi 1

Twentieth Annual Report of the Poor Law Board. PP 1867–8 [4039] xxxiii 1

Twenty-Third Annual Report of the Commissioners in Lunacy. PP 1868–9 (321) xxvii 1

Twenty-First Annual Report of the Poor Law Board. PP 1868–9 [4197] xxviii 1

Twenty-Fourth Annual Report of the Commissioners in Lunacy. PP 1870 (340) xxxiv 1

Twenty-Second Annual Report of the Poor Law Board. PP 1870 [123] xxxv 1

Twenty-Fifth Annual Report of the Commissioners in Lunacy. PP 1871 (351) xxvi 1

Twenty-Third Annual Report of the Poor Law Board. PP 1871 [396] xxvii 1

Ninth Annual Report of the Local Government Board. PP 1880 [2681] xxvi 1

Thirty-Sixth Annual Report of the Commissioners in Lunacy. PP 1882 (357) xxxii 1

Twentieth Annual Report of the Local Government Board. PP 1890–1 [6460] xxxiii 1

Forty-Fifth Annual Report of the Commissioners in Lunacy. PP 1890–1 (286) xxxvi 1

Report of the Royal Commission on the Care and Control of the Feeble-Minded. PP
1908 [4202] xxxix 159

Report of the Royal Commission on the Poor Laws and Relief of Distress. PP 1909
[4499] xxxvii 1

CASES

Anderton *v.* Burrows (1830), 4 Car. & P. 210 (NP)

Bannatyne and Bannatyne *v.* Bannatyne (1852), 2 Rob. Ecc. 472

Brookshaw *v.* Hopkins (1772–4?), Lofft 240 (KB)

Budd *v.* Foulks (1813), 3 Camp. 404 (NP)

Child, Ex Parte (1854), 15 CB 238 (QB)

Eliot *v.* Allen (1845), 1 CB 18, 14 LJ (NS) CP 136

Fell, In re (1845), 3 Dowl & L. 373, 15 LJ (NS) MC (QB)

Fletcher *v.* Fletcher (1859), 1 E & E 420, SC, 28 LJ, NS, QB 134, 5 Jur NS 678,
32 LT 255, 7 WR 187 (QB)

Hadfield's Case (1800), 27 Howell's St. Tr. 1281

Hall *v.* Semple (1862), 3 F & F 337 (QB)

Hodson *v.* Pare (1899), 68 LJ QB 309; [1899] 1QB 455, 80 LT 13, 47 WR 241,
15 LTR 171 (CA)

Lovatt *v.* Tribe (1862), 3 F & F 9

Martin *v.* Johnson (1858), 1 F & F 122

Norris *v.* Seed (1849), 3 Exch. R 782; 18 LJ, NS, Exch. 300, 13 Jur. 830

Nottidge *v.* Ripley, *The Times* 24 June 1849, 7 (QB)

Prodgers *v.* Phrazier (1681), 3 Mod. 43, 1 Vern 12, 1 Equ. Cas. Abr. 277 and
Hale, PC, p. 29 (Ch.)

R. *v.* Hatfield Peverel (1849), 18 LJR (NS) MC 225; 14 QB 298

R. *v.* Clarke (1762), 3 Burr. 1362 (KB)

R. *v.* Ellis (1844), 14 LJ (NS) MC 1

R. *v.* Harris (1867), 10 Cox CC 541 (Central Criminal Court)

R. *v.* Barnsley (1849), 18 LJR (NS) MC 170 (QB)

R. *v.* Inhabitants of Minster (1850), 14 QB 349

R. *v.* Inhabitants of Rhyddlan (1850), 14 QB 327

R. *v.* Inhabitants of St Nicholas, Leicester (1835), 4 LJ (NS) MC 97 (KB)

R. *v.* Jones (1831), 2 B. & Ad. 611 (KB)

R. *v.* Justices of Cornwall (1845), 14 LJ (NS) MC 46 (QB)

R. *v.* Pinder; In re Greenwood (1855), 24 LJ (NS) QB. 148

R. *v.* Shaw (1868), 11 Cox CC, 18 LT (NS) 583, 37 LJR (NS) MC 112, LR 1 CC
145

R. *v.* Whitfield (1885), 15 QB 122 (CA)

Shuttleworth, Re (1846), 9 QB 651, 16 LJ, NS, MC 18

OTHER SOURCES

Adams, John (1989) 'Caring for the casual poor', *Oral History*, **17** (1): 29.

Allderidge, Patricia (1985) 'Bedlam: fact or fantasy', in *The Anatomy of Madness*, Vol. II, ed. William F. Bynum *et al.* (London: Tavistock), p. 17.

Andrews, Jonathan (1991) 'The Glasgow Royal's case notes: what they do and don't convey about the patient's experience of insanity in the nineteenth century'. Paper delivered at a conference on the History of Case Histories. Stuttgart: Wellcome Unit for the History of Medicine (Glasgow) and Institut für Geschichte der Medizin der Robert Bosch Stiftung, 23–25 September 1991.

Andrews, Jonathan (1995) 'The politics of committal to early modern Bethlem', in R. Porter (ed.), *Medicine and the Enlightenment* (Amsterdam: Clio Medica), p. 6.

Andrews, Jonathan (1998) 'Case Notes, Case Histories, and the Patient's Experience of Insanity at Gartnavel Royal Asylum, Glasgow, in the Nineteenth Century, *Social History of Medicine*, **11** (2): 255.

Anon. [John Bucknill?] (1857) 'Tenth Report of the Commissioners in Lunacy to the Lord Chancellor', *Journal of Mental Science*, **3**: 19.

Anon. [John Bucknill?] (1858) 'The new Commissioners in Lunacy', *Journal of Mental Science*, **4**: 127.

Apfel, William and Dunkley, Peter (1985), 'English rural society and the new Poor Law: Bedfordshire, 1834–47', *Social History*, **10**: 37.

Arieno, Marlene A. (1989) *Victorian Lunatics: A Social Epidemiology of Mental Illness in Mid-Nineteenth-Century England* (Selinsgrove: Susquehanna University Press; and London and Toronto: Associated University Presses).

Arlidge, J. T. (1858) 'On the construction of public lunatic asylums', *Journal of Mental Science*, **4**: 188.

Arlidge, John T. (1859) *On the State of Lunacy and the Legal Provision for the Insane, with Observations on the Construction and Organization of Asylums* (London: John Churchill).

Arthurs, Harry W. (1985) *'Without the Law': Administrative Justice and Legal Pluralism in Nineteenth-Century England* (Toronto: U. of T. Press).

Ashforth, David (1976) 'The urban Poor Law', in Derek Fraser (ed.), *The New Poor Law in the Nineteenth Century* (London: Macmillan).

Bahmueller, Charles F. (1981) *The National Charity Company: Jeremy Bentham's Silent Revolution* (Berkeley: University of California Press).

Bartrip, P. W. J. (1983) 'State intervention in mid-nineteenth century Britain: fact or fiction', *Journal of British Studies*, **23**: 63.

Bentham, Jeremy (1798) *Outline of a Work entitled Pauper Management Improved*, reprinted in 1848 in *The Collected Works of Jeremy Bentham*, Vol. VIII, ed. John Bowring (Edinburgh: William Tait).

Berrios, German E. and Freeman, Hugh (eds), (1991) *150 Years of British Psychiatry, 1841–1991* (London: Gaskell).

Bittner, Egon. See Garfinkel.

Blaug, Mark (1963) 'The myth of the old Poor Law and the making of the new', 23 *Journal of Economic History*, **23**: 151.

Blaug, Mark (1964) 'The Poor Law Report re-examined', *Journal of Economic History*, **23**: 229.

Bott, E. (1827) *The Laws Relating to the Poor*. 6th edn, ed. John T. Pratt (2 vols, London: Butterworth).

Brock, William. See Orme and Brock.

Brook, Matthew (1828) *A New Abridgement of the Law*. 7th edn. 8 vols, ed. H. Gwillim (Vols. 2–4) and C. Dodd (Vols. 1, 5–8). (London: Strachan).

Brook, Robert (1573) *La Grande Abridgement*. 2 vols. n.p.

Brundage, Anthony (1988) *England's 'Prussian Minister': Edwin Chadwick and the Politics of Government Growth, 1832–1854* (London and University Park: Pennsylvania State University Press).

Brundage, Anthony, Eastwood, David and Mandler, Peter 'The making of the new Poor Law *redivivus*', *Past and Present*, **127**: 183.

Buck, John (1858) 'Letter', *Journal of Mental Science*, **4**: 309.

Bucknill, John Charles (1856) 'The diagnosis of insanity', *Journal of Mental Science*, **2**: 229.

Bucknill, J. C. (1858) 'The custody of the insane poor', *Journal of Mental Science*, **4**: 460.

Bucknill, J. C. (1858) 'The medical certificates of admission papers', *Journal of Mental Science*, **4**: 312.

Bucknill, J. C. (1861) 'On medical certificates of insanity', *Journal of Mental Science*, **7**: 79.

Bucknill, John. See also anon.

Burn, W. L. (1964) *The Age of Equipoise: A Study of the Mid-Victorian Generation*, (reprinted 1965, New York: Norton).

Busfield, Joan (1986) *Managing Madness: Changing Ideas and Practice* (London: Hutchinson).

Butterfield, Herbert (1931) *The Whig Interpretation of History* (reprinted 1973, Harmondsworth: Penguin).

Bynum, William F. (1981) 'Rationales for therapy in British psychiatry, 1780–1835', in *Madhouses, Mad-Doctors and Madmen: The Social History of Psychiatry in the Victorian Era*, ed. Andrew Scull (Philadelphia: University of Pennsylvania Press).

Bynum, William F., Porter, Roy and Shepherd, Michael (eds) (1985–88) *The Anatomy of Madness: Essays in the History of Psychiatry*, Vols 1–2: 1985; Vol. 3, 1988 (London: Tavistock).

Cage, R. A. (1981) *The Scottish Poor Law 1745–1845* (Edinburgh: Scottish Academic Press).

Campos Boralevi, Lea (1984) *Bentham and the Oppressed* (Berlin and New York: de Gruyter).

Castel, Robert (1983) 'Moral treatment: mental therapy and social control in the nineteenth century', trans. Peter Miller, in *Social Control and the State: Historical and Comparative Essays*, ed. Stanley Cohen and Andrew Scull, (reprinted Oxford: Blackwell, 1985).

Castel, Robert (1988) *The Regulation of Madness: The Origins of Incarceration in France*, trans. W. D. Halls (Cambridge: Polity).

Checkland, S. G., and Checkland, E. O. A. (eds) (1834) *The Poor Law Report of 1834* (reprinted Harmondsworth: Penguin Books, 1974).

Cohen, Stanley and Scull, Andrew (eds), (1983) *Social Control and the State: Historical and Comparative Essays* (reprinted Oxford: Blackwell, 1985).

Comyn, John (1822) *Digest of the Laws of England*. 5th edn. 8 vols, ed. Anthony Hammond. (London: Strachan).

Cornish, W. R. and Clark, G. de N. (1989) *Law and Society in England 1750–1950* (London: Sweet and Maxwell).

Corrigan, Philip and Sayer, Derek (1985) *The Great Arch: English State Formation as Cultural Revolution* (Oxford: Basil Blackwell).

Crowther, M. A. (1981) *The Workhouse System, 1834–1929: The History of an English Social Institution* (reprinted London: Methuen, 1983).

Dean, Mitchell (1991) *The Constitution of Poverty: Toward a Genealogy of Liberal Governance* (London: Routledge).

Dicey, A. V. (1905) *Lectures on the Relation between Law and Public Opinion in England during the Nineteenth Century* (London: Macmillan).

Digby, Anne (1975) 'The labour market and the continuity of social policy after 1834: the case of the Eastern Counties', *Economic History Review*, 2nd series, **28**: 69.

Digby, Anne (1976) 'The rural Poor Law', in Derek Fraser (ed.), *The New Poor Law in the Nineteenth Century* (London: Macmillan), p. 149.

Digby, Anne (1978) *Pauper Palaces* (London: Routledge & Kegan Paul).

Digby, Anne (1982) *The Poor Law in Nineteenth-Century England and Wales* (London: The Historical Association).

Digby, Anne (1985) *Madness, Morality and Medicine: A Study of the York Retreat, 1796–1914* (Cambridge: Cambridge University Press).

Digby, Anne (1985) 'Moral treatment at the Retreat, 1796–1846', in *The Anatomy of Madness*, Vol. II, ed. William F. Bynum *et al.* (London: Tavistock), p. 52.

Dinwiddy, J. R. (1984) 'Early-nineteenth-century reactions to Benthamism', *Transactions of the Royal Historical Society*, 5th series, **34**: 47.

Dolan, Thomas M. (1879) *Some Remarks on Workhouse Hospitals with Illustrative Cases*, (Leeds: Charles Goodall).

Donajgrodzki, A. P. (ed.) (1977) *Social Control in Nineteenth Century Britain* (London: Croom Helm).

Donajgrodzki, A. P. (1977) ' "Social Police" and the bureaucratic elite: a vision of order in the Age of Reform', In *Social Control in Nineteenth Century Britain*, ed. A. P. Donajgrodzki (London: Croom Helm), p. 51.

Donzelot, Jacques (1979–80) *The Policing of Families: Welfare versus the State*. Foreword by Gilles Deleuze. Trans. from French by Robert Hurley (London: Hutchinson, 1980; New York: Random House, 1979).

Driver, Felix (1993) *Power and Pauperism: The Workhouse System, 1834–1884* (Cambridge: Cambridge University Press).

Driver, Felix (1994) 'Bodies in space', in *Reassessing Foucault: Power, Medicine and the Body*, ed. C. Jones and R. Porter (New York and London: Routledge), p. 113.

Duke, Francis (1976) 'Pauper education', in *The New Poor Law in the Nineteenth Century*, ed. Derek Fraser (London: Macmillan), p. 67.

Dunkley, Peter (1980–1) 'Whigs and paupers: the reform of the English Poor Laws, 1830–1834', *Journal of British Studies*, **20**: 124.

Dunkley, Peter. See also Apfel.

Eastwood, David. See also Brundage.

Engelstein, Laura (1993) 'Combined underdevelopment: discipline and the law in imperial and Soviet Russia', *American Historical Review*, **98**: 344.

Fee, Elizabeth (1978) 'Psychology, sexuality and social control in Victorian England', *Social Science Quarterly*, **58**: 632.

Fennell, Phil (1986) 'Law and psychiatry: the legal constitution of the psychiatric system', *Journal of Law and Society*, **13**: 35.

Fessler, A. (1956) 'The management of lunacy in seventeenth century England: an investigation of Quarter-Sessions records', *Proceedings of the Royal Society of Medicine*, **49**: 901.

Fido, Judith (1977) 'The Charity Organisation Society and social casework in London 1869–1900', in *Social Control in Nineteenth Century Britain*, ed. A. P. Donajgrodzki (London: Croom Helm), p. 207.

Findlayson, Geoffrey B. A. M. (1981) *The Seventh Earl of Shaftesbury, 1801–1885* (London: Eyre Methuen).

Flinn, M. W. (1976) 'Medical services under the new Poor Law', in *The New Poor Law in the Nineteenth Century*, ed. Derek Fraser (London: Macmillan), p. 45.

Forsythe, Bill, Melling, Joseph and Adair, Richard (1996) 'The new Poor Law and the County Pauper Lunatic Asylum — the Devon experience 1834–1884', *Social History of Medicine*, **9**: 335.

Foucault, Michel (1965) *Madness and Civilization: A History of Insanity in the Age of Reason*. Trans. Richard Howard (reprint New York: Vantage Books, 1973).

Foucault, Michel (1977) *Discipline and Punish: The Birth of the Prison*. Trans. Alan Sheridan (New York: Random House).

Foucault, Michel (1978) 'The Dangerous Individual', *International Journal of Law and Psychiatry*, **1**: 1.

Foucault, Michel (1978) *The History of Sexuality. Volume I: An Introduction*. Trans. Robert Hurley (reprint New York: Random House, 1980).

Foucault, Michel (1980) *Power/Knowledge: Selected Interviews and Other Writings 1972–1977*, ed. Colin Gordon (New York and London: Harvester Wheatsheaf).

Foucault, Michel (1988) *Politics, Philosophy, Culture: Interviews and other Writings, 1977–1984*, ed. Lawrence Kritzman (New York: Routledge).

Fraser, Derek (ed.) (1976) *The New Poor Law in the Nineteenth Century* (London: Macmillan).

Fraser, Derek (1976) 'The Poor Law as a political institution', in *The New Poor Law in the Nineteenth Century*, ed. Derek Fraser (London: Macmillan), p. 111.

Fraser, Derek (1984) *The Evolution of the British Welfare State: A History of Social Policy since the Industrial Revolution*. 2nd edn. (London: Macmillan).

Fry, Danby (1877) *The Lunacy Acts*. 2nd edn. (London: Knight and Co.).

Garfinkel, Harold and Bittner, Egon (1976) ' "Good" organizational reasons for "bad" clinical records', in Harold Garfinkel, *Studies in Ethnomethodology* (reprinted Cambridge: Polity), p. 186.

Garland, David (1985) *Punishment and Welfare: A History of Penal Strategies* (London: Gower).

Glen, W. Cunningham (ed.) (1843) *Archbold's Poor Law*. 12th edn. (London: Shaw and Sons).

Glen, William Cunningham (ed.) (1858) *Shaw's Union Officers' and Local Boards of Health Manual for 1858* (London: Shaw and Sons).

Glen, William Cunningham (1859) *The Consolidated and other Orders of the Poor Law Commissioners and the Poor Law Board*. 4th edn. (London: Butterworth).

Goffman, Erving (1961, reprinted 1968) *Asylums: Essays on the Social Situation of Mental Patients and Other Inmates* (Harmondsworth: Penguin).

Goldstein, Jan (1993) 'Framing discipline with law: problems and promises of the liberal state', *American Historical Review*, **98**: 364.

Gordon, Colin (1992) '*Histoire de la folie*: an unknown book by Michel Foucault', In *Rewriting the History of Madness*, ed. Still and Velody (London: Routledge), p. 32.

Greaves, George (1861) 'Homes for the working class'. Paper delivered to the Manchester Statistical Society, 8 Apr. 1861.

Greaves, George (1867) *Hints to Qualifying Surgeons under the Factory Acts* (London n.p.).

Green, Bryan (1983) *Knowing the Poor: A Case-study in Textual Reality Construction* (London: Routledge & Kegan Paul).

Grob, Gerald (1990) 'Marxian analysis and mental illness', *History of Psychiatry*, **1**: 223.

Harrison, Brian (1974) 'State intervention and moral reform in nineteenth-century England', in *Pressure from Without in Early Victorian England*, ed. Patricia Hollis (London: Edward Arnold), p. 289 .

Hart, Jenifer (1977) 'Religion and social control in the mid-nineteenth century', in *Social Control in Nineteenth Century Britain*, ed. A. P. Donajgrodzki (London: Croom Helm), p. 108.

Hawkins, James (1868) *On the Desirability of National Education for the Deaf and Dumb Poor* (London: Longmans, Green and Co.).

Hawkins, James (1872) *Are the Beneficient Uses of Public Institutions adequately Supported by their Present Organisation?* (London: Longmans, Green).

Hay, Douglas (1975) 'Property, authority and the criminal law', in Douglas Hay *et al.*, *Albion's Fatal Tree* (reprinted London: Penguin, 1977), p. 17.

Henriques, Ursula (1972) 'The rise and decline of the separate system of prison discipline', *Past and Present*, **54**: 61.

Henriques, Ursula (1979) *Before the Welfare State: Social Administration in Early Industrial Britain* (London: Longman).

Hervey, Nicholas (1985) 'A slavish bowing down: the Lunacy Commission and the psychiatric profession 1845–60', in *The Anatomy of Madness*, Vol. II, ed. William F. Bynum *et al.* (London: Tavistock), p. 98.

Hervey, Nicholas (1986) 'Advocacy or folly: the alleged Lunatics' Friend Society, 1845–63', *Medical History*, **30**: 245.

Hervey, Nicholas Bethell (1987) 'The Lunacy Commission 1845–60, with special reference to the implementation of policy in Kent and Surrey'. University of Bristol dissertation.

Heywood and Massey (1961) *Court of Protection Practice*. 9th edn. (London: Stevens and Sons).

Hilton, Boyd (1988) *The Age of Atonement: The Influence of Evangelicalism on Social and Economic Thought, 1795–1865* (Oxford: Clarendon).

Himmelfarb, Gertrude (1984) *The Idea of Poverty: England in the Early Industrial Age* (London: Faber).

Hodgkinson, Ruth (1966) 'Provision for pauper lunatics, 1834–71', *Medical History*, **10**: 138.

Hodgkinson, Ruth G. (1967) *The Origins of the National Health Service: Medical Services of the New Poor Law, 1834–1871* (London: Wellcome Historical Medical Library).

Hollis, Patricia (ed.) (1974) *Pressure from Without in Early Victorian England* (London: Edward Arnold).

Hunt, Alan and Wickham, Gary (1994) *Foucault and Law: Towards a Sociology of Law as Governance* (London: Pluto).

Hunter, Richard and Macalpine, Ida (1963) *Three Hundred Years of Psychiatry, 1535–1860* (reprinted Hartsdale, New York: Carlisle, 1982).

Ignatieff, Michael (1978) *A Just Measure of Pain: The Penitentiary in the Industrial Revolution, 1750–1850*. (reprinted London: Penguin, 1989).

Ignatieff, Michael (1983) 'State, civil society and total institutions: a critique of recent histories of punishment', in *Social Control and the State: Historical and Comparative Essays*, ed. Stanley Cohen and Andrew Scull. (reprinted Oxford: Blackwell, 1985).

Ignatieff, Michael (1983) 'Total institutions and working classes: a review essay', *History Workshop Journal*, **15**: 167.

Ingleby, David (1983) 'Mental health and social order', in *Social Control and the State: Historical and Comparative Essays*, ed. Stanley Cohen and Andrew Scull (reprinted Oxford: Blackwell, 1985).

Jones, Gareth Stedman (1971) *Outcast London: A Study of the Relationship between Classes in Victorian Society* (Oxford: Clarendon).

Jones, Gareth Stedman (1983) 'Class expression versus social control? a critique of recent trends in the social history of leisure', in *Social Control and the State: Historical and Comparative Essays*, ed. Stanley Cohen and Andrew Scull (reprinted Oxford: Blackwell, 1985).

Jones, Kathleen (1955) *Lunacy, Law, and Conscience, 1744–1845: The Social History of the Care of the Insane* (London: Routledge & Kegan Paul).

Jones, Kathleen (1960) *Mental Health and Social Policy 1845–1955* (London: Routledge & Kegan Paul).

Jones, Kathleen (1991) 'The culture of the mental hospital', in *150 Years of British Psychiatry*, ed. German Berrios and Hugh Freeman (London: Gaskell), p. 17.

Jones, Kathleen (1991) 'Law and mental health: sticks or carrots', in *150 Years of British Psychiatry 1841–1991*, ed. German Berrios and Hugh Freeman (London: Gaskell), p. 89.

Laurence, Ray (1981) 'Models of Madness in Victorian Asylum Practice', *European Journal of Sociology*, **22**: 229.

Lieberman, David (1985) 'From Bentham to Benthamism', *Historical Journal*, **28**: 199.

Lowe, Louisa (1883) *The Bastilles of England; or the Lunacy Laws at Work* (London: Crookenden).

Lubenow, William C. (1971) *The Politics of Government Growth: Early Victorian Attitudes toward State Intervention, 1833–1848* (Newton Abbot: David & Charles.

Lumley, William Golden (1845) *The New Lunacy Acts* (London: Shaw).

Lumley, William Golden (1849) *Manuals of the Duties of Poor Law Officers. Medical Officer* (London: Knight).

Lumley, William Golden (1869) *Manuals of the Duties of Poor Law Officers: Master and Matron of the Workhouse* (London: Knight).

Lumley, William Golden (1871) *Manuals of the Duties of Poor Law Officers: Medical Officer*. 3rd edn. (London: Knight).

McCandless, Peter (1983) 'Dangerous to themselves and others: the victorian debate over the prevention of wrongful confinement', *Journal of British Studies*, **23** (1): 84.

McCord, Norman (1976) 'The Poor Law and philanthropy', in *The New Poor Law in the Nineteenth Century*, ed. Derek Fraser (London: Macmillan), p. 87.

MacDonagh, Oliver (1958) 'The nineteenth-century revolution in government: a re-appraisal', *The Historical Journal*, **1**: 52.

MacDonagh, Oliver (1977) *Early Victorian Government 1830–70* (London: Weidenfeld and Nicolson).

McGowen, Randall (1994) 'Power and humanity, or Foucault among the historians', in *Reassessing Foucault*, ed. C. Jones and R. Porter (London: Routledge), p. 91.

Mackenzie, Charlotte (1985) 'Social factors in the admission, discharge, and continuing stay of patients at Ticehurst Asylum, 1845–1917', in Bynum *et al.*, *The Anatomy of Madness*. Vol. II (London: Tavistock).

McLeod, Hugh (1984) *Religion and the Working Class in Nineteenth-Century Britain* (London: Macmillan).

Malthus, Thomas R (1803) *An Essay on the Principle of Population; or A view of its past and present Effects on Human Happiness; With an Inquiry into our*

Prospects respecting the future Removal or Mitigation of the Evils which it occasions. 1803 edn. ed. Patricia James and Donald Winch (Cambridge: Cambridge University Press).

Mandler, Peter (1990) 'Tories and paupers: Christian political economy and the making of the new Poor Law', *Historical Journal*, **33**: 81.

Mandler, Peter. See also Brundage, above.

Mayer, John A. (1983) 'Notes towards a working definition of social control in historical analysis', in *Social Control and the State: Historical and Comparative Essays*, ed. Stanley Cohen and Andrew Scull (reprinted Oxford: Blackwell).

Mellett, David J. (1981) 'Bureaucracy and mental illness: the Commissioners in Lunacy, 1845–90', *Medical History*, **25**: 221.

Mellett, David J. (1982) *The Prerogative of Asylumdom: Social, Cultural and Administrative Aspects of the Institutional Treatment of the Insane in Nineteenth Century Britain* (New York, London: Garland).

Melossi, Dario (1990) *The State of Social Control: A Sociological Study of the Concepts of State and Social Control in the Making of Democracy* (Cambridge: Polity Press).

Midelfort, Erik H. C. (1980) 'Madness and civilization in Early Modern Europe: a reappraisal of Michel Foucault', in *After the Reformation: Essays in Honor of J. H. Hexter*, ed. Barbara C. Malament (Manchester: Manchester University Press), p. 247.

Millar, Edgar (1996) 'Idiocy in the nineteenth century', *History of Psychiatry*, **7**: 361.

Millar, John (1859) *A Plea in favour of the Insane Poor* (London: Henry Renshaw).

Moir, Esther (1969) *The Justice of the Peace* (Harmondsworth: Penguin).

Mommsen, Wolfgang J. (1980) ' "Toward the Iron Cage of Future Serfdom"? On the methodological status of Max Weber's ideal-typical concept of bureaucratization', *Transactions of the Royal Historical Society*, 5th series, **30**: 157.

Nelken, David (1983) *The Limits of the Legal Process: A Study of Landlords Law and Crime* (London: Academic Press).

Nicholls, George (1898) *A History of the English Poor Law*. 2 vols (New York: Putnam and London: P. S. King).

Nolan, Michael (1825) *A Treatise of the Laws for the Relief and Settlement of the Poor*. 4th edn., 3 vols (London: Butterworth).

Ontario (1990) Enquiry on Mental Competence. 'Appendix III: historical developments in England', in *Enquiry on Mental Competence: Final Report* (Toronto: Queen's Printer for Ontario), p. 324.

Orme, Henry, and Brock, William (1987) *Leicestershire's Lunatics: The Institutional Care of Leicestershire's Lunatics during the Nineteenth Century* (Leicester: Leicesterhire Museums Publication No. 47).

Owen, David (1964) *English Philanthropy 1660–1960* (Cambridge: Harvard University Press).

Parris, Henry (1969) *Constitutional Bureaucracy: The Development of British Central Administration since the Eighteenth Century* (London: George Allen & Unwin).

Parry-Jones, William Ll. (1972) *The Trade in Lunacy: A Study of Private Madhouses in England in the Eighteenth and Nineteenth Centuries* (London: Routledge, and Toronto: University of Toronto Press).

Philips, David (1976) 'The Black Country magistracy, 1835–60', *Midland History*, **3**: 161.

Philips, David (1983) ' "A just measure of crime, authority, hunters and blue locusts": The "Revisionist" social history of crime and the law in Britain, 1780–1850', in *Social Control and the State: Historical and Comparative Essays*, ed. Stanley Cohen and Andrew Scull, (reprinted Oxford: Blackwell).

Poor Law District Conference (1876) *Report of Poor Law District Conferences, 1875* (London: Knight).

Pope, H. M. R. (1877) *A Treatise on the Law and Practice of Lunacy* (London: H. Sweet).

Pope, H. M. R. (1892) *A Treatise on the Law and Practice of Lunacy*. 2nd edn. (1892), ed. Boome and Fowke (London: Sweet and Maxwell).

Porter, Roy (1987) *Mind-Forg'd Manacles: A History of Madness in England from the Restoration to the Regency* (reprinted Harmondsworth: Penguin, 1990).

Porter, Roy (1987) *A Social History of Madness: Stories of the Insane* (London: Weidenfeld and Nicolson).

Porter, Roy (1990) 'Divided selves and psychiatric violence', *Cycnos*, **6**: 95.

Porter, Roy (1991) 'History of psychiatry in Britain', *History of Psychiatry*, **2**: 271.

Porter, Roy (1992) 'Foucault's Great Confinement', in *Rewriting the History of Madness: Studies in Foucault's* Histoire de la Folie, ed. Still and Velody (London and New York: Routledge), p. 119.

Poynter, J. R. (1969) *Society and Pauperism: English Ideas on Poor Relief, 1795– 1834* (London: Routledge & Kegan Paul and Toronto: University of Toronto Press).

Prochaska, Frank (1988) *The Voluntary Impulse: Philanthropy in Modern Britain* (London: Faber and Faber).

Renvoize, Edward (1991) 'The Association of Medical Officers of Asylums and Hospitals for the Insane, the Medico-Psychological Association, and their presidents', in *150 Years of British Psychiatry 1841–1991*, ed. German Berrios and Hugh Freeman (London: Gaskell), p. 29.

Roberts, David (1979) *Paternalism in Early Victorian England* (London: Croom Helm).

Rogers, Joseph (1889) *Reminiscences of a Workhouse Medical Officer*. Edited with preface by Thorold Rogers (London: T. Fisher Unwin).

Rose, Michael (1976) 'Settlement, removal and the new Poor Law', in *The New Poor Law in the Nineteenth Century*, ed. Derek Fraser (London: Macmillan), p. 25.

Rose, Michael E. (1986) *The Relief of Poverty, 1834–1914.* 2nd edn. (London: Macmillan).

Rose, Nikolas (1985) *The Psychological Complex* (London: Routledge).

Rothman, David J. (1971) *The Discovery of the Asylum: Social Order and Disorder in the New Republic* (Boston and Toronto: Little, Brown and Co.).

Rothman, David (1980) *Conscience and Convenience: The Asylum and its Alternatives in Progressive America* (Boston and Toronto: Little, Brown and Co.).

Rothman, David J. (1983) 'Social control: the uses and abuses of the concept in the history of incarceration', in *Social Control and the State: Historical and Comparative Essays*, ed. Stanley Cohen and Andrew Scull (reprinted Oxford: Blackwell).

Rubinstein, W. D. (1983) 'The end of 'Old Corruption' in Britain 1780–1860', *Past and Present*, **101**: 55.

Rushton, Peter (1988) 'Lunatics and idiots: mental disability, the community, and the Poor Law in north-east England, 1600–1800', *Medical History*, **32**: 34.

Russell, Richard (1988) 'The lunacy profession and its staff in the second half of the nineteenth century, with special reference to the West Riding Lunatic Asylum', in *Anatomy of Madness*, ed. William F. Bynum *et al.* Vol. III (London: Tavistock), p. 297.

Sankey, W. H. O. (1856) 'Do the public asylums of England, as at present constructed, afford the greatest facilities for the care and treatment of the insane?', *Journal of Mental Science*, **2**: 466.

Saunders, Janet (1988) 'Quarantining the weak-minded: psychiatric definitions of degeneracy and the late-Victorian asylum', in *The Anatomy of Madness*, ed. William F. Bynum *et al.*, Vol. III (London: Routledge), p. 274.

Sayer, Derek. See Corrigan.

Scull, Andrew (1976) 'Mad-doctors and magistrates: English psychiatry's struggle for professional autonomy in the nineteenth century', *Arch. Europ. Sociol.*, **17**: 279.

Scull, Andrew (1979) *Museums of Madness: The Social Organization of Insanity in Nineteenth-Century England* (reprinted Harmondsworth: Penguin, 1982).

Scull, Andrew (1983) 'Humanitarianism or control? Some observations on the historiography of Anglo-American psychiatry', in *Social Control and the State: Historical and Comparative Essays*, ed. Stanley Cohen and Andrew Scull (reprinted Oxford: Blackwell, 1985).

Scull, Andrew (1984) *Decarceration: Community Treatment and the Deviant – A Radical View.* 2nd edn. (Englewood Cliffs, NJ: Prentice Hall, 1984; and Oxford: Basil Blackwell Ltd.).

Scull, Andrew (1989) *Social Order/Mental Disorder: Anglo-American Psychiatry in Historical Perspective* (London: Routledge).

Scull, Andrew (1991) 'Psychiatry and its historians', *History of Psychiatry*, **2**: 239.

Scull, Andrew (1993) *The Most Solitary of Afflictions: Madness and Society in Britain, 1700–1900* (New Haven: Yale University Press).

Scull, Andrew. See also Cohen.

Shelford, Leonard (1847) *A Practical Treatise of the Law concerning Lunatics, Idiots, and Persons of Unsound Mind* 2nd edn. (London: S. Sweet).

Showalter, Elaine (1985) *The Female Malady: Women, Madness and English Culture, 1830–1980* (reprinted London: Virago, 1987).

Sim, Joe (1990) *Medical Power in Prisons: The Prison Medical Service in England, 1774–1989* (Milton Keynes: Open University Press).

Smith, Dorothy (1974) 'The social construction of documentary reality'. *Sociological Inquiry*, **44** (4): 257.

Smith, Dorothy E. (1984) 'Textually mediated social organization', *International Social Science Journal*, **36**: 59.

Smith, Dorothy E. (1990) *Texts, Facts, and Femininity: Exploring the Relations of Ruling* (London: Routledge).

Smith, L. D. (1995) ' "Levelled to the same common standard"? Social class in the lunatic asylum, 1780–1860', in *The Duty of Discontent*, ed. O. Ashton, R. Fyson and S. Roberts (London: Mansell), p. 142.

Smith, Roger (1981) *Trial by Medicine: Insanity and Responsibility in Victorian Trials* (Edinburgh: Edinburgh University Press).

Still and Velody (eds) (1992) *Rewriting the History of Madness* (London and New York: Routledge).

Suzuki, Akihito (1991) 'Lunacy in seventeenth- and eighteenth-century England: analysis of Quarter Sessions records Part I', *History of Psychiatry*, **2**: 437.

Suzuki, Akihito (1992) 'Lunacy in seventeenth- and eighteenth-century England: analysis of Quarter Sessions records Part II', *History of Psychiatry*, **3**: 29.

Suzuki, Akihito (1992) 'Mind and its disease in Enlightenment British medicine', University of London dissertation.

Suzuki, Akihito (1995) 'The politics and ideology of non-restraint: the case of the Hanwell Asylum', *Medical History*, **39**: 1.

Thane, Pat (1978) 'Women and the Poor Law in Victorian and Edwardian England', *History Workshop*, **6**: 29.

Thomas, William (1974) 'The philosophic Radicals', in *Pressure from Without in Early Victorian England*, ed. Patricia Hollis (London: Edward Arnold), pp. 52 ff.

Thompson, F. M. L. (1981) 'Social control in Victorian Britain', *Economic History Review*, 2nd series, **34**: 180.

Thompson, Kathryn M. (1982) 'The Leicester Poor Law Union, 1836–71'. University of Leicester dissertation.

Tomes, Nancy (1988) 'The Great Restraint Controversy: a comparative perspective on Anglo-American psychiatry in the nineteenth century'. *The Anatomy of Madness*, Vol III, ed. William F. Bynum *et al.* (London: Routledge), p. 190.

Townsend. (1787) *A Dissertation on the Poor Laws by a Well-wisher of Mankind* 2nd edn. (London: Dilly).

Tuke, Daniel H. (1858) 'Does civilization favour the generation of mental disease?', *Journal of Mental Science*, **4**: 94.

Turner, Trevor (1991) '"Not worth powder and shot": the public profile of the Medico-Psychological Association, *c.* 1851–1914', in *150 Years of British Psychiatry*, ed. G. Berrios and H. Freeman (London: Gaskell), p. 3.

United Kingdom. Metropolitan Commissioners in Lunacy (1844) *Report of the Metropolitan Commissioners in Lunacy to the Lord Chancellor* (London: Bradbury and Evans).

United Kingdom. Royal Commission on the Poor Law. *Report from His Majesty's Commissioners for Inquiring into the Administration and Practical Consequences of the Poor Laws.* See Checkland.

United Kingdom. Royal Commission on the Poor Laws and Relief of Distress (1909) *Report of the Royal Commission on the Poor Laws and Relief of Distress* (London: Queen's Printer).

United Kingdom. Royal Commission on the Poor Laws and Relief of Distress (1909) *Minority Report of the Poor Law Commission, 1909* (London: National Committee to Promote the Break-Up of the Poor Law).

Unsworth, Clive (1987) *The Politics of Mental Health Legislation* (Oxford: Clarendon).

Unsworth, Clive (1993) 'Law and lunacy in psychiatry's "Golden Age"'. *Oxford Journal of Legal Studies*, **13**: 479.

Walker, Nigel (1968) *Crime and Insanity in England. Vol. 1: The Historical Perspective* (Edinburgh: Edinburgh UP).

Walton, John K. (1979) 'Lunacy in the Industrial Revolution: a study of asylum admissions in Lancashire, 1848–50', *Journal of Social History*, **13**: 1.

Walton, J. K. (1985) 'Casting out and bringing back in Victorian England: pauper lunatics, 1840–70', in *The Anatomy of Madness*, Vol. II, ed. William F. Bynum *et al.* (London: Tavistock), p. 132.

Watson, Stephen (1992) 'From moral imbecility to psychopathy: prison psychiatry in England 1920–1959', in *Law and Mental Health: Historical, Legal, Ethical, Diagnostic and Therapeutic Aspects.* Proc. of 17th International Congress of the International Academy of Law and Mental Health, 26–30 May 1991 (Leuven: IALMH), p. 61.

Weisbrod, Bernd (1985) 'How to become a good foundling in early Victorian London', *Social History*, **10**: 193.

White, William (1846) *History, Gazetteer, and Directory of Leicestershire, and the small County of Rutland* (Sheffield: for the author).

Wiener, Martin J. (1990) *Reconstructing the Criminal: Culture, Law and Policy in England, 1830–1914* (Cambridge: CUP).

Williams, Karel (1981) *From Pauperism to Poverty* (London: Routledge & Kegan Paul).

Windholz, George E. (1987) 'The explicitly stated rationale for the involuntary commitment of the mentally ill given by the nineteenth-century German-speaking psychiatrists', *Psychological Medicine*, **17**: 291.

Winslow, Forbes, M. D. (1845) *An Act (8 & 9 Victoria c. 100) for the Care and*

Treatment of Lunatics, with Explanatory Notes and Comments (London: Benning).

Wood, Peter (1991) *Poverty and the Workhouse in Victorian Britain* (Stroud: Alan Sutton Publishing).

Wright, David (1993) 'A beam for mental darkness: a history of the National Asylum for Idiots, Earlswood, 1847–1886'. University of Oxford dissertation.

Wright, David (1996) ' "Childlike in his innocence": Lay attitudes to "idiots" and "imbeciles" in Victorian England', in Wright and Digby, *From Idiocy to Mental Deficiency* (London: Routledge).

Wright, David (1997) 'Getting out of the asylum: understanding the confinement of the insane in the nineteenth century', *Social History of Medicine*, **10**: 137.

Zainaldin, Jamil S. and Tyor, Peter L. (1979) 'Asylum and society: an approach to institutional change', *Journal of Social History*, **13**: 23.

Zangerl, Carl H. E. (1971) 'The social composition of the county magistracy in England and Wales, 1831–1887', *Journal of British Studies*, **9** (1): 113.

Index

able-bodied paupers
distinguished from non-able-bodied
80, 261, 264
and new Poor Law 40, 81, 260, 263
outdoor relief, continuation after
1834 80, 261, 264
restriction of relief after 1870 152,
280–2
admission orders, county asylums 152,
172–183, 280–2
Bucknill on 173–4
content of 48, 174–5
recording practices 158–61, 172–4,
182
Association of Medical Officers of Asylums
and Hospitals for the Insane
(AMOAHI) 130–1
Asylum medical officers 17–18, 129–32
casebooks, recording in 168
Poor Law Guardians, relations
with 131–2
training 129
wages 131
see also Buck, Bucknill, Conolly

Bentham, Jeremy 75–6, 77, 82, 85, 100
British Medical Association 127, 130,
136, 140
Buck, John 113–14, 131, 152, 210–11
Bucknill, John 130, 132, 173–4, 212

case books, county asylums 151,
161–172, 249, 278–80
content of 162–7, 168
moralization of paupers in 164–7, 170–2
recording practices 158–61, 165–6,
167, 169
amendment of account to match
results 166
Castel, Robert 10
charitable provision for insane 36, 152,
260, 263
see also private patients

chronic insanity
county asylums, in 203
workhouses, in 207, 221–2, 223
Conolly, John 118
county asylum
administrative structure 10, 20, 32–7,
47–50, 249
admission criteria
cure prospects 156, 202–3, 212
dangerousness 121–2, 124, 174–7
expense 51–3
feigned madness 134, 137
manageability 178–81, 187, 202,
212–3
admission processes 4, 12, 98–102,
153–5
costs of 51, 53
Justices of the Peace and 48, 99,
121–2, 152
medical certification 48, 89–90,
98–9, 152, 173–5, 178–82
relieving officer and 4, 48, 49, 98–9,
101, 153–4
chronic insanity in 203
conditions in 226–7, 246
cure, 17, 19, 36, 86, 88, 93, 124, 155–6,
202–3, 212, 226
discharge 48, 166–7
removal to workhouses 131, 187,
223–4, 256
exclusion from 1834 Poor Law statutory
scheme 72, 84–7, 94
expense of 51–2, 121, 168, 202, 206,
261, 265
discouraging admission 51–3
reimbursement by families of
inmates 41, 157
'failure' of the asylum 19, 20, 241, 245–6
inmates
paupers
definition of 41, 157–8, 204–5
restriction to 42–4
views of admission 12, 132–41

306